THE PRACTICE OF
SOCIAL WORK

THE PRACTICE OF SOCIAL WORK

ROBERT W. KLENK

Huron County Guidance Center

ROBERT M. RYAN

University of Denver

Wadsworth Publishing Company, Inc.
Belmont, California

L. C. Cat. Card No.: 78–129991

Printed in the United States of America

1 2 3 4 5 6 7 8 9 10—74 73 72 71 70

Preface

Controversy thrives among practitioners, educators, and students of the social work profession over the issue of method—which method should be taught and subsequently used in the field. The profession is divided generally into four factions: caseworkers, group workers, community organizers, and social work generalists, who favor a combination of these methods. In editing this book for social work methods students, we have not condemned any method. On the contrary, it is our position that both room and need exist for any workable method. However, we have taken a generalist perspective. Our rationale for such a perspective developed from our teaching experience, in which we found that broad exposure gives the novice the most solid foundation for further study.

The first chapter of this book, *Introduction*, presents our conception of a social work generalist. This conception includes a rationale for the articles that were selected as well as a possible teaching framework.

The next chapter, *Philosophy and Values in Social Work Practice*, attempts to show the breadth of the generalist approach to social work practice, with selections that explain the philosophical bases of the profession and illustrate many of the relationships and processes involved.

Casework, the third chapter, presents the perspectives of the individual approach to problem solving. Our selections emphasize the role of the worker as a problem solver, focusing on the individual in terms of his total environment, his effect on that environment, and its effect on him.

The chapter on *Group Work* examines the use of the group approach in social work practice. Emphasis is placed on the effectiveness of the group in providing a bridge between individual members and the outside world. The diverse functions of groups are shown by the variety of kinds of groups portrayed in the selections.

The next chapter, *Community Organization*, discusses the activities of social workers in using the organizational approach. Emphasis is placed upon the significance of social action in the organizational structure of social change.

Finally, *Future Trends* explores some anticipated developments in the profession. The articles in this chapter deal with some of the implications of social change and historical movements for the future of social work, as well as with some of the current debates and tendencies within social work itself.

It is our belief that no single answer or solution can solve the problems of practice in social work. There is a danger of oversimplification in focusing on the basics of the various viewpoints. However, we hope that, by presenting these basics in a way that is oriented to students, this book will make a contribution to the development of our profession.

Our thanks go to the reviewers, who made many helpful suggestions: Herbert Bisno, Fairleigh Dickinson University; Sidney S. Eisenberg, Sacramento State College; Donald Feldstein, Council on Social Work Education; Lester J. Glick, Syracuse University; Erma T. Meyerson, University of Pittsburgh; Ralph Segalman, University of Wisconsin; and Irving B. Tebor, San Diego State College.

We would also like to acknowledge the patience and contributions of our wives, students, and colleagues, without whom this volume could not have been compiled.

Robert W. Klenk
Robert M. Ryan

Contents

1

Introduction

Within the profession of social work, practitioners and educators are concerned with the development of more effective social work practice. One area of concern focuses on an expanded problem-solving orientation to social work practice in contrast to the more widely accepted individual methods orientation consisting of social casework, social group work, and community organization. A practitioner using the expanded problem-solving orientation is like the general practitioner in medicine; the practitioner using an individual methods orientation would have the medical specialist as a counterpart. We believe that social work, like medicine, needs both general practitioners and specialists in order to develop more effective practice.

The primary criteria used to determine the format of this book and to select articles were those of Hearn's description of a "generalist"[1] and Bartlett's "The Working Definition of Social Work Practice" (see Chapter 2).

Hearn has identified four possible products of the social work education process. He describes these as ranging from generalist

[1]Gordon Hearn, "Toward a Unitary Conception of Social Work Practice" (paper read at the Fourth Annual Student Social Work Conference, University of Washington, School of Social Work, May 10, 1963), pp. 3-4. (Mimeographed.)

to specialist, including the multiple specialist and the specialized generalist. The generalist is likely to be a product of an undergraduate social welfare curriculum; the specialist may have completed doctoral study. This book was compiled primarily for the social work generalist.

The "Working Definition" concerns itself with those elements of social work practice common to all aspects of social work. Method is described as "an orderly systematic mode of procedure" in which the practitioner is concerned with effecting change "(1) within the individual in relation to his social environment; (2) of the social environment in its effect upon the individual; (3) of both the individual and the social environment in their interaction."

Within the context of an expanded problem-solving orientation, the individual social work practitioner must develop approaches for specific problems. Bisno presents one theoretical framework within which the components of social work practice might be viewed:

Social work as a profession
within a
socio-cultural milieu
operating through
organizations and entrepreneurial activities
confronts
problems in social functioning: actual or potential
with a
*goal of maintaining and enhancing the social
functioning of persons, singly or in collective units,*
expressed through social workers occupying a variety of
*occupational roles in various fields of
practice and institutional sectors*
acting within a
system of orientation
by means of the *skilled* use of selected,
but not mutually exclusive nor monopolized
methods and techniques
employed in interaction with
client and other relevant transactional systems
and subject to
evaluation.[2]

Within the context of the above theoretical framework, Bisno suggests nine roles (or approaches) that the generalist may use in the problem-solving process:

[2]Herbert Bisno, "A Theoretical Framework for Teaching Social Work Methods and Skills with Particular Reference to Undergraduate Social Welfare Education," *Journal of Education for Social Work*, 5 (2), 1969, p. 7.

Adversary: Processes, techniques, and skills involving articulation and resolution of conflicts of interests and commitments.

Conciliatory: Processes, techniques, and skills involving the maximizing of associative relationships.

Developmental: Processes, techniques, and skills involving the creating, mobilizing, and use of resources for purposes of development.

Facilitative-instructional: Processes, techniques, and skills involving teaching, supervision, etc.

Knowledge development and testing: Processes, techniques, and skills involving research, evaluation, and dissemination of findings, data, programs, and policies.

Restorative: Processes, techniques, and skills involving the remedying and healing of impaired functioning.

Regulatory: Processes, techniques, and skills involving adherence to rules and norms.

Rule-implementing: Processes, techniques, and skills involving the operationalizing and administering of laws, policies, and programs.

Rule-making: Processes, techniques, and skills involving the making of policies, laws, and other rules.[3]

Through the development of these and other approaches, the social work generalist acquires useful skills and techniques.[4] Part of his skill is an awareness of his own limitations; that is, the ability to identify those aspects of problem areas which are beyond his level of competency and to select appropriate specialists. Where social work specialists are not available, as is often the case, the generalist must be prepared to define clearly those areas where he can have a significant impact.

We view this reader as covering three distinct areas. Chapter 2 focuses on the underlying philosophy and values of all social work practice. The second phase, Chapters 3, 4, and 5, focuses on the traditional methods of social work practice—social casework, social group work, and community organization. However, each of the articles in these sections demonstrates the social work practitioner's use of a particular method in a more expanded problem-solving frame of reference. Chapter 6 represents a new dimension which holds the earlier mentioned values and philosophy relatively constant while viewing the problem-solving process from a generalist frame of reference.

The reader may profitably employ Bisno's or Teare and McPheeters' framework for integrating the ideas in this volume.

[3]Bisno, *op. cit.*, p 10.
[4]Another view of the generalist can be found in Harold L. McPheeters, *Roles and Functions for Mental Health Workers* (Atlanta, Ga.: Southern Regional Education Board, 1969); and Robert J. Teare and Harold L. McPheeters, *Roles and Functions for Social Welfare Workers* (Atlanta, Ga.: Southern Regional Education Board, 1970).

Another way of viewing the interrelationship among articles in different sections is from an expanded problem-solving perspective. The articles in each section were selected to illustrate various problem-solving approaches. Perlman suggests that we not become captives of our own narrow interpretation of method. Briar, discussing social casework, suggests a need for an indefinite number of approaches for meeting human needs and goes on to identify what some of these might be. Tropp identifies five approaches to working with groups, four of which are part of the social group work process. Moore's discussion of community organization calls for an expansion of roles, processes, understanding, and use of community dynamics.

A somewhat different way to relate these articles is from a "New Design" point of view, in which various problem-solving approaches are discussed. Turner calls for new social work approaches in response to changing societal conditions. Janchill presents a new conceptual tool that might be used to expand existing practice theory and to develop further a generalist theory for practice. Strickler and Allgeyer present a new application of crisis theory for work with groups. Warren discusses new priorities in community organization as they relate to changing community patterns. Beck presents a new design for social work practice that suggests a generalist frame of reference.

Still another perspective for relating the articles is to focus on a given social problem, such as poverty. That poverty is an appropriate concern of social work is discussed by McCormick. Fantl, Youngman, and Grosser identify the multidimensional nature of a social problem that necessitates an expanded repertoire of approaches. Purcell and Specht, reiterating the multidimensional nature of social problems, go on to illustrate the interrelationships that exist between different social problems, further demonstrating the need for a generalist approach.

We compiled this reader for the student who, whether at the undergraduate level in a social welfare curriculum, in an agency's in-service training program, or at the graduate level, is new to the social work educational process. Much of this material could previously be found only in journals, which are always in demand and consequently often unavailable. Thus the professional social work practitioner might also find this book useful.

2

Philosophy
and Values in
Social Work Practice

The generalist in social work combines the individual, group, and organizational approaches in dealing with human problems. As Bartlett observes, the problems facing a social worker involve many factors, and their solutions require the ability to transcend any single perspective. As is often said, complex problems require complex solutions.

Thus, the generalist approach grows from a conception of the nature of social work. Tillich sees social work as requiring a broad and deep understanding, one which precludes dogmatism about methods. Such an understanding, he says, affirms the value of the individual and leads to the achievement of the ultimate aim of social work: "namely, the universal community of all beings in which any individual aim is taken into the universal aim of being itself." And this aim "transcends the limits of [social work's] techniques."

A flexible approach to methods is also proposed by Younghusband, who sees the present three social work methods as having a common base: "Any or all of them should be used flexibly in any given situation in whatever would be the most effective form of intervention." When Younghusband defines one of the functions of social work as being "to promote socially

constructive and personally gratifying transactions between individuals, groups and communities . . . ," the generalist approach is implied: though the methods are "distinct, they are not
necessarily separate" because the factors involved in the problems are interconnected.

Perlman sees a danger in being confined by the boundaries of
traditional methods, in that "it is possible that the ways we perceive a situation, and define it, and go about treating it are
shaped a priori by the particular method to which we have allegiance or in which we have skill." She therefore recommends
cutting across traditional lines and sees flexibility and spontaneity as among those qualities needed by one who would produce desired changes.

With respect to the kind of changes social work seeks to produce, a final issue which is presented in the readings bears mention here: Is the task of social work confined to alleviating the
problems which befall the less fortunate members of society, or
should social work also seek to change those aspects of the society itself which contribute to these problems? Turner states the
issue thus: "One of the frequently heard inside criticisms of social
work is that it tries to take responsibility for remaking society. But
also as frequently, social work is criticized by persons outside the
profession for not doing just that."

The generalist seeks to use methods without allowing them to
obscure his vision of the complex realities with which he must
deal. Likewise, we hope, the reader will study these abstract ideas
without losing sight of the flesh and blood reality to which they
refer. This reality is the practice of social work.

Toward Clarification and
Improvement of Social
Work Practice

Harriett M. Bartlett

The central responsibility of a profession is to maintain and promote in all possible ways the effectiveness of its service to society. Because social work grew up in so many separate organizations, there was until recently no channel through which social
work practice could be viewed and acted upon as a whole. It is
true that important steps were taken by certain segments of the
profession. Schools of social work and educators, being a more
homogeneous group within a single organization, were in a posi-

Reprinted with permission of the author and the National Association of Social Workers
from *Social Work*, Vol. 3, No. 2 (April 1958), pp. 3-9.

tion to give much-needed leadership to professional thinking. Some specific fields of practice also, such as medical and psychiatric social work, developed consistent ongoing programs for study and improvement of their work, with standing practice committees which brought out a steady stream of studies and reports. But the building of a professional curriculum or of a total professional program should rest upon understanding of the basic knowledge, values, and skills essential for competent practice, which could not be attained until that practice could be analyzed in some comprehensive and penetrating manner. The problem was recognized some years ago[1] but little progress was made. Educational thinking continued to move ahead so that, with the lag in study of practice, a rather serious imbalance has been developing in the profession.

The major obstacles to movement in the practice area seem to have been the lack of any comprehensive conceptual scheme by which practice could be analyzed and the lack of any channel for consistent and cumulative thinking about practice. Finally, in 1955, when practitioners from all fields came together to establish a single professional organization, the favorable moment arrived. As part of the new organization a permanent working group was set up to concentrate its effort on social work practice, namely, the Commission on Social Work Practice of the National Association of Social Workers. This practice-focused, profession-wide group has been working at its assignment for two years. Out of its experience are now emerging lines of thought and action that are significant for the whole profession.[2]

Trends and Issues

The first attempt to view social work practice in its full scope is almost overwhelming. After deliberation, the best starting point appeared to be the trends and issues of most acute interest to practitioners in the major fields of practice. Here are some examples of the several dozen items that emerged from a discussion of concerns.[3]

[1] Ernest V. Hollis and Alice L. Taylor, *Social Work Education in the United States* (New York: Columbia University Press, 1951).

[2] This paper, which has been prepared at the request of the Commission on Social Work Practice, draws freely on the thinking and formulations of its members. It would be impossible to make specific acknowledgment and this has not been attempted. The expression and some of the thinking are the writer's but the major effort in this article is to set forth the vigorous and creative thinking of this professional group. Of course, a national practice commission has no monopoly in the area of practice on which sections and chapters of the national association and other social work groups all over the country are actively working. However, a national group whose assignment covers practice as a whole is in a favorable position to do what no other single group can do by itself.

[3] Report of Subcommittee on Trends, Issues, and Priorities, Commission on Social Work Practice, National Association of Social Workers, September 1956 and March 1957.

l. Using professional staff in social agencies to best advantage is a matter of great concern because of the shortage of qualified workers. Many workers appear to spend a disproportionate amount of time on writing records, attending meetings, and similar activities compared with the time devoted to serving their clients. This is one of a group of items that falls into the category of those over which social workers have control.

2. Social, economic, and political trends are of major importance in influencing the development of social work practice. The profession has often been in the position of planning and taking action *after* problems have reached an acute state. Such problems as this one fall into a class involving factors and forces *outside* social work. It may be that such problems will have to be broken down into segments—such as one trend, the employment of married women—about which data are available.

3. "Multiproblem" families are another subject of intense interest to practitioners. The disproportion between efforts expended in working with these families and results obtained by present methods calls for further exploration.

This problem is of still another type, which shifts and changes as it is analyzed, partly because the term means different things to different people. It may mean families resistant to casework, or those known to most agencies in the community, or those showing the most severe pathology.

4. A fundamental issue is the inability of the profession to state clearly what knowledge, skill, and values are needed by every social worker for basic competence in practice. This illustrates the class of basic questions regarding professional competence in social work practice on which research is required.

Charting Priorities

So many issues and so many lines of action are possible here that any proposed activity could range all the way from immediate decision to long-range study and research. A first step is to determine what degree of effort should be concentrated on each, and what combination of approaches is likely to bring the best results. Then the various approaches for dealing with the questions—such as immediate decisions, short-term projects, and long-term continuous studies—can be considered.

With persistent analysis, it should eventually be possible to classify major studies that have been made and areas for exploration to show what has been accomplished and where gaps exist. Specific projects undertaken by various kinds of groups—professional bodies, agencies, schools, individuals—can all be set forth. Then it should be possible to determine better the order in which certain problems must be attacked, since the answer to one question often depends upon the solution of a prior, underlying problem.

Such exploration still will not provide the much-needed definitions of social work and social work practice, which are essential but so far have proved unattainable. Social workers have been blocked in the past because they felt no individual or group could attempt to say what social work is. Yet everyone agrees that some statement regarding what is meant by social work practice must be formulated as a base for planning an effective program to improve practice. Such a concept of what practice is should encompass all activities known as social work and all levels of practice whether carried on by trained or untrained workers. All professions arrive at a point in their development where they must accept responsibility for subprofessional and semi-professional personnel in their practice,[4] but social work is just awakening to this recognition. It is obvious, however, that the profession cannot deal with the practice of the subprofessional worker—or even define it—until professional practice is more clearly delineated.[5]

It is with this background, then, that the following "working definition" is offered at this time. First, the goal is limited, so that the attempt is to define only social work practice, not social work in all its manifestations. Next, this statement is just a working definition—to show on what base the Practice Commission is operating. And still further, the formulation can be viewed as tentative, to be revised and refined continuously as knowledge and understanding of practice grow.

Working Definition of Social Work Practice

Social work practice, like the practice of all professions, is recognized by a constellation of value, purpose, sanction, knowledge, and method. No part alone is characteristic of social work practice nor is any part described here unique to social work. It is the particular content and configuration of this constellation which makes it social work practice and distinguishes it from the practice of other professions. The following is an attempt to spell out the components of this constellation in such a way as to include all social work practice with all its specializations. This implies that some social work practice will show a more extensive use of one or the other of the components but it is social work practice only when they are all present to some degree.

[4]Hollis and Taylor, op. cit., pp. 166–173.
[5]Minutes of Meeting of Subcommittee on Use of Nonprofessional Personnel. Commission on Social Work Practice, National Association of Social Workers, September 29-30, 1956.
This working definition was prepared by the Subcommittee on the Working Definition of Social Work Practice for the Commission on Social Work Practice, National Association of Social Workers, December 1956.

Value

Certain philosophical concepts are basic to the practice of social work, namely:

1. The individual is the primary concern of this society.

2. There is interdependence between individuals in this society.

3. They have social responsibility for one another.

4. There are human needs common to each person, yet each person is essentially unique and different from others.

5. An essential attribute of a democratic society is the realization of the full potential of each individual and the assumption of his social responsibility through active participation in society.

6. Society has a responsibility to provide ways in which obstacles to this self-realization (i.e., disequilibrium between the individual and his environment) can be overcome or prevented.

These concepts provide the philosophical foundation for social work practice.

Purpose

The practice of social work has as its purposes:

1. To assist individuals and groups to identify and resolve or minimize problems arising out of disequilibrium between themselves and their environment.

2. To identify potential areas of disequilibrium between individuals or groups and the environment in order to prevent the occurrence of disequilibrium.

3. In addition to these curative and preventive aims, to seek out, identify, and strengthen the maximum potential in individuals, groups, and communities.

Sanction
(i.e., authoritative permission; countenance, approbation, or support)

Social work has developed out of a community recognition of the need to provide services to meet basic needs, services which require the intervention of practitioners trained to understand the services, themselves, the individuals, and the means for bringing all together. Social work is not practiced in a vacuum or at the choice of its practitioners alone. Thus, there is a social responsibility inherent in the practitioner's role for the way in which services are rendered. The authority and power of the practitioner and what he represents to the clients and group members derive from one or a combination of three sources:

1. *Governmental agencies* or their subdivisions (authorized by law).

2. *Voluntary incorporated agencies*, which have taken responsibility for meeting certain of the needs or providing certain of the services necessary for individual and group welfare.

3. *The organized profession*, which in turn can sanction individuals for the practice of social work and set forth the educational and other requirements for practice and the conditions under which that practice may be undertaken, whether or not carried out under organizational auspices.

Knowledge

Social work, like all other professions, derives knowledge from a variety of sources and in application brings forth further knowledge from its own processes. Since knowledge of man is never final or absolute, the social worker in his application of this knowledge takes into account those phenomena that are exceptions to existing generalizations and is aware and ready to deal with the spontaneous and unpredictable in human behavior. The practice of the social worker is typically guided by knowledge of:

1. Human development and behavior characterized by emphasis on the wholeness of the individual and the reciprocal influence of man and his total environment—human, social, economic, and cultural.

2. The psychology of giving and taking help from another person or source outside the individual.

3. Ways in which people communicate with one another and give outer expression to inner feelings, such as words, gestures, and activities.

4. Group process and the effects of groups upon individuals and the reciprocal influence of the individual upon the group.

5. The meaning and effect on the individual, groups, and community of cultural heritage including its religious beliefs, spiritual values, law, and other social institutions.

6. Relationships, *i.e.*, the interactional processes between individuals, between individual and groups, and between group and group.

7. The community, its internal processes, modes of development and change, its social services and resources.

8. The social services, their structure, organization, and methods.

9. Himself, which enables the individual practitioner to be aware of and to take responsibility for his own emotions and attitudes as they affect his professional functions.

Method
(*i.e.*, an orderly systematic mode
of procedure. As used here, the term
encompasses social casework, social
group work, and community organization)

The social work method is the responsible, conscious, disciplined use of self in relationship with an individual or group. Through this relationship the practitioner facilitates interaction between the individual and his social environment with a continuing awareness of the reciprocal effects of one upon the other. It facilitates change: (1) within the individual in relation to his social environment; (2) of the social environment in its effect upon the individual; (3) of both the individual and the social environment in their interaction.

Social work method includes systematic observation and assessment of the individual or group in a situation and the formulation of an appropriate plan of action. Implicit in this is a continuing evaluation regarding the nature of the relationship between worker and client or group, and its effect on both the participant individual or group and on the worker himself. This evaluation provides the basis for the professional judgment which the worker must constantly make and which determines the direction of his activities. The method is used predominately in interviews, group sessions, and conferences.

Techniques
(*i.e.*, instrument or tool
used as a part of method)

Incorporated in the use of the social work method may be one or more of the following techniques in different combinations: (1) support, (2) clarification, (3) information-giving, (4) interpretation, (5) development of insight, (6) differentiation of the social worker from the individual or group, (7) identification with agency function, (8) creation and use of structure, (9) use of activities and projects, (10) provision of positive experiences, (11) teaching, (12) stimulation of group interaction, (13) limit-setting, (14) utilization of available social resources, (15) effecting change in immediate environmental forces operating upon the individual or groups, (16) synthesis.

Skill
(*i.e.*, technical expertness; the ability
to use knowledge effectively and readily in
execution or performance)

Competence in social work practice lies in developing skill in the use of the method and its techniques described above. This means the ability to help particular clients or groups in such a way that they clearly understand the social worker's intention and role, and are able to participate in the process of solving their problems. Setting the stage, the strict observance of confidentiality, encouragement, stimulation or participation, empathy, and objectivity are means of facilitating communication. The individual social worker always makes his own creative contribution in the application of social work method to any setting or activity.

As a way of increasing skill and providing controls to the activity of the social work practitioner, the following are utilized: (1) recording, (2) supervision, (3) case conferences, (4) consultation, (5) review and evaluation.

Teaching, Research, Administration

Three important segments of social work, namely, teaching, research, and administration, have significance for the development, extension, and transmission of knowledge of social work practice. These have many elements in common with social work practice, but in addition have their own uniqueness and some different objectives.

Comment

This manner of going at a social work definition has a number of advantages. Since social work is by its very nature concerned not with single entities but with multiple factors, interrelationships, and processes, a definition stated in the form of a configuration is particularly relevant. There is value in having a structure that can remain constant. We are often confused by definitions because they appear in different forms although their meaning may be similar. The concept of a working definition that is definitely intended to keep growing is also helpful because we can feel less critical and concerned over its early inadequacies. Also, it can more easily respond to growth and change in the profession and the surrounding society.

Long-Range Study

This working definition is a small beginning—but still it is a beginning—toward conceptualization of the basic elements in social work practice. There is general agreement that research is needed to define these elements. Understanding of these elements is needed in order to develop better agency programs, a sound educational curriculum, and competent workers. The diffuse activities now known as social work practice must be analyzed in such a way as to identify the central core. The primary goal is not to improve the status of social work (although this will be a by-product) but to enable its members to render better service because of their increased competence, clarity, and security in their functions. The results of research should eventually distinguish social work from the other helping professions.

The ways in which studies of practice could begin are legion, but probably the most important first step is the determination to undertake ongoing, basic research.[6]

In order to identify the basic elements in social work practice, we must take practice at its most fully developed points, where goals and methods can be clearly distinguished. This means looking at what professionally trained social workers are doing in well-defined social work programs. Only the characteristic social work activities would be studied. This will not necessarily be the whole job—some activities undertaken by social workers in their daily jobs will not fall within the definition of social work practice. Furthermore, studies of particular facets of the problem—such as the untrained worker—will have to be postponed. The first emphasis apparently will be description and analysis, with evaluation of results to come at a later period.

It appears that major effort in the early phase of study must be devoted to developing adequate research methodology. As yet there is no orderly system of concepts or reliable research instruments by which practice can be analyzed. It will be necessary to develop from the working definition of practice a conceptual scheme for classification of conditions (problems) encountered and services rendered in social work practice. Then, and only then, say the research advisers, can adequate research designs for the study of practice be formulated.

Some of the implications of this research approach to practice should be noted. Initial concentration on methodology seems essential to get started at all, but such focus could lead into a blind alley unless properly related to over-all purposes. Even the first step is a commitment. Purposes must, therefore, be carefully formulated. This will not be a single "master plan" but a long-range research effort in which each step must build on the preceding one. It should give us the type of cumulative thinking that social work practice has lacked and needed for so long. To do all this, professional social workers and research experts must work together. Such ongoing study can be a flexible process, growing and changing with social work itself.

Of course, there will be disappointment that we cannot immediately launch into active studies but must devote much effort

[6]Two research experts who are members of the group were asked to formulate an initial proposal, which has been accepted as a basis for action.

to developing study method and design. However, social workers can hardly expect to progress in research until they have a suitable body of concepts and research tools at their command. Actually the struggle to find a method should bring valuable insights regarding practice itself, and vice versa. This two-way interaction between study and service is one of the most encouraging aspects of a good study program. Since the problems are so difficult, there will inevitably be ups and downs, but the general momentum should continue. The profession through its professional association must consider this an indefinite commitment.

Trying to put first things first raises some difficult issues. Many groups of practitioners, as well as social work educators in the current Curriculum Study, urgently need basic criteria regarding knowledge, skills, and values essential for competent practice. But it appears that we do not at this time have that degree of understanding of our practice that will permit valid and authoritative answers to these questions. Neither do we have the tools with which to study and produce answers in a brief period. In the past, the social work profession has been too easily satisfied with short-range explorations and superficial answers to fundamental questions. The time has come when the profession must concentrate on building a long-range program in relation to practice, moving steadily through the necessary steps in logical order. In the end, we shall all be further ahead.

The Philosophy of Social Work

Paul Tillich

I have been asked to speak on the subject "The Philosophy of Social Work." No one can claim to give *the* philosophy of social work, and even *a* philosophy of social work is an enterprise which by far surpasses the limits of my ability and the time given me here.

What I shall attempt is to try to develop some ethical principles of social work which may be useful to reflect on and consider for those who do the work as well as for those of us who are only friends of such work but who may find their problems a mirror of the problems of human life generally.

Looking back in memory and with a little bit of pride at the twenty-five years of Selfhelp, its small beginning, its continuous

Reprinted from *The Social Service Review*, Vol. 36, No. 1 (March, 1962), pp. 13–16, by permission of The University of Chicago Press.

growth, its power to last, I see a healthy tree which never tried to grow beyond the natural strength of its roots, but under whose branches many birds from many countries, and often of surprising varieties, found a transitory refuge. It might well be that this help is partly dependent on a sound philosophy of social work, a philosophy which lives not only in the minds but in the hearts of those who work as part of Selfhelp.

Therefore, when I agreed to speak today about the "philosophy of social work," I was helped by the idea that I did not have to develop concepts out of the air but had only to give a philosophical interpretation of the actual work of Selfhelp and the basic convictions underlying this work—convictions which we have developed, discussed, and transformed during the twenty-five years of our existence.

The basis of all social work is the deficiency of every legal organization of society. A perfectly functioning organization of the whole society, a social mechanism embracing all mankind would not leave room for social work, but such a mechanism is unimaginable. It is prevented by two factors, one which is rooted in what we call today in philosophical jargon "man's existential predicament," his insufficiency. The second factor is rooted in man's existential nature, the uniqueness of every individual and every situation. No total regulation, even if given in the best interest of everybody, ever has adequately functioned either in war or in peace. The disorder produced by totalitarian regulations in Nazi Germany during the Second World War is equaled by the disorder in food distribution in Soviet Russia during the present cold war. Neither intellect nor character of men is adequate to such a task. And even if they were in one part of the world, interferences from other parts would spoil the functioning of a perfect social organization. The fact on which Selfhelp is based, the European immigration, was for a long time beyond the reach of any existing legal organization of social needs. Spontaneous social work was the only way to solve the immediate problem.

But this is a minor part of our question. More important is the fact that even in the best legal organization of social needs, every individual represents a unique problem. Only in a society which suppresses individual claims for help can this problem be put aside, and not only individual persons but also individual situations between persons, or persons and groups, transcend the reach of any legal organization. It is the greatness of man that his freedom implies a uniqueness which prohibits his being absorbed into a social machine so long as he remains man. For this reason social work is more than emergency work, unless one defines

emergency as a perpetual concomitant of the human situation—
and that probably is true.

Certainly all social work tries to make itself superfluous and
many forms of it have done so. And in all our discussions we often
have asked ourselves whether we have already reached that
stage, but each time we found a large number of emergency situations which required the continuation of our way of social
work.

We tried to listen to the situation as we did in the years of our
foundation, and in doing so we tried one of the great laws of life,
the law of "listening love." It is one of the decisive characteristics
of love that it listens sensitively and reacts spontaneously. As one
of our early friends, Max Wertheimer, has indicated, situations
have a voiceless voice. "Things cry," he used to say, but also what
cries most intensively are situations. It was the cry of a particular
situation which we hardly could have ignored and which drove us
to found Selfhelp. And it was not only the beginning of our history in which this happened. Again and again we had to listen
sensitively and to react spontaneously. It is certain that in some
situations we were not sensitive enough and reacted not spontaneously enough, but it was a fundamental principle of our philosophy of social work.

Social work is centered in individuals. The most concrete, and
therefore most important representative of social work is the
caseworker, and for him is valid what is valid for the whole organization in its relation to the individual. He also must listen
sensitively and respond spontaneously. He meets the individual
and he is in the understandable temptation of transforming care
into control. He is in danger of imposing instead of listening, and
acting mechanically instead of reacting spontaneously. Every social worker knows this danger, but not always does he notice
that he himself may have already fallen to this temptation. He
should not make a harsh judgment about it, but from time to time
he should restate the principle of "listening love" in order to dis-
solve any hardening mechanism in those who do social work.

The danger of which I am speaking is a tendency in every dealing with other persons to treat them as objects, as things to be directed and managed. It was always a symbol for me that the patients of the social worker were called cases. I do not know
whether a better word can be found, but the word "case" automatically makes of the individual an example for something
general. Who, I ask all of you, wants to be a case, but we all are
cases for the doctor, the counselor, the lawyer, and certainly the
social worker. He is not to blame for this inescapable situation,

but he would be to blame if in his dealing with the patient, with this case, he makes him into an object for whom everything is determined and in whom spontaneity is suppressed. The question is whether the caseworker is able to see in his patient not only what is comparable with other cases or identical with what he has experienced in other patients, but that he sees also the incomparable, the unique, rooted in the freedom of the patient. It is the amount of love between the social worker and the patient which here is decisive—the listening, responding, transforming love.

Here, when I use the term love, as before, I certainly do not mean the love which is emotion; nor do I think of *philia*—of friendship which only really develops between the social worker and his patient, nor do I think of the love which is *Eros,* which creates an emotional desire towards the patient that in many cases is more destructive than creative; rather, it is the love whose name in Greek is *agape* and in Latin *caritas*—the love which descends to misery and ugliness and guilt in order to elevate. This love is critical as well as accepting, and it is able to transform what it loves. It is called *caritas* in Latin, but it should not be confused with what the English form of the same word indicates today— namely, charity, a word which belongs to the many words which have a disintegrated, distorted meaning. Charity is often identical with social work, but the word "charity" has the connotation of giving for good causes in order to escape the demand of love. Charity as escape from love is the caricature and distortion of social work.

Critical love, which at the same time accepts and transforms, needs knowledge of him who is the object of love. The social worker must know his patient. But there are two different ways of knowing. We may distinguish them as our knowledge of the other one as a thing, and our knowledge of the other one as a person. The first is the cognition of external facts about somebody. The second is the participation in his inner self—as far as any human being is able to participate in another one. The first is done in detachment, through an empirical approach; the second is done through participation in the inner self of the other one. The first is unavoidable, but never enough in human relations. The second gives the real knowledge, but it is a gift given alone to the intuition of love. Here the social worker is in the situation of all of us in our daily encounters with each other. No amount of factual knowledge about each other can replace the intuition of love, which remains love even if it judges.

A refinement of the empirical way of knowing man has been given to us by the psychology of depth, the very name of which

Philosophy and Values

indicates that it will be more than knowledge of an object, that it will know the person as a person, but with the means of analysis of the dynamics of his being. It is a way, one could say, between the two other ones. It is understandable that it was attacked from both sides, and still is, but also that it was eagerly taken over as a tremendous help for social work, as well as for other fields. In earlier years, it often made the social worker into a dilettante psychoanalyst, just as the minister in the alliance of religion and psychological counseling is in danger of establishing himself as a minor psychoanalyst—an attitude against which I have warned my students of theology for thirty years now.

But there are two dangers in this—schematism and dogmatism. It judges the object of analysis according to schemes with a relative validity but never fully applicable, and it is dependent on the doctrines of the different psychotherapeutic schools, usually judging on the basis of one of them. As the best analyst knows, personal participation in terms of mutuality, and this means the intuitive love, is never dispersible. No matter how refined the psychoanalytic matter may be, if you don't have a point of communion with the central person of the other one, all the methods do no good in the long run. Analysis is a tool, very refined, but not without the danger of missing the end by the way in which the tool is used.

This leads to the last and perhaps the most important question—the end, the aim, of social work. The aim has several degrees. The first degree is the conquest of the immediate need, and here the factor of speed is important. The necessity of accepting and being willing to bear the consequences of possible errors, even of helping somebody who doesn't deserve help, must be taken by the social worker. It is analogous with love which has the principle that it is better missing several guilty ones than condemning one innocent one. The second degree is the self-abrogation, the self-conquest of social help, as far as possible, by guiding the person into independence. This is attempted always in all social agencies, but we know it is not always possible. Then there is a third stage about which I want to say a few words. On the basis of the present situation as I have seen it in the young people in all the colleges and universities, and in many other people, we mainly need to give the people of our time the feeling of being necessary.

Being necessary is, of course, never absolute. Nobody is indispensable. Nevertheless, somebody who does not feel necessary at all, who feels that he is a mere burden, is on the edge of total despair. In all groups I found this widespread feeling of not being necessary. There are many reasons for every effect, but one of the reasons for this is that in our secularized society one thing is lost, namely, that, whatever their external destiny may be, people no longer have an eternal orientation, an orientation which is independent of space and time. It is the feeling of having a necessary, incomparable, and unique place within the whole of being. Herein lies a danger for uprooted and migrating millions. It is a danger for mankind itself, namely, to feel that their existence as a whole is no longer necessary. The easy way in which politically we are playing now with collective suicide is analogous to the phenomenon of individuals who have lost the feeling of a necessary place, not only in their work and community, but also in the universe as a whole.

This leads to a final aim of social work. In helping every individual to find the place where he can consider himself as necessary, you help to fulfill the ultimate aim of man and his world, namely, the universal community of all beings in which any individual aim is taken into the universal aim of being itself. That is the highest principle of social work and, of course, transcends the limits of its techniques. It is certainly understandable that this aim is not always conscious to those who have the burden of the daily work. On the other hand, it may give them a spiritual lift in moments when they feel grateful to hear a response from one of thousands whom we may have helped. It may be of inspiration to us to think that we contribute to the ultimate aim of being itself in our small way—and every individual's way is small. To give such inspiration may be a function of an hour of memory such as the present one.

Human Values and the Poor

Mary J. McCormick

The presence of the poor has always harassed the human race. In centuries past Hebrew prophets and Greek philosophers, Roman statesmen and Christian converts deplored the sufferings of the weak and the oppressed. Against the background of the Mosaic law, with its passion for justice, Isaias described the poor as "the rich man's prey" and as human beings whose rights are "ground in the dust." In the Book of Proverbs, Solomon declared that "the poor man's need [is] his peril" and that "to the friendless [the poor] every day brings trouble." The Athenian stranger in Plato's Laws discoursed on "the hard necessity of poverty"

Reprinted with permission of the author and The Family Service Association of America from *Social Casework*, Vol. 46, No. 3 (March 1965), pp. 132–141.

which drives men "by pain into utter shamelessness." Seneca, in his treatise *On the Happy Life*, encourages men to give if, by doing so, they can keep a deserving person from being dragged down by poverty.

Under the Christian law, special emphasis was given to the importance of charity. Christ not only lived and worked among the poor but also maintained a complete identification with them. Throughout His life, He reminded His followers, in a variety of ways, that "you have the poor among you always so that you can do good to them when you will," and there is no indication that He foresaw a time when this would not be so. As a result, those whom He left to organize the Church, charged particular members of their group with the care of widows and orphans because these persons "were [being] neglected in the daily administration of relief." In the 1960's, both the complaint and the action are disconcertingly familiar.

It is unnecessary to recount in this article all the plans and programs that have been directed toward the problems of the poor at various periods in the world's history. The efforts to "do good" to them took shape in the monasteries of the Middle Ages, in the workhouses of the seventeenth century, and in the Poor Law reforms of 1834. They continued in the charity organization societies of the nineteenth century, the family and children's services of the twentieth century, and the Social Security Act of 1935.

Such efforts have stemmed from widely divergent philosophies. Some authorities have held firmly and sternly to the belief that misfortune is solely the fault of the victim and that he must, therefore, be punished. At the other extreme are those who have subscribed to the belief that no person is ever the master of his fate and that personal responsibility should be minimized. Hence, permissiveness has alternated with punishment while the poor have maintained their *status quo*.

These divergent approaches were partially reconciled in the early 1900's when interest began to be directed to the causes as well as the cure of poverty. Supported by developments in the behavioral and social sciences, the experts undertook to examine, on the one hand, those personal factors that might account for the seeming permanence of poverty and, on the other, the shortcomings of a society that tolerated such permanence. The consequent awakening of a social conscience led the United States into an era of legislative reform and voluntary philanthropic endeavor interrupted only by World War I and resumed again in the affluent twenties. During this period, the growth of social work as a discipline in its own right brought with it renewed emphasis on the individual character of social ills. The view was advanced that each problem is experienced differently by each person who has it, that any problem inevitably carries both personal and social implications and must be treated in terms of this knowledge.

Significant as these developments were, it took the shock of a nationwide depression in the thirties and the emergence of widespread poverty before a social security program was enacted. Representing the combined efforts of legislators and social workers, the Social Security Act provided insurance against dependency and help for those who were its victims. In the thirty years since the passage of the Act the coverage of various groups in the population has steadily expanded; the amount of the grants has increased; and the administration of the Act has become more flexible and also more complex. Yet, today, in the mid-1960's, one out of every five Americans is counted "among the poor"; hence President Johnson's declaration in 1964 of an "unconditional war on poverty," which, in his words, "the richest nation on earth can afford to win . . . [but] . . . cannot afford to lose. . . ."[1]

The Battle Front of Human Values

If men and matériel, technical skill and scientific knowledge, public support and private commitment are effective weapons, then victory should be a foregone conclusion, for all of these resources—and more—are present in abundance. In a sense, the multiplicity of resources is equalled only by the multiplicity of the problems they are intended to solve. But wars—at least "conventional" wars—have many battlefields, some of which are less easily identifiable than the destitution of an Appalachia or the explosiveness of a Harlem or a Hunter's Point. In addition to the visible fronts that statisticians, journalists, and social workers describe with such vividness and accuracy, there are other fronts that defy description because they are invisible, intimate, and pervasive. Their boundaries are those *human values* that, among the poor, are too often remarkable only because of their absence. These are, however, the boundaries along which strategic battles must be fought, not merely for the duration of the war on poverty, but for as long as any segment of mankind chooses to pursue the democratic way of life.

[1]Lyndon B. Johnson, "The State of the Union Message," presented at the opening session of the 88th Congress of the United States, January 8, 1964, *U.S. Congressional Record*, Government Printing Office, Washington, D.C., 1964.

Philosophy and Values

The fact that America has chosen this "way" scarcely needs reaffirmation here. "The paramount goal of the United States was set long ago. It is to guard the rights of the individual, to ensure his development, and to enlarge his opportunity. It is set forth in the Declaration of Independence. . . ."[2] The report on national goals, which opens with these statements, proceeds to identify American goals at home and abroad. The first three goals—individual dignity, equality, and effective liberty—serve also to identify the basic values that are in constant jeopardy among the poor and that the current war will have to defend. It is true that there is a distinction between goals and values, but there is also the kind of interdependence that leads, quite logically, to their joint discussion. In brief, goals represent the object of man's desire, the things that he wants because they are pleasing to him. "Values, on the other hand, are defined, sociologically, at a higher level of abstraction, since they lend direction to performance . . .; they offer standards by which social living can be measured."[3]

Individual Dignity

The absence or breakdown of these standards is one of the greatest deprivations that the poor man suffers, a deprivation intimately associated with those violations of human dignity that are the visible signs of poverty—bad housing, deteriorated neighborhoods, unsavory work, unwholesome recreation. All these are counted among the indignities of the poor. It is important to understand, however, that they are, in reality, "accidentals" of violated dignity: they are not intrinsic to dignity per se. For "dignity does not consist in being well-housed, well-clothed, and well-fed. . . . Dignity does not derive from a man's economic situation, nor from his vocation. It does not require a white-collar job or any other status symbol." On the contrary, dignity, as a positive value, "rests exclusively upon the lively faith that individuals are beings of infinite value." Quoting Abraham Lincoln may seem trite, but he did say, on one occasion, "It is difficult to make a man miserable while he feels he is worthy of himself and claims kindred to the great God who made him."[4]

This concept of individual dignity needs little elaboration for members of the helping professions. With a unanimity almost unique among specialists, they accept the fact that a man possesses personal worth simply because he is a man. Consequently,

[2]President's Commission on National Goals, *Goals for Americans*, Prentice-Hall, New York, 1960, p. 1.

[3]Mary J. McCormick, "The Role of Values in Social Functioning," *Social Casework*, Vol. XLII, February 1961, p. 72.

[4]President's Commission on National Goals, *op. cit.*, p. 49.

whatever threatens his sense of personal worth—and poverty today does just that—becomes a challenge to professional dedication and effort. The trouble is that, in the face of the increasing pressures of a crowded, competitive, mechanized world, it is difficult to serve, with real effectiveness, those whose dignity is shattered. Some of them do not know that help is available for the asking; others know but are fearful and suspicious because the help comes from an alien world that seems far removed from the one in which they exist rather than live. For theirs is the world in which, as one journalist has phrased it, "Poverty is dirty, hungry, cold in winter, broiling in summer, and worst of all it is lonely and self-reproaching."[5] They accept misfortune, they bear it without struggle, and they see themselves and their neighbors as worthless failures. The sense of worthlessness and the self-reproach come together in a closed and vicious circle, which is both the cause and the effect of the poverty that seems so final.

Perhaps this is the reason the professions sometimes have as much difficulty helping the poor as the poor have in seeking and using their help. Professional people are committed to an orientation diametrically opposed to the apathy and lack of initiative that seem almost indigenous to poverty. Theirs is a world in which a person is expected to exercise control over his problems and initiative in solving them. He does this by the intelligent use of his own personal resources, augmented, when necessary, by those of the community. The principle of interaction thus comes into play; society assumes a degree of responsibility for the well-being of a member, and he, in turn, perfects that well-being for the good of others as well as himself. When this happens, the common good and individual fulfillment join in a two-way flow of giving and receiving, and, in the process, human dignity is fostered and reinforced. The person becomes increasingly conscious of his own worth, both to himself and to his fellow men. The goals he pursues become more desirable because they are shared; the values to which he subscribes exert greater influence because they are the combined values of the many and the one.[6]

Failure in Communication

These are the convictions that motivate those who offer professional services; and the influence of the convictions is apparent in every stage of the helping process. Paradoxically, however,

[5]Ben H. Badikian, "The Invisible Americans," *Saturday Evening Post*, December 21–28, 1963, p. 37.
[6]McCormick, *op. cit.*, pp. 70-78.

it is precisely in the helping process that such beliefs are apt to become a liability rather than an asset, for, in the interchange of giving and receiving help, culture and subculture meet. The difficulty is that they do not always merge. The professional culture is committed to definite ideas and ideals about personal adequacy as a goal and a value; the subculture of poverty deprives its members of mastery over their own lives. In addition, it repudiates the responsibility that such mastery would entail because, for the poor, "taking a chance hurts too much." Consequently, their response—or lack of it—"may confuse, then alarm, and finally anger" the professional person even while he recognizes the dynamics and sympathizes with the behavior.[7]

The problem then becomes one of finding a solution for this failure to establish communication, for that is the real issue. The poor and their helpers need to become better acquainted, and obviously the initiative has to be taken by the helpers. It is an encouraging fact that social workers, along with the personnel of other professions, are doing this. They are attempting, in many ways, to bridge the gap between the culture of a democracy and the culture of those who, by virtue of a common heritage, should belong to that democracy, but, through the exigencies of their lot, are separated from it. Much has already been accomplished through less formalized interviewing, readier involvement in the lives of the poor, and multiple-client interviewing and other group approaches that encourage mutual participation and understanding.

These attempts have not yet been made on a broad enough front, however. For the most part, they represent the current interests of particular workers or agencies and are carried out on a purely experimental basis. They do not reach enough people, either among the poverty-stricken or the helping professions. Nor do they exhaust the possibilities inherent in a wide range of activities that are only now being explored. Consequently, these efforts alone will not break down the wall that separates so many human beings from the human values of dignity and worth. These values must be supported not only by the elect among the professions but also by a society that accepts as its "first national goal . . . the development of each individual to his fullest potential" and is ready to strive for that goal through concerted action. If the proposed war can consolidate such action, if it can challenge effectively the inward, as well as the outward, manifestations of violated dignity, then, in the words of Walter Lippmann,

[7]Robert Coles, "Psychiatrists and the Poor," *The Atlantic*, July 1964.

"The cause will be good for the poor whom it will benefit. But it will be especially good for the country which, after enlisting [in that cause] will respect itself a good deal more than it now does."[8]

Equality

In the document that marked the birth of the United States, certain truths are presented that are held to be self-evident: that is, they require no proof. These truths are cited so often that repetition seems wholly unwarranted. Yet, there is ample reason, in the mid-sixties, for accepting Henry M. Wriston's statement that "familiarity with words of the Declaration has bred inattention to their full meaning."[9] Perhaps the explanation rests, at least partially, in the fact that the simple, declarative sentences mean, *literally*, what they say: "All men are created equal;" all "are endowed by their Creator with certain unalienable rights;" among these "are life, liberty, and the pursuit of happiness. . . ." *Equality* and *effective liberty* are thereby ranked with *individual dignity* among the possessions that the Creator gave to His creatures and that, by virtue of their origin, are a part of man's inheritance.

It seems pointless to attempt to add to—or elaborate on—the current literature dealing with poverty and what it tells about the *status quo* of this heritage.[10] The contributions during 1964 alone range all the way from the coldly scientific studies of the research analysts to the human interest stories of the feature writers. Books, pamphlets, and government documents have been supplemented by conference reports and statistical findings at every level of sophistication. It is safe to assume that each contributor has something to say about the inequality and lack of freedom that complicate still further the causes and effects of poverty by displacing the positive goals and values that are the counterparts of equality and freedom.

It is also safe to assume, at least for the present discussion, that each of these writers recognizes, from his own vantage point, four major areas in which such negative forces operate: economic opportunity, education, occupation, and the law. It is true that deprivation in any one of these areas carries over into each of the others, for man reacts as an integrated whole, not as a creature of segmented parts. However, there is a kind of "specialized" pov-

[8]Walter Lippmann, "The President and Poverty," The Washington Post Co., Washington, D.C., 1963.
[9]President's Commission on National Goals, *op. cit.*, p. 35.
[10]American Public Welfare Association, *"Poverty": Selected Reading References*, rev. ed., the Association, Chicago, 1964.

erty associated with each, which has its own particular effect on the goals and values of the poor whom it engulfs.

Economic Opportunity and
the Poor

The first of these, economic opportunity, embraces such tangibles as property, income, and money. The impact of poverty on this trio is self-evident. The poor do not own property in a society in which ownership is both a status symbol and a mark of psychological and social security. Neither do they have the occupational choices that belong to a competitive social order or the financial returns that accompany stable employment. Least of all do they have money, which, irrespective of the amount, is identified with some degree of mastery and power. The result of the combined deprivation is the "human tragedy of life without opportunity."

The role of private ownership does not have to be argued here. Such ownership is fundamental to a democratic social order; it belongs among man's natural rights and is, in a sense, a guarantee of economic independence. The individual who owns property is, theoretically at least, in a position to discharge his obligations to himself and to others. Moreover, he can, if he wishes, do this freely and independently and in line with his own best interests, both material and psychological. The resultant action becomes both a matter of status and a mark of inner security because, in performing it, the person testifies to his own faith in himself and his usefulness to others. Within the confines of the same action, he makes use of "the opportunity and the encouragement to work, to play, to create, to communicate, to enjoy beauty. . . ." In other words, he experiences those satisfactions of normal living that are denied the poor because of their poverty, and that the current war must somehow make possible for them if the United States is to perpetuate her image as the land of opportunity.

The same principles operate in the money-income cycle. In the course of the exhaustive studies of the past few years, the specialists have established certain criteria for judging the level of living of a family and used them as guides in setting income levels. In the late 1940's the United States Senate study set the poverty line at a $2,500 annual money income for an urban family of four. Updated for 1960, the figure was increased by about $500. An AFL-CIO study established the figure at $3,000. This amount identifies poverty at its extreme. Families suffer from real hunger, inadequate clothing, deplorable housing; they are denied any of the coveted extras.[11]

[11]Earl Raab and Hugh Folk, *The Pattern of Dependent Poverty in California*, Welfare Study Commission, Appendix G, Consultants' Reports, March 1963, p. 354.

The next, or subsistence, line offers no great improvement. The base figures for it, as established by the same investigators, respectively, are $4,000 and $4,800. These amounts, unsupplemented, will barely feed, clothe, and shelter the urban family of four at a substandard level. An adequate budget calls for an additional $2,000. Money income in the neighborhood of $6,000 should provide a level of living that is modest but sufficient as long as extraneous demands are minimal. This is the marginal line, however, and its hazards are, in reality, serious. It is true that the extra $2,000 brings a different over-all standard of living and some degree of security on a day-by-day basis. It is equally true that this differential brings no protection against the emergencies that may, at any time, precipitate a move to the other side of the poverty line.[12]

The really alarming thing about these figures is that they apply to flesh and blood—to people in numbers so great that "mass poverty" is now an accepted phrase. In the State of California alone, one-half million persons are below the "poverty line"; one million persons are at the level of "bare subsistence"; at least three million are in the "barely adequate" category. In other words, one quarter of the population of a highly affluent state is composed of those who already experience poverty and those who are constantly threatened by it. It is reasonable to assume that economic insecurity such as this will be reflected in the physical and psychological reactions of those who are plagued by it. Among the poor, present fears tend to overshadow future hopes. Consequently, their goals are dictated by expediency rather than by long-range planning; their values are the values of the moment, for "neither memory nor anticipation can do much for them." The current war cannot eradicate the memories, but one of its objectives is to stimulate the anticipation.

Survival and the Ability to Produce

The income picture is further complicated by the twin factors of occupation and education, each of which is, in its own way, a condition of survival. In the United States of the 1960's, survival is dependent, to an unprecedented degree, on the ability to produce. This ability depends, in turn, on the combined assets of training, whether of mind or body or both, and of skill—that is, the smoothness and certainty with which knowledge flows into

[12]*Ibid.* and Mary J. McCormick, "Poverty in the Bay Area," *The Monitor*, San Francisco, October 4, 1963, p. 354.

action. When the flow becomes synonymous with production, the cycle is completed and leads to further action. The person who is the moving force—whether he has produced material goods or mathematical formulas—thus establishes his usefulness and achieves some personal and social independence. He accomplishes this through the effective use of resources that are uniquely his and that have been channeled by him, voluntarily, toward socially satisfying ends.

Needless to say, this is not the pattern among the poor, for the poor of today are the nonproducers. Earl Raab and Hugh Folk, in their report on their study in California, describe poverty as the *status quo* of people who produce at a low level or not at all. These are the people who are not capable, either actually or potentially, of responding to the demands of an economy that, other things being equal, could support them. Who, then, are these nonproducers and "what are the forces which impoverish them and make them dependent?" Of more immediate concern, perhaps, What can be done for and with them? California answers for itself (in the pages of the Welfare Study Commission reports) much as the experts answer for the nation.[13]

At both the state and national level, these nonproducers are distributed, principally, among five population groups. Three of these are the groups for which society has always had to bear the burden: the aged who cannot meet the costs of being old; the mothers of dependent children who are without the safeguards of normal family life; and the handicapped who cannot cope with the demands of a competitive society. The fourth and fifth groups are those about which the planners of the present war need to be actively concerned, if for no other reason than that they are less easily categorized and explained and, so far as remedial measures go, less easily reached.

One of these groups is made up of men and women who, for want of training and skill, cannot compete in a labor market that gives highest priority to such qualifications. These people cannot benefit either from employment demands in general or from specific job opportunities. The other group is something of a mid-century phenomenon and is especially disturbing to those engaged in the helping professions. It consists of the 50 per cent of the population twenty-five years of age or older who have less than a high-school education. Of this group, 15 per cent did not finish grammar school. There is no need to underline the fact that the problem is complicated further by the racial factor; a larger

[13]Raab and Folk, *op. cit.*, p. 347.

percentage of nonwhite than of white persons have not completed high school. The total group, nonwhite and white, is replenished annually by a distressingly high number of school dropouts, both voluntary and requested. These are the "jobless, aimless, hopeless youngsters" who join the nonproductive adults in perpetuating the poverty against which the present war is directed.[14]

The very title of the official document, the Economic Opportunity Act of 1964—which is, in effect, the declaration of the war—indicates the principal battle lines on which the war will be fought, lines that, according to President Johnson, extend to "every private home, in every public office, from the courthouse to the White House."[15] Among the major provisions of the Act are those that establish programs of training, retraining, and relocation for the nation's potential, but currently unproductive, labor force.[16] The Act holds out new hope for those whose skills and abilities have been replaced by machines and for those whose capabilities have never been explored or encouraged. Its aim is "not only to relieve the symptom of poverty but to cure it, and, above all, to prevent it."[17]

Serving the Impoverished

The difficulty is that immediate programs are, of necessity, ex post facto solutions; they must aim, initially, at the repair of damage already done. This calls for great tolerance of the apparent slowness with which remedial and preventive measures become operative, for time is, in itself, an obstacle to rapid progress when human beings are involved—beings who, by their very nature, often work against their own best interests. This means that those who are in key administrative positions as well as those who are involved in direct service will have to recognize and respond to the feelings and emotions of people who are, for all practical purposes, without defined goals and values. These are people who have never known the enthusiasm that is stimulated by challenging, purposeful occupation; they have never had the ego satisfaction of being producers. They are the "impoverished people" who, to place Jerome Cohen's words in another context, "differ greatly in the extent to which they can live beyond the moment." Dr. Cohen is referring to the differences among the poor themselves: "Some use religious convictions to

[14]*Ibid.*, pp. 348–56, 367–68.
[15]Johnson, *op. cit*
[16]Public Law 88–452, 88th Congress, 2nd Session, 1964.
[17]Johnson, *op. cit.*

absorb the pain of the moment. Others have different but equally deep attachments."[18] The point here is that the concept applies, with equal weight, to the differences between the poor and those who, within the present program, are responsible for their betterment—persons who do live beyond the moment. These are the goal-conscious, value-conscious men and women who approach the poor out of a background of middle-class culture in which future goals are the desirable ones and in which success, both personal and social, is evaluated in terms of progress toward, or attainment of, those goals.

Perhaps the real challenge that lies ahead is that of establishing a common ground on which persons for whom goals and values are defined and those for whom they are scarcely realities can meet. The poor must be given a chance to know, as people as well as experts, those who are responsible for helping; the specialist must, on his part, come to know the poor as individuals, not as categories.

This is the kind of reciprocal association that, in her own unique and sensitive fashion, Mary Richmond appreciated so keenly. She called it friendship, but of a special sort; she characterized it as reasonable and orderly, while, at the same time, reflecting "the power of sympathy"; most of all, she saw it as motivated by charity, or love. To her, charity meant "sympathetic and patient appreciation of the lives and aims of creatures least like ourselves." Many years later, and within the contemporary frame of reference, Gordon Hamilton identified "a special kind of love" as an essential element in the helping process: the ingredients, "warmth, concern, therapeutic understanding"; its end result, a relationship (or acquaintance or friendship) in which each person offers to the other something of himself. One uses help when the other cares enough to give it; the other gives out of a conscious willingness to enter into and share the life experiences of a fellow man. The interchange is vital; without it, the process of giving and receiving is no more than a travesty of charity, for it denies man the respect that is both his birthright and his constitutional right.[19]

Legal Protection and the Poor

Protection of constitutional rights is a major goal of the law in a democratic society. Moreover, this protection extends, *de jure*, to

---

[18]Jerome Cohen, "Social Work and the Culture of Poverty," *Social Work*, Vol. IX, January 1964, p. 100.

[19]Mary J. McCormick, "A Legacy of Values," *Social Casework*, Vol. XLII, October 1961, pp. 404–409.

every citizen; it is valid for all times and places. Yet it is an acknowledged fact that, in the world's greatest democracy, "equality before the law has failed to control inequality which is beyond the law." And the victims of this failure are the poor.[20]

The reasons for *de facto* inequality are many and varied. The cost of legal service, like the cost of medical care, is such that private counsel is largely unavailable; the poor man cannot afford it. Meanwhile, the legal aid services at his disposal are overburdened, like the medical clinics on which he relies, and delays are inevitable. Even so, financial costs and delayed action are only a part of the problem. Court dockets are crowded, judges are under pressure, and the "rule of law" becomes increasingly difficult to follow. Presumably, these external hindrances could be corrected or mitigated through administrative changes within the judicial system; for example, informal disposition instead of formal adjudication of cases. The more complicated aspect of the situation, however, is one that only the expressed will of society—perhaps encouraged by the current attack on poverty—can remedy: the *helplessness* of the poor as they are confronted with the need to defend their rights.[21]

Sometimes this helplessness stems from ignorance; the poor do not know what their rights are, much less how to go about protecting them. Sometimes the sense of worthlessness and defeat so characteristic of poverty leaves its victims inert and apparently indifferent. But at other times a more immediate and objective reality (and a more serious one in terms of society's responsibility) accounts for their inaction—the fear that defensive action will jeopardize financial help, especially if that help comes from public funds. Such help is per se within the law; certain aspects of its administration are interpreted by some authorities as being outside the law, to wit, the midnight searches that Charles Reich declares, unequivocally, to be a flagrant violation of the constitutional rights assured by the Fourth and Fourteenth Amendments.[22]

The rationale and the procedure of the searches are familiar. The expressed purpose is to check on eligibility for assistance. Eligibility may be determined by the presence in, or absence from, the home of an adult male who is capable of supporting the

[20]William J. Kerby, *The Social Mission of Charity: A Study of Points of View in Catholic Charities*, Macmillan Co., New York, 1921, p. 74.
[21]Henry H. Foster, Jr., "Social Work, the Law, and Social Action," *Social Casework*, Vol. XLV, July 1964, pp. 383–92.
[22]Charles A. Reich, "Midnight Welfare Searches and the Social Security Act," *Yale Law Journal*, Vol. LXXII, June 1963, pp. 1347–60.

family. "The demand for entry, without a warrant, in the middle of the night or in the early morning, may carry with it the threat, express or implied, that refusal to admit will lead to discontinuance of public assistance."[23] On the basis of careful and explicit legal documentation, Mr. Reich establishes the unconstitutional nature of the procedure: it violates "the right of the people to be secure in their persons, houses, papers and effects, against unreasonable searches and seizures. . . ."[24] These rights, as guaranteed by the Fourth Amendment, "are enforceable against the federal government and, through the due process clause of the fourteenth amendment, against the states." They are violated when "the recipients of public bounty . . . may be forced to endure official . . . prying."[25]

The question then is, as Mr. Reich phrases it, "If the practice of searching the homes of public assistance recipients is unconstitutional, why has it continued so long?[26] Mr. Reich's answer fits the context here. He says,

A major reason is that persons on public assistance are in no position to enforce a constitutional right of privacy. They lack the means and knowledge to litigate constitutional questions. And the available legal remedies are inadequate. . . . [They] are strictly after-the-fact; they do not bar the searches. The only way to bar the searches is to refuse to admit the investigators, and in the present state of the law that means risking the loss of subsistence for the family.[27]

This is just one instance in which protection within the law does not extend to protection beyond the law and the poor are penalized for their poverty. Equality under the law, as a right of the individual and a goal of society, is denied, at least tacitly, and the values surrounding individual dignity are placed in further jeopardy. All this occurs in the United States of the 1960's in spite of the fact that democracy "has a fundamental commitment to equality, in the best and most realistic senses of that word: to equality before the law, equality of political voice, equality in constitutional rights, equality of opportunity, and equality of consideration."[28] The commitment falls short of its mark every time the house of a poor man is invaded and he is defenseless against the invader.

[23]Ibid., p. 1347.
[24]Ibid.
[25]Ibid.
[26]Ibid., p. 1355.
[27]Ibid.
[28]President's Commission on National Goals, op. cit., p. 74.

Self-Determination:
The Root of Effective
Liberty

The British economist Barbara Ward claims that one of the great ideas the genius of the Greeks gave to mankind was that of "the free and responsible citizen participating in a political community based on law."[29] In this constructive, sanctioned participation, the free man enjoys effective liberty—liberty that "requires a continuous exercise of judgment and will" because it is postulated on the rights of others as well as of self. The values surrounding the common good, as well as the personal good, are fostered; the restraints that protect the goals of each are accepted. In the political system and way of life that is called democracy, men guard their freedom through sharing it with others, both at home and abroad. The trouble is that in the United States today this sharing does not extend to at least one fifth of the nation's population—for the poor at home (like the poor of all nations and all ages) do not share, either materially or psychologically, because they are not free!

The war on poverty has as its avowed goal the achievement of freedom in the material order, that is, in the order of opportunity, of work, of law, and of personal worth as related to productivity. Legislation provides the framework; the Office of Economic Opportunity will provide the implementation. But, unfortunately, the programs per se cannot cope with the *intangibles* of poverty—the attitudes and reactions that, perpetuated among the poor through long conditioning, are the real obstacles to sharing. Neither political machinery nor money nor social improvements can, for example, engender in the poor man self-esteem and the self-determination which is the root of freedom and of which he has so long been deprived.

This point is crucial, for responsible, goal-directed behavior is part and parcel of the American way of life; it represents certain sets of values that the normal, balanced person cherishes—the values that belong to personal identity (to being one's self); to reasonable self-sufficiency (to working out one's own problems); and to decision making (to making up one's own mind). These sets of values are so interrelated as to be, for all practical purposes, inseparable. Yet the last-mentioned is probably the most cherished and crucial. Decision making is one of the sharpest demands that the twentieth century imposes on any individual; he meets, or fails to meet, its demands as an inte-

[29]Barbara Ward, *Faith and Freedom*, Doubleday & Co., New York, 1958, p. 56.

grated self through which the whole of his life—physical and mental, conscious and unconscious—is expressed by a single act in which he is a free agent.

Unless this capacity for decision making, which is both a native endowment and a constitutional right, is preserved among those who use it and developed among those who do not, this nation may find herself in the paradoxical position of winning many battles in the material order but losing the war in the psychological one. For in this kind of warfare, time, rather than technique, is the controlling factor. And it takes time to gain an understanding of the goals and values of that freedom that is bolstered, on the one hand, by equality and, on the other, by a sense of personal worth.

To say again that the poor are not free is merely to repeat the obvious; to conclude that the war in their behalf will not be won until they are, is only to be realistic; to foresee the difficulties and uncertainties of the campaign to which the nation is now committed is only to benefit from history. Perhaps there never can be total victory. It is not only possible, but entirely probable, that the poor will be among us always—so that we can do good to them. In proposing to do that good by launching a full-scale attack on poverty, the United States is testifying to her own conscience and challenging her own resources. She is doing so with sincerity, dedication, and strength. In the spirit of these virtues, her leaders can do one thing more—they can recall and, with the insertion of a single word, apply to themselves and their programs and to the poor and their problems the familiar lines from the familiar *Elegy*:

> Let not Ambition mock their useful toil;
> Nor Grandeur hear with a disdainful smile,
> The short and [not] simple annals of the poor.

Intercultural Aspects of Social Work

Eileen Younghusband

A seminar on intercultural perspectives in social work education was held at the East-West Center, University of Hawaii, from February 21st to March 4th, 1966, sponsored by the Council on Social Work Education and the East-West Center and financed by

Reprinted with permission of the Council on Social Work Education from *Journal of Education for Social Work*, Vol. 2, No. 1 (Spring 1966), pp. 59–65.

a grant from the Vocational Rehabilitation Administration of the United States Federal Department of Health, Education, and Welfare with assistance from the East-West Center. The Director was Dr. Mildred Sikkema, and the discussions were led by the Chairman, Dr. Herman Stein, Dean of the School of Applied Social Sciences, Western Reserve University. Among the twenty-two participants were social work educators, sociologists, psychologists, and anthropologists from the U.S.A., Canada, India, Japan, Pakistan, the Philippines, Singapore, and Thailand, including the presidents of the International Conference of Social Work and the International Association of Schools of Social Work from Yugoslavia and the United Kingdom, respectively.

The mixture of cultures and disciplines resulted in very lively discussions in which no holds were barred. The usual danger in such intercultural gatherings is that because they take place between people who have all been educated in the West, they lead either to over-denial of difference or to over-assertion of difference as a matter of national pride. The members of this seminar were too varied and experienced to let either happen.

The agenda for the discussions was made up of the intercultural aspects of social work—values, function, and method. Because nothing was taken for granted, but everything was meant to be analyzed and questioned, it looked at times as though nothing would be left but a few vague generalizations. The group went through the normal group processes of analyzing, discarding, and going around in circles. Finally, in the last few days, it found it was clear about a good many questions with regard to social work values, the relation between social work and the social sciences, and the nature of social work and its desirable course of professional development, together with the uses and limitations of its present three methods: casework, group work, and work with communities.

Social Work Values

Social work values were a constantly recurrent theme all through the discussions, with much pressure exerted by the North Americans on the Asians to examine whether and to what extent the traditional social work values were truly universal or were instead derived from a particular Western culture at a given point in its historical evolution. In essence, the conflict was recognized as being between values regarded as inherent in the individual and values deriving from status, kinship, religious affiliation, and ethnic group membership.

The term "values" itself tended to be rather loosely used to include ethical values or "oughts," people's actual preferences and choices, and cultural attitudes: for example, past or future orientations to time.

The Asians, whether anthropologists or social work educators, took the view that what are often described as Western values, like the worth and dignity of the individual, are not specifically Western, but first emerged in the West in the processes of historical evolution associated with industrialization. They pointed out that previously Western and Eastern values were much the same, and that the values of the educated elite in Asia are closer to those of the West than to peasant populations in their own countries. They also pointed out the similarities shown in attitudes and values by studies of groups that are grossly deprived—economically, emotionally, and socially—in any part of the world, in both urban and rural conditions.

The Asians were much less troubled about the imposition of values than the Westerners and said that if social work values (which derive largely from Greek philosophy, some aspects of the Judeo-Christian tradition, and the Age of Enlightenment) are good values, then it is a desirable social work function to act as a change agent in the spread of these values. In any event, historical evolution everywhere is producing a convergence of values.

There was a good deal of discussion as to how social workers could base their practice upon the principles of individual freedom and choice in situations where decisions are customarily made by authority figures: the head of the family, the wise elders, the head man. Instances were cited of the use for change that can be made of the slack that exists in any social system.

It was agreed that any professional practice must rest upon some degree of common perception of purpose and function between the practitioner and the client and be demanded by the wider community. This creates problems for social work in those situations where people expect authoritarian solutions, expect to be told what the problem is and what they ought to do. This is true especially in community work where people often expect the worker to get things for them or to side with them against some other group rather than that they themselves should be involved in working to meet their needs.

It was agreed that the ultimate aim in social work is the well-being of the individual human being, that nothing should be done to diminish his humanity and everything possible done in the given circumstances to enhance it. As one member put it: "It isn't possible to analyze this value further; it is a value at the end of the line, and one can only assent with a grunt."

There are obviously various derivative or instrumental values related to this. There was much discussion about the derivative value of self-determination and some feeling that this had ceased to be a useful concept, particularly in work with groups and communities where it is not at all obvious who or what is the "self" which determines. Various alternative terms like personality growth, self-reliance, self-enhancement, self-realization, self-fulfillment, and increased capacity for choice were explored. Also, the idea that behind these various terms lay a real experience, a sense of the desirability of bringing more elements in the personality within the central organizing system, of promoting the growth of the self, of a sense of self-worth, of the self as cause, and of enhancing the capacity for responsibility and choice. This of course raised the question of whether personality development was synonymous with self-determination, or whether there are different ways in which the self develops, and thus whether the extended family or other group might be a means to self-development rather than a hindrance. In any event, the whole concept of self-determination may be culture bound; and it is not clear whether it is a goal or a process or both.

Quite early in the seminar it was agreed that social work is committed to social change. This was defined as "change for the better" but although participants kept on coming back to it, they never came to grips with what was meant by "better." The Indian member suggested that it included concepts of individual freedom, of material well-being, of mastery of self, of better opportunities for all, and of better social adjustment.

There were various attempts to list values, in the sense of human needs, like a rising standard of living, or desires like liberty or equality, but with recognition of problems that arise from the clash between values and the dilemma of "what trumps what." This dilemma included the clash between professional and culturally held values. Such a clash occurs, for example, in circumstances where it is assumed that one should get jobs for one's relatives or where one's professional values conflict with the tenets of one's religion.

There was much stress on the increase of rationality (as against prejudice, superstition, ignorance, and traditional procedures) as a value and therefore the commitment of the professions to the increase of rationality, even including, as one member put it: "the rational use of the irrational." At the same time it was clear that the greater the growth and application of scientific knowledge, particularly in the social and behavioral sciences, the greater the need for professional value commitments in order to protect the individual, group, or community from manipulation and exploitation.

This same essential problem of values kept on cropping up in various forms. It was expressed in such questions as should the social worker give expression to his values or only encourage the client to express his, in the hope that sooner or later he will arrive at those of the social worker? This specter of skillful manipulation, of forcing men to be free, of "Daddy knows best" kept floating across all the discussions.

Social Work Function

The function of social work gave the group quite as much trouble as values. Here, too, more questions were arrived at than answers. It became clear that the social work function differs in different parts of the world according to major needs, resources, and priorities in the culture, but the similarities seemed sufficient for the same profession to be recognizable everywhere. At the same time, it was clear that social work is a fluid and emerging profession, and like many other professions, it is not stable either at its center or its circumference.

The social scientist chided the social workers with picking up bits of knowledge from the social sciences and psychology but not developing any "hard" knowledge of their own. Nonetheless, an American sociologist in the seminar suggested that social work has a cluster of activities and values that are not exclusive in content but in configuration, while its aims and methods are not identical with those of any other profession.

Historically speaking, social work began as a social movement but is now developing more clear professional functions and methods. Because of its heavy commitment to certain social values and to social betterment, it is desirable that it should continue to have this social reform element in it. For various reasons, much of the responsibility for this devolves on social work educators. This is because they are expected to be in the vanguard of professional progress, and also because university or other schools of social work are often powerful—partly because they are more neutral than social agencies or professional associations.

The social work function was variously defined as follows: an endeavor to do something rational in the field of social living; to enable people to be able to function more adequately on their own behalf in relation to social problems; to promote socially constructive and personally gratifying transactions between individuals, groups, and communities, including an improvement in their circumstances; and to generate in individuals a capacity to meet multiple role demands.

There was a good deal of discussion about the relation between social role and social work. The concept of social role clarifies the way in which social systems, which consist of enduring patterns of social interaction, are embodied in individual behavior. In other words, social roles are the bridge between the individual and the social system. A key function of social work is, therefore, to help increase opportunities for individuals to fulfill multiple role requirements with satisfaction to themselves and others. This includes helping individuals to achieve adequate role performance and also helping to change any given social system that makes it hard for the individual to perform roles adequately. Social work also comes into action where breakdown of the role performance occurs in crucial or deviant or crisis situations. There is a value element in the concept of social role. It is important to emphasize this because this formulation of the social work function could be used in the interests of bringing about social conformity. In any event, role theory does not necessarily cover all dimensions of human motivations, aspirations, and values.

It was fairly easy to agree that social work is committed to facilitate the meeting of unmet need; to help the underprivileged of any kind, the deprived, and the deviant; to aid in dysfunctional situations, in crisis situations, whether individual or group, and in conditions of violent social change, such as disaster, urbanization, mass migration, or drastic innovation (for example, the social consequences of building a dam).

These all imply direct service of an individual or social therapy type: indeed, the therapy function of social work is the most highly developed so far. But if this is its sole function, then it becomes essentially a peripheral profession, dealing with the deprived, malfunctioning, and deviant, and acting as an adjunct to the professions of medicine and education. Social work is also not as socially useful in this form, particularly in developing countries where mass change is the first necessity, as it would be if it could develop further basic knowledge and practice skills in social administration, social planning, and policy formulation, in working with communities. The task which faces social work—and the most pressing demand upon it—is to develop abilities to act as a regulator of social change. It is not yet clear whether therapeutic treatment skills and social planning and policy formulation can both be accommodated within the same profession, nor whether, as knowledge grows, there will be increasing divergence so that the present common base will be lost in the growth of specialist knowledge.

The analogy of the range of skill and knowledge comprised within the medical profession was often used. The public health model also served to stimulate exploration of the need for an epidemiology of social problems, including the assessment of need and determination of priorities; of strategies of intervention; of identification of "at risk" groups and crisis situations; and of the deployment and use of social workers for preventive as well as treatment purposes. It was agreed that social workers should be located where people came most easily: in well-baby clinics, in schools, in doctors' surgeries, or at other natural points. This should not preclude the setting up of a comprehensive social welfare service.

Social System Maintenance, Control, and Change

The term "client" took some hard knocks. This was partly because in community work, frequently it is not possible to decide who *is* the client, and partly because the term implies a contract to serve a particular individual or group, whereas it is becoming increasingly clear that the appropriate function of social work lies in intervention in a system rather than commitment to a given client. The relevant question may be not "Who is the client?" but "What is the storm center of this particular problem situation, and what method of intervention would be the most effective and at which points?" "For what purpose?" "What kind of change is desirable and possible?" The "client" is thus not a person but a variable in a process.

Within the threefold division of social system maintenance, control, and change, the social work function is primarily concerned with system maintenance and control where large social systems are concerned, but it may also be able to bring about system change (which implies radical discontinuities) in smaller social systems. The concept of dynamic equilibrium suggests that system maintenance includes considerable possibilities for change and adaptation, in which social work should be able to play a useful role in predicting consequences, in planning, and as a regulator and shock absorber, as well as being sensitive always to social welfare needs and resources. For this purpose, it is also necessary for social workers to be aware of the directions in which major structural change is taking place and of its consequences: the consequences, for example, of demographic change or changes in work patterns or in standard of living. Changes in the opportunity, power, and income structures must also be taken into account for their effects on the strategy of social welfare and the practice of social work.

Method and Practice

Trying to clarify emerging or agreed upon social work functions led into discussion of practice and method. After some preliminary struggles with such problems as the role of social workers on planning committees and so forth, it became clear that there was a range of necessary activities which might or might not be an integral part of the social work function as such. It also became clear that social work practice goes well beyond social work methods, though it must be in harmony with the social work commitment to meet need from within a certain value system: for example a committee should *not* be manipulated on the basis of a hidden agenda.

All three social work methods—casework, group work, and community work—are evolving and changing; all take account of the individual in his family and social setting as the ultimate source of reference. Needed are new methods and reformulation of existing methods, as, for example in bringing about and regulating large scale organizational change.

The essence of the casework method is a way of dealing with certain human problems on a case by case basis—the "case" being an individual or family unit. Although the diagnosis is on an individual basis, the treatment may include the use of group work. The cliché that casework is a luxury was examined. It was obvious that it can be afforded to only a limited extent and in developing countries only in particular places, and that there are many higher priorities and more appropriate services in such countries. For example, it is absurd to use trained caseworkers to interview public assistance applicants in dire poverty and primarily in need of food, clothing, and shelter. In other circumstances, it may not be the casework method but the service that is inappropriate, as in starting a child guidance clinic before basic child welfare services exist.

The Asian participants from schools of social work contended that all students should have some experience of casework because this is the analysis in depth of individual human situations and thus the best way to study under the microscope how people and their families react under stress. In casework, all dimensions of an individual's life are seen more effectively than they are in work with groups or communities.

There was almost no discussion of group work, except a brief reference to the value for the individual of group experience as a means of learning how to function better socially. It was regretted that group work had progressed from recreational activities to group therapy without developing a wider range of methods and skills in working with a variety of normal groups, a development that might have provided some of the much-needed practice skills in various segments of work with communities.

So far as community organization and community development are concerned, it is probable that these are not really separate methods, but represent a range of different processes in community work. They have been thought of as different, because community organization developed in urban centers in the United States in work with a diversity of organizations, while community development evolved in other countries in rural conditions where there was little organizational structure. The various senses in which the term "community" may be used were not examined; throughout the discussions, it was used with reference to geographical communities.

Community work may either be task oriented—that is to say the purpose may be a literacy campaign or a campaign to start a clinic or to absorb immigrants—or it may be process oriented, the purpose being to help community leaders to identify the community's most pressing needs. In the first type, outside agents or some group in the community will have decided on a specific priority and be using various methods to persuade the community to accept the service, to undertake the enterprise, or to change the attitudes of the members of the community. In the second, or process oriented type, the emphasis is on helping people to work together to determine their own priorities and to find the resources from within or outside the community to meet them. The process itself, with the resultant growth in people's capacity for decision making and implementation, is the primary aim. A third form consists in enabling groups of people to adjust to the stress of change, as for example, when tenants move to a new housing project.

In developing countries, community development, largely of the process orientation type, is used to increase the country's resources by inciting people to do things for themselves—dig wells or build roads, with some technical help. Thus, they increase resources far more quickly than if they waited until the state had the means to provide these services. This type of community development is usually based on persuading people to become involved in a nationally determined program of priorities.

Unlike casework, community work is not normally concerned with pathology or deviance. On the other hand, it does not always operate in situations where there is agreement about the nature of a given social need or the aims and methods to be employed in meeting it. In conflict situations, the aim is to bring about resolution or compromise without open aggression or ostracism or withdrawal. No matter what the circumstances, the aim is always better allocation of resources, community cohesion, ability to identify and meet needs, and ability to cope with conflict without disruption.

Community workers must constantly guard against having a hidden agenda that they are trying to maneuver the community into accepting; being drawn into taking sides with one group against others; lacking clarity about what processes are at work in the community and what their own aims are in often diffuse situations; or relinquishing their professional role and becoming simply "a good sort" in the community.

It seemed fairly clear in the discussions that the American term *community organization* had much the same meaning as *social administration* has in some other contexts if it is accepted that this latter includes working with different administrative or other groups in a community in order to facilitate a process which results in a better use of resources and improved social relationships.

Though the present three social work methods—casework, group work, and community work—are distinct, they are not necessarily separate. They have a common base; and any or all of them should be used flexibly in any given situation in whatever would be the most effective form of intervention. This raised the difficult question of whether students could be adequately trained in all three methods, and what range of training, including knowledge and practice skills, they could absorb and use effectively. Too wide a range could result in shallow knowledge and performance; too much emphasis on one method might result in over-training but not for the real task. It is quite likely that casework is being over-emphasized in training at the expense of community work. This is partly because casework is very much better developed as a method by comparison with community work in which the clarification of practice skill and understanding of process is still weak. It would also be all too easy to broaden the base of practice at the expense of depth of penetration in social problem intervention.

All through the seminar, participants were conscious of the effects of historical evolution, changing cultural values, the level of economic development, the increase of knowledge and complexity, and the nature and direction of social change as they played upon and molded the values, function, and methods of social work. They were also fully aware of the need for much more social research, including cross-cultural studies. They did not think that in ten days of discussion they added to knowledge, but they did, to their own satisfaction, clarify some issues, shake up and jolt some sacred cows, raise many questions, and see gigantic fresh tasks ahead.

In Reponse to Change:
Social Work at the
Crossroad

John B. Turner

Whether one is discussing the urban crisis, the crisis of the underdeveloped sections of America and of the world, the prospects of war or peace, or the student rebellion, it is painfully clear that the human condition is under severe questioning. It is not at all unusual, therefore, that the social work profession is under scrutiny by the more sensitive of its members as well as by outside critics. The real test of a profession is its ability to be relevant to the problems of society it is granted sanction to remedy. However, in a period when both the condition of mankind and our knowledge about that condition are changing rapidly, the articulation of professional values, if not the values themselves, are called into question.

Social work is not alone in this issue; indeed, all the human service professions are so affected. In addition to social work, the charges of irrelevance of professional practice to social problems are equally applicable to education, health, housing, economics, and law. But company, in this case, is poor solace. The company social workers seek to be among is the company of those professions that are considered relevant and responsive to the values of a humane society. In other words, how is social work, as an organized, community-sanctioned activity, to behave toward the development of more just and egalitarian conditions for all members of society?

The question of relevance, in many ways, is the single most important question to be asked by the social worker, the consumer of social work services, the interested board and committee member, and the public. When service consumers, social work's critics, ask about relevance they want to know whether the service will mean a change for the better for them. Among the most serious criticisms being leveled at social work are these:

Reprinted with permission of the author and the National Association of Social Workers from *Social Work*, Vol. 13, No. 3 (July 1968), pp. 7–15.

1. Large numbers of people who are among the poor, the disadvantaged, and the unfulfilled are either not eligible for existing programs or are not being reached by them, a characteristic that unfortunately is equally applicable to many of the newer programs such as Head Start. It is widely known that only one-quarter of those classifiable as poor are beneficiaries of public assistance programs.[1]

2. The people with the greatest need for help frequently are denied this help. The reasons for this sad state of affairs are several: eligibility requirements, accessibility, custom, and imbalance in the development of services, especially those of the voluntary funded agencies.

3. Some programs actually contribute to the problem or to conditions causing the problem. They either deal with the symptoms instead of the central, more causative problems, or they exacerbate the problem in terms of the administrative policy that is pursued with reference to the problem definition and resource allocation.

Divorcing Social Work from Welfare

If social work is to correct these criticisms and become more responsive to the urban crisis, it must become free of the concept and image of social welfare services. This is more than a semantic quibble. Consider for a moment the traditional view of social welfare. Welfare (both public and private), viewed functionally by the public, is a concept that embraces activities to help individuals who have been unable to benefit from traditional systems established by society to meet basic human needs. When a person is unable to obtain or keep a job, to locate or utilize decent housing, to find or utilize health services, to acquire a useful education, to form and utilize socially productive relationships with others, the welfare system is called into play. But society also has said that the preferred way of meeting human need is through the efforts of the individual without personal dependence on public resources.

The clearest entitlement for help under the present system is to the person who is judged not to be able-bodied and who is considered not capable of taking a place in the labor market. For the person who is apparently able-bodied and in need of help, services are largely oriented to a diagnosis of individual dysfunction. Far too often such services are out of context with the pressing reality of social demands on the individual. For those who fail to respond to or utilize services oriented to arresting individual dysfunction, the impact of services has, in fact, been little more than a dole, maintaining dependency rather than decreasing it. Social

[1] S. M. Miller and Martin Rein, "Social Action on the Installment Plan," *Trans-Action*, Vol. 3, No. 2 (January-February 1966).

work has not been too successful in developing the tools and concepts that equip the profession as a whole to act responsibly in the fullest sense of the term "social rehabilitation." Leonard Cottrell, Jr., in speaking similarly of mental health, put it this way:

Given the professional training, special competence of the psychiatrist, it is almost certain that they will conceptualize the task in terms . . . which [are] heavily oriented towards the goals of early diagnosis and treatment of [the] individual. . . . Although prevention is also a component of medical conceptualization, the basic theoretical orientation of the psychiatrist makes it unlikely that his formulations of preventive strategies will stray very far from a clinical standpoint and consequently are not likely to be comprehensive enough for the requirements of the situation.[2]

Until recently social work has, in effect, ignored those whose problems are essentially a direct or indirect result of a breakdown or gap in social organization for the expected way of satisfying basic human needs.

Social work is handicapped by being wedded to the concept of welfare. Welfare, historically, has too often meant protective caretaking of the non-able-bodied. The concepts of caretaking and rehabilitation are too limited in definition, as it becomes clearer that it is not just people who are deprived, ill, and unskilled, but that our communities, our social, economic, and political structures are also sick, dysfunctional, deprived, in need of crisis intervention, and in need of rehabilitation. If social work is to be more responsive to the human crisis it must operate from a concept sufficiently broad to embrace the range of front-line institutional functions that are required to produce and to maintain a socially productive man in a humanized society.

It is not just that the concept and the system of social welfare seek to administer to the individual almost exclusively, but it is what they do to and for the individual.

1. They place personal inadequacy at the core of the explanation of the failure of the individual to satisfy his needs for housing, health, economics, education, justice, or communal participation.
2. They place emphasis on helping the individual at the point at which his handicaps are already little less than insurmountable. They provide too little too late for most people.

There are two important consequences stemming from the interaction of the assumption about the centrality of personal failure and the lateness of the point of intervention:

[2]Urban America and the Planning of Mental Health Services, Vol. 5, No. 10 (New York: Group for the Advancement of Psychiatry, November 1962).

1. The social worker tends to be located outside the systems in which his skills and knowledge can be brought to bear early enough to make maximum use of motivation and prevent layering of problems.

2. The social worker, as well as his education, tends to underemphasize the importance of substantive knowledge about the normal social systems for satisfying need and the problems attendant to their utilization, such as in housing, employment, and education. Likewise the social worker requires knowledge of the constantly changing efficiency and effectiveness of the housing, educational, employment, and medical systems for responding to the needs of diverse groups.

The implications for action are that social work must shift much of its manpower from its present pattern of deployment within welfare organizations to nonwelfare organizations. Social workers need to be located in and be much more a part of educational, housing, employment, and health systems. Thus, social work services could be used not only in instances of crisis, but should be used to enrich and develop people's lives and in the prevention of social dysfunction. What is needed are an expanded definition of school social work, social workers in job settings, industrial social workers, housing social workers, social workers in city administration, more social workers attached to citizens' groups as bona fide employees of these groups.

The concept of human development is suggested as one concept that merits some consideration in these terms. First, by use of the term human, the value question is immediately brought into focus. To humanize means to make creditable to man, to refine, to civilize, to put into practice the ideals of man; it implies that man's society can be shaped by consciously planned efforts. Second, to participate in human development, by definition, suggests that one must be able to assist people early enough to have a positive consequential outcome with reference to their future growth and direction. It suggests for social workers, therefore, a priority for energy and knowledge allocation.

These social workers would differ from social workers today in at least one important aspect. In addition to knowledge about individual and family functioning, the social worker would need to be knowledgeable about the specific area in which he worked, e.g., housing, health, education.

Guaranteed Jobs

The single most important thing that can be done to revolutionize social welfare and dim its imperfections is to establish a guaranteed job system accompanied by a money equivalent for those for whom no jobs exist, as a basic floor for economic security. Social problems may not be eliminated by placement of every person into some decent job, but this would go a long way toward changing the character of those problems and thus changing the ability of social work to accomplish more nearly what it claims it can accomplish—namely, rehabilitation, control, and prevention with respect to social dysfunction.

Many people, in looking for ways of eliminating the imperfections of the welfare system, seek dramatically different, almost mystical, changes in the way in which services are organized and delivered. There is a serious flaw in many plans offered in response to this search. It is the assumption that welfare, even welfare with a new look, can change the basic character of the hard-core social problems that confront us today. Many of the changes proposed are tactical. But it is not tactics that are required. What is needed are strategies that free social work from the limitations of welfare. Strategies are needed that will regard welfare as only one of several functions under the broader umbrella of human development.

It is important to keep in mind the centrality of income maintenance as a part of any successful program to reduce dependency, to offset powerlessness, and to rehabilitate people before they become consumers of welfare services.[3] Of special relevance for short-range action is the necessity to change the notion of minimum financial assistance, now operative in all programs, to one of adequate financial assistance. Social workers have a moral commitment to make it clear to the public that public welfare services cannot serve as a substitute for an adequate distribution of income to all elements in society. This is especially true for those individuals included among welfare consumers solely because there is no place for them in the job market. For not making this clear in the past, health and welfare organizations now bear the brunt of severe criticism.

Poverty is more than a "blot on the American conscience"—it is hell for 35 million Americans. As Schottland points out: "Up to this time, we have applied half measures to the eradication of poverty and they have, at best, half succeeded, sometimes only serving to perpetuate the disease they were supposed to cure."[4]

In suggesting the guaranteed job as the most important strategy for humanizing the community, the writer is not oblivious of the

---

[3]So All May Live in Decency and Dignity (New York: National Association of Social Workers, 1967). "One-half of all people now living below the poverty line are under 18 years of age."
[4]Ibid.

poor record of present manpower and training programs or unmindful of the increasingly automated world of work. In regard to the first point, our perspective must not be limited to the present products of inadequate schooling—people who have grown up into a world that has denied them the hope of personal economic progression and achievement and therein has effectively denied them the ability to use training when it is finally made available to them.

If the cycle of chronic disengagement from society is to be broken, the United States, as a matter of policy, must provide a man with a job or with its money equivalent. Clearly the most important immediate concern of community action must be to increase the opportunity for jobs and job advancement. The emphasis here must include rational geographic distribution of jobs, the development and creation of new careers, equal access to jobs by all, and special efforts to prepare people to work.

While the responsibility for the provision of jobs, the development of work expectations, employability qualifications, and the upgrading of those who are underemployed can and must be shared among human development institutions, it must be *shared*, not *fragmented*. This sharing requires a major national policy with resources to back it up, to assure every American who can and who wants to work that dignity, status, and rewards will be available to him.

The efforts of the President and the Vice-President, of the Congress, of the Labor Department, the antipoverty programs, and the urban coalition, while reflecting recognition of the need to provide work and work ladders for youths and young adults, nevertheless are still of an insufficient scale to deal with the full dimensions of this problem.

To do these things will not be easy. There will still be opposition from those who do not yet understand the realities of today's world of work. Not all who need and who are able will want to work. Not all people who need help will benefit from this approach. But such a program is a necessary anchor component in a system of universal income maintenance and in human development.

Human service organizations must take the leadership in placing income distribution on the public agenda and must press to keep it there until the American public grapples creatively and effectively with it. Therefore, for social work the prime objective of social action must be the establishment of a guaranteed job system.

Youth and Family
Development

In addition to the questions already raised, there are a few others that must be answered if social work services are to be used more effectively:

1. How can people be motivated to use the services they need?

2. How can resources be organized, over time, for the consumer? That is to say, if the unraveling of service benefits is to be prevented, staying power with a child or family over the period of a generation may be necessary. How can a capacity for generational planning and service be developed?

3. How can services be expanded for full coverage of a high-risk population group? The importance of coverage is routinely underestimated.

To illustrate the importance of these questions, let us take as a risk group those low-income families with preschool children who are likely already to be educationally handicapped by the time they enter school in terms of ability and motivation to learn, physical health, and socialization that in turn affects learning. While aspects of our knowledge about intelligence and emotional growth may be questioned, there is a substantial amount of evidence that the preschool years are highly crucial in the development of individual potential. It is also known that the social and physical environment in terms of its norms, opportunities, and supports influences and shapes the individual's ability to master his life situation. Certainly, then, it makes sense to give the preschool years top priority. But how is this to be done? Is it to be accomplished by working exclusively with the child and excluding the parents, or can one really work with the family as a unit? Can it be accomplished by grouping families geographically, for example, in a housing project, and then bringing a complex of services into these locations? Is it possible to create a school for families—enrolling the entire family—to prepare them for graduation into independent living?

Notwithstanding changes in contemporary family structure, the importance of the family is that it provides certain kinds of resources that are not otherwise available for coping with life. The family can also provide a continuity of resources over a period of generations. In a sense, a family needs to multiply its resources and power over a period of time. Without some mechanisms by which these can get passed along, it is difficult to accumulate a sufficient depth of resources to enable the family to break through to reasonably stable and independent living.

Here reference is made to the mutual-help concept characteristic of many families in which mother, father, brother, and sister sacrifice to some extent so that one member of the family may go to school, obtain needed medical care, locate better housing, go into business, or seek some other family-approved and valued objective.

The family also provides a kind of discipline; that is, it helps in setting long-term goals and in making the necessary sacrifices for achieving them without too much hardship. Thus, its members are enabled to develop skills and resources to cope with and get on top of the system. The family further provides a specific kind of socialization—not just socialization into a class structure, but socialization into a subculture that has developed ways of coping effectively with life.

The family is not being discussed here so much in terms of how well people get along with each other within the family, important as this is, but in terms of whether that family is able to provide *protection*, the *socialization* required for responsible participation in organized life, and the *basic necessities* that people need to cope with life. The family is a cell from which social energy has to come and for which we have not, so far, been able to develop much in the way of substitutes. Policy and programs are needed that seek to strengthen family functioning in these terms.

Thus far it has been suggested that if social work is to respond in a relevant way to the challenge of crisis in urban life, its manpower must be moved into primary systems for basic need satisfaction, including and more effectively linking the functions of (1) service utilization, (2) modifications and improvements in service delivery, and (3) design and development of new policies and programs. The number one priority for the social work profession is social action to help bring about a system of guaranteed jobs as a floor in income maintenance. The number two priority is a policy and program to concentrate preventive and rehabilitation services on the young and their families.

Productive Competition

Another strategic component is the desirability of introducing productive competition into the delivery of human development services. The proposition assumes that competition has a positive value, that it will lead to a better product, to better service for the consumer. It assumes that the sponsor will receive a better profit. To do this, the goals and objectives of service, as well as a description of how services will be delivered, need to be clearly stated and should be a part of the contract between the consumer and the service delivery sponsor. Of equal importance is the requirement that the individual or group contracting for services be in a position to cancel or reject what is considered an unfavorable contract. To do the latter effectively, the consumer must have a real choice among providers of services.

One development that has some potential for helping to bring about some measure of competition is the effort to transfer a greater sense of proprietorship of service from the providers to the consumers of service. However, observations of efforts to achieve greater consumer group involvement lead the writer to conclude that even the most successful efforts still border closely on symbolic participation. How does the welfare agency relinquish its traditional monopoly in making decisions about what services, how much, and who gets them? How can agency administration and policy-making boards achieve greater involvement of consumers and still provide a professional service? The answers are not easy to come by, but there are some principles to guide us in constructing some models for experimentation.

First, what does the service agency require to stay in business? It must have access to resources of personnel, knowledge, expertise, facilities, and, of course, money. It must also have access to the consumers of its services. Without access to resources or consumers, agencies would soon be forced to close their doors.

The table stake for control over access to resources is possession of money or loyalty to those with money. On the other hand, the requirement for control over access to consumers is a monopoly of services or a responsive constituency of consumers. Efforts to provide the consumer a real co-determination *may* have floundered precisely because he has not possessed either control over services or access to consumers. Thus, most efforts to transfer ownership of welfare agencies take on the character of a power stalemate or a rather frustrating standoff.

The welfare consumer does not have control over money, by definition, nor is there any immediate potential for such control. In most instances he does not have access to a responsive constituency of consumers because consumers lack an organizational base. But they do have the *potential* for achieving such a membership base.

If social work is serious about transferring service ownership, the place to begin is to help consumer constituencies become functionally organized, that is, to organize around a concrete gain, not just around representation on agency boards. For example, consumer groups of families with children and with incomes at or below the poverty level might be organized. Such an organization would first need some membership benefit that could come immediately upon affiliation and not require any complicated member-to-member interaction. Conceivably, such a benefit might be in the form of discount purchases on priority items for families such as shoes, medicine, and the like. The group would then begin to develop the cohesion needed to consider more complicated group enterprises such as contracting with welfare and other organizations for services that would be of a more permanent benefit, for example, helping the family breadwinner to become upgraded in his job in order to increase the per capita income of the family or providing educational and health services to preschool children.

In other words, with a meaningful organization base the consumer group is now in a position to negotiate with welfare and related agencies for services. The consumer representative no longer needs to suffer role confusion and conflict as a member of the agency's board or committees; he is now truly the legitimate agent of his own reference group outside the board contracting for what the group needs. Obviously there are other issues to be settled such as staffing the consumer group and financing services, but given this framework these issues appear to be subject to solution.

Personal Responsibility

Although this discussion has been in broad community terms, individual and organizational action are required if strategies such as those discussed are to be put into effect. Putting ideals into practice is a complicated task. If the social work profession is serious about wanting to be responsive to the human condition, it must recognize a few basic requirements:

1. Action to humanize requires (a) doing oneself—whether self is an individual or a corporate body such as a staff or board of an organization—and (b) influencing others—fellow professionals, fellow board and committee members, the United Fund, the welfare council, the city council, the county commissioners, the state legislature. The process of humanization requires a commitment both to individual action and to social action.

2. Humanization requires placing humane values above other values. It is not possible to have one's cake and to eat it too. As long as one is only confronted with situations in which one's ideals do not conflict with other interests, it is relatively easy to act and to try to influence others to behave in ways consistent with these ideals. However, when one faces situations in which one's ideals, if achieved, must take priority over other interests, it is not only much more difficult to act oneself, but it is equally difficult to influence others. Social work cannot succeed in humanizing the community if, when the going gets tough, it turns its

back on humane ideals. The implications of this requirement for community policy have been pointed out by Michael Harrington in his assertion that the leadership of this country proposes making a social revolution without the inconvenience of changing any basic institutions.[5]

3. A third requirement for closing the gap between ideals and the reality of the status quo concerns the function of wealth in terms of knowledge, technology, and working capital. A country with few natural resources, few educated people, and scarce capital cannot hope to reach the same degree of achievement of its ideals as can a country such as the United States. This country is able to spend billions of dollars to conquer space. In 1966 the United States produced 44 percent of everything produced in the world. The country's leaders claim that the gross national product is larger than the gross national products of all Western Europe, Japan, and Canada combined.[6] Truly, the United States does not lack the resources for the humanization of its society. Clearly it has the knowledge, the technology, and the capital required to do the job. For the people of the United States, the process of humanization is not unlike the process of losing weight—it is 99 percent a matter of will power!

Humanization of the community requires the establishment of community policies that persistently seek improvement in the quality of human life, not only in keeping with the dictates of knowledge, technology, and financial resources, but in keeping with our values. Our value structure embraces at least four major notions: (1) participatory democracy, (2) free enterprise, (3) cultural pluralism, and (4) Judeo-Christian morality. But these values are built on and cemented together with two fundamental ideas—*social justice* and *egalitarianism*. History teaches that these ideals can never be taken for granted. From the affairs of the family to the affairs of the state, we must remain ever alert to the demonstration and preservation of these ideals. They are the finest creations of mankind.

Reactions to Change

What are some of the understandable but no less damaging reactions to change that social workers, individually and organizationally, are capable of and against which we must be on guard? First, we are often tempted to preserve the status quo on the basis of maintaining organizational stability. Stability is not an end; it is a means to an end. Organizations are born in response to a need and unless periodically overhauled lose their usefulness

[5]Michael Harrington, "A Subversive Version of the Great Society," in Herman Stein, ed., *Social Theory and Social Invention* (Cleveland: Case Western Reserve University Press, 1968), pp. 47–69.
[6]See Hubert H. Humphrey, "Humanizing the City for Youth," *Social Welfare Forum, 1967* (New York: Columbia University Press, 1967), p. 3.

in terms of their purpose in meeting that need. When, in order to develop new services, the only alternative is to establish new organizations, scarce resources that might better be used to meet other emerging needs are depleted.

A second response takes the form of an automatic bias in favor of programs that emphasize the development of the individual's self-adequacy as a solution to problems that are not basically problems of the individual but rather of our social, economic, and political structure. As pointed out earlier, this too is an expensive response because the case loads get larger and results remain largely irrelevant to the problems. As community criticism about welfare programs and social work services rises, community support begins to fade away.

A third response may be found in organizational provincialism. Here the tendency is to see problems in terms of *ours* and *theirs* regardless of the scope of the problem, its causes, and the variety of special disciplines and special interests needed to resolve it. Once organizational claims are staked out, they tend to hold forever. When caught up in the fallacious logic of this response, agencies and citizen action groups usually discover too late that they need each other. It is this response that frequently leads to meaningless distinctions between public and voluntary sponsorship of programs.

A fourth reaction takes the form of individual and organizational silence. It is the problem of speaking up, speaking out, and speaking for, as well as responding to others who are speaking out against the need of society to be more responsive to the human condition. One cogent phrasing of this obstacle may be found in the words of a Jewish refugee from a Nazi concentration camp: "It is not your enemies that you must fear for they will only kill you; it is the persons who are neither friend nor enemy, who remain silent and who, by so doing, create the climate where your enemies can kill you and your friends can betray you." And this too is an expensive response to choose because it drives men to desperate acts when caught in the attack of their enemies, the betrayal of their friends, and the inaction of the silent and indifferent.

Conclusion

One of the frequently heard inside criticisms of social work is that it tries to take responsibility for remaking society. But almost as frequently, social work is criticized by persons outside the profession for not doing just that. Social work as a profession is

unique in that by definition it is inextricably linked with responding to the total range of human dysfunction, individual and
communal. The future of social work stands at the crossroad
where one path will lead it to an increasingly minor responsibility
for remedying human ills and the other path will lead to vigorous
and immediate efforts to achieve a more responsive role. To follow the latter path, social work, its practitioners, and its organizations must bring into balance its expertise and methods of problem intervention with expertise and substantive knowledge
about social problems and their solutions.

If social work, its practice, and its education can achieve this
balance of expertise; if social work can effectively expand its operations into educational, occupational, and health settings; if it
can establish a family and child development service concept directed toward doing more than repairing what has broken down;
if it can fuse its penchant for social action with expertise about
deciding outcomes—then the profession will have indeed successfully met the test of being relevant to the human condition.

Social Work Method:
A Review of the Past Decade

Helen Harris Perlman

A review should be done in a period of tranquility, with things
settled down, at some place of distance from that which is being
observed and analyzed in order to get perspective and to see patterns. If these are necessary conditions, this review of social work
method is done under the worst of circumstances. Perhaps in no
previous span of ten years have there been so much surge and
change in social work, so many forays into new areas of action
and thought as in this past decade. Armies of caseworkers shift
from individual to group treatment, group workers shift from socialization to therapeutic activity, community workers split into
phalanxes of "developers," "planners," "organizers." Everyone's
banners cry "onward!" or "unity!" And in this melee of surge and
sound the writer scrambles about, an overstimulated, under-
equipped observer trying to see where social work methods are
today.

This introduction is my confession that I have not been able to
find a coherent framework within which to view methodological

Reprinted with permission of the author and the National Association of Social Workers
from *Social Work*, Vol. 10, No. 4 (October 1965), pp. 166–178.

trends in the past ten years. I have talked to practitioners and to teachers, reviewed the literature, twisted and turned my sights. The one certainty I have captured is that of uncertainty, of change, movement, fluidity, and breakthrough. It is said that in some sciences knowledge doubles every ten years. I do not think social work's knowledge has doubled in this past decade. But it is clear that its push to know, its efforts to explore knowledge, its self-demanding aspirations for extending, identifying, organizing, and testing its functions and its practices have proceeded by geometric leaps. I do not presume to know whether this is good or bad, whether it is a situation for professional self-congratulation or for viewing with alarm. All I can promise is that what follows is one social worker's willingness to share a view of kaleidoscopic movement in social work's modes of action, in its three major methods of intervention: casework, group work, and community organization.

First I invite you to listen to the changing vocabulary of social work. The thrust is from passive to active voice, from past imperfect to present imperative tense, from ideas of adjustment to those of coping, from social workers as enablers to social workers as change agents, from client as having self-determination to client as change target, from compromise to manipulation of power, from co-ordination to innovation. I do not mean that all these are antithetical ideas or that in other guises they have not figured in social work considerations before. But words have consequences and the emphasis on the aggressive, innovative, intrusive mode is strong among us now; it reveals our press and inclination.

Changes in Casework

The surge of new ideas, the shift of focus, the play of new approaches are many and plain to be seen in the method called "casework." Even a superficial glance will reveal these movements—some of them trends, some merely oscillations. There has been a shift in theory framework—from id to ego psychology. The caseworker's attention is increasingly on the nature and efficacy of the individual's conscious and just-preconscious behaviors, on the mechanisms by which he protects, adapts, or copes with both the internal and external stresses he encounters. Those functions of the ego that have to do with perception and cognition and interpersonal competence, those feelings that have to do with motivation for change, those interactions between self and object that are called "social functioning"—these are increasingly in the center of casework's study and influence efforts.

Consonant with this (whether as cause or consequence or both it is hard to know) is a shift from focus on intrapersonal conflict to focus on conflicts in interpersonal transactions, from person viewed against the background of past and in the central spotlight, center stage, to person viewed as part of an interacting role network in which he is both acted upon and acting, both being and becoming.

Underpinning these new perspectives are certain expanding concepts from the theory of what we call "social science." Perhaps "science" is a euphemistic appellation, promising more than it can give surety for—but more of this later. At present, by whatever name, the theory and findings of person-to-group in a transaction are base-points for change in casework's focus and treatment methods. Family structure and interplay, culture and class norms as behavior determinants—these, among other ideas, permeate the caseworker's office talk at the least and his thinking and experimental action at the most responsible level.

Related to this focus on person-in-social-functioning (whether "social" is defined as one person in interaction with one other or as one person in that amorphous organism called society) is the upsurge of interest in the poor and the culture of poverty. The psychodynamic impact of long and chronic impoverishment, the culture of social work itself and the acculturation of its practitioners, questions of where casework comes in or gets off in the sudden popular espousal of the cause of the now all-too-visible poor—all these figure with new prominence in casework discussion. It was one segment of casework that provided the first professionalized push toward the poor before they became the darlings of the press and politics. In spots across the country casework experiments were being tried early in the fifties to reach the hard-to-reach, to plan what are now called "intervention strategies" but what were then called aggressive or assertive efforts to motivate the unmotivated, to socialize the socially disorganized and unwilling clients of courts or family and child welfare agencies. As these efforts were made and as difficulties were encountered they served to raise many still unanswered questions in casework about the aptness and applicability of the traditional casework model for the needful but inarticulate, apathetic, or openly resistive population.

Partly rising out of these questions and experiences, partly stimulated by concurrent public health–mental health action researches, there have poured into casework ideas of crisis treatment and prevention. These ideas, too, challenge the traditional casework treatment model. And they challenge the structure and programs of many agencies that use casework as their major mode of problem-solving. Concepts of crisis or of prevention, when they are understood in depth, push for redefinitions of both casework means and ends. They require rethinking of casework's ideas of what is to be diagnosed and what is to be treated and what treatment consists of. They tie in with a firm grasp of ego psychology, with many social science insights, with poverty problems and manpower shortages. Thus one sees a whole network of recognized and/or unnoted connections pushing and shoving at the formerly orderly method of operation called casework.

But we are not yet done. Manpower shortages in casework combined with fragments of social science ideas about socialization, reference groups, role networks, therapeutic milieus, family transactional and communication systems have somehow coalesced in an uneasy combination to create a major methodological shift. Reference here is to the phenomenon of work with groups by caseworkers everywhere—in family and child welfare agencies, residential centers, psychiatric and general hospitals and clinics. Purposes of work with groups range from information-conveyance to decision-making to therapy, in numbers varying from the dyad of a marital problem to the triad of an Oedipal problem to the octet (or more) of strangers gathered together about some problem common to them all. Indeed, the use of group interviewing by caseworkers seems to have risen to fad dimensions and the caseworker who does not carry at least one group is just plainly out of style. (Or perhaps he is in the next decade's avant-garde!)

Casework's Use of Groups

The use of group sessions by caseworkers has had many spokesmen in casework's literature and many values attributed to it as a substitute for, or as a supplementary method to, the one-to-one interview. These attributed values range from expedience and economy of time and effort to the connections assumed to exist between the group process and ego support, between group participation and facilitated social functioning, between enhanced communication and enhanced happiness. (Someone should say something about the possibility that there are some things in interpersonal life that are better uncommunicated either by word or action. It is *what* is communicated, not alone the phenomenon of communication, that is our treatment concern.)

No one can deny that there exists an association between and among these phenomena. But there have been as yet few attempts to articulate and test what the explicit connections are. In what ways, for example, does ego psychology relate to the use of group interviewing? What different purposes are served by group interviewing from those served by individual interviews? What different outcomes are anticipated? What different expectations in terms, for example, of relationship to the caseworker, of client's self-understanding versus, say, his self-management? For what sorts of problems is the individual best dealt with in the group? Should the decision to use one-to-one or one-to-group interviewing be made in relation to problem type or in relation to goal? In short, in casework's rather sanguine taking on of group interviews there is roused a beehive of questions yet to be asked and answered.

Caseworkers writing on the use of groups do not seem too troubled about group dynamics or group process in their difference from the one-to-one interview. Questions such as what is the nature of "groupness," what principles govern the social worker's relative activity or passivity in the group, what techniques further intercommunication among group members rather than dialogues held with the caseworker in the presence of others—these and like questions have not seemed to plague caseworkers to the same degree or extent that questions about principles of individual interviewing plague group workers who are moving in casework's direction. "Group process" is called by name in casework writings. But what this process is and what group dynamics are as differentiated from individual dynamics have yet to be identified and grappled with.

Certainly at the points when the caseworker takes on a group and the group worker lifts out single members from his group for individual interviews differences in methods grow blurred. Perhaps this presages a merging and integration of the methods of casework and group work. Certainly it requires further work at what is already taking place in a number of schools of social work across the country: examination of the specific and generic elements in each method, looking toward possible combinations. Because we sometimes lose sight of the obvious it is here pointed up: the likenesses between casework and group work at levels of commitment, conviction, and knowledge of man and society are easily seen and affirmed. But it is the knowledge of transactional processes and the means by which these are managed—the know-how and skill of *doing*, the differences between interviewing one-to-one and one-to-group, the principles that govern what is done and how it is done—these have yet to be explored and articulated so that we can know what makes casework and group work alike and also different.

The Thrust of Research

Of the many changes to be seen in the casework method over the past ten years space here permits lifting out only one more—the remarkable thrust of research in this practice method. Prior to this decade research in social work had focused chiefly on the nature of social problems and agency operations. Within the past ten years some outstanding researches have focused on the casework method—that is, on the relation between what the practitioner does and its outcome. The shifts in the research microscope's focus are not our story here. What is of import is the fact that research in a process or method can come about only when there is established a firm base of regularities of practice. Regularities rise up out of practice that has been conceptualized and to some extent systematized. Casework, for a number of reasons, is the social work method that has most fully explicated and organized its practice rationale. This is what has readied its practice for testing and research scrutiny and, further, this is what gives its practitioners the courage—for it takes courage—to open up their practice to critical study.

Impact of Social Science Theory

The impact of social science theory on casework is plain to see. Because the problem of its absorption and use in practice is the same for the several methods, it will be dealt with later. Here it need only be noted that concepts such as role, class, reference group that place and explain the individual in his social context have been used in casework for expanding its diagnostic understanding. But the use of such understanding for treatment actions is not as yet clearly manifest. The question is whether we are nursing an illusion to the effect that understanding a problem in different perspectives really tells us what to do and how to do it. Does the incorporation of social science content into casework—or group work or community work—contribute to the development of our skills and techniques, to the processes by which we attempt to effect change?

Changes in Group Work

When we turn to group work we see that it, too, is in rapid movement, undergoing almost revolutionary changes. It has burst the too narrow seams of its basketball uniforms and arts-and-crafts smocks; increasingly it appears in the contrasting symbolic garments that bespeak the poles of its present scope—the authority-cool white coats of hospital and clinical personnel and the play-it-cool windbreaker of the street corner gang-worker.

The past decade's changes in group work are changes in its territorial domains, in the problems it considers to be amenable to its skills, and in its modes of action. Its domain has widened from agencies for youth development, character-building, leisure-time activities—the activities focused on enhancement of social functioning and enrichment of opportunities—to include those agencies and places that are set up to rehabilitate or restore or reform such social functioning as is held to be problematic, impaired, deficient. It has taken on the problems of malfunctioning of the individual as they are manifest in his alienation from groups or in his interpersonal—which is to say his "group"—transactions. It has extended its repertoire of professional actions to include a range of therapeutic methods of influence. From the moment of its professionalization group work sought to identify and "diagnose" the individual members of groups. In this sense group work always individualized. But the actual treatment of the individual group member for his particular problems and the relation of such treatment of personal problems to group membership and process—these are in the center of group work concerns today.

As group work has been introduced and has proved useful in psychiatric and other rehabilitative centers it has inevitably become infused with ideas of therapeutic milieu, of individual psychopathology and psychodynamics (as they are expressed and affected by the group), and even with the study-diagnosis-treatment model that casework inherited (with some chronically awkward consequences) from those same settings. At the risk of oversimplification it may be said that at one of its surging edges group work is increasingly involved with the persons, places, problems, and even some of the processes that not too long ago were assumed to "belong" to casework.

Reaching Out to the Hard-to-Reach

But there are bents in other directions too, tugs by forces both within and outside social work. Group work actually never left the neighborhood house, never left the disinherited population. Yet, the influence of the settlement house waned as house residents "settled" but populations moved, and neighborhood houses sometimes found themselves, by urban rot or renewal, bereft of a neighborhood. Moreover, the gap between social work and the poor grew wider as social workers struggled for professional status, for clients who were "in" members of the community, who were approachable, accessible, understandable. Within the past decade, owing in part to the new respectability of the poor, in part to conscience-nudgers within its own ranks, group work, like casework, has turned again to work with the most needful, to reverse what Vinter called the "retreat from those most in need." Infused now with new insights about the effects of social class, culture, ethnicity upon the motivations and communications of the long-poor and long-outcast, one sector of group work has turned afresh to attempting to engage the disengaged, the alienated, the delinquency-prone young people in today's slums.

Paralleling casework's reaching out to the hard-to-reach, group work has stepped up its reaching out in hitherto untried ways to the hard-to-engage youth. Delinquents or potential delinquents, socially alienated or socially threatening gang groups, young people who have "dropped out" not only from school but from all regularized, socially valued roles—these are again in the practice concerns of group work and at the growing edge of its experiments. These groups are problematic in more ways than one. To work with them requires creative synthesis of both sociodynamic and psychodynamic knowledge and particular awareness and management of the gap that exists between the values and norms ·of the socially alienated and those of social work. Moreover, such dual perceptions and management require security and freewheeling capacity in the group worker. He must often be "detached" from an agency and all its security appurtenances and at the same time remain "attached" to professional values; at the same time he must become "attachable" to the distrustful, uncommunicative, often antagonistic persons who are his potential clients. This is no small task.

Problem of Self-Definition

When one looks at this range of practice embraced by group work it is easy to understand the run of high feeling in its ranks about its definition and identity and the push by its leaders and formulators to develop further its practice models and principles. In the examination of its writings one sees some internecine struggles over whether its major commitments should be on the continuum of education-to-therapy or on the continuum of education-to-socialization. And sometimes these issues and questions are made murky by confusing personalities with positions.

Nomenclature and the meanings that are contained in names are in the center of group work discussions. What is "group work" to "group counseling" to "group therapy" to "group dynamics" to "group process"? The echoes of like questions in casework sound fainter now than they did ten years ago, it may hearten group workers to know. It is not that questions such as where casework leaves off and psychotherapy begins have been resolved neatly. Rather it is that there has been some acceptance of the fact that there are more ways to help people than we have dreamed of. It is that perhaps the questions of boundaries are far less important than the questions of whether we can indeed translate professional purpose into such practice and service as will meet not categories of method but client need.

Awareness of Individual Psychology

Add to its self-definition and identity struggles the new awareness in group work of individual psychology, of the relatedness between intrapersonal needs and interpersonal behavior. Increasingly interested in the individuals who make up the group and concerned with how to deal with them individually when this seems called for, group workers look toward casework's area of special knowledge and technique. One gets the impression that somehow group workers are more respectful and tentative in their approach to working with individuals than are caseworkers in their approach to the group. One reason probably is that as group workers approach treatment of the individual they do so because of his sickness or malfunctioning; this is uneasy ground. On the other hand, as caseworkers approach the group, they move into what seems, on the surface at least, to be a diluted, safety-in-numbers situation. Whatever the causes, group work is involved in the effort to incorporate more fully and firmly into its methodology the knowledge of how to deal with the individual person who from time to time may need to be lifted out of group sessions into the one-to-one encounter.

It would be a service to all social work methods if group work did not too immediately and slavishly imitate the casework model; if, rather, it asked and answered some questions of its own. Its use and patterning of the individual interview, for example, might be shaped by such questions as the following: the relation between what is done in the individual interview to the purpose for which the person is being kept in the group, the effect on the relationship between group worker and other members of his group when one member has been taken on for special treatment, at a more theoretical level the connections between those social science concepts that have long under-pinned the group work method and the concepts of individual psychodynamics that are coming to have increasing play in group work thinking, and the connections between both these bodies of theory and the group process by which planned change can be made to occur. What is suggested is that group work's present thinking on its problems of method development and practice theory might serve all three social work methods if it did not too quickly surrender its uniqueness for the comfort of prefabricated action principles of another method.

On one of its pushing-out edges of practice, then, group work is increasingly overlapping with the casework method. At its opposite frontier it overlaps with community work. The boundaries between group work and community organization have always been fluid and close. With the renewed interest in settlement house activities and the experiments by group workers in moving out into the community for the redirection and reorganization of indigenous groups there is a growing common ground. So we turn to look at the community organization method, the third of social work's major practice methods.

Changes in Community Work

Perhaps the community organization method epitomizes the changes and conflicts in social work practice today. Its methodological struggles and its pressing questions may be seen as heightened versions of theory and practice problems in casework and group work.

To begin with, it is not simply a rhetorical question to ask, "What is community organization?" The *Social Work Year Book, 1957* contains one article on community organization.[1] The 1965 *Encyclopedia of Social Work* carries three articles on three different but manifestly interrelated areas of community work: "Community Development," "Community Organization," and "Community Planning and Development."[2] The author of "Community Development"—a term lucky enough to have the identifying stamp of "international usage" on it—points to the problems inherent and unresolved in differentiating these three

[1]Campbell G. Murphy, "Community Organization for Social Welfare," in Russell H. Kurtz, ed., *Social Work Year Book, 1957* (New York: National Association of Social Workers, 1957), pp. 179-185.
[2]Charles E. Hendry, "Community Development," Meyer Schwartz, "Community Organization," and Jack Stumpf, "Community Planning and Development," in Harry L. Lurie, ed., *Encyclopedia of Social Work* (New York: National Association of Social Workers, 1965), pp. 170-208.

branch-outs from what had been considered a practice unity. For purposes of simplicity an embracing name and one that ties in most readily with casework and group work will be used here: "community work."

Viewed from the vantage point of interested ignorance, the thrust in community work, like those in casework and group work, is a response both to internal and external stimuli that made existent boundaries too tight and old roles too limiting. The external stimuli are those that have become commonplace in the daily lives of all our citizenry: challenges to develop ideas, plans, programs, policies, new structures, new "targets" for coping with economic, educational, and cultural poverty and for socially alienated and socially antagonistic groups.

The idea of the "Great Society," the opening of federal concern and coffers for the creation and management of new programs for social welfare, the self-assertion and active organization of those sectors of society that for years had been depressed and silent—these are all-but-revolutionary upheavals. Suddenly social work finds that the intents and resources it had long called for are almost to be had. Almost to be had—not for the asking, but for the invention and presentation of bold, imaginative programs, preferably those that come with how-to-do-it directions. This is a major challenge to community workers. Add to this the widespread rise of vigorous young leaders at universities, in churches, in grass roots (or perhaps one should say instead "street pavement") organizations—all of whom are organizing, advocating, researching, and giving service—and the position and functions of the professional community worker are jostled as well as challenged.

The shift, then, seems to be from community organization as a method that has largely, although never exclusively, been involved in the co-ordination of existing services to the development of new kinds of structures and functions; from the redistribution of voluntary funds to the invention of programs and structure that can fruitfully utilize the millions of tax dollars that are ready to be poured into social welfare programs; from the concept of "citizen participation" that identified "citizen" in Platonic terms as one of the elite, one held to be "fit" to govern, to the concept of citizen participation as including those who are assumed to be the beneficiaries of service, now viewed as potential "indigenous leaders"; from consultation and standard-setting functions to social planning and action functions; from a sense of "community" as a small, stable, circumscribed unit to a recognition of the open and broken and expanding boundaries of present-day communities; and finally to awareness that "community" is a concept that demands a new definition and vision. Thus the social work method called community organization, which has in the past largely suggested a replenishment and tidying-up within a bounded area of given circumstances and conditions, has stretched and opened to include concepts of community development and planning and action, all with progressive, participant connotations.

The author of "Community Planning and Development" lists twenty-two "central issues" as yet unresolved in community work. They are questions far more upsetting to the equilibrium of its practitioners than those that alternately nettle and excite group work and casework, questions that express some of the paradoxes inherent in the traditional model of this method.

Persons, Problems, and Place

Who, for example, is the client of the community worker? Many community workers reject the use of that designation completely because of its connotation of dependency. But even if one uses it in its more general sense, as meaning "one who employs the services of a profession," who is the client? What group of persons make up the client-system of the community worker? Is it those who hire him or those for whose supposed benefit he is hired?

In the event of conflict of interest, with whose side is he allied—with those who employ him or those whom he is supposed to help? Put crudely: in a power struggle between opposing forces in a community, a militant neighborhood council, let us say, and the governing board of the neighborhood house that originally gave encouragement and house-room and a community worker to aid "indigenous participation," with whom will the community worker align himself?

For the community worker who is a professional social worker, what problems are most appropriate? Among the galaxy of social welfare problems and programs—the restitutive needs, the coordinating necessities, the social policy-making, the planning and engineering of action programs, the organization and support of voluntary efforts—which among these ought to be the priority or ascendant concerns of the community worker? Does this decision relate to power or skill or auspice?

What is the place, the auspice that hires the professional community worker? As long as community work remained within the safe boundaries of organized chests and council agencies it was in the ordered, relatively comfortable position of its sibling

Philosophy and Values

methods, casework and group work, shaped and channeled by its sponsorship. With its sallying forth into new areas and ventures it steps off from its familiar floor boards, with some gain in a heady sense of freedom but some loss of backing and certainty. Goals, structures, and functions are "set" by the setting in which the social worker is employed. So, too, are the worker's ways of working, his actions toward change. As he becomes the organizer of a new kind of community service, for example, a community mental health center for which patterns are only now in the making, what does he do, with and for whom, and by what methods?

These questions of problems-to-be-worked, persons-to-be-worked-with, and place all bear on process and on social work values as well. Power as a social force has pushed its way into frank and uneasy recognition by community workers. Power structures, power conflicts, power play are considerations that must be in the very center of any community-wide intervention strategy, whether political, economic, or social. The social scientist offers ways by which power phenomena can be understood and even manipulated. But between understanding and manipulation lie the considerations of professional ethics and human relationships. The social worker's pause to weigh and choose among relative values may become both his glory and his bane.

Turn to the Social Sciences

Perhaps even more than in casework and group work, community work has turned in the past decade to the social sciences for illumination. The findings of social science may have particular relevance for community work because they are so often focused on the large social scene and on its systems and trends. Power structure and dynamics, bureaucracy and its workings, the idea of social systems, these constructs and others are both underpinning community practice and shaking it up. New dimensions of goal and tasks are revealed by new knowledge. But, as has been said for casework and group work, this expanded and deepened understanding has not yet flashed directional arrows that point to what to do and how to do it. Community work has yet to coax out of its knowledge the principles that will guide its special actions.

Defining the Method

Within the past few years faculties of schools of social work, individually and in concert under the aegis of the Council on Social Work Education, the National Association of Social Workers through its productive commissions and committees, and groups of community workers on their own have taken on and wrestled with the problems of defining and delineating the method called "community organization" or "community action," of identifying its special social work characteristics, and especially of trying to extract and name its particular techniques. If it is to be taught in schools of social work its content must be clarified and its "strategies of intervention" must be cast into some systematic organized form. On the one side lies the danger that in the eagerness to find likeness among social work methods community work might be pushed and stuffed into treatment models that do not suit its specialness. On the other side lies the danger of ambiguity masquerading as flexibility.

Furthermore, the student of community work may be given little or no training in the depth experience of the one-to-one or one-to-small-group encounter and problem-solving that has been held to be the nucleus of social work learning. It is possible that such direct work with the people who actually suffer the problems with which social work is concerned is the crucial experience that results in the vital and telling difference between a bright young sociologist who enters community work and an equally bright young social worker who adds to his brightness and youngness a feelingful knowledge of the emotional and personal impact of social problems. These educational considerations and many others lie ahead for those who look to the development of community work.

Because community work is the most complex among the social work methods, because its operations are far more variegated and far less subject to worker control than those involved in casework or group work, and because it is currently in a phase of redefinitions and new insights, the probability is that its operational theory will be some time in developing.

Development of Practice
Theory

All three social work methods—casework, group work, and community work—thus have as their major task ahead the development of their practice theory, the theory that explains and guides their action. What the social worker does and how he does it—this is what will spell the special identity of the social work profession. We are surely and even rapidly adding to our store of knowledge; we have given tongue and heart to what we believe in and hold to be good; but the what and the how of carrying knowledge and belief into action—these are yet to be formulated. And this is difficult. Among the many problems that rise up as soon as one speaks of "method" are two that merit some further comment. One is that of the uses of social science. The other is that of whether social work methods are more alike than different from one another, more generic than specific, or the other way around.

Part of the problem in the actual use of social science theory for action purposes is not in the theory but in ourselves. Our difficulty is our overwhelming sense of needfulness—the feeling that somehow we have failed to find the keys that unlock the right doors to human behavior. This combines with the hope that someone else holds these keys. Once we thought sociology held them; then we thought psychoanalytic theory held them; now we seem to think social science holds them. We are not even sure what social science consists of, what combined bodies of knowledge are its constituents and whether all of these bodies can claim the rubric "science." But we reach out avidly, eager to know better in order to do better.

The caveat we must hold before ourselves is against letting the need blind us. Words seem to hold magic, and the use of words like "communication" and "transaction" and "client-system" and "role network" may infuse us with a heady sense of having something to conjure with. We can weave word-spells around one another, but unless we plumb these words for their particular meaning, for what phenomena they express, and then for what their implications for action are, we will find ourselves disappointed again that what we thought was gold is dross. Something of this sort has begun to happen in work on family diagnosis. It somehow does not quite tell us what to do about family treatment. We have a whole bagful of new words with their attendant manifest meanings by which to talk about family organization and processes, but we have yet to distill from those words their implications for treatment actions. We might even find, if we look hard, that we have some throwaways among them.

Furthermore, what is called social science is not all of a piece. It is not a nice, unified system; it ranges across varied phenomena in a vast field. Naturally, then, it holds contradictory findings and hypotheses, and many empty spaces, too. We will not find complete coherence in social science concepts and theory; moreover we must recognize that its findings are not of equal import to us. Some of its knowledge is more and some less useful to our purposes. Some ideas relate more closely to one method in social work than to another. It is our particular and identified practice problem that should determine what we look for in any body of knowledge, social science or any other. Selectivity based on our knowledge of what we are after, what we lack, what we need to understand, and on the relevance or fit of any given bit of knowledge for our work—this is our necessity.

Finally, the most difficult problem in the incorporation of social science into social work method is the problem of translating what is understood into principles of action. One of the major differences between social science theory and psychodynamic theory is that the latter, whether orthodox or heterodox, is derived from action, from efforts at intervention in psychological processes. Psychoanalysis started as research but turned out to be a therapeutic process. Psychodynamic theory has been elaborated and extended, to be sure, by speculation, extrapolation, experiment, and literary and dramatic analogies. But basically it is a practice theory, continuously tested in a process of transactions between a treating person and his patient or client. This is why psychodynamic theory so readily yields up practice principles, why it is so readily translatable into guides for doing. Doing reveals dynamics. (This is probably one reason why casework's development of its practice theory came earlier and more easily than that of other social work methods.) Psychodynamic theory is chiefly, though not completely, based on actual intervention. Social science theory is chiefly, though not completely, based on study that yields explanations.

Social science has studied and sought to explain the existence of social phenomena, to measure their frequency, extent, and regularity, and to postulate cause-effect relationships. The units studied have been large so that quantification would support generalization. With some notable exceptions in action programs, the researcher has been an objective observer of what was being studied, outside the process, dedicated to avoiding such interventions or action as might change the nature of what was being studied. Thus, there is an understandable gap between social science findings and their applicability to social work actions. Treatment or intervention strategies do not freely flow out of these findings. Whatever action guides they hold have to be teased out and translated into action terms.

The further probability is that for the most part it will take action to produce action theory. Description and study of practice, its regularities, the relation between what the social worker does and what happens—these operations in social work's several methods will need to be scrutinized, identified, formulated, and connected. In short, we shall probably have to search at our own doorsteps for the principles that explain what and how we do.

The second problem in method formulation today is that in our eagerness for "togetherness" and in the battering push on schools of social work to prepare versatile social workers, not narrow technicians, we may too quickly crystallize and box in our methods. This problem deserves a paper on its own; here it can only be touched.

**Need for Diversity in
Methods**

At a high level of generalization it is easy to see a common pattern in casework, group work, and community work. For all of them there is a generic, that is, an inclusive or general base. This consists of our knowledge of man in society, of social welfare programs and purposes, of our values and ethical commitments, and of our problem-solving process that follows the logic of identification of the problem-to-be-worked, its study, its assessment, and the making of decisions and choices about modes of action. But all this offers only the most general outlines of practice. At the moment of going into action—at the moment when a live social worker engages himself with his live client—whether that client is one person, a group, or interacting groups—for the purpose of changing behavior or conditions, then his method becomes specific, particular, differentially shaped, and acted out. The ways a social worker translates his understandings into actions, how he handles himself and the people and circumstances he aims to change—these constitute his technical know-how. It is this know-how that needs to be named, explained, and regularized.

The danger is that in our effort to find social work "all of a piece" we may try too quickly and too hard to push and fit new, emergent, as yet insufficiently tried modes of practice into established or old molds. And we may lose, thereby, the richness and potentialities of diversity in practice.

One sees, for example, a continued eyeing of casework for its fairly neat array of action principles. Sometimes that eyeing is admiring. It says, "How orderly you are. We too can fit into your scheme." Sometimes that eyeing is baleful. It says, "What a poor scheme you work by. It doesn't provide a hint about social reform or prevention." Both positions are in error. The casework model is a clinical model. It is focused on clear and present malfunctioning in single units of person or family. Its purpose is to give help when such an individual unit experiences and feels present problems. Its actions are founded on conceptions of the motivating powers within individuals and of how those powers are enhanced by relationship, on notions of the releasing and reorganizing values of identification, of talk, of emotional expression followed by reflective consideration, and so on. As a clinical model it has validity. For certain persons with certain problems this one-to-one model cannot readily be disposed of.

On the other hand, when casework moves into dealing with other sorts of problems—for example, those of crisis situations—and with certain kinds of people—for example, the socially antagonistic and alienated—and with new sorts of goals—for example, that of prevention—its clinical model may well need radical change. This change needs to occur, for instance, when caseworkers begin to group their clients as is the trend today. What assumptions are they making about the nature of relationship in the group as same or different from relationship in the twosome, about group members as sources of supplementary ego supports, and so forth? In short, the clinical treatment model cannot simply be extended to embrace other kinds of units and ends; on the other hand, it should not be held wanting because it does not shape treatment actions for which it was never intended.

If this need for working out differentiated treatment models based on differentiated persons, purposes, and programs holds within one method, casework, it suggests that among the three social work methods even greater diversity may be needed and found. We should not too readily expect that our action theory will neatly fall into the same molds for all three methods. Perhaps we should ask ourselves in what ways an action model for therapeutic purposes is likely to differ from one that has educational purposes, and this model from one that has planning-prevention purposes. Maybe the way to go about identifying social work practice activities is not within the traditional boundaries of casework, group work, and community work at all, but across lines, by asking ourselves what kinds of problems call for what kinds of service and actions. It is possible that the ways we perceive a situation, define it, and go about treating it are shaped a priori by the particular method to which we have allegiance or in which we have skill. Perhaps—if we are bold enough to face uncertainties—treatment or intervention or planned change will defy being bound by laws or principles of governance. Perhaps knowledge and understanding plus ethics and values need only to be joined with courage, flexibility, and creative spontaneity to produce desired changes. Or perhaps, once we have genuinely and precisely described what and how we do rather than prenamed it and cast it into a method category, those detailed descriptions of new modes of action will reveal certain repeated patterns that can be put together and explained toward a generic social work theory of action.

The great federal programs for poverty prevention and for education and training call for versatile social workers. Our present-day articulated repertoire of actions is a limited one. It needs expansion, experiment, ranging, even to risking some crazy-creative combinations that may develop and add to our ways and means of helping and changing. The characteristic of experiment as differentiated from trial and error, of course, is that underlying the former is a hypothesis, an idea about cause-effect relations, and a structured way of describing and then examining what has been done, and how and why. With this approach we will have more precise descriptions of our various practice methods. Then we can seek to articulate the practice principles they suggest.

The plea is obvious. While we give ourselves to the difficult task of developing the methods of social work we should guard against crystallizing too quickly. We should observe and describe our doing in some detail before we clap it into definition and category. We should recognize and tolerate, and even welcome, the range of differences among our several methods before we package them under generalizations that blur out those differences. Let us remind ourselves that the practice of medicine embraces both the surgeon and the psychoanalyst; teaching contains the professorial lecturer and the remedial tutor; law holds the trial lawyer and the taxation expert. Each pair is part of one profession, but they would be hard put to it to find uniformity in what they actually do. What we must recognize is that different problems and different purposes call for different interventive means and actions. Out of diversity comes richness and range; the identification of the underlying system can follow after.

Concluding Comments

It would be satisfying to be able to sum up this review of social work methods in a tidy, integrated conclusion, and to add a touch of wisdom. If ever I thought I was wise, this survey of our practice has humbled me. I am not sure I have seen straightly or clearly; I am afraid I have done no one full justice. But one impression comes clear. When in 1952 I urged that we "put the social back in social work" I thought it was a lost cause. Today there is a ground swell toward this goal in every part of our practice, thrust up by passionate belief and firmed up by knowledge and reasoned appraisal. True, we are at the moment when the surge and ferment in our methods make them not yet ready for neat ordering. But their present disorder is the symptom of vigorous breakout from confining forms. It holds the potential of reorganizations and combinations of old tried and true methods and of unfenced space for experiments and innovations in action.

To the labor of examining, challenging, diversifying, assessing, and firming-up social work method our ten-year-old professional association—the National Association of Social Workers—our schools of social work, the Council on Social Work Education, and our forward-looking practitioners and agencies are all joined. The social climate has never been more invigorating. There is nothing to do but to get on with it, doggedly, and with high heart.

Selected Bibliography

Boehm, W. W., "The Nature of Social Work," *Social Work*, 3 (2), 1958, pp. 10–18.

Boehm, W. W., "Social Work: Science and Art," *Social Service Review*, 35 (2), 1961, pp. 144–152.

Coughlin, B., "Value Orientation in Social Welfare," *Social Welfare Forum*, 1967, pp. 115–126.

Fantl, B., "Integrating Social and Psychological Theories in Social Work Practice," *Smith College Studies in Social Work*, 34 (3), 1964, pp. 161–251.

Gordon, W. E., "A Critique of the Working Definition," *Social Work*, 7 (3), 1962, pp. 3–13.

Gordon, W. E., "Knowledge and Value: Their Distinction and Relationship in Clarifying Social Work Practice," *Social Work*, 10 (3), 1965, pp. 32–39.

Kahn, A. J., "The Societal Context of Social Work Practice," *Social Work*, 10 (4), 1965, pp. 145–155.

La Barre, M., "The Strengths of the Self-Supporting Poor," *Social Casework*, 49 (8), 1968, pp. 459–466.

McCormick, M. J., "The Role of Values in Social Functioning," *Social Casework*, 42 (2), 1961, pp. 70–78.

Pumphrey, M. W., "Transmitting Values and Ethics through Social Work Practice," *Social Work*, 6 (3), 1961, pp. 68–75.

Stretch, J. J., "Existentialism: A Proposed Philosophical Orientation for Social Work," *Social Work*, 12 (4), 1967, pp. 97–102.

3

Casework

The individual approach is that method of social work practice which focuses on individual problems. Even here, however, the person is considered not in isolation but rather in an environment which affects him and which he affects. Perlman explores the relationship between the person and the situation as it applies to the individual approach. She sees an integrated approach as necessary for achieving the goals of an individual approach, which she describes as helping "individuals to cope more effectively with their problems in social functioning." Reynolds, in discussing the historical development of social casework practice, also suggests the need for a broader perspective in the individual approach.

The therapeutic function of casework, discussed by Briar, tends most to focus on the individual. But Briar sees "clinical" casework, with its therapeutic approach, as only one valid approach. "I have in mind no fixed list of casework functions," he writes, "because the central point is that these functions arise in response to the needs of the persons we seek to serve and the conditions of their lives. . . ." Consequently, the social worker may be required to involve himself in family treatment or in social policy making.

Other authors in this section also point out that to help an individual, the social worker must often deal with a whole, complex situation. Rapoport, in discussing crisis intervention, emphasizes that the steps required to alleviate immediate stress may be either client-centered or situation-centered or both, depending on the problem. Sax sees the possible uses of family treatment to effect changes in an individual.

The authors in this section, then, portray a changing conception of the individual approach: a movement from a clinical approach to a more encompassing individual-in-relation-to-his-total-environment orientation. Such an emphasis on the broad approach is, as we have said, characteristic of the social work generalist.

The Social Casework of an Uncharted Journey

Bertha C. Reynolds

In Mary Richmond's day, about the turn of the century, it seemed simple to establish a protest against harsh deterrent treatment of people who were economic failures, and against demoralizing and irresponsible charity. Finding individual families in the mass, searching for causes, and influencing character development seemed sufficient to supplement needed social reforms. It was only later that we did a finer sifting and picked individuals out of families, and then located within individuals the ego-functioning we thought we might assist.

No one would challenge today the underlying assumption that has been growing all these years—that basically people make their own adjustments, that skilled help can do no more than assist at points where their own resources fail. What we consider here—based on a record of the author's own experience—is whether in fifty years new light has been thrown upon social work practice and even upon some of its underlying assumptions.

These years have been a time of intensive as well as rapid change. The world has never been the same since World War I and that was only the ripening of changes occurring over centuries. In social work, certain trends have been truly revolutionary. For instance:

1. We became ashamed of and repressed consciousness of social class. Mary Richmond could write happily about philanthro-

Reprinted with permission of the author and the National Association of Social Workers from Social Work, Vol. 9, No. 4 (October 1964), pp. 13–17.

py—the privileged giving to the underprivileged and building bridges of understanding between the two through volunteer "friendly visitors." World War I was the turning point from this orientation to a concept of democracy that minimized social class. We came to believe that social casework, if it were indeed a valid concept of scientific social adjustment, ought to be applicable to people in difficulties whatever their social status. We began with families of servicemen; we extended casework to middle-class families with child guidance and marital problems, and to people of all ages with emotional difficulties. When the Great Depression resulted in governmental taking over of a limited responsibility for subsistence needs of masses of people, voluntary social agencies felt that they could, and must, shift their concern to problems other than economic. The people who had economic difficulties (and who would once have been considered "lower class") were now just sifted out of social work consciousness that could feel itself to be not "class conscious" but democratic.

2. During the period of two world wars and a depression, social casework, which theoretically was for everybody who needed help, became more and more restricted to those whose economic needs were cared for otherwise, and who had enough leisure and verbal articulateness to explore their own personal difficulties with a skilled professional person. This shaped a definition of social casework as a certain kind of practice, applicable to a certain kind of people, and usable only in a setting which produced certain conditions, among which were time for extended interviews, freedom from too great environmental pressures, and a certain level of intelligence. In a school of social work covering the entire country, I was concerned that the majority of people in need were served by public assistance and large medical agencies, where the conditions for this kind of casework practice did not obtain. Either the definition of social casework was too narrow to cover its potentialities for service to the majority of people in need, or else its potentialities were really limited and some other discipline must be invented to serve the total population. Some years of investigation of the possibilities in what was called "short-contact interviewing" convinced me that what I understood to be casework principles were applicable to every sort of situation in which a skilled professional person meets a person in need of help. In practice the definition has been too narrow, and has a far wider range than thought possible.

3. There have been in psychiatric social work certain assumptions of universality that were challenged by my experience in the Depression years. Freud's philosophy, expressed in *Civilization*

and *Its Discontents* and in his generalizations from practice, seems to find a built-in conflict in everyone between the primitive instinctive desires and the restraints of civilized life. The constructs of *the id, the ego,* and *the superego* were useful to explain these conflicting elements. The ego, the balancing adjustment factor, became the locus of success or failure in living, and ego psychology became the field of operation of psychiatric casework.

The experience of social agencies in the Depression, however, challenged in several ways the assumption of a prevailing neurosis associated with civilization. The need for the necessities of life, which befell millions in a crisis of unemployment, was not appropriately treated or alleviated by "There is something wrong with your adjustment; let me help you." In fact, when the mores made income failure equivalent to personal inadequacy, the priceless personal ingredient of self-confidence was not enhanced by an insistence that to be helped one must first admit failure and seek help on someone else's terms. Who were we to offer help to people differing in no way from those of us who had lived successfully except that they had lost and we retained a job? Nevertheless, the preferred mode of practice featured a series of weekly interviews over a rather long period as the alternative to diagnosing the person's problems as unsuitable for casework help. The paradox appeared in this young profession that, while the majority of so-called social workers did what needed to be done in mass programs which could not provide the settings for what was called casework, the training in professional schools was geared to the few who sought work in these settings. Along with this there was a haunting difficulty in defining how the work with emotional problems was different from the role of a psychiatrist. To be blunt—social casework as seen by the mass of social workers was so defined as to be, for both client and worker, a plaything for the rich. Yet these workers were shaping the new public programs of assistance and health care without much help from the schools.

4. Social casework had to be differentiated not only from psychotherapy but from social welfare, which has had a significant development in the last thirty years. In Mary Richmond's day, to take responsibility for bettering the lot of poor people was to try to solve intelligently *all* their problems, finding resources as one could in themselves or in the community. The Depression made absurd the hope that private philanthropy could take care of almost every problem. It became clear that if it was not demeaning for a total community to see that pure water was available to everyone, why did this not hold true for food when there was no

other way of obtaining it? If education was provided for children, why not health care to make it possible for them to learn? If mass disaster kept recurring, why not mass insurance against such destruction of people? So social casework, a method of helping, came to be attached to welfare services which were not themselves casework, but a discharge of governmental responsibility. When Mary Richmond objected to government pensions for widowed mothers because she thought them a step backward away from individualized service, she did not see that a civilized society requires both an administration efficient enough to see that thousands of mothers had income with which to care for their own children and a skilled service available to mothers who need it in order to adjust the program to individual needs as well as to help individuals to function at their best. When I investigated the various sorts of short-term services in mass agencies for welfare, social casework turned out to be a definable skill present in the simplest services if the professional person had the sensitivity to use it as well as in the complex situations touched off by emotional conflicts.

The social casework of Mary Richmond's day could not be practiced now. Its assumption of class stratification would be considered condescending and we demand a democratic approach to people. We do not now consider as part of social casework the dispensing of the necessities of life, homes for children, hospital care, and employment—although government programs for these things are not fully adequate and desperate needs are still unmet. Social casework has come to be recognized as a professional practice—we all want it to be available to everyone who needs it.

A Personal Philosophy

What we are not clear about is who does need it. What criteria mark situations appropriate for social casework, and are mass programs of welfare services able to supply a setting for it? Part of our trouble is in definition of social casework. Is it a limited skilled treatment of ego-functioning in individuals who seek that treatment? Or is it a professional way of dealing with people in trouble, people of all sorts and in all sorts of circumstances? I shall use the rest of this paper to try to make clear the concept of social casework to which I came, and which is set forth as it grew in *An Uncharted Journey*. This concept grew because it became apparent to me how much people were able to do for themselves. To think in terms of adjustment rather than maladjustment, health instead of pathology, to find conditions of normal living (or even ways of compromising with conditions that are not fully favorable), to win with each person his own best balance—this is the philosophy of social work to which I came out of many mistakes and much tribulation. The book tells the story. Only a few of the most important points are stressed in this article.

1. The Importance of Social Diagnosis

It is not just harking back to Mary Richmond to say that when a person in trouble meets a professional person dedicated to helping, the first question to ask is, "What is the matter?" We have sometimes not asked it in detailed fashion but only sorted cases by some technical device. It is not simple to find out the real trouble. Often the person himself does not know, for his conscious awareness is pretty well limited to what he can deal with. If he needs professional help, it is to apply another, trained intelligence to the complex of realities which is his trouble, and see how to deal with it.

We should not assume that invariably the trouble is in the ego-functioning of the person, convenient as it would be to have a formula to apply. There are many other important questions to be answered. Is this living organism in a reasonably healthy relation to physical nature—is he fed, making his living, progressing appropriately to his age, or is he hungry, frustrated, lacking in vigor, angry, and misusing his energies? Then—is this social being relating to others in a healthy way filling his various roles? What are his potentialities? Where has his trouble blocked him in realizing them?

Diagnosis by a professional person implies a body of knowledge and a trained skill that a person in trouble cannot command within himself. Of what does the knowledge and skill of the social caseworker consist? I have come to challenge too much reliance on Freudian psychology with its assumption that neurosis is preconditioned by civilized society. A different view of history is that man is a part of nature and healthy adjustment to it is "natural" for man. If his development is a *leap* upward from the rest of nature, no less is it a natural process. An animal with a developed hand and larger brain and articulate speech could become what man is today only by evolving a *social*, co-operative way of life. We need not fear, but rather turn to use what human society adds to man's stature and potentials for living.

We have to be aware that social institutions evolved by the tyranny of the strong over the weak are not always favorable to healthy social life, that inhumanity of man to man exists and has become frightful in our time. A diagnosis of an individual's un-happiness, therefore, cannot ignore a diagnosis of the sickness of society and what it is doing to the person's life. This combined social diagnosis (man in society and society pressing upon him) is a prerogative of social casework which overlaps with no other form of professional service. Whether we meet troubled people in counseling, or in a long line of applicants for public assistance, or in a hospital clinic or a court or a school, this function of seek-ing out "What is the matter?" is our uncontested area of service.

2. The Importance of Relationship

Another milestone after Mary Richmond was the new awareness of "relationship" touched off by Virginia Robinson. Not to be di-verted by the peculiarities of some interpretations, the accessibili-ty of a professional person, emotional nearness, has always been at the very heart of psychiatric social work. As I once said, one can give coal with a cold heart, but cannot so give understanding. We have slowly learned not to be afraid of warmth, as if it would be-fuddle our intellectual objectivity. We still have difficulties, however, in getting close to people, even physically. We inter-pose secretaries, intake procedures, offices, and clinics until sometimes it seems only the boldest can get through to reach help.

One great help in overcoming distance is a frank recognition that one's way of life does largely determine how one thinks. The most dangerous assumption is that there are no social classes in America, and hence no differences of outlook. To overcome real differences we have to be taught, case by case, how the client does think and feel, and by the client himself.

3. Potentials for Change in Troubled Persons and Their Situation

Social casework does not stop with diagnosis, though we tend to become baffled when asked what it is we do to change whatever it is that blocks health and happiness for a person. If we have learned in fifty years not to think we can play Providence with material gifts, or with a foster home, a job, medical treatment, or the more elusive psychotherapy, what can we do? In the 1920's we irritated our clients by elaborate diagnostic studies that pointed to telling them what was the matter, after a staff conference of experts, hoping that thereafter they could solve their own prob-lems. If that does not work (as too often it does not), if we cannot solve problems for them, if we cannot make people over as we have hoped psychiatry might, what then?

The Asset of Humanity

I do not have all the answers. A few things I am sure of, however, even though some are assumptions and different ones from those upon which much of social work practice is based:

First, nature works with, not against us, for health of body and mind, even against great odds. Witness the youths who do *not* become delinquent or neurotic, the slum-dwellers who go on to contribute mightily to their generation, the loving and resourceful parents, the heroic defenders of right living in all walks of life.

Second, in contrast to saying, "You have failed. Are you willing to let me help you?" the first question to ask is, "You have lived so far. How have you done it?" and go on from there. The activity of the person is crucial especially in his social relationships, no matter how he has feared and bungled them. Just as man became man in learning to co-operate with his social group in making a living, so he survives individually by the social relationships which bear him up and enable him to develop as a person. We therefore study those social relationships, how they work for health and how they are blocked or even destructive.

Third, how does a relationship to a professional person help one in trouble to use his own powers of adjustment? We no longer think it is a sentimental adjunct of service that a scientifically trained person must outlive or even that it is love—a mystical, unknown power—that makes our world go round. We now know enough to realize that social relationships are decisive in human survival and growth, and that this professional relationship is one of a special kind. At least it is protected from the crass self-interest that often mars the helpfulness of friends; it is based upon the best psychological and social understanding our education can give us; it enhances whatever personal gifts we have; it is made available by organized services and, hopefully, is to be found more reliable than spontaneous good will. We have evidence in our practice that a relationship to a professional person can restore self-confidence, relieve paralyzing fear, release energy, and can stimulate in the client his own intelligence and resourcefulness.

Fourth, beyond this dynamic potential of a relationship, what can we offer? We have come to see that we cannot make anyone over. The person must live his own life. All that the society of which he is a part can do is to create better conditions with which he may shape his life. We, as representatives of that society, may, in limited ways, mobilize resources within and outside himself for happier use of what is there in his social world. So, although our relationship to the client is dynamic, personal, often reaching him through his unconscious as well as his conscious desires with understanding and upbuilding, our professional service is always *social*. We understand him only in his activity in his own social setting. We help him find health instead of misery, victory instead of defeat, in the very setting or in such a changed setting as society is able to offer him. We are ever and always a *go-between* profession, seeking an understanding of how a fellow human being is able to live his life in the social group which makes life possible for him.

Fifth, this is to say nothing of social change, which was an impelling consideration in much of my professional life. As a social caseworker, I could not ignore what the social system was doing to individuals and families and social groups. As a social caseworker, I had to differentiate between what a person could change in his situation for himself and what was forced upon him by a cruel and exploitative society. The fact that casework could only help with "fringe benefits" while vital needs went unmet in the face of hunger and joblessness was perhaps beyond any competence of mine. As a human being, however, it was my business to understand and to care. As a social caseworker, too, I could not be indifferent to the fact that my professional functioning was often blocked by impossible living conditions. Once I became sensitized to what people were doing for themselves in the struggles of the 1930's, I could not fail to see that social casework had here its greatest ally—the active will to live of humans whose intelligence could now be used in organized effort with their fellows.

That asset of humanity cannot be lost, only temporarily mislaid. It is the prevailing resource of any helping profession—the *vis curatrix naturae* on which the greatest in medicine have always relied.

The Current Crisis
in Social Casework

Scott Briar

It is said that social casework is in deep trouble. It is said that caseworkers are destined for extinction. It is said—and this criticism cuts deepest of all—that casework is not responsive to the needs of the persons it claims to serve. These criticisms, with

From *Social Work Practice, 1967* (New York: Columbia University Press, 1967), pp. 19–33. Reprinted with permission of Columbia University Press.

many variations, can be heard from persons outside the profession, from other social workers, and even, though more softly, from some of our fellow caseworkers. In fact, just a few months ago, Helen Perlman felt moved to ask whether casework is dead.[1]

As a teacher and practitioner whose professional career has been centered on social casework, I am distressed by these criticisms. Unfortunately, what distresses me most is that I find myself compelled to agree with many of these criticisms. Casework *is* in trouble. And unless casework cures its own ills, it could very well be destined to become, at worst, a relic of a past era or, at best, a marginal activity in the profession. But I am not willing to stand idly by to watch this prophecy come to pass. The initial vision that gave rise to social casework was based on an important insight into the human condition in modern society, namely, the realization that if social welfare programs are to be genuinely responsive to the needs of persons, they must be individualized. If that insight is forgotten, the profession as a whole will be the worse for it.

The recent criticisms of social casework have taken two principal forms. One questions the very existence of casework by arguing that a case-by-case approach to social problems is at best inefficient and at the worst, hopeless and perhaps even harmful. The second declares that casework simply is not effective, a criticism that is perhaps even more fundamental than the first.

The argument against the case-by-case approach to social problems has appeared partly as an accompaniment to the rising tide of interest in social change and social reform. I want to emphasize that I see no grounds for anything but enthusiasm and optimism about this trend and the promise it portends for the profession and for social welfare. It is a welcome development, not only because social reform activities have too long been neglected, but also because there can be no doubt that many of the problems of concern to the profession will not yield to direct service alone but require intervention at other systemic levels in the social order.

In some of the burgeoning literature on the need for social reform, however, there has appeared a strand of strong and sometimes shrill criticism of social casework. Some of this criticism is well deserved, but some of it heaps on social caseworkers responsibilities they never presumed to carry, and some of it reflects a disquieting naïveté about what social change can realistically be expected to accomplish. But more important is that the

[1]Helen Harris Perlman, "Casework Is Dead," *Social Casework*, XLVIII (1967), 22–25.

growing emphasis on social change as a strategy for alleviating social problems has evoked from many caseworkers a defensiveness about their own activities. And this defensiveness threatens to block more constructive responses by caseworkers to the changes occurring in the profession.[2]

It is important at the outset to be clear about the legitimate grounds for a critique of the casework enterprise. It is fair to criticize casework—or, for that matter, group work, community organization, and social reform—for failing to accomplish what it claimed it could do; in other words, for not being effective. If caseworkers have claimed to be able to help persons with certain kinds of problems and the evidence shows that they have not done so, then caseworkers better return to the drawing board and look for other ways to accomplish their aims. It also is fair to criticize caseworkers if they lose sight of the problem, the need, the person, and the task in a preoccupation with techniques, ideologies, and theoretical concepts. In other words, if it is true, as some have argued,[3] that caseworkers, rather than devising methods tailored to the client's needs and expectations, have expected clients to adapt to the caseworker's methods, then caseworkers should pause to remind themselves that their first commitment is to the client. And, finally, it is fair to criticize casework if it cuts itself off from persons who need its services. That is, if it is true, as it appears to be, that persons who could benefit from the services of caseworkers are systematically deprived of them, then we must alter the methods of delivering and offering casework services so that they are available to such persons.

It is *not* responsible, on the other hand, to criticize social casework for failing to fulfill responsibilities it never promised to discharge—for failing, for example, to eliminate poverty, do away with delinquency, or end illegitimacy. It is possible that some caseworkers have made such rash and immodest claims, but I do not believe the field of social casework has seriously taken these responsibilities upon itself. Consequently, it is absurd to point to the continued existence of social problems as a sign of the failure of casework. Nevertheless, the misconceptions implicit in this line of argument point to the need for a clearer statement of what it is that caseworkers *are* supposed to do.

[2]Berthe Gronfein, "Should Casework Be on the Defensive?" *Social Casework*, XLVII (1966), 650–56.

[3]Richard A. Cloward and Irwin Epstein, "Private Social Welfare's Disengagement from the Poor: The Case of Family Adjustment Agencies," in Mayer N. Zald, ed., *Social Welfare Institutions* (New York: Wiley, 1965), pp. 623–44.

The dominant preoccupation of social casework over the past thirty-five to forty years has been devoted to the development of the therapeutic function of social casework, or what has come to be called "clinical" casework. I have no quarrel with clinical casework—most of my own practice is of this sort—except that I do not think clinical casework is nearly as effective as it ought to be. Caseworkers can no longer afford to ignore the implications of studies such as the recently published *Girls at Vocational High*.[4] The findings of that study may seem discouraging, but they cannot be written off as due to inadequacies in research design and technology. For what confronts us is not one study but a long list of studies with equally distressing results. Hunt, Kogan, and their co-workers labored long and hard at the Community Service Society in New York City to measure the outcome of casework and found an average movement of only one step on the movement scale, a result that, at the least, should have stimulated a searching reconsideration of the clinical casework approach developed in that agency and widely promulgated in the field.[5] This is not to say that casework is never effective, and it is important to be clear about that. Any caseworker can cite cases from his own experience to show that casework is effective, sometimes dramatically so. What the research indicates is simply that our batting average is too low—not that we never succeed but rather that we succeed too infrequently.

The research on the effectiveness of casework is only a small part of the story. Research on the effectiveness of psychotherapy is both more extensive and, in some respects, more rigorous than the outcome studies of casework.[6] I know that many caseworkers are quick to insist on the difference between clinical casework and psychotherapy, but it is demonstrable that the theory and techniques of treatment that inform clinical casework practice were not developed independently but carry a heavy debt to psychotherapy, and to psychoanalytic psychotherapy in particular. Thus, studies that question the efficacy of dynamic psychotherapy also challenge the foundations of clinical casework. And

[4]Henry J. Meyer, Edgar F. Borgatta, and Wyatt C. Jones, *Girls at Vocational High: An Experiment in Social Work Intervention* (New York: Russell Sage Foundation, 1965).

[5]For a review of this research, see Scott Briar, "Family Services," in Henry S. Maas, ed., *Five Fields of Social Service* (New York: National Association of Social Workers, 1966), pp. 16–21.

[6]The literature on research on psychotherapy is too vast to be summarized here. A recent review of major studies of traditional psychotherapy is available in Hans J. Eysenck, *The Effects of Psychotherapy* (New York: International Science Press, 1966). An excellent source for current developments in research on psychotherapy is the chapters on psychotherapy in the *Annual Review of Psychology* published each year by Annual Reviews, Inc., Palo Alto, Calif.

the plain facts are that the effectiveness of the traditional psycho-therapies, the so-called "dynamic" psychotherapies, is in grave doubt. Even defenders of the traditional psychotherapies who have surveyed this body of evidence can find only weak support in a few isolated studies and for the remainder can only question the validity of the research itself, a weak and no longer sufficient defense.[7]

Moreover, at least as far as casework is concerned, it is not simply that effectiveness is less than satisfactory, but other research has shown that the model of clinical casework dominant for many years is suitable for no more than a fraction of the clients who come to us. We now know that even in the presumably ideal conditions of the private family service agency, the conception of casework as a prolonged series of interviews between the caseworker and an individual who is seeking help with emotional or interpersonal problems appears to be applicable to at most 25 percent of the clients who seek help from such agencies.[8]

But the findings I have all too briefly summarized here should not be viewed as cause for despair. The response required is of quite another sort. The message of these findings is that caseworkers should embark on a period of active and vigorous innovation and experimentation, in a search for more effective models and methods for the conduct of clinical casework. Fortunately, some promising directions for experimentation have already appeared. Caseworkers in many places are experimenting, for example, with short-term methods of intervention. But experimentation with short-term approaches has not proceeded at a pace commensurate with their obvious relevance to the reality that a large proportion of the encounters between caseworkers and clients are of brief duration. If we are to give short-term methods the attention they deserve, we have to modify our tendency, as Lucille Austin notes, to regard them "chiefly as a matter of expedience."[9] Family treatment represents another area of active experimentation in social casework. Unfortunately, however, the family therapy movement also illustrates a characteristic weakness of innovative efforts in social work, namely, the failure to conduct systematic evaluations of effectiveness. Despite the enormous effort that has been devoted to family diagnosis and treatment over the past ten to fifteen years, the number of at-

[7]See, for example, Robert Wallerstein, "The Current State of Psychotherapy: Theory, Practice, Research," *Journal of the American Psychoanalytic Association*, XIV (1966), 183–225.

[8]Briar, *op. cit.*

[9]Howard J. Parad, ed., *Crisis Intervention: Selected Readings* (New York: Family Service Association of America, 1965), p. xi.

tempts to assess its effectiveness systematically can be counted on the fingers of one hand.[10] Thus, we continue to expand family treatment only on the basis of faith and the missionary zeal of the practitioners who have become committed to it. Faith, however, is not enough. The crucial questions to be asked of an intervention method are not "Does it sound good?" or "Is it fascinating?" but "Does it work?" and "Is it more effective than other methods?"

Appearing on the horizon are some even more fundamental innovations in treatment models and techniques. I have in mind a variety of new therapeutic strategies based on theories that depart radically from the psychoanalytic formulations that have dominated psychotherapy and casework for the past thirty to forty years. One illustration of these new departures is the attempt to apply sociobehavioral theory to social work practice. When one first hears it, the language and metaphors of this approach may seem strange or even disagreeable, but do not turn away if they do. Or, at first glance, it may seem that this theory simply puts new labels on old, familiar ideas, but that impression, too, would be invalid. The sociobehavioral approach has already had wide application and is based on theories that are backed by extensive research.[11] The results thus far are impressive, sometimes dramatically so, and perhaps the most promising aspect of sociobehavioral theory is that it suggests a strategy for the development of practice knowledge that is more systematic than those we have followed in the past. We cannot afford to ignore any perspective that is demonstrably successful or that appears to promise a more effective strategy for developing the body of knowledge we need in order to improve our effectiveness. Finally, I would mention the important innovations now being formulated in response to our increased understanding of the realities of casework with the poor.

My intent in these comments on clinical casework is to make two general points. The first is that current attempts to disparage the therapeutic function of social casework are invalid and misdirected. Clinical casework represents an essential function carried out in relation to important human problems. For that reason, the demand for caseworkers to perform this function should continue to increase, if—through more vigorous innovation and

[10]One of the better exceptions is Robert MacGregor, et al., *Multiple Impact Therapy with Families* (New York: McGraw-Hill, 1964).
[11]See, for example, Leonard Krasner and Leonard P. Ullmann, eds., *Research in Behavior Modification* (New York: Holt, Rinehart and Winston, 1965); and Leonard P. Ullmann and Leonard Krasner, eds., *Case Studies in Behavior Modification* (New York: Holt, Rinehart and Winston, 1965).

systematic experimentation—caseworkers can discover ways of performing this function more effectively.

My second point is that the general field of psychotherapy is in a state of exciting ferment and experimentation. Unfortunately, however, many caseworkers are effectively isolated from these developments, for it still is true that caseworkers by and large keep abreast primarily of those developments in psychotherapy that are within the psychoanalytic tradition, broadly defined. This restriction is becoming increasingly dysfunctional for clinical casework, since, as Ford and Urban recently concluded in their excellent review of developments in psychotherapy, "the innovative steam has gone out of the psychoanalytic movement. Major theoretical and technical advances in the future will probably come from other orientations."[12] In order that we can benefit from those advances in the general field of psychotherapy that may be applicable to casework practice, it is essential that we find ways of keeping informed about the many new developments in that closely related field.

I said that the disparagement of clinical casework is misplaced. The proper target of these critics, in my opinion, is the strong tendency to equate clinical casework with casework, the tendency to regard the therapeutic function as the *only* function of casework. To make this equation is to constrict the range of functions of casework and thereby to make it less flexible and less responsive to changing needs and conditions. The founders of social casework had no such narrow conception of the functions of the social caseworker. (By founders, incidentally, I have in mind persons such as Mary Richmond, Porter Lee, Edith Abbott, Shelby Harrison, and Bertha Reynolds.) The therapeutic function was part of their vision of social casework, but it was only one of several functions they thought caseworkers should perform. However, the history of social casework is in large measure a history of progressive constriction, elimination, and reduction of the functions of casework to the therapeutic or clinical function.[13] The other functions of the casework enterprise envisaged by its founders have either atrophied or have been relegated to marginal activities subsumed under the catch-all phrase, "environmental manipulation." I believe this trend ought to be reversed, not simply because the founders had a broader conception of the

[12]Donald H. Ford and Hugh B. Urban, "Psychotherapy," in *Annual Review of Psychology: Volume 18, 1967* (Palo Alto, Calif. Annual Reviews, Inc., 1967), p. 333.

[13]Bertha Reynolds's autobiographical book, *An Uncharted Journey: Fifty Years of Growth in Social Work* (New York: Citadel Press, 1963), is in part a chronicle of one person's efforts to maintain a broader conception of the casework mission in the face of her colleagues' more successful attempts to constrict it.

caseworker's mission, but because changing conditions and changing conceptions of the problems facing the profession require an expanded conception of casework.

Two functions that were explicit components of the casework enterprise in its early history have since atrophied. I select these two functions only as examples; they are not the only functions that have been neglected.

One is a function that currently is being revived under the rubric of "social broker."[14] The justification for this function resides in the fact that there are many persons who need services but do not know that these services are available; many others know that the services are available but do not know where to obtain them; others who know where to obtain services do not know how to get them or else face obstacles in seeking and obtaining them; and still others do not know how to gain the maximum benefits available to them. This function is vastly more important today than it was when Mary Richmond and her colleagues were preoccupied with it, because the maze of social welfare programs is far more complex and the social agencies are larger and more bureaucratic than they were in her day. Fortunately, however, we have an advantage not available to Mary Richmond, namely, a substantial body of knowledge concerning the dynamics of the welfare system and its constituent agencies. This body of knowledge could be applied—though by and large it has not been—to the performance of the social broker function, much as we have applied social and psychological knowledge in our performance of the therapeutic function.

The problem of getting what one wants and needs from the public welfare agency, the health department, the vocational rehabilitation agency, the psychiatric hospital, the public school—and on and on through the array of organizations with which persons must negotiate to get what they need—is no simple matter, as everyone knows from his own encounters with large, complex organizations. Increasingly, if a person is to gain from these agencies the benefits to which he is entitled, he requires an informed and skilled guide who knows the social welfare maze, knows the bureaucracy, and knows how to move it to get what the client needs and deserves. In our personal lives, we may be able to negotiate effectively with the organizations that directly affect us because we know how, the businessman is able to hire specialists to deal with the organizations on which he de-

[14]For other discussions of this concept, see Charles F. Grosser, "Community Development Programs Serving the Urban Poor," *Social Work*, X, No. 3 (1965), 15–21; and Paul Terrell, "The Social Worker as Radical: Roles of Advocacy," *New Perspectives: the Berkeley Journal of Social Welfare*, I, No. 1 (1957), 83–88.

pends for services and benefits, but many of the persons we seek to serve lack the knowledge, skills, or resources to negotiate effectively with the organizations on which the satisfaction of their needs may depend.

Currently, the broker function is being revived, but only to a limited extent. As an outgrowth of the war on poverty, new careerists are being trained to perform this function. But evidence already is accumulating to indicate that subprofessionals can perform this function effectively only with professional guidance and direction and that in some instances they cannot perform it very effectively at all, partly because some of the problems encountered require the application of considerable skill and knowledge.[15] Recognition of the importance of this function also is evident in the growing interest in the creation of neighborhood information and referral centers. Thus far, however, discussion of such centers has been focused more on organizational considerations than on the roles to be performed and the knowledge and skills required for their effective performance.

Another function that was highly visible early in the history of social casework subsequently not only declined in significance but came to be regarded by some as inconsistent with the proper conduct of casework practice. Some of the early leaders in casework saw one function of the caseworker as that of a person who actively fought on the side of his client to help him meet his needs, realize his hopes and aspirations, and exercise his rights. The caseworker was to be his client's supporter, his adviser, his champion, and, if need be, his representative in his dealings with the court, the police, the social agency, and the other organizations that affected his well-being. In other words, the caseworker was to serve not only as a therapist or as a social broker, but also as an active advocate of the client's cause in relation to the various social organizations.[16] Currently, we are being told by lawyers, who at last are becoming interested in social welfare problems in sufficient numbers to make a difference, that performance of the advocacy function by social workers is essential both for the client to get what he is entitled to receive and for the social welfare system to operate as it is supposed to, especially as it becomes more institutionalized. For instance, fair and equitable procedures in an organization will remain such only if its clients

---

[15]Sherman Barr, "The Indigenous Worker: What He Is Not, What He Can Be," Fourteenth Annual Program Meeting, Council on Social Work Education, 1966.

[16]For other discussion of the advocacy role, see Grosser, *op. cit.*; Terrell, *op. cit.*; Earl C. Brennan, "The Casework Relationship: Excerpts from a Heretic's Notebook," *New Perspectives; The Berkeley Journal of Social Welfare*, I, No. 1 (1957), 65–67; and Scott Briar, "The Social Worker's Responsibility for the Civil Rights of Clients," *ibid.*, pp. 89–92.

are able to insist that the procedures be honored and to call the organization to task when it becomes lax. But many of the persons whom caseworkers seek to serve, especially among the poor, will not exercise their rights, press their claims and needs, or appeal actions that adversely affect them unless someone performs the role of advocate, because many of these clients are too apathetic, feel too powerless, or are too uninformed to do so. Moreover, effective performance of the advocacy function would help to insure that agencies are attentive and responsive to the needs and desires of clients.

One example will illustrate the importance of the advocacy function. The California State Department of Social Welfare provides a fair hearing procedure to be used by a welfare recipient when he believes that the welfare agency has erred or has taken improper action in his case. There are over one million welfare recipients in California. During a one-year period, from 1965 to 1966, only 1,098 recipients, or less than one tenth of one percent of all recipients, used the fair hearing procedure. There is no doubt that the proportion of recipients who have legitimate grounds for requesting a hearing is substantially greater than one tenth of one percent. For one thing, this proportion is substantially below the rate of error in the agency's favor typically found in sample case record audits. What prevents more recipients from using this procedure? Based on some research I am currently completing, I would say one reason is that only a tiny fraction of recipients know about the fair hearing or how to apply for it, in spite of the fact that they are routinely given information about this procedure.[17]

A substantial proportion of recipients who obtain fair hearings win their appeals. And the recipient's chances of winning are doubled if he brings along someone to represent him. The recipient can select anyone he wants as his representative; rarely does he bring a lawyer, but the hearings are informal and a lawyer's skills and knowledge ordinarily are not necessary to represent the client. The client's caseworker frequently is required to be present, but he is expected to represent both the client and the agency, which prevents him from serving as his client's advocate. Bear in mind that the stakes for the client may be quite high, namely, the means to feed, house, and clothe his family. I suggest that the caseworker ought to be free to represent his *client's* cause in such situations. And the agency should want to have this function performed in order to discharge its commitment to the welfare of its clients.

[17]Scott Briar, "Welfare from Below: Recipients' Views of the Public Welfare System," *California Law Review*, LIV (1966), 370–85.

Finally, it should be emphasized that performance of the advocacy function to the point where the client has the experience of making his wishes felt and having them acted on can enhance, sometimes dramatically, his sense of confidence, competence, and mastery and reduce the feelings of apathy and impotence many of our clients experience in their dealings with the organizations that affect their lives.

It also is important to see both the social broker and the advocate functions in a somewhat broader context. In my view, these functions must become institutionalized if the social welfare system is to operate as it should, no matter how well planned or enlightened it is otherwise. It would be a naive and tragic mistake to view these as residual functions that need to be performed only because the social welfare system has not yet been perfected. On the contrary, the social welfare system cannot be perfected unless these functions are performed effectively. To argue otherwise is analogous to arguing that the fact that plaintiffs and defendants still need attorneys when they go to court is symptomatic of imperfections in the court system, that if the court system were perfected, lawyers would be unnecessary. The opposite is, of course, the case. That is, the court system as a system cannot operate properly unless the functions assumed by lawyers are performed.

I have discussed three functions that originally were conceived to be integral components of the caseworker's mission: the therapeutic function, the social broker function, and the advocacy function. Subsequently, casework became preoccupied with the therapeutic function at the expense of the others. The therapeutic function flourished and underwent sophisticated theoretical development to the point where it seemed to some that this was the *only* function of casework. Recently, research has raised grave questions about the effectiveness with which caseworkers perform their therapeutic function. I have argued that our response to these questions should be vigorous innovation and systematic experimentation. I have also argued that we need to expand our conception of the casework mission to include other functions, not simply because they are part of our historic heritage but because the needs of our clients and the conditions of their lives require that we assume these responsibilities. Moreover, we should devote to these other functions the same measure of thought and skill we have long devoted to the therapeutic function, for the tasks these other functions impose on us are no less difficult or demanding than those we encounter in our therapeutic work.

I do not mean to imply that these three functions are the only ones I have in mind in calling for an expanded conception of social casework. I discussed the social broker and advocate functions as crucial examples to make the case for an expanded conception of casework. But there are other functions that caseworkers need to perform. For example, there is the vital and indispensable role that social caseworkers should be playing, as practitioners, in social policy-making. Caseworkers have virtually unique access to information indispensable to the development of sound social welfare policies and programs.

Moreover—and I cannot emphasize this point too strongly—I have in mind no fixed list of casework functions, because the central point is that these functions arise in response to the needs of the persons we seek to serve, the conditions of their lives, and our understanding of these needs and conditions. Consequently, as these needs and conditions and our knowledge of them change, our responses to them should be modified accordingly. It also follows from that, of course, that not all these functions are needed by every individual or family nor will any one caseworker necessarily perform all of them.

An expanded conception of social casework has many implications that deserve more detailed discussion than is possible here. However, two general implications are of crucial importance. First, vigorous innovation and experimentation in treatment methods and participation in the activities required in performing the advocate and social broker functions require that caseworkers have much greater professional autonomy and discretion than now prevail in many, if not most, social agencies. Ninety percent or more of all caseworkers practice in bureaucratic organizations, and the demands of such organizations have a tendency to encroach upon professional autonomy. Every attempt by the agency to routinize some condition or aspect of professional practice amounts to a restriction of professional discretion, and for that reason probably should be resisted, in most instances, by practitioners. But it will not be enough to resist bureaucratic restriction. We will need to roll back the restrictions that already constrain practice in order to gain the freedom essential to experiment, to discover new and better ways of helping the clients to whom we are primarily responsible. There are, of course, realistic limits to the amount of autonomy and discretion an organization can grant to the practitioner, but no one knows just where that limit is, and we cannot know until we have tried to reach it. It may be that when this limit is reached we will find it still too confining to engage in the kind of practice required to help some of our clients.

The second general implication is that the remedies I have proposed require a much closer relationship between practice and research than we have achieved thus far, because research is an indispensable tool in our efforts to improve the efficacy of casework. The relationships between the practitioner and the researcher continue to be problematic. There are good reasons to believe that in the long run the best solution to these problems may be to develop both sets of skills in the same person.

A brief quotation from Alfred Kahn concisely expresses a basic assumption underlying everything I have said:

Crucial to social work is an integrative view of needs. . . . The real commitment, and the unique nature of the entire social work institution . . . is not to any one method or even one concept but rather to human need. The role is dynamic—and never completed. The danger is the loss of that flexibility essential to the recognition of new horizons and the undertaking of consequent responsibilities.[18]

If we take seriously the view that the central commitment is to human need and if we keep our attention focused squarely on the needs of persons and the responsibilities these needs impose on the profession at all levels of systemic intervention, I believe the result must be an expanded and dynamic conception of the scope and multiple functions of the endeavor we call social casework.

[18]Alfred J. Kahn, "The Function of Social Work in the Modern World," in Alfred J. Kahn, ed., *Issues in American Social Work* (New York: Columbia University Press, 1959), p. 16.

Crisis-Oriented Short-Term Casework

Lydia Rapoport

There is a good deal of current interest in the use of brief case-work treatment—from both a pragmatic and a theoretical point of view. On the pragmatic side we have been pushed by considerations of expediency to be more innovative about ways and means of serving larger numbers of people more quickly and more effectively. On the theoretical side, we are pressed to re-examine our basic assumptions, conceptual models, and operating principles which have guided traditional practice, in order that we may produce conceptual tools that will be more responsive to changing social needs and commitments. Our professional history suggests that often practice in fact precedes theory-building. The pragmatic or useful leads us on, while the theoretical ra-

Reprinted from *The Social Service Review*, Vol. 41, No. 1 (March 1967), pp. 31–43, by permission of the author and The University of Chicago Press.

tionale is formulated later. Ideally, practice and theory should be partners. In reality there are time lags: What we do and what we say we do are often at variance. We are suffering from just this kind of time lag in regard to brief casework treatment. Much is being done that is experimental and innovative, but little of it is reflected in our practice theory in any systematic way. This paper is an attempt to highlight the relevant issues and to point to those areas in which traditional theory fails us.

Brief casework treatment is certainly not a new interest or a new area of practice. It has been inherent in the very nature of casework theory, which has embedded in it a concept of focus implying some sense of limit.[1] An examination of the literature of the past thirty years shows periodic reference to brief treatment. Increasing systematic attention has been paid to the fate of many cases after intake. We became more concerned with our own "dropouts." It is a well-known fact that a large proportion of clients discontinue service during the intake process or after having had just one or two interviews. These clients were often labeled as being unmotivated or uncooperative or resistant to service, but follow-up studies showed that these individuals or families believed that they had gotten something out of the experience. They even claimed improvement in their situations or attitudes. Social workers tended to be dubious about this finding, whether it was based on self-assessment or on more objective evidence. It may in fact be true that clients got something that was valuable to them. The most important point is that these findings took us by surprise: Brief intervention was not part of our plan and, therefore, not part of purposeful professional activity.

Theoretical Fallacies and Myths

Despite the persuasive needs for brief intervention, other counter-pressures stand in the way. For example, one frequently has to make a case for brief casework treatment. There seems to be a good deal of resistance, which may be based on the perpetuation of theoretical assumptions which are more in the nature of myths that have stood in our way and have prevented fresh and creative thinking about brief treatment.

[1]For example a social psychiatrist constantly used the term "focused casework." I pointed out to him that this term is a redundancy, that, since there is no such thing as unfocused casework, the term does not need to be qualified. Perhaps, by contrast, in regard to the nature of psychotherapy, one needs to qualify the process by specifying the concept of focus.

Depth and Length of Treatment

There seems to be a hierarchy of values regarding the psycho-therapies, especially in relation to the dimensions of depth and length. "Depth" most often refers to the stratum of personality to be tapped, namely, either the "system unconscious" or the in-stinctual forces in the personality. Only psychoanalytic treatment methods yield direct access to this stratum.[2] Hence psychoanal-ysis, placed at the top of the hierarchy, has been madé the pre-ferred model for therapeutic intervention. One still hears rec-ommendations for many clients and patients that the treatment of choice is long-term treatment or psychoanalysis, *if* it were avail-able, and *if* the patient were motivated, etc. Having to counter-pose so many conditional factors suggests that there is a fallacy in this thinking. The alternative to "depth" one often hears is the term "superficial." However, a more fruitful and less value-laden concept might be "complexity." Thus, refined attention to mat-ters of ego-organization and emotional and social functioning requires understanding and dealing with complex organization in the personality which is unrelated to questions of depth or superficiality.

The Nature of Treatment

There is the myth regarding the lasting nature of treatment. Discussions about briefer forms of treatment always elicit ques-tions concerning whether any changes brought about are lasting. This question reveals another erroneous assumption, namely, that if change is going to be lasting it can be achieved only by a long process. There is another, more important fallacious as-sumption embedded in the question of the lasting nature of change. It presupposes a static life-model: that life-circumstances and experience are predictable and stable, and that, once con-flicts have been resolved, no major problems in adaptation will arise. Examined in this light, such an assumption is absurd. We do know that life-circumstances, whether in part predictable or whether entirely unpredictable, carry with them a potential for healthy growth and change, as well as a potential for stress and maladaptation. Furthermore, successful adaptation requires more than successful conflict-resolution. It also requires a potential for adaptive and coping mechanisms which are stimulated and shaped by both outer circumstances and inner resources.

[2] Anna Freud begins her classic book, *The Ego and the Mechanisms of Defense*, with the following: "Many analysts had conceived the idea that, in analysis, the value of scientific and therapeutic work done was in direct proportion to the depth of the psychic strata upon which attention was focused" (New York: International Universities Press, 1946, p. 3).

Another related myth concerns the nature of change as "cure." The concept of cure, borrowed from medical practice, is different from the concept of restoration of functioning. The concept of cure evokes the surgical model of medicine.[3] In surgery one can remove or excise something and, in many instances, effect a cure or restoration of health. This rather static concept in fact does not fit many conditions of physical disease. For example, in states of acute infectious disease we find an acute flareup in an organism previously in a state of health or in some state of relative equilibrium, followed by a diminution of acute infectious symptoms and a return to the previous state of functioning. This model of acute infectious disease is more akin to the life-model with its fluctuations of stress and adaptation.[4] It is also more congenial to the purposes of social work.

Cause

The concept of cure is linked inextricably with another important concept—that of cause. Here the myth is that in order to bring about a cure one must at least know and get at the causative factors. The relationship of cause and cure also comes from medicine, with its doctrine of specific etiology, which came into vogue with the development of the germ theory of disease, which has been most effective in the control and cure of infectious diseases. It should be noted that, before the germ theory of disease came into being, disease was considered to be "due to a lack of harmony between the patient and his environment."[5] Despite the quaintness of the language, this formulation has a very modern ring. It is not uncongenial to social work thinking.

The concept of specific etiology is also limiting in another way. It tends to lead to a reductionist type of thinking by encouraging a search for a single cause. The fact is that in the area of social problems, be they matters of mental illness or delinquency, we are always involved in trying to understand and deal with a complex system wherein causation must be viewed as multiple. Such a point of view has a good many positive implications for intervention. In medicine it suggests, for example, that disease processes in the absence of a specific single known cause can still be con-

[3] From personal communication with the late Dr. Mary Sarvis.

[4] David M. Kaplan, "A Concept of Acute Situational Disorders," *Social Work*, VII (April 1962), 15-23; Bernard Bandler, M.D., "The Concept of Ego-supportive Psychotherapy," in *Ego-oriented Casework: Problems and Perspectives*, ed. H. J. Parad and R. R. Miller (New York: Family Service Association of America, 1963).

[5] Rene Dubos, *The Mirage of Health* (New York: Harper & Bros., 1959).

trolled through intervention at various points in the natural history of the process by several seemingly unrelated procedures. This model of intervention is basic to public health activities, with their focus on prevention and control. In social work practice, on the community as well as the individual level, a good deal might be achieved in intervention and control without knowing precisely all the causative factors at the base of the problem.

Structure and Tradition

There are other kinds of myths which are less rooted in certain methodological conceptions but are more the outgrowth of usage and tradition. These are matters of structure and style of working. Practice is also operationalized from these through the delineation of organizational principles that guide procedures. Such principles have often become confused with principles growing out of the attempt to operationalize method theory. Furthermore, they have sometimes become invested with a theoretical authority which is inappropriate and stultifying. For example, we have developed over the years a complex rationale for making a formal study which we call "intake"—the beginning and the more formal aspect of the diagnostic procedure. We have used information-gathering to make a differential diagnosis that should guide us in developing a differential treatment approach. How much of this work is necessary and useful, and how it is to be achieved will be discussed later. At this time, mention will be made only of some of the many problems this procedure has created. We know that in order to carry out a complicated intake procedure we have to involve the client in a waiting period at various points in the helping process. We have rationalized the waiting period (which makes us all uncomfortable) by saying that it can be used to test out the client's motivation and, furthermore, to evaluate how he manages his anxiety. However, we have failed to realize that by the time a client is seen for diagnosis, after a waiting period, or for treatment after an even longer wait, he is no longer the same person as when he first applied for help. We have failed to note that his symptomatology may have shifted and that something has probably happened to his defensive system, namely, that he is more guarded and better defended against his initial anxiety, and, most important of all, that something may have happened to his accessibility which may make it more difficult to work with him effectively and economically.

There is another more subtle problem in how a protracted diagnostic procedure and the waiting list, by fostering, in essence, a regressive type of transference, operate negatively and militate against the achievement of our goal to help people attain maximum independent functioning. The fact is that a prolonged period of diagnostic study puts the client in an essentially passive position. Furthermore, an implicit promise and message system is being enacted: The client promises to give a good deal of information in exchange for the "promise"—actually an implicit assumption—that he will be taken care of. We reinforce this by telling him that we will let him know later our recommendations and treatment plan. The waiting period tends to reinforce his passivity and dependency expectation: In exchange for willingness to wait we offer long-term treatment.[6] It has also been suggested that the waiting list actually serves to screen in a certain type of more hostile, dependent, masochistic, or overintellectual client who is quite agreeable to making this kind of silent bargain.

Another example of how structure has become confused with aspects of method theory is the use of the interdisciplinary team, particularly in child guidance work. Many people are now questioning its efficacy, from many points of view. There was a time when the rationale for having members of a team work with the same client or family was based on the sharper difference in training and the greater lack of knowledge in our respective professions. This situation has changed. Today's mental health professional workers have better grounding in dynamic psychology and psychopathology, and all are increasingly more socially oriented. We are becoming aware that much of interdisciplinary work is costly and wasteful. There is a need, of course, for medical responsibility in certain kinds of settings. Also, interdisciplinary teamwork is justified and necessary when there is clear delineation of function based on specialization. The negative feature of non-functional teamwork for the client is the lack of continuity of contact with one person, the diffusion of affect that comes with the need to repeat one's history to a variety of people, and the delay in beginning an active process of problem-solving.

The above two examples attempt to show that certain intake procedures and the use of the clinical team are not fundamental to the theory of casework methods, but are structural arrangements which have been operationalized and then rationalized as being principles of casework method.[7]

[6] I remember with embarrassment now my work years ago as intake supervisor in a clinic, when I told people that since their problem took a long time to develop it would take an equally long time to unravel. It sounded reasonable and made sense, but because of my basic orientation at the time I did not realize that I was reinforcing the client's self-image of being "sick," which then generated a certain set of expectations.

[7] It might be added that we have trouble in other contexts in distinguishing concepts and principles that are part of an integrated practice theory: ideas are offered as practice principles that are no more than an expression of personal style of a gifted practitioner.

Essentials of "Crisis Theory"

Although interest in brief treatment is not altogether new, current thinking has been set into a new context, that is, within the framework of crisis theory. Many of the phenomena observed in the past when people responded positively to brief intervention can now be understood through an explanatory system which was previously not available to us. This explanatory system is referred to by some as "crisis theory," as developed largely by its major theoreticians, Dr. Erich Lindemann and Dr. Gerald Caplan. Some of the salient theoretical points about the nature of crisis will be reviewed briefly to serve as an underpinning for our understanding of brief treatment.[8]

We believe that the concept of crisis is useful in casework, particularly in short-term work and in focusing intervention. The term "crisis" has been used loosely and interchangeably with other concepts; it has been confused with notions of stress, problem, or need. The term "stress" is often used to describe both precipitating event and the consequent subjective state of feeling with which the individual responds. As precipitant, stress generally is used to imply a negative or pathogenic state; it is considered to be some kind of burden or load which presses down on the individual and creates a negative effect on his functioning.[9] In contrast, the term "crisis" refers to the state of the reacting individual. The state is one of upset. There are certain characteristic signs of this state of upset: there are emotional signs, such as tension, anxiety, shame, guilt, or hostility. There may also be evidence of some cognitive confusion, and even perceptual confusion if the state of crisis is severe. The state of crisis in which the individual finds himself is the result of stress. A stressful event develops into a state of crisis only if a person lacks the capacity to cope with or master the event. It is assumed that the crisis requires a novel solution and that the individual or family does not have available such solutions within the normal range of problem-solving

The field of family therapy might be cited as an example in which a good deal of confusion reigns and much sifting needs to be done to separate theory from personal style.

[8] For a fuller treatment of this material see Lydia Rapoport, "The State of Crisis: Some Theoretical Considerations," *Social Service Review*, XXXVI (June, 1962), 211–17; also in *Crisis Intervention: Selected Readings*, ed. Howard J. Parad (New York: Family Service Association of America, 1965), p. 22.

[9] Eli M. Bower states in regard to stress: "Of all the metaphors the human behavioral sciences have borrowed from their sister sciences and from literature, none has been more in the need of habitation and name than the concept of stress. Yet in the past its metaphorical habitation has mostly been in the house of hardship, retardation, insult, and affliction, and its name has been synonymous with noxiousness. . . . Stress as the grand metaphor of life and living has found little if any place in a philosophy or psychology of normal development and health." He regards the process of living as stressful; he uses stress to mean responding to stimuli. ("The Modification, Mediation, and Utilization of Stress during the School Years," *American Journal of Orthopsychiatry*, XXXIV [July, 1964], 667–68.)

mechanisms.[10] John and Elaine Cummings add an interesting distinction between "problem" and "crisis." In their view, a person confronted with a problem is also faced with elements of novelty. However, he can solve this through the use of new combinations of coping mechanisms available to him in his ego sets. In contrast, a crisis requires the learning of new ego sets or roles and their integration into the ego. The Cummingses explain further that an ego-damaged person will experience even simple problems as crises.[11]

Another useful notion is that a crisis is not an illness, nor is it to be equated with psychopathology. It may be superimposed on psychopathology. The difficult task in intervention, then, is to sort out and to deal separately with a crisis and its effects from the chronic or underlying psychopathology. This formulation of crisis does not prejudge the outcome. Furthermore, in contrast to the concept of stress, with its pathogenic potential, the state of crisis is seen as having a growth-promoting potential, provided that certain favorable factors are operating. In other words, the outcome to a crisis may be in the direction of greater strength and mental health rather than in deterioration or pathology.

It might be well to review the kinds of crises and how they may be classified. First, there are the developmental crises which are bio-psycho-social in nature and which have been well identified by Erikson.[12] These, of course, refer to the maturational stages and developmental tasks that are linked with them. We see these most clearly because they are fundamentally biological in nature. Of course the transitions in maturational stage also require social adaptation and some kind of role transition. Second, there are crises of role transition that are not related to the developmental phase as such. While pregnancy and the assumption of the role of motherhood has its biological underpinnings, there also is a requirement of social adaptation. In contrast, a crisis due to the requirements of role transition from active worker to retired individual is not so much biologically based as socially determined. It is the society that defines when the person is old or can be put "on the shelf." Another example of a crisis that may be induced through role transition not linked to age or developmental phase is the promotion of a line worker to a supervisor or administrator, which involves increasing responsibility and authority and may

[10] Howard J. Parad and Gerald Caplan, "A Framework for Studying Families in Crisis," Social Work, V (July, 1960), 3–15; also Parad, Crisis Intervention, p. 53.

[11] Ego and Milieu (New York: Atherton Press, 1963), p. 55.

[12] Erik Erikson, "Growth and Crisis of the 'Healthy Personality,' " in Personality in Nature, Society, and Culture, ed. Clyde Kluckhohn, Henry A. Murray, and David M. Schneider (2d ed., rev. and enl.; New York: Alfred A. Knopf, 1953), chap. iii.

bring with it feelings of tension, anxiety, and the possibility of crisis. Third, there are the accidental crises, often called "hazardous events," that occur in the life of any individual or family. These are adventitious or chance matters such as the loss of a job, the death of a loved one, the premature birth of an infant, and so on.

It should be emphasized further that a crisis presents a problem in the current life-situation. Nevertheless, the current problem may be linked with old conflicts which may or may not have been satisfactorily resolved in the past but which in any case are to some extent reactivated by the current stress. This reactivation of old conflicts is likely to arise because the stresses leading to a crisis very often serve as a threat to the gratification of instinctual needs. From this point of view a crisis may be conceptualized as representing (1) a threat, either to instinctual needs or to the sense of integrity; (2) a loss involving either a person or a feeling of acute deprivation; or (3) a challenge. Each of these three states has a typical or characteristic accompanying affect. For example, if the crisis situation is experienced primarily as a threat, it will be accompanied by a great deal of anxiety. If the crisis situation is experienced primarily in terms of loss, it will be accompanied by depression and mourning. If it is viewed as a challenge it may be accompanied by some anxiety, but with it there will be some mixture of hope and a release of greater energy or drive for problem-solving.

It has also been noted that the state of upset is limited in time. This is a very important notion. The acute phase of a crisis does not go on indefinitely, because somehow the individual or family pushes toward re-establishing itself and achieving some kind of new equilibrium. However, the new equilibrium established may be healthy or pathological. The natural history of the crisis, with its built-in time limits, suggests that one has to intervene during this period if one is going to influence outcome in a brief or economical manner.

There is another important notion in regard to outcome or the resolution of the crisis which may be difficult for the conventionally trained clinician to accept. We are told by researchers that the outcome of the crisis is less dependent on the person's personality structure or the specifics of his psychopathology than on the current state of his ego strengths.[13] This is not new to social workers, who are always making appraisals of ego strengths. An additional important dimension is the symbolic significance of the crisis to the individual and its link with past conflicts: What

[13]Kaplan, "A Concept of Acute Situational Disorders," op. cit.

does the current crisis trigger off which was not well resolved in the past? Another factor on which prognosis depends is the nature of the current socio-cultural milieu: What supports can the environment offer, such as strengths in the family, basic institutions, and other environmental opportunities?

Implications for Treatment

Thus far no attempt has been made to specify the time involved in "brief" treatment. Practice varies considerably. One empirical study currently in progress may at least describe common practice in agencies as to actual duration of time and whether time is set in advance. The time element alone does not characterize and distinguish brief treatment from other treatment modalities. In order to understand the nature of brief treatment various other parameters also need to be examined. A central requirement is the need for genuine acceptance of the concept of limited goals. Although most of the principles and techniques in our present treatment methodology are relevant and useful, we do need a reordering of what we have, as well as a decided shift in emphasis.

Certain basic principles requisite to goal-focused and time-limited treatment may be delineated as follows:[14] First, in order to help people who are in a state of crisis, we need to have rapid access to them—and, conversely, they need to have easy access to us. A previous statement of mine, now often quoted, is also relevant here: "The person or family in crisis becomes more susceptible to the influence of 'significant others' in the environment. Moreover, the degree of activity of the helping person does not have to be high. A little help, rationally directed and purposefully focused at a strategic time, is more effective than more extensive help given at a period of less emotional accessibility."[15] This suggests that one should make use of anxiety when it is at its height. A corollary to this principle is that there needs to be continuity of contact, and a use of time structured as to its limits and, within such limits, flexibly arranged.

Second, treatment should be highly focused and segmental. This too is not a new idea. The focus is on the present, and the segment to be dealt with is the precipitating stress and its consequences for the individual or family. There have been interesting

[14]Helen Harris Perlman has written on this subject: "Problem-solving must include . . . conscious, focused, goal-directed activity between client and caseworker. . . . The work of problem-solving in the caseworker's mind must, if it is to be effective, be a systematically organized process" (*Social Casework: A Problem-solving Process* [Chicago: University of Chicago Press, 1957], p. 87).

[15]Rapoport, "The State of Crisis," *op. cit.*, p. 217.

studies showing that the detailed exploration and understanding of the precipitating stress and its specific meaning is often, in itself, of such great therapeutic value that no further help may be needed.[16] When possible and necessary, there should be a clarification of the linkage of the current stress and upset with a previous, old, preconscious, or unconscious conflict that was not entirely successfully resolved. The kind of material necessary to make this linkage often comes out surprisingly readily when the person is in a state of crisis. At such a time the usual defenses are weakened, and the person is less guarded against the revelation of such pertinent information, which ordinarily is repressed or suppressed.

Third, communication should be addressed to certain aspects of the ego, such as the defensive system which needs to be strengthened; the cognitive system, which needs help with intellectual mastery through explanation and clarification; the affective system, in order to lower tension, anxiety, or guilt; and the adaptive and coping parts of the ego, which need strengthening and enlargement. Although the worker addresses himself to the ego, his attention is heavily focused on the communication of the client's preconscious and its patterning, for this is the source from which it is possible to draw some rapid assessment of the special meaning of the recent stress and the reason for the current state of crisis.

There are certain techniques within our technical repertoire which are especially pertinent in brief-treatment work with people in a state of crisis. In general, the approach needs to be more active and directive than in traditional work. Implied is the greater use of authority. Advice-giving, which for a long time acquired a kind of taboo for historical as well as theoretical reasons, is being re-examined for its utility. Advice-giving can be used in a very potent way, especially if its dynamic meaning can be anticipated by taking into account the client's unconscious needs and impulses. Another use of authority is expressed in what might be called psychological manipulation, or what I sometimes call the controlled use of magic. This is not as diabolical as it may sound. For example: A Mexican woman came to see a worker who fortunately had lived in Mexico for several years and understood some important cultural factors. The client was in an acute psychotic state, with florid paranoid ideation and feelings. Afraid that she was being poisoned, she refused to eat. As an immediate first-aid approach, the worker told her authoritatively to go home

---

[16]B. L. Kalis et al., "Precipitating Stress as a Focus in Psychotherapy," *Archives of General Psychiatry*, V (September, 1961), 219–26.

and cook for herself and told her exactly what ingredients to put into this Mexican dish. In essence she was putting her weight and protection behind this, but she was also saying that the client could exercise some controls over her own fate and that the worker would stand behind her. As an additional source of support, the worker gave the client an amulet (given her by another Mexican client), which was supposed to have magical properties to keep her from harm. The real magic was the worker's understanding and willingness to use her authority as protective ego. The woman went home, pulled herself together, cooked and ate a meal, and stabilized herself until some reasonable psychiatric care could be arranged for her.

The management of time is an important consideration. Here, as in other aspects of this work, we can learn a good deal from the functional approach. Time needs to be used to provide structure and limits, which are reassuring to an ego that is decompensating. Time limits also operate as leverage and as pressure to get on with the problem-solving task.[17] They also serve as relief to the client against anxiety about getting involved in a dependency situation and serve as counterforce against the client's self-concept of being emotionally "sick." Time limits can also be used, along with other techniques, to prevent tendencies toward development of a regressive transference.

Another goal is the enlargement of the client's sense of autonomy and mastery as fast and as far as possible. In this goal, too, time can be an important variable. The client should be able to set the frequency and length of time—within agreed-upon limits—like a self-demand schedule. We must have enough faith and be sufficiently free from anxiety ourselves to accept the client's time schedule. There is, after all, no magic in weekly appointments; these may fit our patterns of working, but not the client's immediate needs. The client may need three appointments in a row, or one each day for a week. The point is that time is a useful instrument in helping with the management and control of various feelings.

Another emphasis in brief-treatment work is the greater engagement of the perceptual and cognitive functions of the ego by describing, defining, and reordering recent experiences. Such work helps to lower anxiety, reduce confusion, and enhance cognitive mastery as first steps in problem-solving. In addition to the restoration of previously useful and adequate defenses, atten-

[17]Multiple-impact therapy is one experiment with a different use of time and intensity. See, for example, Agnes Ritchie, "Multiple Impact Therapy: An Experiment," *Social Work*, V (July, 1960), 16–21; and Harold Goolishian, "A Brief Psychotherapy Program for Disturbed Adolescents," *American Journal of Orthopsychiatry*, XXXII (January, 1962), 142–48.

tion is given to finding new adaptive patterns as ways of handling conflict or finding solutions. The enhancement of coping patterns is achieved by a process that has a decided educational component, such as anticipatory guidance, rehearsal for future reality, learning new social and interpersonal skills, and enlarging the capacity for anticipatory thinking and prediction. In some instances, the educational process may be less verbal and more based on identification. Here, the worker consciously offers himself actively as a model for identification and encourages the rehearsal of behavior and attitudes in regard to new roles.

The ending process, which is anticipated if not actually predetermined, also should be given more conscious attention. Termination takes place when a previously defined goal has been reached or when the client begins to find solutions. We do not expect him to work through all his problems. We do have a concept of an "open door," which enables the client to return for further work when he needs it. Acceptance of the life-model of problem-solving and a door that is really open should make it easier for the client to return without a sense of shame or failure. It should also be of help to the worker. At present, many workers feel a sense of guilt and failure if a client returns for more help. We tend to view his return negatively; we expect that a problem solved should stay solved for all time. His return could be viewed positively. Experience has shown that clients who return after a brief period of help need even briefer help in the second round. They may return because of similar stress, yet the crisis is often less intense. They may use the second experience to consolidate their gains. Sometimes the need for help the second time may be entirely unrelated to the first situation. It is then dealt with in accordance with current need.

We also need to consider for whom brief casework is the treatment of choice. From one point of view all people can benefit from brief and focused intervention, particularly in times of stress. At such times, brief treatment offers what Dr. Mary Sarvis called simply "the useful next step."[18] Perhaps it is begging the question to suggest that brief treatment is useful for everyone. We should distrust any approach that is offered as an undifferentiated panacea. More important, failure to identify the specificity of a concept or the differential application of an approach causes either to lose its essential utility.

We know that brief, goal-focused intervention is useful for the person with an essentially good ego who is under considerable

[18]Mary A. Sarvis, M.D., et al., "A Concept of Ego-Oriented Psychotherapy," *Psychiatry: Journal for Study of Interpersonal Processes*, XXII (August, 1959), 277–87.

external stress. It has also been surprisingly effective with the person of borderline character who may be on the verge of a psychotic episode with a breakthrough of primitive impulses. Here, active intervention can often quickly restore crumbling defenses and return the individual to a previous level of functioning. Here we have two examples of people, at widely separated ends of the mental health continuum, who can make good use of brief treatment.[19] For each, the essential goal is restoration of prior adequate functioning, within the limits of present capacity. If the goal is enhancement of functioning by elevation of maturational level or by resolution of some types of internal conflict, then a longer period of treatment is necessary in order to dislodge infantile fixations or other maladaptive, habitual modes of response. What is worthy of further research, however, is the observation that, at certain times, in certain situations (all of which need to be defined), brief treatment has the potency to do more than restore functioning. It can actually produce profound changes in the personality by facilitating some rapid reorganization of psychic structure and energy. It is my speculation at present that this is more likely to happen at times of maturational crises, such as at adolescence, when the personality is in a greater state of flux.

Another way to approach this question is to ask: When is a crisis not a crisis? This question is posed in order to reserve the concept of crisis for those specific situations for which it was designed. For example, there are people in a chronic state of crisis, for whom it is a life-style. Indeed, for many of these people the crises are self-generated rather than accidental and serve the purpose of warding off deep unconscious anxiety and depression. These people generally suffer from character disorders. They are not the ones we can help with brief crisis-oriented intervention, as we have defined it. We may be able to offer some kind of first aid at such time, but we know that these people may return at each crisis point but will probably not be available for any sustained work. Another example which illustrates the need to define the state of crisis more narrowly is the situation of those unmarried mothers in which we can conjecture that the pregnancy was an expression of emotional conflict. In such an instance, the pregnancy is not the crisis for the girl (although it may be for the family or community). In fact, we often note that during the period of the pregnancy the girl is calm, bland, anxiety-free, and sometimes even contented. The crisis probably existed before conception

[19]Many of the contributors to *Short-Term Psychotherapy*, edited by Lewis R. Wolberg, M.D. (New York: Grune & Stratton, 1965), take decidedly opposite views on the question of the treatment of choice in regard to the degree of psychopathology. The issue therefore needs to remain open for further systematic exploration.

and may have led to the pregnancy. However, that was not the time that social workers were around to intervene. Another crisis may be generated at the time the girl is confronted with the need to make a decision to relinquish or keep her baby. Here, if the crisis is well handled, we may have a chance to solve a present problem and even resolve a latent conflict.

Implications for Traditional
Casework Theory

Although it was stated earlier that the work of brief treatment with people in crisis can be guided by concepts and principles that are available to us within traditional casewo.k theory, nevertheless this approach does raise some serious challenges in regard to present casework history. A few of these issues will now be discussed.

Diagnosis

In considering the issue of diagnosis, we are on treacherous ground. The usual diagnosis is based on psychosocial description or psychiatric nosology. Neither is too useful in brief work with people in states of crisis. It is very difficult to evaluate the previous or usual state of the personality of the client when he is at a point of high upset. We need a way of diagnosing acute situational stress and a way of classifying hazardous events and people's responses to them. This is an unexplored area. We also need a way of rapidly appraising the state of ego-functioning. It is hard to relinquish the idea of formulating a diagnosis that is genetically based if one is schooled in a developmental psychology. We are taught to formulate explanations of causal phenomena by way of reference to origins. "Why" is answered by "how he got that way." This is an incomplete formulation. According to one psychiatrist, "genetic accounts can be enlightening but all too frequently they 'explain away' without really explaining."[20]

What can be the sources of information and data for diagnosis in brief treatment? Since time is of the essence, we do not have the leisure for history-taking, with its vertical and horizontal exploration of life-experiences and with later verification of hypotheses. We need to rely much more heavily on marginal clues in the presenting behavior, the quality of interaction with the helping person, and on aspects of preconscious communication. In addition, an important source of information, which also serves

[20]John A. MacLoed, M.D., "Some Criteria for the Modification of Treatment Arrangements," in Parad, *Ego Oriented Casework*, pp. 165–76.

as conceptual framework, is knowledge regarding typical crisis behavior and necessary problem-solving tasks. Such knowledge is being more systematically formulated. It provides a kind of map that serves as guide to rapid formulation and strategic intervention.

Relationship

Another issue is the centrality of the concept of relationship in casework treatment. We are accustomed to thinking that the positive relationship is the chief tool, if not the dynamic force, in treatment. There is a temporal component suggesting that it takes time to develop a "meaningful relationship" and that one cannot treat without it. Relationship is a rather fuzzy concept, since we cannot state with clarity what aspect of relationship, what kind, what symbolic value, what degree of intensity, and so on. I should like to raise the question of whether one can treat without the so-called relationship, or, more accurately, whether there are components of "relationship" that can be maximized for use. For example, the worker's authority of competence and expertness may be used more powerfully to capitalize on the client's readiness to trust and to submit out of a feeling of confusion, helplessness, and anxiety. Such an approach may serve even a deeply suspicious client who, in a crisis, longs for protection. It is suggested that one can take advantage of the regressive impulse without permitting a regressive transference to develop. Avoidance of regression is important in order to discourage dependency and to protect and enhance self-esteem. Perhaps the component of attachment in relationship is less crucial than the degree of involvement, however brief.[21] Attachment is less necessary, since treatment does not depend on a "corrective emotional experience" (which was of essence in Alexander's concept of brief treatment) or on the "working-through" process.[22] It depends instead more on cognitive restructuring and unlinking the present context from past concerns.

Other Questions

Several other concepts come into question. The role of motivation and our rigid thinking about it has led into therapeutic

[21]In a recent study of brief treatment, Malan quotes an astute observation of Dr. Michael Balint—that the therapist's enthusiasm has a direct bearing on the process and outcome of therapy, since it brings with it a corresponding heightened excitement in the patient, with the result that repressed feelings come easily to the surface and are experienced with an intensity and completeness so that the further "working through" process may not be necessary (D. H. Malan, M.D., *A Study of Brief Psychotherapy* [London: Tavistock Publications, 1963]).

[22]Franz Alexander, M.D., "Psychoanalytic Contributions to Short-Term Psychotherapy," in Wolberg, *op. cit.*

binds.[23] Perhaps not many people are motivated to change their ways of behaving and feeling, but all people in distress are motivated to get relief from suffering. This is our starting point with people in crisis.

A related question refers to the dynamic force that brings about change. In psychoanalysis it may be energy released by the working-through of the infantile neurosis brought to the fore by a regressive transference which this method of treatment explicitly induces. Self-understanding or insight is also an explicit goal in psychoanalysis. In keeping with our notions of the hierarchical value of the psychotherapies, we have tended to overvalue the power of insight. Sometimes insight is no more than hindsight. In brief treatment we might say the goal is "foresight"—the enhancement of anticipatory awareness to be used in problem-solving. We capitalize on the dynamic force for change made possible by the disequilibrium of the crisis that produces a fluid ego state. The goal of brief treatment is action and the furtherance of rapid behavioral change with positive reinforcement.[24] This involves more complex processes than those formulated by the behaviorist or neo-behaviorist school and should be based on understanding of psychodynamics.

Another concept that needs re-examination is self-determination. This may well run into conflict with points made earlier about greater use of worker authority and more directive action, including suggestion, advice, and even psychological manipulation. At the same time the need for maximizing autonomous action was stressed. Both things pertain. At a point of high anxiety and confusion there is need for protective action. Autonomous action can begin with reduction of cognitive and affective confusion when there is clarity regarding choices and the consequences of alternative courses of action.

This paper has attempted to place short-term casework into the framework of crisis theory and to delineate some pertinent central concepts. It has made note of impediments to its further development based on adherence to other conceptual models. Many aspects of traditional casework theory are relevant to brief approaches; other concepts need re-examining for their relevance or utility in this newer treatment modality.

[23]Genevieve Oxley, "The Caseworker's Expectations and Client Motivation," *Social Casework*, XLVII (July, 1966), 432–37.

[24]For a masterful elucidation of the role of action see Allen Wheelis, M.D., "The Place of Action in Personality Change," *Psychiatry*, XIII (May, 1950), 135–48.

A Discussion: What Is
Family-Centered Casework?

Patricia Sax

It seems justifiable at first glance to use the term *family-centered casework* as a generic term, because it appears to be used to designate the same behavior that is suggested by the multiplicity of variant terms that appear in the literature—family treatment, family therapy, family social work, family-group counseling, family-group treatment, integrative therapy of the family unit, family counseling, multiple-client interviewing, and so on and on. In other words these terms appear not to be used differentially. But differentiation of some sort is clearly necessary when one considers, for example, the two extremely disparate interpretations of the single term *family-centered casework* that have appeared in the literature. The first interpretation places emphasis on direct or indirect treatment of the individual members of a family. The second emphasizes that the family is the unit for diagnosis and treatment. All other interpretations seem to fall somewhere between.

Though the manifest behavior of workers embracing one or the other of these two points of view could be expected to be similar, their nonmanifest behavior surely would not be. And it is this nonmanifest behavior, specifically the result of perceptive and cognitive functioning, that results in a diagnosis and the establishment of treatment goals that give the manifest activity its direction, as well as its pace and tone. Perception—the taking in of information—is selective, and this selectivity is based on, among other factors, what one is consciously looking for. In addition, one's frame of reference predetermines to some extent one's cognitive functioning—the meaningful evaluation and interpretation of data, and the purposive activity that follows.

Analysis

In an attempt to clarify the different meanings ascribed to the concept family-centered casework, I shall undertake in this article to analyze the concept word by word.

Especially pertinent to a discussion of the term *family* are some thoughts of Aneurin Bevan:

Reprinted with permission of the author and The Family Service Association of America from *Social Casework*, Vol. 48, No. 7 (July 1967), pp. 426–428.

He . . . must also be on his guard against the old words, for the words persist when the reality that lay behind them has changed. It is inherent in our intellectual activity that we seek to imprison reality in our description of it. Soon, long before we realize it, it is we who become the prisoners of the description. . . . Social institutions are what they do, not necessarily what we say they do.[1]

Many writers in social work journals, particularly prior to this decade, have interpreted the term *family* to imply a collection of biologically or legally related individuals living, usually, under a common roof and having certain emotional bonds, whether positive or negative. The recognition of the effect that parental care and attitude have on the children has been a part of this traditional model along with the recognition of the effect of shared experience and social, economic, and cultural influences. The emphasis in this interpretation is on the individual who is affected by internal psychic forces and external environmental forces, both within and separate from the context of his family. The literature before and through the mid-fifties gives the impression that the family is viewed as having certain responsibilities and functions and that the degree of adequacy with which these are carried out has a direct effect on the child. There is no emphasis on the child as an influencer.

One can see the influence of Freudian doctrine in this description of the family. Its significance in the context of this discussion is that it emphasizes the individual. It does not, however, preclude concern for each individual within the family group. This idea is typified in the following statement:

. . . efforts to influence family life in the interests of the child must be based upon an understanding of the needs and strivings of each family member, especially of the parents, as well as upon an understanding of the value of the parents to the child in his development.[2]

Within this frame of reference a family-centered focus can be interpreted as incorporating a concern for the rights, responsibilities, needs, and strivings of each member of the family. It could mean an intellectual awareness that would influence the caseworker's treatment of an individual member of the family. Since social workers have emotional investment in their work, however, the particular family member who is the client is many times the central concern; although lip service may be paid to the concept of family-oriented or family-centered casework, sometimes

___

[1] Aneurin Bevan, *In Place of Fear*, Simon & Schuster, New York, p. 14.
[2] Mary E. Rall, "The Casework Process in Work with the Child and the Family in the Child's Own Home," in *Casework Papers 1954*, Family Service Association of America, New York, 1955, pp. 31–32.

treatment efforts with other family members are actually a kind of environmental manipulation. Perhaps this is a pitfall that must be avoided, but the recognition of a potential pitfall does not negate the worth of this entire conceptual model of the family.

The other major, and more recent, conceptualization has been expressed thus:

> The family is not simply a collection of individuals: it constitutes a true small group, a dynamic entity with a life, structure, and institutions of its own. Within the family, the action of any member affects all, producing reactions and counteractions, and shifts in the family's equilibrium. Reciprocally interrelating roles must be found, or the personality of one or more members will become distorted. [3]

This concept emphasizes "the family as a system, the psychosocial integration of the individual within that system, and the continuing transactional relationship between family group and individual person." [4] Viewing the individual's relationship to his family in this frame of reference has the effect of drastically altering the meaning of the term *family*, and consequently, the meaning of the term *individual* undergoes a similar alteration. If the individual is no longer seen as a distinct entity but as an integral component of a system, his behavior is seen "not only as a function of [his] internal psychic economy . . . but also as a function of the family group." [5] The hypothesis that a client's problem is a symptom directly related to some dysfunctioning within the family as a system carries with it the necessity of dealing with the system directly in order to bring about improved social functioning. The alternative, if one accepts this hypothesis, is that "improvement in the mental health of the member defined as 'sick' would very frequently be countered by an outbreak of disturbance elsewhere in the family system." [6]

Within this frame of reference, heavily influenced by sociological and social-psychological thinking, *family-centered* must imply *family-system-centered*. Therefore, conscientious casework in the first phase of studying the problem would require gaining a clear understanding of how the particular family's system of interaction operated. This entails confronting the family group directly. The implications for treatment are even more far-reaching: the Midwest Seminar on Family Diagnosis and Treatment, under the auspices of the Family Service Association of

    [3]Theodore Lidz, Stephen Fleck, and Alice R. Cornelison, *Schizophrenia and the Family,* International Universities Press, New York, 1965, p. 353.
    [4]Frances L. Beatman, Sanford N. Sherman, and Arthur L. Leader, "Current Issues in Family Treatment," *Social Casework,* Vol. XLVII, February 1966, p. 75.
    [5]*Ibid.*
    [6]Florence Rockwood Kluckhohn, "Family Diagnosis. 1. Variations in the Basic Values of Family Systems," *Social Casework,* Vol. XXXIX, February-March 1958, p. 63.

America, came to the conclusion that "family treatment is distinguished from individual treatment with a family orientation by the fact that the caseworker *enters directly into the interaction between family members.*"[7] In this context *centered* cannot refer simply to an intellectual awareness of the system; it necessarily implies multiple-client or family-group interviews, since it is the interaction between family members that is the focus.

The meaning of the term *centered*, then, is dependent upon how one chooses to define *family*.

The last phase of this word-by-word analysis is an examination of the term *casework* in the light of the foregoing discussion. The differing frames of reference presented both seem to be compatible with the statement that "the aim of casework is to restore or reinforce or refashion the social functioning of individuals and families who are having trouble in their person-to-person or person-to-circumstance encounters."[8] The issue that poses the problem relates to the basic nature of casework. Some writers define casework as work with the individual and contend that it is the individual-to-individual relationship that distinguishes it from group work. According to this view, "family-system-centered" work might indeed be considered group work. The Family Service Association of America has stated that "the term 'client' may apply to one or more family members."[9] This does not clarify the issue. Perhaps family-centered casework is a hybrid falling somewhere between traditional one-to-one casework and group work. Perhaps we must redefine our professional specializations.

Summary

Two distinct conceptualizations of the family lead to two intrinsically different helping processes, both of which can be called family-centered. The one emphasizes the individual in the family, approaching the family as a collection of individuals with needs and assets. It does not preclude the use of family-group interviews but maintains a focus on the individuals in the family, as individuals. The other, based on a view of the family as a complex system, approaches the behavior of an individual family member as not entirely meaningful except as it relates to the family system of interaction and family interrelationships. It requires treatment not of the individual, but of the system. The waters are

[7]Otto Pollak, "Entrance of the Caseworker into Family Interaction," *Social Casework*, Vol. XLV, April 1964, p. 216.
[8]Helen Harris Perlman, "Social Casework," in *Encyclopedia of Social Work*, Harry L. Lurie (ed.), National Association of Social Workers, New York, 1965, p. 704.
[9]Family Service Association of America Committee Report, "The Content of Family Social Work," *Social Casework*, Vol. XXXVII, July 1956, p. 320.

further muddied when one attempts to put this dichotomy into some meaningful relationship with the term *casework*, for, in a sense, the second helping process may indeed be a kind of group work.

Perhaps it is fortunate that there is no "right" answer and that the individual practitioner must resolve these issues for himself. If anything else were the case, the dynamic nature of the profession would be in jeopardy. It is, however, incumbent upon the profession to attempt to clearly delineate the issues involved. More clarification and definitiveness, and less advocacy, are needed for this task.

Preventive Intervention

Berta Fantl

The term "preventive intervention" may take on more specific meaning as those equipped with knowledge of individual psychodynamics move into an era in which sociocultural factors can be comprehended with pertinence and greater differentiation. Environment is no longer seen as restricted to what is accessible to immediate perception and open manipulation.[1] A new kind of awareness of the person-in-the-situation configuration is evolving which is significant for helping professions concerned with broad human issues.[2]

Conspicuous features of our time are the rapid changes in family and community life, the growth of bureaucratic structures, the professionalization of services, and the cultural and educational assimilation of different ethnic groups in urban centers. Along with these changes we are experiencing a new broadening of community responsibility for those in crisis or in a permanent dependent status—new at least in this country. It is not as if all the old patterns had vanished, but life has become complicated enough for the sophisticated and educated, let alone those whose earlier experiences have had little emotional enrichment and who have lacked opportunity to develop differential skills and competence for new kinds of social living.[3] The complexity of city life, the pattern of taking and sharing in new community

Reprinted with permission of the National Association of Social Workers from *Social Work*, Vol. 7, No. 3 (July 1962), pp. 41–47.

[1]Herman D. Stein, "The Concept of the Social Environment in Social Work Practice," *Smith College Studies in Social Work*, Vol. 30, No. 3 (June 1960), pp. 188–210.

[2]Bertram Beck, "Prevention and Treatment," based on the work of the Subcommittee on Trends, Issues, and Priorities of the NASW Commission on Social Work Practice, 1959. (Mimeographed.)

[3]Nelson N. Foote and Leonard S. Cottrell, *Identity and Interpersonal Competence* (Chicago: University of Chicago Press, 1955).

structures, the establishment of new and meaningful interpersonal relationships in family affairs and organizational systems, cannot be left to chance alone. Simpler tasks than these we do not expect to accomplish without support and guidance, and without margin for experimentation and error.

Concept of a Neighborhood

In the fall of 1958 a small unit of social workers left the centralized downtown school child guidance services in which they had been working to take up residence in a lower-lower-class district. Psychological testing and psychiatric consultation were provided from the central agency by request. This move reflected a growing sense that clients who normally would not flock in significant numbers to the doors of social agencies need to be studied and more fully understood in their natural setting, and that social workers and their agencies need to become part of the neighborhood in order to make services available which are physically as well as psychologically accessible, when crises arise that readily motivate clients to use help—if help can be offered in a style congenial to their spontaneous ways of expressing problems as well as solving them.

Concern soon shifted from the traditional one-to-one relationships and work with "collaterals" to a broad awareness of the daily life of clients, their immediate dilemmas and crises, their family ties or lack of them.[4] Once enmeshed in the human problems of the neighborhood, the consideration arose of how much or how little casework services for a few families would accomplish in view of the type and number of problems encountered and the over-all needs of the neighborhood. This is not meant to imply that there is not a crying need for more and better diagnostic and treatment facilities for clients with emotional problems. But with social problems as they increasingly exist, every social agency needs to take an honest look at how well it serves the population it thinks and says it is serving, and whether in our present knowledge and skills there is perhaps room for innovations of service that might benefit larger numbers of people, in different dimensions of human behavior and relations.

Once the major areas of strength and weakness of the neighborhood were identified as compared to the rest of the city, as well as major social institutions, the composition of ethnic groups, the neighborhood pattern, and ways in which people communicated and related to each other, a new conception evolved

[4]Berta Fantl, "Casework in Lower Class Districts," *Mental Hygiene*, Vol. 45, No. 3 (July 1961), pp. 425–438.

of the work to be done, which, despite gaps and imperfections, seemed more realistically related to the welfare needs of the total neighborhood than were the traditional clinical services. Casework services continued to be provided for a limited number of clients, and increasing time was spent in collaboration and consultation with some of the "caretaking agents" who exercise a profound influence on the lives of clients.[5]

A keen awareness developed of the existing social distance between clients and the caretaking agents, their prejudices about each other, and the breakdown of meaningful communication, which seemed to defy every effort and good intention of either party for a more positive interaction that might make full use of the meager number of services available in the neighborhood. One was aware not so much of lack of interactions as of opposing interaction and negative attitudes. Invariably prejudices and stereotyped perceptions were intensified by fear of "what people might think"—ignorance of another way of life and hopeless discouragement after repeated failure to establish rapport. People were often not sure what was expected of them, or how to act or what to say, or how to time their requests.

It is perhaps of interest to note that, as the social workers gradually became recognized and accepted by the client group as persons from whom one could "get help," the first few self-referrals were requests for help in conveying ideas and information to the schools, to public welfare officials, or to the police, or questions regarding them. It became apparent that not just the "doing of things" is important in initial relationships with multiproblem clients, but also ability to convey the feeling that we are not afraid to grapple with the complicated role relationships and interactions of their social environments.[6] These clients may not have had opportunity to develop the type of personality structure that fosters introspection and psychological awareness more commonly attributed to middle-class clients; be this as it may, most of them showed considerable awareness and discomfort about some of the more obvious social and cultural factors that interfere negatively with their social relationships and functioning.

Prejudices and stereotyped perceptions may have deep psychological roots; yet one gained the firm conviction that with patient, skillful, repeated intervention, and given a minimum of favorable attitudes, prejudices and stereotyped perceptions could

[5]Gerald Caplan, *Concepts of Mental Health and Consultation* (Washington, D. C.: U. S. Dept. of Health, Education, and Welfare, 1959).

[6]For a similar conceptualization of differential interventions see Ludwig Geismar, "Three Levels of Treatment for Multiproblem Families," *Social Casework*, Vol. 42, No. 3 (March 1961), pp. 124–128.

be sufficiently modified to permit more satisfying behavior. One saw teachers become less discouraged with their jobs, policemen discover that they and certain groups of children did not need to be enemies—or at least not all the time—and the school social worker feeling at home in situations which not long before had been incomprehensible and would therefore have resulted in closing a case through the withdrawal of either the client or the agency.

Emerging Focus

Although an effort was made in the same way to understand other social institutions, it seemed logical as a school agency to try especially to understand the social structure and position of the schools in the neighborhood.

Such questions were asked as: How, on the whole, do school people in our neighborhood view their pupils and their families? How do the various ethnic groups view education as a goal for their children? Are there conflicting aims in the over-all educational system which put unbearable pressure on administrators and teachers, making a favorable response to their pupils more difficult? At what points does the value system of the educator conflict with those to be educated? Why is there such great turnover of teachers, nurses, and social workers in a neighborhood like this? Why is the neighborhood so little challenge to anyone? When and at what points are expectations about each other not met? What is the status problem in working in this district?[7]

We were concerned with what the low self-concept of our clients might mean to their interpersonal relationships and interactions. Were they taking out social and emotional frustration on each other? Was the societal strain (poverty, unemployment, discrimination) so high that impulsive behavior was one way of releasing tensions—taking also into account that waiting for any kind of gratification was not the usual neighborhood pattern? Many Negro clients maintained that living in the South had not been "too bad." Was it so bad that they needed to use denial as a defense, or were role expectations fewer, more personal in nature, better defined, and thereby less confusing? Could one realistically expect less stealing and violence (which might reflect a change of values) so long as social conditions did not leave room

[7]Elizabeth D. de Losada and Berta Fantl, "Working Papers." Unpublished manuscript, 1958–1960. We wish to express our gratitude to Edmund H. Volkart, Ph.D., professor of sociology at Stanford University, California, for his sustaining interest in our work and for the opportunity to discuss this type of question with him.

for equal and useful opportunities and outdated laws did not "fit the crime"?[8] Not only individuals but whole neighborhoods need to find their identity in society, and we need to understand the latent function performed by these "bad" neighborhoods in relation to the rest of the city.

By such questions one would not expect to find specific answers to problem situations in their own way as unique as individuals under close analysis. But the questioning broadened our psychological frame of reference to include the social systems, norms, values, and customs of the recipients of general welfare services and the helping professions; it provided a beginning for a more appropriate and flexible approach to mastering the environment while meeting inner personal needs.

Focus was on the problem situation, on the quality of interaction, on possible problems in communication. One tried to understand the inner and outer stresses to which people were responding and the expectations they had of themselves and of others. By disentangling, clarifying, and supporting complicated role relationships in the context of sociocultural factors and personal needs, it was hoped to re-establish an equilibrium for better communication and social functioning, and more mutually satisfying relationships. Recognizing the gaps and limitations of our present conceptual frame, the ultimate goal was to create a more benign neighborhood climate for clients by widening understanding of psychological, cultural, and social factors in the light of recent knowledge.

Sometimes it seemed that the mere presence of the social workers, their desire to understand, and their frank appraisal of what could be done or what did not seem possible brought a lessening of tension. More often they were more than mere listeners and observers. While paying attention to the minute details of what was going on between people and the types of stresses they were reacting to, they often intervened carefully with words or actions, taking pains not to overdo and letting the client or consultee handle the situation the moment he seemed able to, yet leaving the door open for further intervention for the same or other problems.

Case Excerpt

The following case excerpt can illustrate only a few among several points which are the concern of this paper.

[8]Richard A. Cloward and Lloyd E. Ohlin, *Delinquency and Opportunity* (Glencoe, Ill.: The Free Press, 1960); Erik H. Erikson, "On the Nature of Clinical Evidence," *Daedalus*, Proceedings of the American Academy of Arts and Sciences, Vol. 87, No. 4 (Fall 1958).

Tony

The counselor of a high school phoned the school social worker when she learned that the couple she had asked to come to school as Tony's parents were in fact foster parents, and that the public welfare department was planning to place Tony with his father, who had been released from prison a few months previously after serving a ten-year sentence for murdering Tony's mother, in Tony's presence, when the child was 3 years old. As distant relatives, and with their own children nearly grown, this couple had taken Tony into their home, showered him with affection and much later, when their finances were no longer sufficient, asked the public welfare department for financial assistance, to which they were entitled as foster parents.

The counselor, who also carried teaching responsibilities, was not only new in her position as "personal problems counselor"; she was also new to the district and not without anxiety and inner tension in meeting her professional obligations. She had asked Tony's "parents" (they had registered him as their child) to come to school, since she considered him emotionally disturbed and in need of professional help. Tony was just sitting, not learning, and was completely inarticulate when questioned by teachers, although seen talking a few times to his classmates. The foster parents presented their story in poorly spoken English, with many gestures and references to the Lord. The counselor, bewildered and upset, wavered between deep sympathy and utter disbelief that so much human tragedy could be possible, of which only the barest details are reported here.

The social worker went over to the school immediately; the foster parents, without really knowing who she was, repeated eagerly and helplessly some of their story. A few telephone calls to public welfare and the probation department confirmed what they had to say. In one department the case load had not been covered because of a long-standing job vacancy, while in the other the worker was new and unfamiliar with his case load; there had been no planning for co-ordination of services. Tony's father showed a long history of emotional outbursts and instability; living by himself and without a steady job, he was left without the support of a worker who might have helped him to get re-established in the community. The foster parents had sought physical protection from him because he was threatening them, but the police had not believed them "because people come with stories like this every day."

After this crisis was settled through appropriate interventions by the school social worker, when it had been clarified who was going to do what next, she noticed that the family had been repeatedly out of money and food and that the $70 they were receiving monthly from the public welfare department for Tony's care was their only steady source of income. (In order to save this amount the public welfare department had "considered" placing Tony with his father.) The foster mother was in need of an operation and unable to carry on with her job; the foster father had suffered two strokes several months earlier which disabled him. His social security payments had not come through. Dressed in his best suit, he had gone downtown several times to settle this matter. Again his limited ability to express himself in the situation and his lack of sophisticated know-how prevented him from dealing effectively with the bureaucratic structure of our social agencies. Because of complications in verifying his birth, it took the school social worker several weeks to locate his application and see that it was moved into the right channels.

Possible Lines of Intervention

One point about this case not unlike other cases is that there was a family in extreme despair, hanging on to each other and surrounded by agencies set up to protect and help people to function more adequately. Yet because of the complexity of structural processes inherent in any large-scale organization, agencies frequently create a climate that defeats much of their original intent. Frequently they are dealing with people who have never had opportunity to acquire the skills and competence to relate in the more impersonal and differential ways to the various officeholders of our growing bureaucratic structures. It is of no use to stay away from these situations and say, "If only the other agencies (police, court, public welfare, and so on) knew what they were doing!" and "We are the only ones who know what is right," since one must realize that all agencies, including our own, are interrelated in the client's social field. If structural or educational changes are necessary, we ourselves must become involved in this aspect of the client's life as one among several ways to bring about change.

1. The school social worker, in her dual role as a caseworker with clients and as a consultant to school personnel, saw several possible avenues for intervention. She could have "reached out" to this family, establishing a continued casework relationship and, with some awareness and attention to the social situation, focusing mainly on the psychological make-up of the clients. By "strengthening their ego" through primarily psychological means she might have hoped that eventually they would be able to deal more effectively with relationships in their environment.

In all probability this approach would have failed, since the worker very quickly recognized that "ego strength" was not lacking, but that these clients had never had the socializing experience to know how to handle themselves in these types of situations. It cannot be said too often or emphatically that not being able to make the right connection in our social systems (including social agencies and clinics), or not following the right societal track from our point of view, is *not necessarily* a sign of poor ego organization.

In this case the point is perhaps plain, but the same often holds true in less extreme situations. Recent studies of character disorders which elaborate on the individual's psychodynamics without looking at the elements in the environment pertinent to his problem miss important clues for psychological treatment, social intervention, or a combination of both. "More casework services" or even "selected case loads"—as a highly desirable and well-intended aim—will not meet our expectations without development of problem formulations and treatment approaches as appropriate for specific client groups as they are realistic for casework. Moreover, as we shoulder the heavy responsibility of being consultants and collaborators in other agencies, we need to clarify what conceptual framework to adopt when the behavior and problems of clients are defined and discussed and social issues are at stake—even when nontechnical language is used, and though the clients are in need of psychological treatment.

Social policy and casework practice with clients of lower classes operate under the same roof. The increasing interdependence of man in relation to man and man in relation to his wider environment, as well as his internal functioning, need the most careful and flexible exploration. The point is not that any one conceptualization is "right" while others are wrong; but to find the conceptualization that will provide us with the most helpful leads in looking at the total needs of clients.[9] It is of little comfort to know that other professions are searching for similar reformulations, differentiations, and refinements. Albert Cohen in recent writing has the following to say: "A major task before us is to get rid of the notion . . . that the deviant, the abnormal, the pathological and, in general, the deplorable always come wrapped in a single package."[10]

[9]How can we think in the framework of "limited goals" for the neediest in our midst and for families burdened with a constellation of troublesome problems, when "expanding goals and sight" are needed? How is it that as social workers we need to be reminded that "constructive attitudes" are essential for working with certain client groups?

[10]Albert K. Cohen, "The Study of Social Disorganization and Deviant Behavior," in *Sociology Today* (New York: Basic Books, 1959), p. 463. This is not unlike what Fritz Redl has to say in more psychological terminology, describing delinquent types, in *New Perspectives for*

2. As a school consultant the social worker could have focused mainly on the conflict situation of the counselor as it related to her professional role. By recognizing her anxiety in being confronted with a perplexing situation and relieving some of her guilt for not being able to handle the situation more adequately—and, in general, through emotional support and some clarifying information—the counselor might have been enabled to deal more effectively with the clients. There were many other cases in which just this occurred.

In this instance the role of the counselor was extremely taxing, in a position new to her and a district quite different from her own background and previous professional experience. Her professional training had prepared her to meet parents who would recognize her as an educator and be concerned about the emotional aspects of their child's nonlearning. Instead she was presented with a family constellation and background she did not expect, while the foster parents in their personal way looked to her as a last resort for help, after telling their story to a number of people. It was not that the counselor was basically inflexible about her role or that she lacked emotional warmth. But it often happens in lower-lower-class districts that the social distance and discouragement between clients and the caretaking agents—whether teachers, social workers, or others—are very great, and the perception of each other becomes blurred. In addition, the types of problems encountered are often dramatically aggressive; they are differently handled and seemingly unrelated to one's own social and emotional world, so that one's defense system may become quite threatened. The fluid give-and-take of feelings and words urgently needed with these clients *could not be produced without more adequate understanding and genuine empathy* for the various aspects of the total situation.

3. By remaining centered on the clients' needs, but focusing on the problem situation in all its emotional, social, and cultural facets, the school social worker decided to relieve the counselor of a pressing task which was more than she could be expected to handle at the moment. By intervening at this point the social worker established immediate rapport, not only with the foster parents but also with the counselor, with whom she had worked before. Through the disentangling of role relationships, the clarification of tasks and responsibilities, the re-establishment of channels of communication, and a sensitive awareness of the spoken and unspoken feelings of all persons involved, the family

Research on Juvenile Delinquency (Washington, D. C.: U. S. Dept. of Health, Education, and Welfare, Children's Bureau, 1955).

received the help they needed most. After the counselor got a "feel" of the neighborhood and the particulars of Tony's situation, she established good rapport with the foster parents, who often came to see her to discuss informally various events of their life.

Since Tony was a fearful child with emotional problems, and no treatment facilities were available for this type of "unmotivated" family, the social worker saw him for diagnostic purposes while the counselor explored resources within the school which would give him some opportunity to develop academically, emotionally, socially, and physically. Frequent and increasingly frank discussions with the school social worker made it possible for the counselor to air some of her own feelings of professional disappointment, her high self-expectations, and her physical fears of the neighborhood. Clarification of some of her misconceptions as they related to particular situations of children and their families lent support to the positive concern of the counselor for her students. After she had experienced the satisfaction and security of handling a few cases well, her warm and spontaneous behavior reappeared and she became keenly interested in her students and an active participant in neighborhood affairs.

Conclusions

This case is not set down as a success story, and deals with only one aspect of the work.[11] The experience of finding and mobilizing potential resources in a neighborhood said to have few potentials was most rewarding. This mobilization occurred through social action, work on community committees, or—as has been suggested here—through work with caretaking agents and short-term contacts with clients during varied crisis situations.

With this broader conception of the work a different type of social worker evolved—one who saw himself as a part of the client's social field, who was ready to enter and deal with crisis situations in a new context and was perceived by others in that way. Being accused of "superficiality" and "lack of depth" in treatment became inadvertently a compliment, as the realization grew that casework sensibility, awareness, and skills can be used in more ways than one to enrich different dimensions of human behavior and help to unfold human relationships.

What emerged from this venture into social and cultural horizons was not the generality still attributed to social science theory, but the richness it added to a limited understanding and way

[11]For other aspects see Fantl, "Casework in Lower Class Districts," op. cit.

of dealing with human problems. A more positive perspective was also gained on the inner strength of individuals and their drive for adaptation in an increasingly complex world.

Casework Practice and
Social Policy Formulation

Harry Specht

Gordon Hamilton continuously stressed the relationship between casework practice and social policy formulation. In 1952 she wrote:

> One cannot successfully solve problems of interrelationships without a sound economic and political structure, but it is also true that one cannot solve—and this is less readily granted—economic problems without profound understanding of human behavior and psychodynamics. These two complementary areas must be integrated for policy and program . . . social workers must find more successful ways of bringing their insights into social legislation. . . . Informed social action can proceed only on deepening knowledge of the personality which determines and is determined by its society, as well as on the more familiar and accepted data of political and related science.[1]

The need for social workers to play a more direct role in the formulation of the social policies that guide social service institutions increases as these institutions grow larger and more complex.[2] Too frequently, though, the charge to the practitioner is delivered in oversimplified cliches that ask professionals to "get into the political arena" or learn to deal more effectively with the "community power structure."[3] In general, the call is for more social action and a more aggressive professional stance in policy formulation. However, the demand for this new stance can be demoralizing to professionals, particularly such practitioners as the social worker in a hospital or family counseling agency. At best, a general call to arms without more specific instructions

Reprinted with permission of the author and the National Association of Social Workers from *Social Work*, Vol. 13, No. 1 (January 1968), pp. 42–52.
[1]"The Role of Social Casework in Social Policy," *Social Casework*, Vol. 33, No. 8 (October 1952), p. 317.
[2]Social policy refers to the goals of social transactions in private and public institutions serving human needs. "Goal" is used as the major referent of policy because it suggests that concepts of organization, structure, economics, and administration be viewed as independent variables that affect policy, but are not themselves policy since goals remain constant, whether or not they are actualized. For a differentiation of social policy and economic policy, see Kenneth E. Boulding, "The Boundaries of Social Policy," *Social Work*, Vol. 12, No. 1 (January 1967), pp. 3–11.
[3]Alan D. Wade, "The Social Worker in the Political Process," *Social Welfare Forum, 1966* (New York: Columbia University Press, 1966), pp. 52–67.

about which arms to use or how to use them is only temporarily inspiring and, at worst, likely to leave many feeling inadequate.

This inadequacy occurs in part because, as Donald Howard puts it, ". . . of the failure to stress social policy formulation as a process rather than in . . . exclusively substantive terms."[4] That is, there is a tendency to conceive of participation in social policy formulation as requiring expertise in a major area of service, a comprehensive and extensive knowledge of a field. But if policy formulation is recognized as a process that can be taught to *all* in a profession, and if it is seen as a process that entails many different tasks and roles, then all professionals can learn to utilize the process so that they can contribute to it in ways most appropriate for them.

A second reason for the practitioner's sense of inadequacy in dealing with social policy formulation is that it is not as well defined as other professional tasks. In casework, for example, the actual doing (counseling) and the units with which one does it (cases) are relatively clear. Many of the methods used in direct practice allow professionals to work within a series of fairly well-defined roles that usually have a high degree of consonance and frequently can be filled by one person. However, as shall be explained in this paper, the process by which policy is formulated involves a wide range of roles that often strain against one another and must be filled by several people. In addition, the caseworker must see these roles in the context of the societal forces that necessitate change in social welfare institutions. Therefore, the author has provided a brief review of the major forces generating change in this society before moving on to a discussion of the policy formulation process.

Forces Generating Change

The first of these forces is the combined effect of automation and an expanding labor force, both of which produce an over-abundance of goods and a shortage of jobs. Increasingly, it will be in the human services that much of society's work remains incomplete—the health, education, social welfare, recreation, and other professions—where society can and should use its surplus manpower. This, of course, will necessitate great change in the organization of social welfare services. There are not enough professionals to meet present demands and there is little likelihood that this situation will change in the near future. Therefore,

---

[4]"Social Policy Formulation as Process" (Los Angeles: UCLA School of Social Welfare, February 1965). (Mimeographed.)

a reexamination of professional functions and the development of a more creative use of subprofessionals and workers in new careers, to do much of the work the professionals may be doing unnecessarily or for which there is not the professional manpower, will be necessary.

The press for civil and social rights in this era will make further demands on the service professions. Society will need to speed up the creation of new mechanisms to meet needs, such as a guaranteed minimum income; the separation of income maintenance programs from social services, as suggested originally by Gordon Hamilton; and the whole host of noneconomic services presently being experimented with in the Office of Economic Opportunity and Model Cities programs.[5] Increasingly, social work will require programs that encourage self-help and allow for citizen participation so that clients, rather than being passive recipients of services that often do not meet their needs, may participate in designing and implementing programs that do.

These problems will demand a more enlarged role of government in meeting social needs than do the already burgeoning and complex programs. New forms of government to deal with the problems of metropolitan areas and joblessness and to coordinate and humanize public services will be called for. The problems encountered in policy formulation must be assessed in light of these forces generating change.

Social Policy Formulation Model

In this paper the various stages of the policy formulation process, the tasks involved at each stage, the institutional resources needed to carry out these tasks, and the professional roles required at each stage will be identified. Following this, the strategic points at which the caseworker can play a role in policy formulation will be considered. By utilizing the model, the gaps in role sets of professional groups concerned with policy formulation may be found.

Many authors have developed models of policy formulation along similar processual lines to the one proposed here.[6] The purpose of this paper is to identify the different professional tasks and roles relevant at the several stages of the process. It is this notion of *difference* that is most important for understanding the relationship between practice and policy formulation.

[5]Gordon Hamilton, "Editor's Page," *Social Work*, Vol. 7, No. 1 (January 1962), pp. 2, 128.
[6]See, for example, Elizabeth Wickenden, *How to Influence Public Policy* (New York: American Association of Social Workers, 1954); and Robert E. Agger, Daniel Goldrich, and Bert E. Swanson, *The Rulers and the Ruled* (New York: John Wiley & Sons, 1964).

Table 1 identifies all the elements mentioned. The process may be summarized as uncovering both incipient and unmet needs and blazing a trail of advocacy toward new methods of meeting those needs. It might take place in a variety of settings—in one small agency, in one department of a large agency, or in a nation-wide bureaucracy—or the different resources and subsystems of only one institution or a wide variety of institutional resources and organizations might be involved.

The reader should bear in mind that the model only suggests the various stages through which policy moves; it does not take into account the question of *who* generates interest in and takes initiative for carrying the process forward. The force generating change might be the practitioner, the professional association or another voluntary association, the administrator, or an interested citizen. Regardless of where the desire for change originates, all these elements are part of the process once it is started.

Whether someone introduces a policy goal from outside the institution or it originates from within, it must at some time become the preference of a person within the decision-making structure to become a part of the process. Otherwise, it will remain stillborn in the mind of its originator.

The following two case examples will illustrate the process. One concerns a caseworker in a city welfare department. The worker's interest in policy stemmed from an administrative ruling that transferred the authority to grant funds for "special needs" from the line supervisor to the senior supervisor. As a result, clients had to wait for unnecessarily long periods to receive funds. These amounts, although usually small, were often needed for family emergencies. The worker questioned the policy at a lower-level staff meeting and was told the issue was settled and closed to further discussion. This response revealed a second policy issue—one relating to administration—the absence of means by which the professional staff could participate in policy formulation. Clients were, of course, emphatically excluded from any participation. These practices resulted in the agency's having policies that were frequently rigid, unyielding, and unresponsive to client needs.

The other example involves a caseworker in a voluntary agency that frequently dealt with runaway children who was distressed by the physical mistreatment of children in the county probation department's residential institution, which was operating with poor facilities and insufficient funds. Finding the institution's administrator defensive and unwilling to bring these problems to the authorities' attention, the worker sought counsel from other

TABLE 1. Stages of Policy Formulation

Stage	Tasks	Institutional Resources	Professional Roles
Identification of problem	Case-finding, recording, discovery of gaps in service	Agency	Practitioner
Analysis	Data-gathering, analysis, conceptualization	Research organization (e.g., university)	Researcher
Informing the public	Dramatization, public relations, communications (writing, speaking)	Public relations unit, communications media, voluntary associations	Muckraker, community organizer, public relations man
Development of policy goals (involvement of other agencies)	Creating strategy, program analysis	Planning bodies, voluntary associations	Planner, community organizer, administrator
Building public support	Developing leadership, achieving consensus	Voluntary associations, political parties, legislative and agency committees	Lobbyist, community organizer, public relations man
Legislation	Drafting legislation, program design	Legislative bodies, agency boards	Legislative analyst, planner
Implementation, administration	Program-organizing, administration	Courts, agencies	Administrator, practitioner, lawyer
Evaluation, assessment	Case-finding, recording, discovery of gaps in service, gathering data	Agency, research organization	Practitioner

social workers. This small group informed the social action committee of their local NASW chapter, which helped organize a broadly based citizens' group to deal with these problems.

First Stage: Identification of Problem

The basis for institutional policy change is in some problem identified as an unrecognized or unmet need in the community, a need the originator of the policy goal believes the institution is responsible for meeting. The perception of the problem and the institution's responsibility are related to the political, economic, social, and institutional forces that come to bear on the perceiver; what is perceived to be a problem will depend on the institutional position of the initiator. So, for example, it is possible that concerns for institutional maintenance might guide the perceptions of professional administrators more than their feelings of responsibility for providing better service to clients. (The welfare department caseworker was concerned about his client receiving benefits promptly; the administrator was interested in keeping the costs of the special needs program as low as possible.)

Tasks that must be completed during this stage are case-finding, recording examples of unmet needs, and discovering gaps in services. The institution itself is the resource to be utilized during this stage, and the practitioner role is most important. Gordon Hamilton noted that skill in determining how family functioning, personality development, and intergroup relations are affected by policy is the most important contribution the caseworker can make in this endeavor.[7]

It is in their functions as advocates and social brokers for their clients that caseworkers will most likely be involved in the policy formulation process. Scott Briar has discussed these functions as part of the caseworker's professional role, pointing out that caseworkers bring to them ". . . a substantial body of knowledge with which to understand the dynamics of the welfare system and its constituent agencies."[8]

However, to use such knowledge in this process requires a professional orientation that views service to one's client as the foremost professional responsibility. The welfare department caseworker's colleagues, for example, felt he had "betrayed" the department when he pressed his criticisms of department policy.

---

[7]Hamilton, "The Role of Social Casework in Social Policy," p. 319.
[8]Scott Briar, "Dodo or Phoenix? A View of the Current Crisis in Casework," *Social Work Practice, 1967* (New York: Columbia University Press, 1967).

Because discussion was foreclosed at the staff level, he presented the issues to the mayor's commission on welfare in co-ordination with an NASW representative, urging its members to intervene in the department's handling of the matter.

Many social workers will ask at this point: How does one weigh the importance of working within the agency structure as against going outside the system as the welfare worker did? But a too narrow view of the system prejudices the case against workers who take action on their clients' behalf. These workers view the agency as part of—really only an agent of—a larger system of state and federal government. The worker *was* working within the structure, just as Benny Parrish and Harold Supriano were working *within* the system when they conflicted with their welfare departments.

Benny Parrish, a caseworker for the Alameda County Department of Social Services, refused to participate in a mass morning raid on the homes of recipients of AFDC grants (then called Aid to Needy Children) to find out if there were any "unauthorized males" present because he believed that such a raid was in violation of the recipients' privacy. For this reason he was discharged for insubordination in 1964. Harold Supriano, a caseworker for the San Francisco Department of Social Services, was discharged shortly before completing his probationary period for several reasons, including his after-hours participation in a community organization that encouraged low-income residents to organize to protest police brutality abuses.[9]

As it turned out, the courts made it clear in the Parrish and Supriano cases that it was the agencies who were out of line—who were not working within the system—and whose behavior was illegal. Professional social workers will be able to help clients obtain their rights only when they are able to absorb the strain and conflict that occur when they mediate the interests and rights of clients. The profession, through its educational institutions and professional association, must provide the mechanisms to help its members do so.

Practitioners, then, can play an important role in the policy formulation process and must be alert to the potential for change in certain aspects of their practice. As a case in point, there are many problems that practitioners regularly confront in their day-

[9]In *Parrish* vs. *Civil Service Commission of the County of Alameda*, 35 U.S.L.W. 2583, Cal. Sup. Ct. (March 27, 1967), the court decided in favor of Parrish. In April 1967, the judge of the Superior Court for the City and County of San Francisco, before rendering his decision in *Harold Supriano and the San Francisco City and County Employee's Union, Local 400* vs. *San Francisco Department of Social Services* (Case No. 566214), called the city's attention to other recent court decisions involving workers' rights and urged the city to settle the case out of court.

to-day work to which these new conceptions of services are relevant. For example, new careers concepts can be useful in dealing with problems of overly large case loads, hard-to-reach clients, waiting lists, staff that are hard to reach because of turnover and personnel shortages, and apathy and alienation in the community to be served.

Second Stage: Analysis

Having identified a problem, it is necessary to develop some factual data about the number of people who are affected and a clear-cut statement of how the problem is actually being measured. Gathering data may not require highly scientific and formalized research procedures. For example, the caseworker at the city welfare department figured the cost to the agency in man-hours of implementing the less desirable special needs policy and how much time clients had to wait for funds. An $8.00 special needs grant for one client, he found, cost the agency over $100 in staff time, and the client was kept waiting for an unnecessarily long period—over six hours for a transaction that could have been completed in a few minutes. When his research was presented to the mayor's welfare commission, its members were horrified and immediately took the matter under consideration.

In the other case illustration, the citizens' group concerned about the probation department set up meetings in various sections of the city to which it invited all youths who had been at the institution and wanted an opportunity to speak about their experiences and grievances; scores of youngsters came. These meetings provided much of the raw data for the citizen committee's work.

The kind and quality of the information-gathering function will change as the process evolves. The citizens' committee used a fairly informal procedure in their early work. Later on, as some of the issues became clear, the committee directed its energies toward bringing in a highly respected professional standard-setting agency to evaluate the community's probation program.

From a processual point of view, the knowledge required is *how* to move from an expression of concern about unmet needs to an organized (and frequently complicated and/or expensive) program of information-gathering. The institutional resource is a research operation—consultation with an agency research department or a university research center; the professional role is that of researcher.[10]

[10]By "professional roles" is meant those roles that must be filled in the policy formulation process. The concern here is to identify the tasks with which professionals in the institution to

Third Stage: Informing the Public

The public is the various subsystems in the institution or general community that must be informed of the problem. The size of the public—as big as the community at large or as limited as the administration of an institution—depends on the nature of the problem or the stage of the process. The task is to present the problem in a form that will capture the interest and attention of the public by use of appropriate media.

The institutional resources are these media. They might be channels within the institution (public relations department, staff meeting) or outside institutional resources (the press and television). Although the form of action may vary, this is the stage at which counterdemands will essentially determine the extent to which activity in the following stages is to be consensual or conflicting.

For example, the welfare worker only asked the mayor's commission to consider the impact of the special needs policy on clients. His reasoned presentation to the commission was sufficient to spur them to work for changing the policy. Although a local newspaper did print the story, that was not a scheduled part of the worker's plan. But the citizens' committee was attempting to demonstrate the inadequacy of the funds allocated by the county for probation. To do this required its challenging the entire system's functioning. That is, the departmental administrators, the juvenile court judge, the juvenile justice commission, and the county officials all recognized (but not publicly) that the probation department's financing was inadequate. However, they did not want to take responsibility for bringing this to the public's attention since they would then have to demand additional funds. Thus, the citizens' committee intentionally sought and received widespread coverage by the news media.

The necessary professional roles differ from those previously mentioned. The muckraker, community organizer, and public relations man (each with different roles) bring the institutional problem to the public's attention.

This step precedes the next stage—developing policy goals—because while the parties who are initiating change may have specific policy goals in mind, they will have little meaning to the relevant public until it is aware that a problem exists. For example, the mayor's commission could not become interested in

---

be changed must be prepared to deal, whether or not the roles are actually filled by professional social workers.

rearranging responsibility in the welfare department until it understood the problem; the citizens' committee could not begin to suggest changes in policy until it had persuaded the public there was reason to examine present probation policy. One further reason for this order is that the parties who participate in seeking policy change will want to be involved in shaping goals. Anyone who initiates change without this realization is likely to find himself without the support he will need later on.

Fourth Stage: Involving Other Organizations in Developing Policy Goals

Many solutions will be offered for dealing with the problem, all of which must be sifted, analyzed, and shaped into a strategy so that the goal will actually provide a solution to the problem. Essentially, a strategy is a set of program goals based on a theory of the problem's origins.

Different voluntary associations and planning bodies are likely to participate at this point, including those that function within and outside the institution. This is the point at which the professional association, as a voluntary organization, can become most actively engaged in policy formulation.

Alan D. Wade's case history of the NASW Chicago Area Chapter's fight against Governor Kerner's attempt to slash the welfare budget in 1962 illustrates the important role of voluntary associations in policy determination.[11] In that undertaking, the chapter made extensive use of a wide range of other organizations at several stages of its effort. Another instance, reported by Marjorie D. Teitelbaum, illustrates that much of the effort of an NASW chapter's attempt to influence standards used in selecting a state social welfare director went into working with other organizations.[12]

The important role of voluntary associations in the determination of social policy cannot be overestimated. It is through their associations with others that Americans make their needs known in political life. The classic theoretical view of the operation of a political democracy is somewhat misleading in this regard.[13] In that view, it is the direct relationship between the legislator and the voter that is the chief determining factor in policy formula-

[11]"Social Work and Political Action," *Social Work,* Vol. 8, No. 4 (October 1963), pp. 3–10.
[12]"Social Workers in Social Action: A Report from Maryland," *Social Work,* Vol. 9, No. 4 (October 1964), pp. 100–107.
[13]Betty H. Zisk, "Formation of Public Policy: Constitutional Myths and Political Reality," in John H. Bunzel, ed., *Issues of American Public Policy* (Englewood Cliffs, N.J.: Prentice-Hall, 1965).

tion; such intermediary mechanisms as interest groups, political parties, lobbies, and pressure groups are viewed invidiously, as "selfish interests."

However, in reality direct relationships with legislators through elections or their letter writing are not effective simply because elections deal with too many issues to be considered conclusive debates on any one issue. While the town meeting view of government is worth cherishing as part of the past, it is not a helpful model for contemporary government.

Generally, legislation is handled through a complex committee system and the factors of time, distance of the central government from the local community, and largeness of government make it next to impossible for the individual to affect policy. It is through organizational interests of all sorts that the interplay between claimants and decision-makers takes place. Any movement for change, whether for reform or reaction, that fails to take account of this fact of American political life cannot succeed.

Professional roles required are those of planner, community organizer, and administrator. But it would be well to bear in mind that strategies must change as goals change. For example, policy issues relevant to new careers programs might move from (1) the viability of using the poor to serve the poor in selected, specialized communicating roles, to (2) using the poor to assume some responsibility carried by professionals in all aspects of service, to (3) utilizing the re-examination of the staffing patterns in social services as a mechanism for broadening community participation in designing and implementing programs. Each of these policy goals is vastly different and will require the work of different people in their formulation.

Fifth Stage: Building Public Support

Many different subsystems of the institution and the community will have a stake in policy formulation. The originator of the policy will have to find those groups in the system that can support the goals described in the previous stage and translate them into instruments for action. That is, a consensus must be achieved among those groups who can support the policy.

Compromises may be made at this stage and the processes of bargaining, exchanging, and persuading will be used. The welfare worker, for example, gained sufficient support for his position by working only with an NASW representative who attended welfare commission meetings. Their posture before the commission was worked out quickly and with relative ease. On the other

hand, the citizens' committee decided at the beginning of its activities to seek the support of many civil rights groups and local
child care agencies because of the difficult political route it was
attempting to navigate. The committee worked many weeks before coming to an agreement on tactics and a position that was
acceptable to all members. In Chicago, Wade reports, the battle
to resist cuts in the welfare budget required mobilization of
forces throughout the state, and much of their work was directed
toward co-ordinating the thinking of the many groups and
organizations involved.[14]

The culmination of this stage is the creation of a platform by
the group supporting the goals, whether it is a political party or
the administration of an agency setting forth a general statement
of direction. As Teitelbaum notes: ". . . the basic position
statement of the [NASW] chapter . . . served as the framework
for the position taken by the other groups . . . whose support was
enlisted."[15]

Major tasks involved at this stage are the cultivation of leadership for the coalition and utilization of skills for negotiating a
consensus among the supporting groups. Thus, the citizens'
group, in dealing with the probation department, selected independent, aggressive leadership rather than the reasoned professional approach used by the welfare department worker. Its previous experience in dealing with the probation department in a
co-operative and nonthreatening manner had been unsuccessful;
its members believed their energies would be sapped in further
delay if such an approach were attempted again.

The history of the development of social policy in medical care
for the aged demonstrates that leadership and coalitions change
as issues and goals change.[16] In the 1930's the issue was whether
medical insurance of any kind was acceptable; major leadership
was provided by professional groups using fact-finding and educational methods. In the 1940's, when both hospital and medical
insurance on a voluntary basis were well established, the issue
was the adoption of a national system and whether it should be
compulsory or voluntary; the labor movement and the American
Medical Association became the chief opponents and provided
the leadership. In the final stages of the fight, in the early 1960's,
the question of federal sponsorship was settled; the issue was
which mechanism: social insurance, public assistance, or some

[14]Wade, "Social Work and Political Action."
[15]Teitelbaum, op. cit.
[16]Eugene Feingold, Medicare: Policy and Politics, A Case Study of Policy Analysis (San
Francisco: Chandler Publishing Co., 1966).

other scheme? The major leadership, in addition to labor and the AMA, was political.

Voluntary associations, political parties, legislative committees, and committees of boards of directors are the institutional resources most likely to be active. The professional will be called on to fill the roles of lobbyist, community organizer, and public relations man.

Sixth Stage: Legislation

The program must be formulated in statutory terms, whether it is written as a law for consideration by some legislative body or as a statement of program to be considered by an agency board of directors. Legislation must be drafted that will describe the allocation of responsibility for the program and, to a greater or lesser extent, will deal with organizational structure, financing, and program operation.

Gilbert Y. Steiner, in his analysis of the politics of social welfare, points out that specific knowledge of both social welfare and political science is required to negotiate the legislative policy-making process.[17] The legislative analyst and social planner are the professional roles required in this stage.[18]

Seventh Stage: Implementation and Administration

Depending on how detailed the legislation is, a large part of the process of policy formulation may be left for this stage, when the concrete policies of program may be established by practice, precedent, and experimentation. A good example is the Economic Opportunity Act of 1964, in which the policy referring to "maximum feasible participation" of the poor was quite vague; the practical details of implementation were left to the program administrators.

Policy formulation may take place informally within the structure of government without fanfare or public proclamation when formal changes in the law are not required, but rather a demand is made for an altered pattern of action within the law. In the cases of the welfare worker and the citizens' committee, no changes in law were required to put the policies they supported

[17]*Social Insecurity: The Politics of Welfare* (Chicago: Rand McNally Co., 1966), esp. chap. 10, "Relief Policy Reconsidered."

[18]Wilbur J. Cohen, "What Every Social Worker Should Know About Political Action," *Social Work*, Vol. II. No. 3 (July 1966), pp. 3–11.

into practice. The tools needed to implement their policy goals were already within the administrative discretion of the agencies. The citizens' committee did, later on, win the support of a state assemblyman who developed legislation that gave the state youth authority increased power to investigate the kind of conditions being protested.

Also, it succeeded in presenting the problem to the county board of supervisors, which debated the feasibility of a study by an independent organization. Afterward, the grand jury, social planning council, bar association, and many other agencies became involved. The citizens' committee seems to have lost in their effort to have an outside national agency do the study. However, the community is now committed to a study by *some* social agency, and even if it is not the one selected by the committee, the community has learned a good deal in the process.

The chief tasks at this point are administrative and programmatic, getting the program organized and policy clarified. The institution and the courts are the chief resources for determining policy; the primary professional roles are administrator, practitioner, and lawyer.

The courts become a major significant institution for determining policy because it is by establishing a system of rights and guarantees through appeals and judicial precedents that a body of administrative procedure and law evolves for any social program. Thus, social service personnel must be able to utilize the skills of lawyers in determining how policy goals can be effected through legal mechanisms such as appeals, rulings, and litigation.

Eighth Stage: Evaluation and Assessment

In a sense, the goals of social policy are ever receding. New programs create new expectations and needs and uncover additional unmet needs. Programs themselves become a major element in the "demand environment" of policy. For example, the passage of the Medicare bill has created the need for a vast increase in the number of nursing homes; this new need has given rise to many other questions of social policy regarding private agencies, standard-setting policies, and financial arrangements.

This stage requires an assessment of the impact of policy and an evaluation of how effectively the policy meets the problem. Actually it is the first stage all over again, for the process of policy formulation is ongoing and has neither a discreet beginning nor an end.

Implications for Casework

The model of the process should draw the attention of case-workers to the series of roles professionals fill in the formulation of policy. Several gaps may exist. If professionally trained social workers are not prepared to undertake these tasks, their assignment will fall to other professionals who may not be fully able to represent the interests of the profession. Therefore, the profession must be concerned about whether educational preparation of professionals helps to build both a basic knowledge about the social policy formulation process and specialized training for roles that are not presently being filled (e.g., carrying out the legal tasks in policy formulation). Or, in the absence of professionals who can fill such roles, means of teaching the skills required to work co-operatively with other professionals must be devised.[19]

The past decade of ferment, change, and achievement in civil rights has exhilarated all people who are dedicated to serving others. As the country now enters a period of political reaction, social workers must develop knowledge by which to use their professional skills and must consciously capitalize on all that has been learned in these last years to participate actively in, illuminate, and enhance the policy formulation process in this revolutionary era.

Gordon Hamilton believed this was the difficult responsibility and the exciting challenge of casework:

Political democracy and civil liberties must fight every inch of the way and one can expect no easier road for social welfare. . . .
In short, everyone wants welfare until it is made clear what it means to socialize the inner drives and the real wants, to accept ourselves and not only our neighbors but those "outgroups" which comprise other nationalities, races, and classes.[20]

[19]The inability of many social workers and lawyers to communicate with each other is a good example of this kind of knowledge gap. See Homer W. Sloane, "Relationship of Law and Social Work," Social Work, Vol. 12, No. 1 (January 1967), pp. 86–93; and Paul E. Weinberger and Peggy J. Smith, "The Disposition of Child Neglect Cases Referred by Caseworkers to a Juvenile Court," Child Welfare, Vol. 45, No. 8 (October 1966), pp. 457–464.
[20]Theory and Practice of Social Casework (2d ed.; New York: Columbia University Press, 1951), p. 10.

Systems Concepts in Casework Theory and Practice

Sister Mary Paul Janchill

The person-in-situation concept is easily identified as the critical base from which the social work profession has steadily

Reprinted with permission of the author and The Family Service Association of America from Social Casework, Vol. 50, No. 2 (February 1969), pp. 74–82.

evolved its theory, its art, and its method of practice. In less than half a century since the publication of Mary Richmond's work, a social work literature expanding and developing the concept has come into being. The concept continues as the central dynamic that organizes the tension of the profession to redefine itself in relation to its values, the process by which it gives service, the basis of the skills it seeks to develop in its practitioners, and the relevance of its methods to the attainment of its goals in today's world.

The history of casework can be traced along the path of two converging motifs. The first of these crystallized social work's understanding of broad social forces in the course of the industrialization of the Western world as these affected man. Attempts were made to discriminate the institutional patterns shaped by new production methods, population shifts and migrations, and cultural change, as well as their immediate impact on individuals and families. Retrospective evaluations of these early efforts to distinguish the individual in the environment often take note of a certain motive and need to define the "worthy poor" in the search to comprehend a social problem. Nevertheless, the emphasis was placed on obtaining a factually detailed social history of the client in order to understand the unique situation of the individual, including his feelings and emotional reactions to his environment. Richmond stressed that "broad generalizations about relief, about family life, about desertion, widowhood, immigrants, and the rest" by "wholesalers" were not meaningful either in understanding or treating individual persons.[1] Rather, diagnosis and treatment plan depended fundamentally on locating an array of specific social factors that come to bear on a person's problem. Understanding of "the personality as it now is, together with the ways in which it came to be what it now is," requires a knowledge of the person's life experience.[2]

Richmond's essential formulation that personality growth occurs through "adjustments consciously effected" between the individual and his environment was virtually eclipsed by the revolutionary impact of psychoanalytic theory, which resulted in the development of the second major motif. Though the Great Depression kept alive the need for direct environmental intervention, it led to a shift in values. There was a growing conviction among caseworkers that the salient features of need were to be understood in the personality of the client: the forces *within his*

[1]Mary E. Richmond, Some Next Steps in Social Treatment, in *Proceedings of the National Conference of Social Work* (University of Chicago Press, Chicago, 1920), 254.
[2]Mary E. Richmond, *What Is Social Case Work?* (Russell Sage Foundation, New York, 1922), 103.

psyche that served to establish a given relationship between him and his environment.

Gordon Hamilton, in a succinct historical analysis, rendered for today's caseworker the meaning that Freudian theory brought to casework practice, affecting the whole process of study, diagnosis, and treatment and recasting the very definition of task for the caseworker by shifting the focus from *problem* to *person* and from the socioeconomic frame of reference to the psychosocial.[3]

For the purposes of this article it is sufficient to recapture the perspective psychoanalytic theory gave to the understanding of an individual, who was no longer viewed simply as a type in relation to temperament, occupation, ethnicity, and economic status. Rather than being seen as a static aggregate of attributes, personality came to be seen as a dynamic unit of forces standing in relationship to the outside world and at the same time to the self. Freudian theory greatly illuminated the meaning of human behavior by explicating goal-attainment operations on unconscious levels. It explained how contradictory goals that arise in the mind breed conflict and how this conflict is reflected in social relationships. It led to an awareness that emotional energies are manifested in diverse ways and that those that are not volitionally directed may persist and act as chronic stimuli, affecting the individual's social interaction and causing physical alterations. In regard to the developmental pattern of human life psychoanalytic theory showed that sexuality is an aspect of growth from infancy onward and that because it responds delicately to disturbances of personality it often reflects difficulties in the growth process. These insights led to the adoption of a completely new stance by the worker, who began to listen to the client not only to learn facts but also to discover unconscious distortions reflected in various mechanisms of defense.

Limitations of the Knowledge Base

In the past decade there has been increasing question concerning the use of the psychoanalytic framework in casework. Caseworkers increasingly tend to view Freudian theory as not entirely sufficient for the explanation of the total range of behavior they observe, and the need for an expanded knowledge base is becoming apparent. There is, in particular, a search for conceptualizations of environment, and person-in-environment, to com-

[3]Gordon Hamilton, A Theory of Personality: Freud's Contribution to Social Work, in Howard J. Parad, ed., *Ego Psychology and Dynamic Casework* (Family Service Association of America, New York, 1958), 15.

plement the Freudian formulation of intrapsychic processes. For despite an avowed conviction, stated in most expositions of casework, that all casework is psychosocial, that problems are to be understood in terms of both inner and outer factors, and that the caseworker's focus is on the person-in-situation, a persistent pattern of dichotomizing internal and external dimensions manifests itself in the study of psychodynamics and in the delineation of psychotherapeutic methods and goals. There have been notably few attempts to integrate both dimensions in the formulation of diagnostic and treatment classifications. A review of the treatment classifications made by Mary Richmond (1922), Porter Lee (1923), Fern Lowry (1936), Grete Bibring (1947), Lucille Austin (1948), Florence Hollis (1949 and 1964), Gordon Hamilton (1951), and Eleanor Cockerill (1952) have at least one thing in common: Treatment geared to environmental problems is distinguished from treatment geared to psychological problems. As recently as 1964, however, Frances Scherz questioned whether environmental services can be considered treatment and took the position that they cannot.[4] Indeed, the rationale for methods of treatment classification seems to flow from the point of view described by Isabel Stamm:

> Treatment has at times been described as though it were a continuum with measures designed to reduce environmental stress at one end, measures to support and strengthen adaptive functioning somewhere in the middle, and, finally, at the other end a precious therapeutic segment dedicated to the resolution of instinctual conflicts.[5]

Such thinking is based on the assumption that the true goal of therapy is to achieve client insight into the manner in which unconscious conflicts are implicated in affective and cognitive life. In general caseworkers have not explored psychological theories for different interpretations of insight and have tended to keep its definition within the psychoanalytic model. In 1956 Austin pointed out that insight is "developed in different methods of psychotherapy through the use of several techniques,"[6] that there are different kinds of insight, and that insight varies according to the individual who is the client. Social work's lag in developing Austin's leads nevertheless persists. The writings of Carl Duncan and W. Edgar Vinacke, citing other authors, stress the relationship of thinking to the external world as well as to inner processes and requirements. Vinacke, in particular, views insight

---

[4]Francis H. Scherz, reviewing Florence Hollis' *Casework—A Psychosocial Therapy*, in *Social Service Review*, 38:207 (June 1964).

[5]Isabel L. Stamm, Ego Psychology in the Emerging Theoretical Base of Casework, in Alfred J. Kahn, ed., *Issues in American Social Work* (Columbia University Press, New York, 1959), 84.

[6]Lucille N. Austin, Social Caseworkers, in Qualifications for Psychotherapists, a symposium, *American Journal of Orthopsychiatry*, 26:51 (January 1956).

in a broader context than the analytic, explicating other forms of insight that are basic to problem-solving and that may be highly relevant to treatment task formulation.[7] Duncan suggests that perhaps subjects "could be trained in reorienting as a method of understanding, and that such a skill would transfer to a wide variety of problems."[8] He discusses J. P. van de Geer's phenomenological theory of problem-solving, which asserts that situations differ in "transparency" and that explanation of some factors results in a reduction of the "nontransparency" of others. Though this approach is not alien to casework, there is little conscious, planned use of methods that would relieve the tendency to separate the inner and the outer in a therapeutic focus.

The consequences of casework's limited theoretical framework and accepted knowledge base are reflected in the current clamor for a redefinition of the task and role of the practitioner. There is growing awareness that the theory upon which social workers rely for practice addresses itself to the individual's mediation of external reality while that reality situation is relatively unspecified and only grossly understood. Social workers have engaged in extended debate about the ensuing limitations of the casework method and the restricted client groups it reaches. They have taken positions that range from a heated defense of practice as it is currently constituted to radical proposals for a restructuring of practice.[9] It is not difficult to identify, in all the arguments, a commitment to the interpretation of the person-in-situation concept.

This . . . is the struggle between the individual and the social, the one and the many, the psychological and the economic, the inner experience and the external event. The developmental view of social work shows what we have seldom been willing to admit, that no great personality in social work has been able to carry both these opposing tendencies in equal development within the self, but that leadership in social work has flourished through individuals who have carried with passionate devotion either one side or the other of this conflict. . . .

Casework is clearly that branch of social work which carries forward, protects, and lives out in thought and activity the single strand of devotion to the separate, single human self: the worth of the one. Other branches of social work, such as community organization, program making, social action, all by their nature belong to the opposite tendency which places upon the broad program, the external adjustment, the economic solution, the higher value in interest and feeling.[10]

[7]W. Edgar Vinacke, The Psychology of Thinking (McGraw-Hill Book Co., New York, 1952), 160–94.

[8]Carl P. Duncan, Recent Research on Human Problem Solving, Psychological Bulletin, 56:424 (November 1959).

[9]See Helen Harris Perlman, Casework Is Dead, Social Casework, 48:22–25 (January 1967).

[10]Anita J. Faatz, The Nature of Choice in Casework Process (University of North Carolina Press, Chapel Hill, North Carolina, 1953), 10.

In developing her thesis, Faatz identifies casework as a process in which the client is helped to achieve internal choice through the sharing that takes place in the worker-client relationship. Her standpoint is in the tradition of the functional school of social work, which includes the Rankian emphasis on the will and choice. Nevertheless, because of the logical consequences of a dichotomy of person and situation, her point of view is shared by many practitioners of the diagnostic school as well.

There are, of course, a great many others in the social work profession who do not concur, and some have contributed to the development of interactional references. Herman Stein, for example, presents a dynamic interpretation of the person-in-situation concept in his clarification of the concept of environment. He begins by identifying the boundaries of the concept that have been proved outdated: "(1) The social environment seen as restricted to what is accessible to immediate perception, and open to direct modification . . . ; (2) the social environment seen as external to the individual [a view which does not take account of the personality-transforming potentials of social-cultural forces] . . .; and (3) the social environment perceived as static."[11] Stein examines certain issues of social class stratification, ethnicity, family structure, and role organization in the social agency itself for their dynamic significance and influence on behavior.

Although such relevant issues have now been delineated, the following difficulties remain:

1. The contributions of the social sciences relating to social class, the structures of role and status, the social organization of the family, and the influences of reference groups and ethnicity are found not in any organized body of theory but as many separate contributions from a variety of disciplines. Because of the lack of a coherent theoretical framework incorporating the various contributions, some social work educators tend to omit them from systematic consideration; others place them side by side, as it were, with the psychoanalytic theory of personality. Omission, of course, exposes the student to error, while "adding" social science theory to a psychoanalytic frame of reference has limited value, and environment thus becomes a secondary consideration.

2. There are aspects of environment that are relatively concrete, static, and still significant, as Stein recognizes, in casework treatment.[12] The profession is left with some of the original problems and value considerations in placing environmental manipulation in perspective.

3. The unorganized selection of unorganized theory makes it difficult to communicate to students and new practitioners the knowledge base for

[11]Herman D. Stein, The Concept of the Social Environment in Social Work Practice, in Howard J. Parad and Robert R. Miller, eds., Ego-Oriented Casework: Problems and Perspectives (Family Service Association of America, New York, 1963), 68.
[12]Stein, The Concept . . . , 68.

which they are professionally accountable. Specifically, the identification of the referents for the basic concept of person-in-situation are as yet unclear.

General Systems Theory

It has been proposed that a bridge is needed between psychoanalytic theory and social science theory. Ego psychology and role theory have been most frequently suggested as supplying that bridge, but these appear to fall short of the need. Although both are vital contributions to the knowledge of personality and behavior, they are not in themselves able to incorporate material from the sciences in a sufficiently systematic way. The need, in my view, is not for a theory or a bridge, but for ways of conceptualizing that bring phenomena and events into dynamic relation to each other, taking time span into account and encompassing the steady inflow of life.

General systems theory may effectively meet the profession's current need for conceptual tools that activate an understanding of the relational determinants of behavior in the person-in-situation configuration. Systems theory is not in itself a body of knowledge; it is a way of thinking and of analysis that accommodates knowledge from many sciences. It offers a framework in which social interaction can be objectively and comprehensively understood without jeopardy to the work of individualization.

Systems, defined by Ludwig von Bertalanffy as "sets of elements standing in interaction,"[13] apparently have some properties and structural uniformities in common. The study of these has become the interest of biologists, physiologists, physicists, engineers, economists, mathematicians, psychologists, sociologists, social psychologists, and a small but growing number of social workers.[14] All have become involved, for example, in the study of homeostasis or equilibrium and the processes and mechanisms contributing to it. Systems theorists work from the assumption that "the essential problems are the organizing relations that result from dynamic interaction and make the behavior of parts

[13]Ludwig von Bertalanffy, General System Theory, in N. J. Demerath III and Richard A. Peterson, eds., *System, Change, and Conflict* (Free Press, New York, 1967), 115–29.
[14]See Gordon Hearn, *Theory Building in Social Work* (University of Toronto Press, Toronto, 1958); Donald E. Lathrope, Use of Social Science in Social Work Practice: Social Systems, in *Trends in Social Work Practice and Knowledge* (National Association of Social Workers, New York, 1966), 212–26; Alan F. Klein, The Application of Social System Theory to Social Work, paper presented at the annual program meeting of the Council on Social Work Education, New York, N.Y., January 25–27, 1966; Carel B. Germain, Social Study: Past and Future, *Social Casework*, 49: 403–09 (July 1968); and William E. Gordon, Basic Constructs for an Integrative and Generative Conception of Social Work, paper presented at the annual program meeting of the Council on Social Work Education, Minneapolis, Minnesota, January 26, 1968.

different when studied in isolation or within the whole."[15] Their frame of reference also requires that environment is taken into account in identifying and explaining the character and properties of any system. The functional relationships between a given system and its environment (constituted by other systems) become the indicators for an analyst or observer of needs and fulfilling processes.

A first level of analysis in systems theory consists in the specification of open versus closed systems. The latter are self-contained, isolated from their environment in the sense that they do not depend on that environment for sustainment, and their constituent unit elements are encompassed within a fairly impermeable boundary. By contrast all living organisms are open systems, which are characterized by an active exchange of energy and matter with the environment. The unit elements of such open systems not only have innate capacities for growth and elaboration but are also capable of increasing differentiation, specialization, and effect through environmental exchanges. The qualitative as well as quantitative potentials for individualization and development are implicit in this concept of open system and its dependence on a supporting environment. The analogy of the open system has the virtue of a metaphor that allows choice in the unit of attention (the personality system of an individual, a family, an organization or agency, a total society, or any subsystem of one of these), as well as requiring the relating of that unit to an environment in the form of other systems.

Daniel Katz and Robert Kahn, in an application of systems theory to the behavior of persons in organizations, present a cogent summary of nine characteristics of open systems, derived from many systems theorists, such as James G. Miller, von Bertalanffy, Floyd H. Allport, and Talcott Parsons.[16] The nine common characteristics are presented below with a few selective indications of knowledge areas that are relevant to their use in conceptualizing the person-in-situation configuration.

Importation of Energy

The intrinsic characteristic of life is seen as that of dynamic forces. These forces enable the organism to adjust itself to changing conditions. The importation of energy feature of the open system suggests there is need for knowledge of the sources of energy whereby any organism maintains integrity as it confronts internal and external changes. Psychoanalytic theory has been

[15]von Bertalanffy, General . . . , 115.
[16]Daniel Katz and Robert L. Kahn, The Social Psychology of Organizations (John Wiley & Sons, New York, 1966), 19–26.

drawn upon in developing understanding of how the instincts serve as sources of psychic energy. Further search is needed in psychology and the other sciences to see how cognitive faculties, open to influence by the instincts, may themselves serve as distinct sources of energy. Social encounter, generally, shapes the affective life from which action itself springs, and energic inputs need to be studied in that context. Sociology, social psychology, and cultural anthropology, for example, are of value in understanding how the expectations of others are inputs for an individual in the process of identification, internalization of values, and adaptive and creative activity. Importation of energy suggests an analytic reference for the ways in which the environment serves the individual and is used by him. Specifically in casework, this orientation permits an assessment of an individual's resources in terms of his inner psychic equipment as well as all the outer sources that make contact with the affective life.

Through-Put

Through-put is used to denote the process by which the system acts upon the energy imported—the transformation of energy. Once again, psychoanalytic theory sheds much light on the distribution of psychic energy, accounting for it in genetic terms, psychic economy, and topographic and structural dynamisms and laws. On the one hand it illustrates some total systemic effects of object cathexis and, on the other hand, the withdrawal of cathexis. Mechanisms of defense may also be understood in relation to a through-put process. Indeed, insofar as psychoanalytic theory regards the mediation of stimuli and of conflict, it is very valuable here. Additional knowledge is needed, however, for an understanding of internal changes that take place under the influence of role interaction. For example, the mother-child relationship cannot be understood in isolation; the mother must be seen in hyphenated relation to the father, the grandparents, and all her other role partners in all her statuses if one is to achieve an understanding of the characteristics of her relationship with her child.[17] The social sciences demonstrate that the manner in which an individual negotiates his environment is more than, but inclusive of, his inner psychological mechanisms. Talcott Parsons stresses the fact that human motives and values cannot be understood except in terms of the interaction of the personality system, the cultural system, and the social system.[18] Robert Merton, among other sociologists, has also cautioned about the

[17]Robert K. Merton, *Social Theory and Social Structure,* rev. ed. (Free Press, New York, 1957), 368–84.
[18]Talcott Parsons, *The Social System* (Free Press, Glencoe, Illinois, 1951).

limitations of psychological explanations of behavior that can be better understood in the light of social science. Hypersensitivity in an individual, for example, can be identified as a personality trait stemming from unconscious guilt and the use of projection as a defense. Or, as Robert Merton points out, the same trait may be interpreted sociologically as the product of activated statuses, as when race is constantly made salient for a Negro, either by negative discrimination or the "suffocation of respect," in a variety of cues that tell him he is different.[19] A spate of organizational studies of mental hospitals and treatment centers illustrates the impact of systems on personality. Exacerbation of pathology has been seen in some instances, while in others ego repair and growth are induced.[20] A systems reference is indispensable to the understanding of role interaction and role performance, whether an individual or a family is the center of focus.[21]

Output

The issue of human action in *behavior* of some kind is suggested by this characteristic of systems, and an immense literature has developed on the language of behavior in psychological and interpersonal terms. Functional analysis, as a sociological method, shows that behavior can also be understood by its consequences for another system. Social work has yet to exploit these insights in attempting to understand psychodynamics and symptomatology. Depression, for example, may be interpreted in psychoanalytic terms: object loss, the incorporation of the object so that there is no longer any difference between the self and the object, and punishment of the incorporated object that was originally the subject of ambivalent feelings. Another way of interpreting depression is by means of its latent functional consequences: the control it gives the patient in environmental systems, such as the family and employment. Systems analysis, then, may be a reference for a larger view of symptomatology. The notion of an output that activates another input also enriches understanding of role complementarity and role induction. Communications theory and learning theory would undoubtedly have greater applicability when used with a systems reference.

[19]Unpublished lectures, Columbia University, 1966.

[20]Alfred H. Stanton and Morris S. Schwartz, *The Mental Hospital* (Basic Books, New York, 1954); Erving Goffman, *Asylums* (Doubleday & Co., New York, 1961); David Street, Robert D. Vinter, and Charles Perrow, *Organization for Treatment: A Comparative Study of Institutions for Delinquents* (Free Press, New York, 1966); and John Cumming and Elaine Cumming, *Ego and Milieu* (Atherton Press, New York, 1963), are some examples.

[21]Irma Stein, The Application of System Theory to Social Work Practice and Education, paper presented at the annual program meeting of the Council on Social Work Education, New York, N.Y., January 25–27, 1966.

This concept involves the notion that "the product exported into the environment furnishes the sources of energy for the repetition of the cycle of activities. The energy reinforcing the cycle of activities can derive from some exchange of the product in the external world or from the activity itself."[22] This concept leads to examining an output as it becomes involved in interpersonal exchanges to identify how it is reinforced and becomes reinvested with energy. The phenomenon of the double-bind exemplifies this characteristic as a pathogenic kind of communication sustaining a cycle of interaction. Such phenomena are identifiable only within a systems reference, since effects for another environment are revealing of the dynamisms involved. This point of reference promises a rich yield in the study of worker-client expectations, definitions that come to be given to the motivated client, issues involved in intergroup and racial conflict, and latent consequences of designated social work programs and policies.[23]

Negative Entropy

The concept of negative entropy puts a minus sign to the characteristic of closed systems that causes them to move inexorably to decomposition or disintegration, since their impenetrability precludes any new input from the environment. An open system, by contrast, can achieve negative entropy by importing more energy from its environment than it spends. This is a natural area of concern in casework. The health of the individual is seen to be essentially dependent on his openness to new sources of energy in the environment—including its being an outlet for the spending activity of the individual or other unit in focus. Robert White stresses the inherent drive of the organism to have effect,[24] which clearly requires a mutual presence of the individual and an environing system in which the spending of energy is reciprocated, reinforced, and rewarded. The concept of negative entropy has enormous value for guiding the therapeutic task in social work. It is in this perspective—and based on a larger knowledge of social interaction—that supportive treatment needs to be redefined. The notion of support is currently linked

[22]Katz and Kahn, *The Social Psychology . . .*, 20.

[23]See Winifred Bell, *Aid to Dependent Children* (Columbia University Press, New York, 1955), which illustrates how the ADC program unwittingly put a premium on fatherless families.

[24]Robert W. White, Motivation Reconsidered: The Concept of Competence, *Psychological Review*, 66: 297–333 (September 1959).

with specific techniques within the casework relationship, as opposed to broader attention to environmental inputs that are system-supporting and life-enriching.

Information Input, Negative Feedback, and the Coding Process

Not only energy but also information and regulating signals from the environment constitute adaptive inputs for a system. Allowing a client to express negative feelings, locate his complaints or conflicts, and sift his experiences has traditionally been part of casework. A complementary approach might consist in identifying and releasing feedback mechanisms from other systems so that they reach the individual or group in focus and become operative. Knowledge of the dynamics of social stratification, role organizations, and the structure of authority is of value.

Steady State and Dynamic Homeostasis

The concept of homeostasis or dynamic equilibrium is central to any theory of systems. A tremendous intellectual effort has been exerted in all the sciences in elucidating the concept. Psychoanalytic theory uses homeostasis as a powerful referent in the explication of integrative, restorative, and compensatory functions within the human psyche. Recently physiologists and biologists have joined psychiatrists in studying the biopsychosocial contributions to equilibrium in the phenomenon of dreams. Charles Fisher and William Dement report studies that seem to validate Freud's theory that dreams are a kind of safety valve for the partial discharge of instinctual energy and that they serve a conservative, economic function in preserving sleep. Experimental studies show that when dreaming (rather than sleep itself) is prevented or frustrated, the individual builds up a deficit that he tends to compensate for by dreaming longer in subsequent periods of sleep. When the deficit is not made up, emotional impairment is likely to result.[25] There is a growing literature on homeostatic mechanisms in family interactions, but such analysis needs to be expanded through understanding of intersystem transactions and the place of conflict in a moving equilibrium. Systems theory is valuable in the general area of accommodation to new inputs of several kinds and the process of reorganization toward a steady

[25]Charles Fisher and William C. Dement, Studies on the Psychopathology of Sleep and Dreams, *American Journal of Psychiatry*, 119:1160–68 (June 1963).

state that is never the same as the beginning point in the action cycle. This is an important perspective in crisis intervention.

Differentiation

Systems theory calls attention to the tendency of self-elaboration within an organism, as contrasted with the differentiation and specialization that results from the development of external relations. In the physical sciences there has been much interest in studying the relationship of the molecular environment of the brain to actual cognitive processes. Social workers stand to enrich diagnostic and treatment approaches greatly by drawing on a wider knowledge base in the social and behavioral sciences to learn how environmental systems shape patterns of growth and differentiation.

Equifinality

The principle of equifinality indicates that a certain final state can be reached from differing initial conditions and by a variety of paths. It finds its validation in modern ego psychology—and in various sciences—and it is so harmonious with values in social work that it hardly needs elaboration. It is proposed as a subject for renewed cathective interest by caseworkers that should lead to creative experimentation in methods by which human growth and happiness may be influenced and achieved.

Conclusion

The above comments on the nine characteristics of systems are brief and suggestive, but they may serve in the selection of a framework that accommodates knowledge from many sciences. General systems theory may be seen to have the following potential values for social work:

1. Whereas the present disease model implicit in the study-diagnosis-treatment formulation requires a normative appraisal and reference to pathology, general systems theory may make possible a more value-free exploration of the relational determinants of behavior through its focus on a synchronic analysis of interacting systems. It seeks first to locate the forces that are reaching the person, emotionally and socially, without supposing pathology at the outset.

2. Replacing a linear approach to causation, general systems theory emphasizes an understanding of cause by the observation and interpretation of functional consequences, both manifest and latent. It directs the practitioner to see that the reason for behavior may emerge by tracing the function of such action for *another system*, rather than its expression in the person or system of origin.

3. General systems theory could push the development and systematization of knowledge by relating processes to outcomes, thereby enhancing predictive ability for designated interventions in a system relevant to the person-in-situation configuration.

4. General systems theory presents the challenge of identification and selection of appropriate points for intervention but leaves open the question of strategy and technique. It may therefore permit greater creativity in task and method development. It may help to correct social work's current tendency to dwell on process and technique in such a way as to identify them with goals they are meant to serve.

5. General systems theory may assist in the appraisal of those elements in the person-in-situation configuration that are enduring or rigid, or that are fluid or accessible in a reorganization of equilibrium. Such appraisal may be particularly helpful in the study of crisis states.

6. Systems theory could provide a richer understanding of symptomatology by seeing symptom in terms of function for and across systems.

7. General systems theory could be very valuable in substituting an enriched metapsychology for the current leanings toward psychic determinism and a closed energy system and thereby widen the scope of clinical social work practice. It allows for consideration of multiple energic sources for the adult as well as for the child, and this has many implications for the programing of services and social policy determination.

Systems theory has had much to offer many scientific disciplines. It may well serve social work in the resolution of the perennial conflict of the many and the one, with the result that the person-in-situation concept can be grounded in meaning and effective practice.

Selected Bibliography

Beatman, F. L., Sherman, S. N., and Leader, A. L., "Current Issues in Family Treatment," *Social Casework,* 47 (2), 1966, pp. 75–81.

Briar, S., "The Casework Predicament," *Social Work,* 13 (1), 1968, pp. 5–11.

Cowan, B., Currie, M., Krol, Roza, and Richardson, J., "Holding Unwilling Clients in Treatment," *Social Casework,* 50 (3), 1969, pp. 146–151.

Fantl, B., "Casework in Lower Class Districts," *Mental Hygiene,* 45 (3), 1961, pp. 425–438.

Garrett, A., "Historical Survey of the Evolution of Casework," *Journal of Social Casework,* 30 (6), 1949, pp. 219–229.

Germain, C. B., "Social Study: Past and Future," *Social Casework,* 49 (7), 1968, pp. 403–409.

Glasser, P. H., and Navarre, E. L., "The Problems of Families in the AFDC Program," *Children,* 12 (4), 1965, pp. 151–156.

Gottlieb, W., and Stanley, J. H., "Mutual Goals and Goal-Setting in Casework," *Social Casework,* 48 (8), 1967, pp. 471–481.

Kaplan, D. M., "Observations on Crisis Theory and Practice," *Social Casework*, 49 (3), 1968, pp. 151–155.

Mayer, J. E., and Rosenblatt, A., "The Client's Social Context: Its Effect on Continuance in Treatment," *Social Casework*, 45 (9), 1964, pp. 511–518.

Mayer, J. E., and Timms, N., "Clash in Perspective between Work and Client," *Social Casework,* 50 (1), 1969, pp. 32–40.

McIsaac, H., and Wilkinson, H., "Clients Talk about Their Caseworkers," *Public Welfare,* 23 (3), 1965, pp. 147–154.

Meier, E. G., "Interactions between the Person and His Operational Situations: A Basis for Classification in Casework," *Social Casework,* 46 (9), 1965, pp. 542–549.

Miller, R. B., "Family Life Education: An Experiment in Agency Outreach," *Social Work*, 13 (4), 1968, pp. 72–77.

Morris, B., "Crisis Intervention in a Public Welfare Agency," *Social Casework,* 49 (10), 1968, pp. 612–617.

Neff, M. E., "Helping Low-Income Families Use Donated Foods," *Journal of the American Dietetic Association,* 45 (4), 1964, pp. 358–361.

Oxley, G. B., "The Caseworker's Expectations and Client Motivation," *Social Casework*, 47 (7), 1966, pp. 432–437.

Perlman, H. H., "Can Casework Work?" *Social Service Review,* 42 (4), 1968, pp. 435–447.

Reid, W. H., "Characteristics of Casework Intervention," *Welfare in Review*, 5 (8), 1967, pp. 11–19.

Sachs, V. K., "Crisis Intervention," *Public Welfare,* 26 (2), 1968, pp. 112–117.

Scherz, F. H., "Family Treatment Concepts," *Social Casework,* 47 (4), 1966, pp. 234–240.

Selby, L. G., "Supportive Treatment: The Development of a Concept and a Helping Method," *Social Service Review,* 30 (4), 1956, pp. 400–414.

Sunley, R., "New Dimensions in Reaching-Out Casework," *Social Work,* 13 (2), 1968, pp. 64–74.

4

Group Work

The group approach is used by the generalist to deal simultaneously with individual problems and with interpersonal and societal factors which may be involved in them. In the section on casework, the use of groups for solving individual problems was mentioned. Similarly, Vinter here sees "the group as the means by which the worker can meet individual goals."

But the group approach is more than attention to many individuals. In the group process, what happens among the members of the group may be of primary importance. Tropp asserts that "people can and do help each other in vital ways through group experience"; Schwartz focuses on "the group as a system of mutual aid" and sees "the group and its living experiences" as crucial.

Konopka suggests a psychological basis for the importance of the group process by relating it to such human needs as "the need to belong" and "the need (for people) to cooperate with each other." The group experience, as it meets these needs, can enhance an individual's social functioning. This, in turn, can help group members "to cope more effectively with their personal, group or community problems."

The articles in this section illustrate some of the variety of groups that can be employed by social workers. Differences in group composition, for example, can be seen in Mandelbaum's description of a group of parents of retarded children. An advantage of using the group approach with people is that meaningful contact with others who share one's problems helps one, by coming to terms with their problems, to break out of the isolation which the problems may have created.

A link between the group approach and the broader community is sketched by Wilson. She sees the knowledge of the behavioral sciences as having changed the concept of the people "from one of the individual and society (i. e., government) to a network of interlocking groups which constitute society." The group, then, is conceived to be an element of the broader society, and it is concluded from this that a successful group experience helps to integrate the individual into his community or society. As Youngman says, the group relates people "not only to each other, but to society. . . ."

Social Group Work: Trends and Developments

Gertrude Wilson

American social work is part and product of the larger social and cultural setting in which it lives. While it helps shape the larger society, social work reflects more than it determines the nature of the whole. It cannot be understood apart from its social context. And the more we understand its links to society and culture, the better we will see opportunities for affecting the development of welfare services and the profession of social work.[1]

An examination of the nature of current theories and practices of a part of the profession of social work necessitates a view of this part against the profession as a whole and the social-culture setting which affects it and which it affects, currently and in the recent past.

Social Work and Social Change

Social forces affecting large collections of people are recognized by their effect upon some people, as seen by others, *one* at

Reprinted with permission of the author and the National Association of Social Workers from *Social Work*, Vol. 1, No. 4 (October 1956), pp. 66–75.

[1]Harold L. Wilensky and Charles N. Lebeaux, "Industrialization and Social Welfare," Preliminary Draft, prepared at the request of the U. S. Committee, International Conference of Social Work (New York: Russell Sage Foundation, 1956).

a time. People in trouble need help. Some observers will be stimulated to help meet the immediate problems. Others will be stimulated to try to stop the causes of the problems. Some will be moved to work in both directions simultaneously. Jane Addams might be classified in the category. In the *Atlantic Monthly* of February 1899, under the title of "The Subtle Problems of Charity," she commented that more thought is given to what a man ought to be than of what he is or of what he may become. The following year, Mary Richmond wrote in *Charities* (February 10) that the settlement movement has shown that the personal shortcomings of the poor are not in the great majority of cases, as was formerly believed, the cause of poverty.[2]

During the first twenty years of this century, while the agencies developing social casework services continued to devote the larger proportion of their workers' time to working with people on an individual-by-individual basis, there was an increasing participation of other social workers in working "for and with the masses." The personnel of social welfare organizations, both volunteer and staff, continued to reflect sharp differences of opinion between the people who identified with agencies devoted to changing the "social order," and those agencies where the workers were developing "the art of bringing about better social adjustments in the social relationships of *individual* men, women or children." By 1915, the division was sharp, and in a paper at the National Conference of Charities and Corrections, Miss Richmond defended social caseworkers from current criticism when she said that during the year "books had been published by social workers in which the broad statement had been made that community action for the common good is far more important than successful casework." She continued,

Whatever social reform eradicates, abolishes or prevents, the two great facts of human variation and of variable human response to stimuli would seem likely to remain. . . . The champions of casework are the champions of social reform. . . . They have welcomed and still welcome every change that will tend to make health as contagious as disease, that will increase industrial opportunity, dignify leisure, and enrich the mental and social life of man.[3]

Here Miss Richmond is saying the social caseworkers welcome the results of the work of other social workers, but there is no indication that participation by social caseworkers in the processes of social change, other than on the individual-by-individual basis,

[2]Florence Sytz, "Social Casework," in *Social Work Year Book 1951* (New York: American Association of Social Workers, 1951).

[3]Mary Richmond, *The Long View* (New York: Russell Sage Foundation, 1930), pp. 376–377.

was envisioned. Later, Miss Richmond added this dimension to the social caseworker's function when she said, "I've spent the first twenty-five years of my professional life in an attempt to get social casework accepted as a valid process in social work. Now I shall spend the rest of my life trying to demonstrate to social caseworkers that there is more to social work than social casework."

As knowledge from the social sciences, psychology, and psychoanalysis became more general among social workers, the concepts and consequently the principles and techniques used by social workers were affected.[4] Social concepts,[5] which made possible the analysis of the social processes through which change takes place, brought the importance and significance of small and large groups into prominence. New knowledge about motivations of human behavior not only provided new insights to the problems which individuals experience as *individuals* but made interpretation of interaction of individuals in groups much more meaningful. The gestalt of the concept of "the people" began to change from one of the individual and society (*i.e.,* government) to a network of interlocking groups which constitute society.[6] With knowledge of the labyrinth of groups through which social change gradually takes place came the recognition that people can be helped to participate in more rapid social change if they learn how to give direction to group activity aimed to achieve their desired result.

People critical of the social reformer's methods of "doing for" other people, but eager to participate in processes of social change which would eliminate the causes of some of the social problems, turned to the social and psychological scientist for basic knowledge. In such knowledge, guides were sought for further development of principles and techniques for social work practice. Through concerted attention given to the significance of primary groups to society grew, among other organized efforts, the progressive education movement within the educational profession and the idea of a specialization to serve groups within the profession of social work.[7]

[4]Grace Marcus, "The Status of Social Case Work Today," and Grace Coyle, "Group Work and Social Change," in *Proceedings of the National Conference of Social Work* (Chicago: The University of Chicago Press, 1935).

[5]Charles H. Cooley, *Social Organization* (New York: Charles Scribner & Sons, 1900); and Earle E. Eubank, *The Concepts of Sociology* (New York: D. C. Heath & Company, 1932).

[6]Mary P. Follette, *The New State* (1920) and *Creative Experience* (1924) (New York: Longmans, Green & Company).

[7]Grace L. Coyle, "Social Group Work," *Social Work Year Book 1951* and *1954* (New York: American Association of Social Workers).

Clara A. Kaiser, "Group Work Education in the Last Decade," *The Group,* Vol. 15, No. 5 (June 1953).

Professional Identification

In the beginning, the people who participated in formulating and analyzing concepts, developing principles and devising techniques for carrying them out were identified with the professions of education, social work, and/or applied social and psychological sciences.[8] They were employed in many different social welfare activities, in organizations with purposes related to specific problems of labor, legislation, housing, minority opportunities, and other problems. They were employed in settlements, worker's education, parent education, adult education, public recreation, and national agencies such as the YM and YWCA, Scouts, and the public schools. While professional education for group workers early found a niche in a school of social work, there was a great difference of opinion among those interested in developing methods of working with groups as to the professional identification of its practice. During the second quarter of this century, about half the schools of social work introduced a curriculum for this specialization. It was not, however, until the establishment of NASW that social group work came to be fully identified as a *social work* specialization within the social work profession as a whole.[9]

Although there have been many differences of opinion as to the professional identification and education of workers for the practice of group work, there has been little disagreement in the literature about its basic assumptions: (1) that a sense of belonging is essential to the happiness of all human beings; (2) that certain life experiences and social situations interfere or deny to many individuals the opportunity to have this sense of well-being; (3) that principles and techniques for helping people to develop a sense of belonging through participation in a group can be developed from concepts drawn from the social and biological sciences,[10] and on the basis of our thinking about our experience in practice; (4) that these concepts, principles, and techniques can be learned by people who have the qualifications for helping others to make the necessary social adjustments to participate creatively in groups; and (5) that the welfare of society is dependent upon the constructive nature of the interacting processes of its many small groups.

[8]Identification of the contributors and their committee in *Decade of Group Work*, Charles E. Hendry, ed. (New York: Association Press, 1948), reveals the wide range of fields from which participants in formative years of group work theory and practice were drawn.

[9]October 1, 1955.

[10]Grace L. Coyle, *Social Process in Organized Groups* (New York: Richard R. Smith Publisher, 1930).

W. I. Newstetter, *An Experiment in the Defining and Measuring of Group*. Western Reserve University, 1938.

Gertrude Wilson and Gladys Ryland, *Social Group Work Practice* (Boston: Houghton Mifflin Company, 1949).

Conceptual Framework

The development of a conceptual framework from which principles and techniques of practice are identified, tested, and transmitted to other people is continuous and never-ending. Concepts from political science, sociology, economics, anthropology, social psychology, and psychoanalysis are "tried for size" against live situations found in groups being served by imaginative, experimental workers seeking to improve their ways of working with groups. Principles and techniques have been and are being developed both deductively and inductively, and some are borrowed from progressive education teachers, caseworkers, and other "helping" professions. Experimental recording of narrative records was carried on early in order to have some material more objective than memory against which to test the use of the concepts and better understand their meaning as operationalized in principles and techniques. By the time the first course was organized in a school of social work, there was considerable material to be drawn from pioneer workers, especially those in the YWCA, YMCA, settlements, adult education, and worker's education. The first group work students began writing narrative records describing their work with groups. Some agencies soon recognized the contribution of record-writing to the quality of the services provided to groups. These recordings[11] of students and workers have provided the most significant substantive material to date upon which current principles of practice are based. Within the last decade, there has been increasing interest in testing the practices which have been established empirically through the techniques of experimental research. Some of the studies of small groups carried on by social psychologists and sociologists[12] have provided an experimental foundation for the principles and techniques used by the social group workers, but few such studies have been made by social group workers themselves.[13] These studies also provide new insights into the group process which provide stimulus for modifying old principles and techniques and the development of new ones.

[11]Grace L. Coyle, *Studies in Group Behavior* (New York: Harper & Brothers, 1937).

Clara Kaiser, *The Group Records of Four Clubs*. School of Applied Social Sciences, Western Reserve University, 1930.

Ruth Perkins, *Magic Casements* (1927) and *Program Making and Record Keeping* (1931) (New York: Woman's Press).

[12]See bibliography in Paul Hare, Edgar F. Borgatta, and Robert F. Boles, *Small Groups, Studies in Social Interaction* (New York: Alfred A. Knopf, 1955).

[13]Juanita Luck, *A Study of Peer Relationships with Children in Their Latency Years*. Ph.D. thesis, University of Minnesota, May 1954.

Helen Northen, *The Effectiveness of Social Group Work in the Development of Qualitative Participation*. Ph.D. dissertation, Bryn Mawr College, June 1953.

Etta H. Saloshin, *Development of an Instrument for the Analysis of the Social Group Work Method in Therapeutic Settings*. Ph.D. dissertation, University of Minnesota, 1954.

Social Process

The responsibility of formulating and then operationalizing the concepts helpful to learning how to become an enabler in groups has been carried largely by people identified with programs of leisure-time, educational, and recreational activities. As the group worker became knowledgeable of the significance of the concepts which brought increasing understanding of the social processes which occur in groups, he identified with these ideas and they became to him *group work content* rather than *generic content* for use of anyone who seeks to function more effectively as a member, leader, or enabler. The allocation of the concepts relative to understanding the social processes in group life to group work is illustrated by the fact that very few schools of social work offer this material as generic for all students, but instead require or offer one semester in group work to all students not specializing in it.

Identification of group workers with the use of the social process in all types of groups is further illustrated in the report of the Committee on Function of Social Group Workers of the AAGW issued in 1948:

> Through his participation the group worker aims to affect the group process so that decisions come about as a result of knowledge and a sharing and integration of ideas, experiences, and knowledge rather than as a result of domination from within or without the group. Through experience he aims to produce these relations with other groups and the wider community which contribute to responsible citizenship, mutual understandings between cultural, religious, economic, or social groupings in the community, and a participation in the constant improvement of our society toward democratic goals.

This statement does not identify or describe social group work as a specialization in social work—instead it describes not only the goals of participation of any social worker in groups, but also of any professional or lay person who may work with any type of group. To all of them, understanding as many of the basic concepts and how to operationalize them in their activities are beneficial. It is important, however, to point out that the basic values of the social work profession of respect for human beings and their right of self-determination are violated if enablers to groups are "trained" in use of techniques without understanding the principles and basic concepts from which they are drawn.[14]

---

[14]Genevieve Carter, "The Concept of Measurability of Need for Social Work Services," in *Group Work and Community Organization, 1953–1954* (New York: Columbia University Press, 1954), p. 73.

Such training raises the flood gates for streams of "manipulation" rather than "enabling" people to participate in decision-making processes which safeguard their rights of self-determination.

From many basic concepts upon which principles of effective work with groups is based, ten concepts have been chosen which relate specifically to "group," each of which leads to other concepts; all of them provide illuminating insights to the intricate processes of interpersonal relations which occur in groups of people.[15] These concepts help us to see selectively and understand and communicate what goes on in the group process. To this extent, they help us to develop and refine principles and techniques.

Concepts

Some of the concepts from which principles of work with groups are drawn (a concept is an abstract idea of universal significance):

A group is the interaction of a collection of human beings.

All groups are alike and all are different.

All groups have a purpose but not necessarily conscious, which is expressed in the substances of the interaction.

All groups originate either as "psyche" or "socio" groups; the first drawn together for purposes of personal satisfaction, and the second because of an external educational interest or common task.

All groups experience conflict and exercise controls—the equilibrium or homeostasis of the group.

All groups have two kinds of structure: (a) interpersonal relationships seen as the process of acceptance creates isolates, pairs, and triangles; and (b) division of labor through which roles are assigned to "get things done."

All groups use a decision-making process based on elimination, subjugation, compromise, integration, or combination thereof.

All groups reflect the social status system of the community and create their own in the decision-making processes.

All groups develop morale or *esprit de corps* which distinguishes each from all others.

All groups tend to develop traditions.

These concepts are some of those which are essential to understanding any type of group; they provide a basis from which *any person* working with a group in *any capacity* may develop principles and techniques for working with them for *any purpose, i.e.,* to control, manipulate, or enable them. When principles and

[15]See bibliographies in Wilson and Ryland, and in Hare, Borgatta, and Boles, *op. cit.*

techniques are developed from them for use by social workers, the value system of the social work profession has a determining influence upon the formulation of principles and *how* the techniques for implementing them are used.

Principles

Some social work principles based on these concepts (a principle is the operationalization of a concept translating it into action):

The enabler:

Respects all human beings and their social organizations through respecting their right to manage their own lives.

Accepts each individual and group as unique and the right of each to be different from every other.

Feels *with* the individual and the group without necessarily feeling *like* them.

Adjusts his behavior to his understanding of the behavior of the group.

Accepts and handles negative and positive feelings for the benefit of the group.

Diagnoses where the group is and helps it to move on from there.

Supplies the group, when needed, with factual material and helps the members recognize issues without indicating solutions.

Stimulates the group to consider implication of issues and new horizons.

Supports the group in making and carrying out decisions consonant with individual and social welfare.

Recognizes the structure of interpersonal relations as an influential factor in group decisions.

Helps the group to divide responsibility and involve as many as possible in planning and executing a program.

Respects and uses the structure established by the group for division of labor.

Expects conflict and helps the group to use it constructively.

Accepts his role of authority when necessary without passing judgment.

Understands the social status system of the community and neighborhood and helps individuals to live with it or to help to change it, when change is necessary to safeguard the right of self-determination and the welfare of the community.

Techniques

Some techniques (a technique is a specific way a principle is applied): In human relations there are usually many techniques for applying a single principle. Techniques are chosen in light of the purpose of the group and the workers' understanding of the people and the social situation in which they are involved. They are not applied automatically in the practice of social work.

The enabler:

Knows the name of each individual in a group and addresses him according to the accepted way in his culture.

Is able to discuss matters of interest to members' daily life, not just the program or affairs of the group.

Considers the schedule established by the group as important an item on his schedule as any other obligation.

Arrives first in order to observe who comes with whom, who sits with whom, who agrees with whom for purpose of identifying subgroups.

Gives sociometric tests.

Uses buzz sessions to secure more participation in activity.

Uses blackboard (or helps group's leader to use it) as a method of helping groups keep on the subject in a discussion.

Uses visual aids.

Arranges chairs in a circle.

Stimulates new interest by exhibits.

Uses role playing.

This list of techniques could be extended ad infinitum.

Socio-psychological concepts, like all other concepts, are man's abstractions of his observations tested by the scientific method as to their universal significance without reference to the value system of the people or the social situation they describe. Their significance lies in the leads they provide to the applied scientists or practitioners for the formulating of principles of *how to do something* with people and groups. A member of a professional discipline examines them to find how he can use their meaning in order better to give the service of *his discipline* (which has a value system) to the people whose problems lie within his professional competence.

Each of these few selected principles emanate from one or more of the quoted concepts, but they each carry meaning beyond the concepts themselves because they reflect the value system of social work. As a social work principle, it is not enough to say that the worker, recognizing that a group is interaction, affects its processes. He does this with respect to the rights of the participating members as human beings for self-determination, and with respect for and within the limitations of purpose for which the group is organized. In other words, how he affects interaction comes from the value system of social work, but knowledge of the nature of interaction in any group, as learned from the social scientists, gives direction and concreteness to his activity.

The techniques listed, on the other hand, are not value oriented, and unless they are used in relation to social work principles, they will not provide social work service. The use of techniques without consciousness of their appropriateness to the particular group situation has as much potential of *interference* as of *assistance* to a group in the accomplishment of its objectives. There is no purpose served, for example, in a worker's using a variety of techniques to identify the subgrouping within a group unless he has an understanding of the meaning of the relationships they signify; how they may advance or hinder the progress of the group; and how to help them to maintain their identity and, at the same time, contribute to the progress of the group. So with each technique—it represents the substance of what a worker does. The kind of help he gives a group, however, is dependent upon his understanding of the principles that guide his choice of techniques.

Generic Knowledge and Skills

Further examination and discussion of these concepts, principles, and techniques would reveal that this list represents knowledge and skills needed by every social worker, whether he works with a group with recreational, educational, or social adjustment purposes, or a group of applicants to become adoptive parents, foster parents, a study committee of a mental hygiene society, the board of an agency, a committee of a neighborhood council, a section of the welfare council, or the welfare council itself. Social workers also need this knowledge and skill to work with nonsocial work groups in the community which seek to lessen the maladjustments in the current social situations. Social change pressured by technology, mobility, threat of war, social cleavages, urbanization, and spatial communication present a challenge to all socially conscious people, but a special challenge to social workers who are daily in personal contact with the consequences of social change. The responsibility of working with community groups in changing the "situational field"[16] is one

[16]See Leonard S. Cottrell, Jr., "The Analysis of Situational Fields in Social Psychology," *American Sociological Review*, Vol. 7 (1942), pp. 370–382.

held by all social workers and is not primarily the responsibility of social group workers.

Observation of social work practice and curriculum content of most schools of social work seems to indicate that there is greater awareness of the *responsibility* of social workers to work in and with groups than of the prerequisite knowledge and skill for fulfilling this responsibility. This is an appropriate time for an examination of the content of courses in group work, similar to the examination of the courses in casework which occurred about twenty years ago when these courses were carrying the major responsibility for teaching the understanding of individual human behavior. When this content was recognized as generic and developed in separate courses, the teachers of casework were freed to teach the social casework process per se. Recognition of knowledge and understanding of the basic concepts, principles, and techniques of working with groups as generic will likewise free the instructors in social group work to teach the distinctive characteristics of the social group work process.

Distinctions and Definitions

The distinction between social group work practice and work with groups is one which is needed, not just in relation to our professional organization and the curriculum content which supports the profession, but also in the fields in which we practice where we are in daily contact with workers who serve groups, not only as part of social work practice, but who work from an orientation different from that of social work. Such distinctions are postponed for later consideration on the theory that we must first agree on what we do that is distinctive within our own profession before we can undertake the task of identifying similarities to and differences from other professional work with groups. A first step in this direction has been taken by the Group Work Section of the NASW through a questionnaire aimed to disclose evidence of agreement and disagreement around the meaning of social group work as shown in the opinions of the members and in the agency's related policies and procedures as reported by them.

In contrast to the statement of the AAGW on the "Function of the Social Group Worker," many authors of books and articles present social group work as centered upon the growth or adjustmental problems of the members of the groups served with the assumption that group experiences that help members to grow and thus improve their social adjustment are contributions to the welfare of society. The extent to which the definitions given by the authors listed below are shared by the majority of practitioners is unknown.[17]

Whatever the definitive statement of social group work practice may be, if it is to cover an area of professional practice it must designate the nature of the problems for which the service is designed, and describe specifically the principles and techniques applicable to helping people overcome them. Whether these problems are defined in terms of "social adjustment" or "growth" or some other terminology is of less significance than coming to grips with the fact that we work with people who have problems and our services are aimed at helping them to minimize or solve them.[18]

The following assumptions are proposed to help clarify and define social group work practice:

1. That understanding the nature of group interaction (the group process) and the dynamics of human behavior is a prerequisite for anyone who successfully fulfills the role of an enabler for a group.
2. That the role and responsibility of an enabler is determined by the primary purpose for which the group is organized.
3. That when a group which is organized to accomplish a predetermined task (such as a class, an agency staff group, an agency board, or a committee of a welfare council), the primary responsibility of the enabler is to help the members to accomplish this task.
4. That the enabler who works with a task-oriented group uses his understanding of the dynamics of human behavior and of the group with consideration of the adjustmental problems of the members, but he does not change the purpose or the content of the group's program for the purpose of helping the members with their individual problems.
5. That when a group is organized for the purpose of providing an opportunity for members to use the group experience for adjustmental purposes (personal growth and change), the first responsibility of the enabler is to diagnose (identify) the unique problems of each member in the group.
6. That the enabler who works with a growth-oriented group carries the primary responsibility of affecting the interaction as expressed in the program content toward the resolution of the problems of the members. The program content is subject to change at any time in accordance with the problems of the members.
7. That the adjustmental problems of members fall within the full continuum from common human problems to those caused by physical, social, emotional, and/or intellectual accidents, illness, or defects.

[17]For example: Grace Coyle, Group Work with American Youth (New York: Harper & Brothers, 1948), pp. 26–31.

Gisela Konopka, Group Work in the Institution (New York: Whiteside, Inc., 1954), p. 25.

Alan F. Klein, "Recreation and the Welfare Dollar," The Group, Vol. 17, No. 2 (December 1954).

Helen Phillips, Achievement of Responsible Behavior Through Group Work Process (Philadelphia: University of Pennsylvania School of Social Work, 1950), p. 2.

Harleigh B. Trecker, Social Group Work (New York: Whiteside, Inc., 1948), pp. 8–9.

Social Work Year Book 1954, op. cit., p. 480.

Wilson and Ryland, op. cit., p. 60.

[18]Klein, op. cit.

In other words the distinction may be found in the difference between the nature of the task-oriented group as compared to the growth-oriented group. In the former, the group-enabler's *primary* responsibility is to support the group to accomplish its task; in the latter, the enabler's *primary* responsibility is to help members to use the group experience to resolve problems which are interfering with their personal growth and their social adjustment.

Just as the principles and choice of techniques of working with any group are affected by the value system of social work, they are likewise affected by the more specific purpose of social group work service. Diagnosis is the core of practice. It is not sufficient to be well grounded in understanding the dynamics of human behavior.[19] The social group worker serving a "growth-oriented" group understands as much as he can about the specific problems of each member in the group he is serving. This involves a study of each individual to secure as much understanding of the meaning of his manifest behavior as the combination of accessible facts of his life experience and theory can provide. The study is continuous but the use of principles and techniques at a given time is determined by the result of the study at that time. Knowledge and understanding of the problems of the members determine (a) the techniques of using program content,[20] (b) the direction of the interacting process between members and between individual members and the worker,[21] and (c) the extent to which members can be helped to secure a feeling of belonging and acceptance of responsibility toward the group.[22]

During the thirty years in which we have been endeavoring to establish a conceptual frame of reference for the practice of social group work, we have been hindered by the variety of usage of the words "group work." It has become a *label* for a "catch-all" of functions rather than a term to designate professional service

[19]Wilson and Ryland, *op. cit.*, pp. 73–76, Chap. 4. Henry S. Maas, "Evaluating the Individual Member in the Group," in *Group Work and Community Organization*, 1953–1954, *op. cit.*

[20]Paul Gump, "Observational Study of Activities for Disturbed Children," in *Group Work and Community Organization*, 1953–1954, *op. cit.*

Paul Gump, "The 'It' Role in Children's Games," *The Group* (February 1955).

Juanita Luck, "A Study of Peer Relationships," *The Group* (February 1955).

Gladys Ryland in Wilson and Ryland, *op. cit.*, Part II, Chapters 6–10.

[21]Wilson and Ryland, *op. cit.*, The Fun Club (Children), pp. 352–369; The Glamour Girls (Teen Age), pp. 421–434; Heights Recreation Club (Young Adults), pp. 457–462; The Elite Woman's Club (Adults), pp. 493–514.

Henry Maas, "Personal and Group Factors in Leader's Social Perception," *Journal of Abnormal and Social Psychology*, Vol. 45 (January 1950), pp. 54–63.

[22]Wilson and Ryland, *op. cit.*, pp. 63–73; particularly chart, p. 68.

Saloshin, *op. cit.*

Phillips, *op. cit.*

with definite discrete meaning. It is currently used to describe (1) a job classification of workers, (2) a field of work, (3) a classification of agencies, (4) a philosophy or movement, in addition to (5) a method which was the original intent of the words. Attempts have been made by some of us to keep the original use of the term by adding the word *social,* and thereby indicate that social group work is a method used by social workers, professionally educated to use it as a specialized social service in a variety of settings.

It is, of course, self-evident that no sound conceptual frame of reference can be developed to apply to an area of work which covers everything and anything which might be included in the job load of a worker or the variety of occupational skills and techniques needed by agencies to fulfill their purposes. If social group workers are to practice from a commonly accepted conceptual frame of reference, the first step must be the acceptance of the limitation of the term as one descriptive of a specialized *method* of serving people in groups. The term does not describe other group methods which social group workers use in such functions as *administration* and its various work with boards and committees, *supervision* whether it be individual or group, *public relations*, or in work with the variety of groups which are part of the *community organization* responsibilities which every social worker carries. These other functions are no less important, but they are not the practice of social group work but rather of social work, and they take generic social work knowledge and skill which is essential to a social group worker in the performance of his total job, and they are functions common to all agencies, hospitals, and institutions providing social services.

In a paper presented to the National Conference of Social Work last year in San Francisco, Irving Miller discussed a possible dichotomy between social goals and the process of becoming professionalized. He says, "Inherent in the nature of professionalism is the development of technical skills and technical knowledge, preferably unique and distinguishable from other technical knowledges and skills . . . the demands and processes of professionalization seem at points to be in conflict with our social movement origins and tend toward conservatism and caution."[23]

It is important for us to recognize that all of social work has "social movement" origins. All social workers have an inheritance

[23]"A Critical Appraisal of Some Aspects of Social Group Work Theory and Practice," in *Group Work and Community Organization, 1955* (New York: Columbia University Press, 1955), pp. 70–71.

from the past and an obligation to the future to participate in the processes of social change which will "lessen the group tensions between the conflicting parts of society" and which will help to shape a society which purposefully aims to reduce the number of unhappy and maladjusted individuals in it.[24] To meet these obligations, we cannot sidestep, avoid, postpone, or leave to others the painful necessary intellectual task of the scholar, as well as of the practitioner, as we continue to develop the concepts, principles, and techniques of the social work profession and of the social group work specialization in it.

[24]Grace L. Coyle, *Group Work with American Youth* (New York: Harper & Brothers, 1948), p. 26.

The Group: In Life and in Social Work

Emanuel Tropp

There is a gnawing dissatisfaction among young people today with the directions that modern life is taking, and this dissatisfaction has burst forth vividly in the phenomenon known as the happening. Originally taking the shape of bizarre occurrences among the most avant-garde segments of the up-coming generation, the happening has been settling more widely into a pattern that has more far-flung significance, becoming a direct form of free human communication in a group. Young people have been saying that all the natural juices have been drained out of living —which has become packaged, planned, synthesized, controlled, and just plain dull. In their desire to be truly alive, our successors in the human enterprise are informing us that we have been guilty of, or accomplices to, the act of removing those precious ingredients in human relationships that make them spontaneous, natural, relaxed, unpredictable, and, therefore, exciting. The generation now in the saddle, which has prided itself on doing so much for mental health, has been accused of turning health into sheer, unrelieved boredom.

It is not surprising, then, that we find young people desperately seeking to find intimate groups in which they can share spontaneity, intimacy, dialogue, existential encounter—in other words, something that is really and truly happening, not the counterfeit they see all around them. They see their elders acting out community patterns with less and less conviction, in organizational

Reprinted with permission of the author and The Family Service Association of America from *Social Casework*, Vol. 49, No. 5 (May 1968), pp. 267-274.

forms that are shallow and futile and in a manner increasingly resigned and cynical. They sense a kind of giving-up by the older generation of any hope for satisfying and productive human relations. For themselves, however, they refuse to give up. They insist on the search for interpersonal and group relations that will combine meaning, vitality, and effectiveness.

The relevance of the seemingly far-out concept of the happening to the values and purposes of social work can be quickly seen. For the social work profession is committed to a central role of helping people cope more effectively with their interpersonal relations. And effective coping today emerges as a problem not only for sick or maladjusted or deviant people, but for just about everyone. Now, to help people cope, those close on our heels in the rush of time are saying: "Let us stop talking about it. Let us do it. Let us make it happen."

The Meaning of the
Happening for Social Work

There is something special about a happening that has a most important message, if one will only listen and hear. It is not a party, with scheduled games, prizes, and all the predictable niceties. It is a spontaneous set-to that gives people the chance to be authentically themselves, with all their strengths and their weaknesses, all their groping and their idiosyncracies, all their sense of wonder, and all their remarkable capacity to change and to grow and to contribute to one another—without Big Brother's having mapped it out fully in a master plan, in advance. To translate the message into social work terms: If one would help people in their social functioning, what better way to do it than to give them the opportunity to *make it happen*, not after they leave the agency, but while they are enjoying its hospitality, with the worker as part of the common enterprise, in groups in which they share with others some common concern.

Now what does this mean for the social worker's professional role? Does he take on the title of group therapist, with all the legerdemain, the mystique, and the glamour that supposedly accrue to this high position—a role that strikes fear into the hearts of many who contemplate it and yet has great appeal to others who see assuming it as an entry to a new secret order? What is the mysterious phrase *group therapy* all about after all? As we examine the current use of the term, it turns out to mean just about everything—and therefore nothing. To many, unfortunately, this thing called group therapy constitutes a strange process whereby a group leader arranges people in some complex preplanned pattern, puts them through their paces, and then proceeds to make the most miraculous things happen. Since everyone would like to be thought to have such magical powers, it has come to pass that all the uses of groups in social work today are being stirred and blended into some sort of representation of this one giddy alchemy, euphemistically called group therapy.

In the very act of looking at this "group therapy," one senses a sudden switch from the atmosphere of the happening—the freshness, the excitement, the drama of real life—to the atmosphere of the laboratory and the clinic. And though it may be valid to hold on to a somewhat clinical stance in a one-to-one relationship (though some are beginning to question this too), it should be clear now that to maintain this stance in the setting of the group is to destroy the essential value of the real-life event.

Carol Meyer recently asked why it was that audiences laughed at the social worker in the film "A Thousand Clowns."[1] At the risk of answering the obvious, it could be said today that the leading character in the film, in his off-beat way, represents the vibrant, alive qualities of the young generation and that any attempts by the social worker to deal with this lifelike quality by "interpreting" it as projection, displacement, and all the rest appear absurd. And such attempts will no doubt eventually be laughed into oblivion. An individual person facing a social worker's awesome arsenal of interpretations may be at a loss to cope with it or may learn, as Thomas Szasz says, to play the worker's peculiar game; but, in a group, real life had better be turned on if the *worker* wants to retain his mental balance.

The analyst Hyman Spotnitz describes his sense of wonder at the change that took place in him as he began to conduct group sessions. He says: " . . . the brighter atmosphere and more spontaneous emotional processes were at one and the same time more relaxing and more invigorating. The dramatic spirit of the interaction, the repartee and the intensity of the feelings coming to the fore made more of me come alive. . . ."[2] Marjorie Montelius also discusses how the group experience is a humanizing one for both the client *and* the worker.[3] Ludwig Binswanger refers to the same sort of experience when he speaks of the need of the analyst to become an "existential partner" of the patient,

[1]Carol H. Meyer, "Casework in a Changing Society," *Social Work Practice, 1966*, Columbia University Press, New York, 1966, p. 11.
[2]Hyman Spotnitz, *The Couch and the Circle*, Alfred A. Knopf, New York, 1961, p. 19.
[3]Marjorie Montelius, *Working with Groups: A Guide for Administration of Group Services in Public Welfare*, U.S. Department of Health, Education and Welfare, Washington, D.C., 1966, pp. 9–10.

on a common plane of human existence—two human beings trying to accomplish something together.[4]

Styles and Values in Social
Group Work

Today, in the arena of social group work theory, there are two
polar views, and various people take stands at stages in between.
There is Robert Vinter, at one end, who sees the group as the
means by which the worker can meet individual treatment goals
—carefully studied, diagnosed, and prescribed for each individual in the group—by unashamedly manipulating the group and
its members to achieve these highly particularistic and differentiated goals. In 1959 Vinter honestly faced a dilemma that he was
unable to resolve: If the natural forces of group life are the most
potent means for effecting individual change in the group, how
can the worker justify becoming deeply involved in controlling
and fragmenting the group process?[5] The truth is that this dilemma is probably unresolvable. The manipulative clinical stance
seriously weakens or destroys the very group forces that are so
potent. Such practice is not only self-defeating, because it violates
the nature of the medium, but also, understandably, productive
of undue anxieties among social workers who contemplate the
possibility of leading a group. To be able to juggle the complexi-
ties of many individual variables simultaneously with the com-
plexities of group relationships is indeed a superhuman undertaking—and it is really not even a desirable one.

At the other pole is William Schwartz, who has developed the
concept of the group as a system of mutual aid and who sees the
group and its living experiences as the crucial focus for the
worker.[6] He sees the worker and the members as engaged in a
common enterprise, that of carrying out the group's purpose. He
sees the individual members as growing essentially through their
group-oriented efforts. Now, Schwartz's position, vis-à-vis Vinter's,
holds within it something far more important than a technical
difference. It is a philosophical difference—the value orientation—that is strikingly at issue. To Schwartz, the group is not a
mélange of wholes and parts to be arranged, taken apart, put
back together, and generally manipulated by a social worker in

[4]See Floyd W. Matson, The Broken Image, George Braziller, New York, 1964, p. 238.
[5]Robert D. Vinter, "Small-Group Theory and Research: Implications for Group Work
Practice Theory and Research," in Social Science Theory and Social Work Research,
Leonard S. Kogan (ed.), National Association of Social Workers, New York, 1960, pp. 123-34.
[6]William Schwartz, "The Social Worker in the Group," in New Perspectives on Services
to Groups: Theory, Organization, Practice, National Association of Social Workers (for
National Conference on Social Welfare), New York, 1961, pp. 7-17.

accordance with his own goals for different individuals; to him, the group is an organic whole that develops a life of its own and an integrity of its own, which the worker had better respect if he is to be useful.

Have social workers not always said that their fundamental tenet was respect for the dignity and integrity of the individual? When dealing with a group, should they not embrace an analogous tenet, respect for the integrity of the group? The group is not an inanimate collection of nuts and bolts to be treated like a tinkertoy. There are very real group feelings, group attitudes, and group beliefs to which members develop deep ties, and, in fact, it is these very ties that make the group such a strong helping agent. Thus, respect for the integrity of the group is a *sine qua non* in social group work, and we must keep this kind of respect alive if we are to keep in mind what social work is all about. Is such respect not very much in keeping with the renewed respect for the balance of nature and the "wisdom of the body," for which we owe so much to Rachel Carson and Walter Cannon? Just as modern science is learning once again to help the body to mobilize its natural forces to heal itself, so we are again learning that the natural forces of the group hold the key to individual growth and that the worker's main role is to help the group use these natural forces.

Given these perspectives, can social workers still view a group approach mainly as a means of reaching more people at one time? If this were so, a group would be merely a kind of multiplication table. The real point is not that a group approach serves more people, but that it serves them in a very different way from an individual approach—and that is the root of what it is all about. Only in an orientation or information group meeting, where the same facts can be given at the same time to more than one person, can a group approach be seen as an economy measure. In most other groups, economy is an illusion, because group service is not of the same genre as individual service—and it is most often provided in addition to individual service, not in place of it.

Another view of groups is that they offer convenient stage settings in which one can watch the actors move around and thus learn more about them. While this may be so, it is hardly a valid reason for the use of the group method; it is an auxiliary gain, a lever to help, not the help itself.

When one gets down to the central core of what really happens that makes the group experience so meaningful and so useful, one discovers the simple truth that people with similar interests, similar concerns, or similar problems can help each other in ways that are significantly different from the ways in which a worker can help them in a one-to-one relationship. This is not to say that the group method is better—simply that it is different; and because it is different, it may be more effective for certain purposes. The key difference is that the members of the group take help from one another. And this is the way it has always happened in life: people have, from time immemorial, helped each other, sans benefit of therapy. Just as people do not have to be taught to breathe, so they move to help each other.

The Gifts of the Group and
Their Meaning for the Worker

To be in a group means to have the resources available to satisfy some of the most fundamental human needs. It means, first of all, belonging, which itself says a great deal, because all human beings have a deep need to belong, to others and with others. Belonging implies acceptance by others, and that acceptance is a basic kind of affection from one's fellow human beings. To be in a group also means having opportunities for self-expression under circumstances in which others can appreciate it, so that it becomes achievement and brings recognition—and these are great supporters and strengtheners of that precious feeling of self-worth so necessary for mental health. Finally, to be in a group means having the opportunity to experience that important communal balance of freedom and limitation, which is at the root of social responsibility, one of the hallmarks of social maturity.

The group is not only an alliance through which normal needs can be met; it can also be a natural healer of hurts, a supporter of strengths, and a clarifier of problems. A group may serve as a source of strength and support for those whose inner strengths have been weakened. It may serve as a sounding board for expressions of anxiety, hostility, or guilt. It often turns out that group members learn that others in the group have similar feelings weighing them down in their aloneness, that they are not so different or so alone—and learning this in live confrontation with one's peers is a most powerful change-inducing experience. In fact, one of the key virtues of the group method is that people are indeed readier to take help from one another than from a worker.

Further, in a group, one may discover that one does have differences from others and that one must contend with these differences in the process of group conflict and group criticism. As this is discovered, one may either affirm one's differences or see a necessity for changing. Thus, the give-and-take of group life can deeply affect one's attitude toward oneself and toward others. It leads to an increased capacity for objective judgment, increased self-control, clearer perspectives on one's own needs, greater acceptance and understanding of the situation in which one finds oneself, more effective use of the services being offered, and, finally, increased social responsibility and preparation for more effective living in the larger society.

Thus, if groups have the capacity, as systems of mutual aid, to help people in such fundamental and powerful ways, it behooves a social worker who wants to lead a group to view this phenomenon with the respect it deserves—not with fear or trembling as if faced with some mystique, but with a healthy appreciation of the central fact that people can and do help each other in vital ways through group experience, and that, if he wants to help people through the group method, he must learn how to help *groups* to be effective.

As the potential leader begins to see the real meaning of group life, it comes to him that his place in it is quite different from what he had imagined. He is not an observer, watching guinea pigs in an experimental cubicle. He is not a puppeteer pulling the strings of responsive but lifeless dolls to produce whatever motions he has deemed best for them. He is not a master planner feeding large masses of complex data about the group members into a computer that will inform him just what each member should do to solve his problem.

If he really knows and respects what a group is all about, he will see that *real* life is *really* happening and that he is *really* a part of it and that it is exciting and dramatic and unpredictable and wonderfully human in the ways in which spontaneous human beings can be when they are sparked by some common concern. Most stimulating of all, he will discover that he is, willy-nilly, a part of this real human drama and that he is not separated as a worker, but suddenly quite humanly alive in the group, in the spirit of the common undertaking. And then his role in this vital atmosphere becomes clearly that of helping the group as best he can to use its natural qualities of mutual aid to help its members.

In this very natural, very alive context of a genuine happening, the worker further discovers, much to his relief, that he need not quake in awe of his own amazing powers, that the group finds its own ways to make its life proceed, sometimes with him, sometimes against him, often despite him, and sometimes even to help *him* do his job. The group does not wait breathlessly for his every move. This does not mean that he is expendable, or unimportant:

it simply means he is not a god. His skill will be most effectively used in helping the group to be strong and to achieve its purpose and in helping individuals to play significant and satisfying roles in the process.

The Keys to Clarity: Purpose, Function, and Structure

All that has been said thus far may hold true generically with regard to most group approaches, but there are distinct and crucially important differences in basic group approaches that must be understood in order to know when to use which approach and when not to, and when one may blend approaches and when this is not feasible. To achieve such an understanding, one must look at the group's purpose, function, and structure.

The *purpose* of a group—why it is formed—is the principal element to be defined. It may be that the agency's idea of the group's purpose and the group's idea are not identical; but at the point at which they meet, an effective definition of the group's operational purpose can be found. If a group leader has not thought clearly about purpose, he will find himself drifting with the group into irrelevant, unproductive, and meaningless areas, into confusing situations and shaky operational patterns. Everything must start from the question that Schwartz keeps asking: "Why are we here?" And it is sound practice for the worker to keep checking himself against that question and to confront the group with it from time to time.

Having determined the purpose for which the group has been organized, the worker can clarify its *function*—what the group members are supposed to do to carry out that purpose. Are they gathered to discuss personal problems, or is it permissible for them to spend the sessions playing poker? Are they to be trained as homemakers, or can they change themselves into a winetasting club? Does anything go, or is there flexibility only within the bounds of purpose and function? If the worker is not clear about function, he will not be able to help the group conduct meaningful activities; for there is a world of possible group activities, but only some are relevant to any given group function.

Once the worker knows what a group is supposed to be doing, he can think clearly about *structure*—how the group will do it. If it is to be a training group, then someone has to be a teacher. If it is to be a social action group, then some form of self-government should be planned. If it is to be a counseling group, then a skilled professional discussion leader (of a special type) must be in charge. In each instance, the worker's role is different. A group can be effectively related to the realities of its existence only when it knows what its powers are and to what extent and in what ways they are limited by the leader. The group may be virtually self-directing, or the leader may exercise almost total control of its activities, or the group may operate in a realm between the two extremes. Too often group members are allowed to float in a sort of limbo, never certain whether the leader's assurances that it is really *their* group are true—and the leader, in fact, becomes uncertain after a while whether he really means what he says or not. The suppressed resentment of such a group at being either misled or confused or toyed with then becomes a new problem that the group *and* the leader could very well have done without. The worker may eventually have to spend several sessions clarifying the issue for the group, and thus the group and leader are both kept busy with an issue that is really not getting them anywhere except back to a better start.

Five Group Approaches

The *why* and the *what* and the *how* can be used for screening the five group approaches in common practice today. First, and perhaps simplest, is the *group education* approach. In its most rudimentary form, it may be a one-time assemblage of a group of people who all need the same information about an agency or institution, for example, at the beginning of their contact with it. We need not look condescendingly at work with such a group. A group of patients entering a hospital can gain much more than information from such a meeting. They learn that they are not alone. They see others like themselves. They experience the bond of physical closeness, of eye-to-eye contact, of sharing an experience. They gain some sense of security and identification and belonging and a sense of completion in that they have been told the terms of their contract. Even with an insensitive leader, there is something of value to be gained. But a sensitive leader who knows both the potential and the limits of such a group meeting can make the experience a truly helpful one to the patients by his way of handling the subject matter and by his expressions of empathy.

Such a one-time orientation program is not, of course, the only kind of group education. One of the most common forms, and distinctly more complex in regard to technique, is what has come to be known in family service agencies as family life education, which should not be confused with group counseling. A typical family life education program is made up of a relatively short series of lecture-discussions for a limited number of parents on a relatively specific subject, such as "How To Handle Your Adolescent Child." In such a program each session is usually started by a speech, a film, a playlet, a panel discussion, or some other device, after which there is discussion, conducted by the worker as group leader. The focus of the discussion is usually limited by the worker to a particular topic or closely related matters—"Should teen-agers be required to help with work around the house?" for example. Thus, the discussion is subject-oriented, not person-oriented. Group members who seek answers to private problems are appropriately directed to other resources, for it is not the function of the group to discuss intimate problems; the participants did not assemble for that purpose, and the leader is not prepared to work at that level. Still, in a family life education group there is considerably more interaction and involvement than in a group gathered for purely informational purposes, and so greater scope and depth.

The second group approach is known as *group counseling*. Firmly established today in family service agencies, child guidance clinics, residential treatment centers, public welfare agencies, and elsewhere, this approach is more individualized than group education. In the family agency, for example—by way of interesting comparison with the family life education model described earlier—a group of parents may be assembled to discuss the particular problems they are having as parents of adolescents. Usually these parents are selected for such a group from the caseload, whereas no problems are required as the ticket of admission to the education group and the members may not have had any connection with the caseload. And it is in this connection that the elusive distinction between purpose and function stands out most clearly. Whereas the parents in both groups would have the same general purpose (to discuss relationships between parents and adolescents), it would be the function of the educational group to discuss broad issues and the function of the counseling group to discuss the members' own very individual problems. In group counseling, a meeting does not start with a lecture, like an entertaining cultural night out; the point is to get right down to the specifics of the personal problems that brought the participants together. Discussion of broad issues may possibly become an evasion of the group's true function, whereas raising questions about one's own child is exactly in keeping with it—the reverse of the situation in the family life education meeting. In this context, it can be easily seen how the function of the group determines the role of the leader and the nature of the skills he needs. In the education group, he is conducting a general mental-health-oriented discussion, whereas in the counseling group he must be alert to the needs of the individual members and to the possibilities at hand for using their interaction helpfully.

The third approach, called *group psychotherapy*, is attended by the most confusion of all. In its essential form, as stated by its main proponents, it is a group method for the treatment of individuals with psychiatric disorders, and it aims at achieving basic personality change, which none of the other group approaches attempts. Whereas other group methods may seek to change behavior patterns, they make no claims to changing the basic personality structure. In group psychotherapy such change is accomplished through group discussion geared to the development of insight into the unconscious causes of behavior, the resolution of internal conflicts, and the modification of defense patterns. It is based on skilled handling of transference in depth, involving the use of fantasy, free association, and dreams and other unconscious material. It is a method that is generally used by professional people who are qualified, to begin with, to undertake individual psychotherapy—usually psychiatrists, sometimes clinical psychologists, and sometimes specially qualified social workers. What has created so much confusion is that some psychotherapists have conducted group sessions that have been no more than group education or group counseling and have labeled them group psychotherapy. To avoid such misconceptions, one must look at what is actually taking place—and use the phrase *group psychotherapy* most cautiously. Moreover, it should be remembered that group psychotherapy, whatever its advantages, also has its limitations; it is not appropriate for all occasions. And it should not be automatically considered the most advanced group method simply because it digs deeper into the psyche (or claims to do so).

Group recreation is the fourth approach. To many people, this seems to be the same as group work, simply because group work has unfortunately been associated by the public in the past with just playing games. However, the resemblance is really quite vague. In group recreation, participants engage in various play activities, under the direction of a leader. Group recreation tends to produce a relaxed kind of informal interaction; it stimulates interests; and it provides outlets for nonverbal expression and for the channeling of feelings. In some agencies a recreation approach is used with latency-age boys and called activity group therapy (although that may be conducted in the style of social group work).

Finally, there is *social group work*, one of the three basic methods of social work. In the course of applying this method, all the other approaches (except group psychotherapy) come into play as part of the total process. The social group work method aims at the full utilization of forces in group life to bring about social growth in the individual members. It is in the process known as group-goal-achieving that these forces are at their maximum, the members being most fully engaged with each other and with the group as a whole.[7] This process involves common decision and common action toward the accomplishment of common goals, shared by the members for the group as a whole. In the course of guiding this process, the group worker uses a variety of group experiences and program media, including social action, community service, and cultural, educational, social, and athletic activities. The group is involved in discussion and decision-making about the specific goals it wishes to achieve. It may also find itself, in the course of its life, discussing general matters of concern to its members or specific matters dealing with the problems of individuals, but these discussions will have arisen naturally out of the work the group has cut out for itself and the relationships that ensue. An example of the group work process in action is a ward council of patients in a hospital who meet to discuss the conditions in which they are living and to make recommendations to the hospital for specific improvements in policies and programs. The group work method thus includes, in addition to goal-achieving by the group, the dimensions of group recreation, group education, and group counseling, but any of these methods can be used separately.

Summary

This survey of the group, in life and in social work, has viewed it in a variety of contexts—the contemporary world of the happening; the innermost meaning of the group experience; the reasons for using groups in social work; the common human needs that are met in groups; the place of the leader in the group; the importance of purpose, function, and structure; and finally the diversity of group approaches. It started with a statement of basic conviction that *people can be helped to help each other;* this is the heart of the matter, and all else is commentary.

---

[7]For a more detailed treatment of this position, see Emanuel Tropp, "The Further Development of Group Work as a Separate Method," *Social Work Practice, 1966,* Columbia University Press, New York, 1966, pp. 44–53.

Social Group Work: A
Diagnostic Tool in Child
Guidance

Sallie R. Churchill

The treatment plan for each patient at the Pittsburgh Child
Guidance Center is based on an interdisciplinary diagnostic
evaluation. Traditionally such an evaluation includes a social history and a psychiatric and psychological evaluation of the child.
Two additional methods, a social group work evaluation of the
child and a family observation,[1] now are being used selectively.
This paper will discuss how diagnostic groups began at the clinic,
the types of such groups, preparation of children for the group,
plans for group meetings and observations made in the group.
Examples from clinical practice will be used.

Social group work as a diagnostic tool emerged to meet a clinical need. Group work is a treatment method frequently used
with school-age patients diagnosed as having neurotic, transient
situational and/or minor character disorders. Caseworkers, psychologists and psychiatrists needed diagnostic information about
such children and knew that this information was available in the
data from the treatment groups.

Disturbed peer relationships are among the most frequent
symptoms for which children are referred. Diagnosis of the problems of the child should include adequate data about peer
difficulties. The traditional model often fails to provide these. Our
reporters, parents, teachers and children themselves rarely give a
clear picture. Often they give conflicting reports. The individual
evaluations clarify why such problems arise in terms of intrapsychic stress but frequently fail to clarify how they are manifested
socially and how they create secondary social problems.

The group worker can provide additional information. For example, the group report may show that a child behaves in a grossly different manner with children, or with children and an adult,
than he did when he was seen individually. The group report can
confirm or may deepen other staff observations. It does complete
the diagnostic picture regarding peer relationships.

Though diagnostic groups seem an answer to an existing clinical need, the introduction of a new method is not always easy or
welcome. Resistance to change by some staff members, trainee

Reprinted with permission of the American Orthopsychiatric Association and the author
from *American Journal of Orthopsychiatry*, Vol. 35, No. 3 (April 1965), pp. 581–588. Copyright,
the American Orthopsychiatric Association, Inc.

[1]Drechsler, R. and M. Shapiro. *1961*. A procedure for direct observation of family interaction in a child guidance clinic. Psychiatry. *24*: 163–170.

difficulties in sharing patient responsibility, parental concern about missed school time and parental fear of group contagion occasionally can prevent placement of a child in a diagnostic group. If group work diagnosis is to be used with a child, the need for such an evaluation must be recognized by one of the professional workers and must be accepted by other staff members and trainees.

Diagnostic and Treatment
Groups in Diagnosis

The goal of the diagnostic group is to evaluate the problems of each member. The group serves as the milieu in which observations are made. The group process is the vehicle which provides observable experiences. The primary concern of the group worker is the individuals within the group rather than the group itself.

One social group worker selected a small, short-term group including no more than six members and meeting for no more than four sessions. A small group provides the greatest opportunity for the children to be involved in an interacting system, too few members for the children to assume such formal roles as team members and assurance to the child that he will not be overlooked in the crowd. To observe the process of group behavior a series of meetings is necessary, but there must be few enough to prevent the children from investing too much in the group experience itself.

Since observation of individual functioning within the group process is the primary task of the group worker in a diagnostic group, a carefully balanced group is not so necessary as in a treatment group, where the primary task is manipulating the group process. Children can be included in the same diagnostic group if there are no counter-indications regarding specific children being together. Severely bizarre, physically handicapped and retarded children are not accepted in diagnostic groups.

Two types of age groupings have been useful: (1) children within a two-year age range and (2) children who range in age over several years on a fairly continuous basis, provided that there is no more than one year's difference between any child and the child closest to him in age. The choice of grouping is based on the patient population.

Groups of one sex usually are best. Several diagnostic groups with both boys and girls have been tried. In general such groups split into two permanent subgroups with the boys in one and the girls in the other. This split seems to cut down the freedom of the children to interact in the group and to place marked limits on the bahavior manifested.

As the demand for group work evaluation of children has increased, temporary placement of children in ongoing treatment groups has been used for diagnosis. Placing a child in an ongoing treatment group requires careful evaluation of both the child and the existing group. Not all treatment groups can tolerate a new child nor can they tolerate the loss of a member without damage to the treatment process. It may not be possible to admit specific children to specific groups. For some children temporary membership in a treatment group is emotionally harmful, but they can benefit from being part of a group in which all members begin and end at the same time. In deciding to place a child in an ongoing treatment group, the primary concern of the group worker is with the welfare of the treatment group regardless of the need or readiness of the child to be diagnosed.

Preparation of the Child
for the Diagnostic Group

The child who has had trouble with other children usually finds a diagnostic group an easily comprehensible procedure. Peer relationship problems generally are painful to the disturbed child himself as contrasted to many other referral problems which cause pain to the school personnel or to his parents. A byproduct of the group diagnostic procedure has been to help a resistant child accept the interest of the clinic in helping him.

Both the parents and the clinic should prepare the child for the group experience. The caseworker interprets the group to the parents in the hope that they will explain the group to the child (but often they do not). The clinic preparation of the child varies according to the needs of the child, the preference of staff members, the point in the diagnostic procedure at which the group is introduced and the type of group being used.

When a diagnostic group is the initial clinic experience for all members, the preparation for the group is the responsibility of the group worker and can be done in the first meeting. He informally meets each child in the waiting room prior to the first meeting, introduces himself and then introduces the children to each other. Together all walk to the meeting room where the group as a whole is told the reasons for its existence and the basic rules. During the first session the worker explores with the children why they are coming to the clinic, including "what their parents have told them," and their concerns and fantasies about the clinic and group experience.

Since the group sessions may fall at any place in the diagnostic process, some children may have had previous clinical appointments. The total diagnostic procedure, including the group, should be discussed in the first interview with the child. Some staff members feel that this introduction should include an introduction to the group worker and/or a brief tour of the meeting room.

Many children show anxiety about entering a new group. The child's therapist or the group worker should explain to an anxious child the nature of the clinic group: a protected group with a worker who knows that the child has had trouble getting along with other children. The child who has had almost continuously disappointing experiences in peer relationships may frankly fear another unprotected group situation. It is necessary to help him see that group experience at the clinic will differ from group experiences he previously has had. Some therapists hesitate to use the group experience when a child expresses anxiety about it; they assume that his expressed anxiety is the problem without exploring the possibility that the child is expressing fear of something else, the nature of which he does not understand. When a child expresses extreme anxiety and reasonable efforts to clarify the nature of the protected group experience fail to reduce this anxiety, it is important to work out these feelings with the child. The group experience for this child may be temporarily dropped.

When a child is assigned to an ongoing treatment group, the group worker must have some direct contact with him individually before he is admitted. He must meet the group worker and see the meeting room. He should not be faced with a totally new situation in which all the other children are familiar not only with the room and the worker but with each other. The group members too need to be prepared for the new member. Generally they watch for the new child in the waiting room and initiate social intercourse before the group session begins. The group worker should observe this premeeting activity and be prepared to offer the new member support should it be necessary.

Group Planning

The diagnostic meetings are planned so that each child is exposed to specific emotional and social tasks and stresses. The series of four meetings permits an evaluation of the pattern of the child's behavior, his ability to maintain certain behavior and his adaptive ability. The functioning of each child in each group session is measured against expectations for children of his own age, sex and cultural group.

The following broad outline for the four sessions provides similar experiences for each group. The specific activities vary with age, sex and even the seasons of the year. In the first meeting the worker uses crafts, games and activities which are potentially highly interesting, provide opportunities for both individual and group activity and offer safe ways for constructive isolation. In the second session the worker increases the demand for peer interaction and the need for social skills, such as participation in group games or sharing of equipment. The degree of change and the pressure exerted by the program will be based upon an evaluation of individuals in the first meeting. Differential demands can be made upon each member within a small group and different demands are made upon different groups. In the third meeting the social behavior of the members is tested in the community outside the safety of the meeting room by a trip to the store, to the museum or the ball park. On this trip the worker will gain information about the ability of each child to handle such social tasks as crossing the street, watching out for pedestrians and the like. After the third session the group worker reviews his impression of each child with the rest of the diagnostic team. Together team members determine what the group worker needs to investigate further. The final session is planned so that the observations needed for each child can be made. During all four sessions the group discusses the purpose of the group, how the group is related to the total clinic procedure, how the members feel about coming to the clinic, how they view their own problems and what help they themselves want.

When a child is seen in an ongoing treatment group, the group worker has less freedom to adjust the content of group sessions to a standard pattern. Evaluation of the child is based on the child's ability to manage his experience within the existing group. In some ways the provocative behavior of the child may stand out more clearly. The breadth of specific experiences will be limited for a treatment group will have more cohesiveness and self-direction than a newly formed diagnostic group. In addition, the treatment group is likely to use group pressures to force the new member to adjust to its behavior.

In all diagnostic group sessions the social group worker plans to take an active role as a helping adult, supporting, interpreting, limiting and giving information as well as equipment. The role remains consistent throughout the four sessions and is made explicit to all members initially. The worker uses program to manipulate and to influence the group process, to produce demands for social skills and to reduce tension.

Collection of Data

Group diagnostic data are gathered clinically rather than in a standard research procedure. The group worker is a direct worker; that is, the intervener, limiter, enabler and the like. He is the planner and the provider. He selects the group members. He also is the diagnostic observer. Planning a specific milieu and program provides structure for the group sessions and permits a general range of observations similar from diagnostic group to diagnostic group but the actual activities in each meeting always are subject to limits and changes which are deemed clinically necessary. Within the group meeting the worker must be flexible with reference to the individual needs of each member.

The social group work report on a child provides clinical information. It is presented on a descriptive, impressionistic and interpretive level. The data are subjective. The group worker has been involved in the process which he is evaluating. He is observing emotions, reactions and interactions on both a quantitative and qualitative level. The date presented are selected by the group worker and related by him to what he perceived as the treatment needs of the patient. Often he predicts from the group sample of behavior to other social situations. For example, he reports how he believes a child will behave in other group situations.

Observations

What does a social group worker report? Primarily, his report is an evaluation of the pattern of behavior of a child in three areas: (1) relationship to other children, (2) relationship to an adult in the presence of other children and (3) the child's knowledge and use of social skills, for example, physical and developmental tasks and expected peer roles. These patterns of behavior are reviewed in several contexts: (1) initial approach to the group situation, (2) ability to change over a period of four sessions, (3) stresses which precipitate regression, (4) behavior which provokes unhappy or unpleasant reactions from others and (5) the child's reaction to group pressure. It is as important to observe the impact of a child's behavior on other children as to observe the child's behavior.

The group worker is trained to understand unconscious motivation determining behavior, but this is not the area of his diagnostic responsibility. His responsibility is to evaluate social functioning and to differentially assess the adaptability of the disturbed behavior, the clarity of reality-based reactions, the social hunger and the motivation for change. The group worker attempts to learn the nature of the social situations which cause a child to become less anxious or more symptomatic. Finally he tries to identify how the behavior of a child unknowingly provokes negative reactions to the child.

Specific examples of the observations the group worker makes can be enumerated, and two examples of diagnostic group work reports on two children seen in diagnostic groups can illustrate some of the points made.

The specific evaluation is made in terms of such patterns as interaction, reaction, provocation, modification and intensification. For example, in regard to the child's relationship to other children at the initial group meeting: (1) Can he show that he wants a relationship? (2) Can he accept friendly overtures? (3) Does he provoke feelings of protectiveness? (4) Under what situations can he relate and to whom? (5) Can he maintain relationships when tension is high? Or in his relationship to an adult in the presence of other children over the period of four meetings: (1) What is the pattern of relating to the group worker? (2) How does a child use the proffered relationship? (3) Is this a child whom adults like in a one-to-one situation yet who shows gross problems in the group when he must compete with other children for the attention of the adult? (4) Do his feelings toward the worker shift when the worker gives to, compliments or supports another child? (5) Do his dependency demands vary with the reality of the situation? In his knowledge of and use of social skills in the context of stress: (1) Can he accept appropriate roles in basic games? (2) Does he quit a game if another child gets a favorite role? (3) Will he disrupt activity when he doesn't want to play? (4) Are his social handicaps caused by lack of knowledge which can be remedied? (5) Do confused moral attitudes cause emotional rejection of activities?

Parts of group work diagnostic reports on two children seen in diagnostic groups illustrate how this theoretical analysis of observations into areas of relationship, contexts and behavioral patterns blends into an integrated whole when the behavior in the group of an actual child is described.

Sylvia is an eight-year-old Jewish girl referred to the clinic for sibling rivalry and conflict with parents. The caseworker requested a group diagnostic because Sylvia was in trouble whenever she was with other children.

As Sylvia entered the group, she acknowledged that there were difficulties with children, but did not admit to any part in any of these difficulties. She stated, "I don't have trouble with children; they have trouble liking me. If they tried harder, they could like me."

The most outstanding aspect of Sylvia's adjustment to a peer group was her tremendous use of denial. She lied with regularity. This was neither a protective measure nor one of confusion of reality. It seemed to be more a manipulating technique. Sylvia was constantly aggressively defensive. She immediately denied having done something whether she had done it or not; she instantly projected the blame to another child in the group. This was not a fearful denial of a child who anticipated she was at fault. Rather it seemed to be her major way of managing children.

Sylvia was an accurate observer of all that went on in the group. In any situation where it was possible she tattled. She was an astute observer of all rules regarding the other children. Whenever arguing a subject she would go back to the previous week, selecting distorted incidents to document her stand. Whether she was right or wrong, she attempted to out-argue each child on any issue which she created.

Sylvia was tremendously intrusive. She was jealous of any worker-child interaction or child-to-child interaction. She would intrude by joining, interrupting or distracting the worker or one of the interacting children. She had very few play skills and could only play if she were boss. The only "satisfactory" play experience she had was when she would offer to play with one child in a defiant effort to show an active rejection of another child. Although she showed phobic reactions to the elevator in her contacts with both her psychiatrist and her psychologist, the elevator caused no sign of fear in the group meeting, when she was competitive to see who got on first, who got off first or who pushed the most buttons.

Sylvia definitely wanted to be liked by the worker but she did not know how to go about it. She could not believe than an adult could be consistent. She never gave up the chance to win an argument, which she started, continued and then usually ended by having a temper tantrum.

In group discussion there was competition with the other children for the worker's attention. She gained this attention mostly by breaking group-room rules or doing something she knew the worker had specifically asked her not to do. If the worker ignored these infractions, Sylvia would bring them to the worker's attention, loudly stating she had not done it.

Sylvia found it impossible to share with the children. She never had enough. She could not share tasks, food, activities or attention. She ate a phenomenal amount of food. She had very few craft skills or activity skills. She was constantly verbally aggressive. She was extremely intelligent and could assess how to annoy people with tremendous skill.

The other children initially attempted to find a way to play with Sylvia. At first they seemed to want to be accepted by this bright little girl. Gradually they began to withdraw and allow her to isolate herself. By the fourth session they were complaining to the worker when they found themselves deprived of cookies, equipment or attention from the worker.

Second Case

Leon is a ten-year-old boy who was referred to the clinic for school behavior problems, immaturity and sibling rivalry. He was referred to the group for diagnosis by the psychiatrist who could not see the problems which the school and the parents complained about in his individual sessions. Leon's behavior was markedly different over the four-week period. In his initial approach to the group he seemed to reach out to play with the other children with a high level of social graces. He attempted to relate to the healthiest boy in the group. This lasted only half of the meeting. He challenged Mike to a game of chess which he played with great skill and craftiness. When he found that Mike was an equal competitor, he became disinterested and lost on purpose. He was aloof from the other boys and looked disdainfully at them in their participation in the active games of tag and dodge-ball. He refused to participate in refreshments because the food was not kosher, yet he "stole" cookies several times.

In the second and third meeting Leon seemed to be tense and anxious. He was asked to play games by the other boys but would participate only in table games. Whenever intelligence played a factor, he could beat the boys easily. When forced to play a game of luck or physical skill, he became impatient and usually quit. He began to tell the boys that their games were stupid and he didn't want any part of their crazy games. He began to try and test the boys' intellectual knowledge by asking questions regarding math, chemistry and history. By the fourth session he could make no attempt to play with the other boys. He was no longer asked to play, yet he could not stand the isolation and tried to keep contact with the other boys by poking fun at them. He ate an enormous amount of cookies. He refused to sit down and eat with the boys because they "hated him."

With the worker Leon kept his distance. Any direct interaction with the worker seemed impossible for him. His only direct approach to the boys was when he wanted them to communicate with the worker for him. This included such obvious behavior as asking one of the boys to ask the worker if Leon could go to the men's room.

Summary

This paper reports on social group work as a method used to diagnose disturbed children at the Pittsburgh Child Guidance Center. It shows how the need to understand the social behavior of children led to the use of diagnostic groups. The kind of groups used, the preparation of the children, and the planning for these groups are described. Finally data made available through group work diagnosis are discussed and illustrated.

Bibliography

(The following are articles or books which could provide additional information about social group work and social group work in child guidance clinics.)

1. Churchill, S. R. 1959. Prestructuring group content. Social Work. 4: 52–59.

2. Coyle, G. 1948. Group Work with American Youth. Harper and Row, Publishers. New York, N. Y.

3. Ganter, G. and L. Irons. 1955. The coordination of group work and casework. Amer. J. Orthopsychiat. 25: 138–147.

4. Ganter, G. and N. A. Polansky. 1964. Predicting a child's accessibility to individual treatment from diagnostic groups. Social Work. 9: 56–63.

5. Jones, H. Mimeographed reports on the Newton Baker Project. Judge Baker Guidance Center. Boston, Mass.

6. Konopka, G. 1963. Social Group Work: A Helping Process. Prentice-Hall, Inc. Englewood Cliffs, N. J.

7. Konopka, G. 1949. Therapeutic Group Work with Children. University of Minnesota Press. Minneapolis, Minn.

8. Schwartz, R., G. Patterson and E. Von der Wart. 1956. The integration of group and individual therapy. Amer. J. Orthopsychiat. 16 (3): 618–629.

9. Vinter, R. 1959. The essential components of social group work practice. Mimeographed paper. University of Michigan, School of Social Work. Ann Arbor, Mich.

10. Wilson, G. and G. Ryland. 1949. Social Group Work Practice. Houghton Mifflin Co. Boston, Mass.

The Group Process in Helping Parents of Retarded Children

Arthur Mandelbaum

When parents are confronted with the fact that their child is retarded, they often enter a period of mourning and grief, accompanied by emotional isolation and loneliness. They feel like exiled aliens in a world that has turned suddenly and unexpectedly cruel and harsh. Such loneliness, tinged with vague, obscure, and little understood feelings of guilt and shame, tends to lead to silence. Communication becomes unbearably difficult and isolation increases.

The human spirit, however, with its vast capacity for enduring stress, develops inner defenses and methods of dealing with sorrow. One human attribute is restlessness, a refusal to be content with the world as it seems. Parents of retarded children have a way to express their discontent, their wish for creative action, by joining together in an association of parents of retarded children. The purpose of such an association is to sustain and strengthen individual parents who are trying to handle similar problems and, thus, to halt the unbearable feelings of being alone and isolated. By thus joining together, parents not only meet important needs they have in common, but also use their collective strength to help their retarded children. They organize and build day-care

Reprinted with permission of the author and the U.S. Children's Bureau from *Children*, Vol. 14, No. 6 (November-December, 1967), pp. 227–232.

facilities and training centers, urge the public schools to include special classes for retarded children, raise money for research, and persuade legislatures to pass laws aimed at improving State institutions.

All these efforts have salutary effects—the parents emerge from their isolation, and services for retarded children improve. But what of the parent's interior life, their inner feelings? As Bernard Cohen has noted, "the stability of the interior environment is the condition of free life."[1] How can such troubled parents be helped to find inward stability and freedom?

One way found to be effective in helping such parents come to terms with themselves is to bring them together in small selected groups under the leadership of a professional person who can help them share common educational, social, and emotional experiences in a way beneficial to each member of the group.

The following analysis of the process that takes place in such groups is based on my experience as a social caseworker who has worked with several small groups of parents of retarded children in the past 7 years—some made up of mothers and fathers, some of mothers only. The groups met once a week for 1½ hours each session. Some groups ran for six sessions; some for 10 or 12 sessions; some, even longer. The members of the groups themselves determined how long they needed to continue meeting together.

The group process is used to help each member to bring forth his concern, anger, and thoughts so that gradually his strength comes to the fore and he can use it more creatively and independently in handling the social and emotional problems stemming from his child's retardation. If the group members can express both their positive and negative feelings and the leader is not critical, hostile, authoritative, or judgmental and is skillfully able to ease communication, then each can grow through the experience. As each member gradually gains more knowledge of himself and of the others in the group, he expresses himself with greater freedom and spontaneity. He learns his wife has feelings he did not know she had and had not recognized in himself. He also learns that she and others have feelings that he thought existed only in himself. He begins the difficult task of learning to listen to *others* talk about *their* feelings, not only to himself. He listens to ideas expressed in a continuous, evolving process and gradually becomes aware of the intense feelings behind them and of how little he knew of this before. He may then come to understand some of the sources

[1]Cohen, Bernard: In the foreword of "An introduction to the study of experimental method" (Claude Bernard). Dover Publications, New York, 1957.

Group Work

of his own angry feelings and to sense that they are rooted in irrationality, disillusionment, and failure to realize his dreams.

Some Themes

Perhaps the most significant aspect of a group process is the opportunity it gives the parent to further resolve his grief. This is necessary before the parent can release his capacity for profound understanding. As Solnit and Stark have said:

Coping with the outer reality of a child with a congenital defect and the inner reality of feeling the loss of a desired normal child requires a great deal of mental work. Such psychic work is slow and emotionally painful, and it proceeds through the gradual and repeated discharge of intense feelings and memories. These mental and emotional reactions enable the parent to recognize and adapt to the reality of the retarded child.[2]

In many young or comparatively young parents who have the major part of their lives still ahead, the trauma they experienced when they first learned of their child's mental defect remains a raw wound.

Mrs. A. spoke dramatically of a dream she had had several months before the birth of her child. In the dream she climbed up to a balcony and then dropped the baby over, shattering him to bits.

Several persons in the group gasped, and several other mothers said quickly that they too had had premonitions of disaster before the birth of their children.

Mrs. A. said that while she was pregnant she had seen a TV program concerning the mercy killing of a mongoloid baby. She recalled being greatly upset and thinking, "How dreadful if my baby would be like that." She described her feelings when she learned that her baby was "like that": "I was in shock, I couldn't believe it, I couldn't think."

Mrs. E. told of an experience her sister-in-law had had with an impersonal and busy doctor. His way of letting her know of her misfortune was to remark casually as he left her hospital room, "You have a retarded child."

A shocked silence followed. Mrs. F. said softly, "I imagine it must be hard for the doctors also."

After some moments of further discussion, the worker asked whether the parents thought it was hard for a doctor to tell parents they had a retarded child.

Mrs. G. said her doctor had tried to tell her a little every day about her baby's condition. She thought he was afraid she might not be able to take it. Finally one day she said to him, "For goodness' sake, tell me the truth." He did. Her husband, who already knew, brought her books on the subject. But that proved to be the wrong thing to do. Her husband meant well, but some of the books contained wrong information.

[2]Solnit, A. J.; Stark, M. H.: Mourning and the birth of a defective child. *In* The psychoanalytic study of the child, vol. 16. (Ruth S. Eissler et al., eds.). International Universities Press, New York. 1961.

Mrs. B. said she also read books about retarded children; some of these books were sentimental and phony, but, "I did learn a little about the subject."

Mrs. C. shrugged, "I was in shock, but I got over it right away."

Mrs. G. laughed in a challenging, anxious, skeptical way. Mrs. C. insisted, "But I did. I realized it was not too bad to have a blind child because they can do many things for a blind child. I didn't know then he was also retarded."

Mrs. D. said that for a long time her doctor did not know about her child's condition because "doctors still don't know many things."

Mrs. G. described how hard it was for her to tell her mother about her child's condition. Tears came to her eyes as she related how both she and her mother wept. This led her to talk about how the child cried almost incessantly. She said she needed to keep faith in God.

Some parents express their fear of having more children and their envy of other parents:

Mrs. A. said that when she sees other couples having healthy babies, a pain hits her; she thinks she is jealous. Mrs. B. said she is jealous, too, but that she knows it is wrong to have such feelings.

The discussion then turned to parents who have normal children and complain about them or abuse them. The feeling that "they do not know how lucky they are" was expressed vehemently and often.

Some themes, common to all discussion groups of parents of retarded children, are introduced with insistent force early in the group process: feelings of isolation, of loneliness, and of inability to communicate with others are quickly recalled.

Many parents tell about how impossible they found it to speak to anyone after the shock of learning about their child's condition. It seemed to them then that there was no one available to listen, at least no one capable of understanding. Professional people could not understand—they seemed, in a sense, like the parents themselves, human, fragile, fearful, lacking the courage to face the problem, to speak about it, to talk honestly, directly, and kindly. As outsiders, they could not *really* understand.

Then the parents begin gradually to bring up their feelings of anger and frustration, forbidden, dreadful feelings that produce a sense of guilt they have tried to control or deny. Some parents think that perhaps the angry feelings within themselves have a magical power and may have impaired the fetus at conception or during gestation. Some wonder whether their child's retardation is not a punishment from God because of their past sins, or whether God has not blessed them by giving them a retarded child as a symbol of innocence, purity, and holiness.

Parents always express these thoughts about God tentatively, with awe toward mysterious, seemingly irrational forces and at the same time with bitterness, irony, and doubt. The question persists: "What did I do to have had this happen to me?"

Feelings Toward the Children

Feelings toward the retarded children gradually emerge. Some parents see the children as grotesque objects to be hidden from public view and from friends and relatives. As such feelings come to light, they become attached to the parents' self-image. The parents feel inwardly grotesque and are afraid of being regarded as genetically imperfect, contaminated, and inextricably identified with the damaged child.

Mrs. Z. said angrily that before her retarded child was born, her mother-in-law boasted that among her 14 grandchildren there was "not one crooked finger."

Mrs. Z. said with a laugh that she thought there was a little of the mongoloid in all of her other children too, as several of them had the simian line and blunted fingers. After the birth of the retarded child, her mother-in-law would not go near him. She suggested that the Z.'s place the child in an institution and was disappointed when they took him home. Once when the father was going to visit a relative, she urged him to take one of the normal children along so that "they could see you are capable of having normal children."

As the parents describe the cruelty of others toward them in their misfortune, many reveal their own harsh and punitive views of themselves. These are gradually modified by the gentle, kind, perceptive judgments offered by other members of the group.

Mrs. S., in an angry voice, told about taking her retarded daughter to a party and, after leaving her side for only a few minutes, being accused by the child of trying to abandon her. Mrs. J. described her embarrassment when she took her retarded son to get a haircut and he tried in his jumbled speech to talk with the barber. Mrs. V. told how *her* son had run excitedly into the living room speaking incoherently when the family was entertaining company. When she tried to calm him down, he had become so excited that she had to send him to the basement. Mr. and Mrs. F. admitted rather shamefacedly that they never took their daughter anywhere because she was so obviously retarded. Mrs. S. confessed that when she took her daughter anywhere she had a strong impulse to shout, "She's a retarded child!" and had real difficulty in controlling it. The group, shocked, fell silent.

The worker pointed out that all the parents apparently had these feelings of embarrassment and discomfort and asked what understanding, what thoughts they had about them.

Mrs. F. said "shame and humiliation." She said she felt like hurling something at them, those who looked at the child, those who thought she was different; she wanted to attack them and defend her child. Mr. V. said "resentment and anger" for having such a child. Mrs. E. said, "I want to say to them, well, what are you looking at?" Mrs. T. said, excited-ly, "I used to do that, think that. I used to stare at them, but now I avert my eyes." Mr. F. said, "I am guilty of that, too. Inside you feel inferior, ashamed."

Mr. T. said they had left their daughter Betty at a party that night with great apprehension, for they had never left her at a party before. "My mind is there while I am talking," he said. "Betty talks, talks, talks. The people we usually leave her with when we come here are out of town. It is important to come here; we have never talked about our feelings about her with anyone else before, never even with relatives or friends." Mr. F. said, "We come here for the child as well as ourselves."

Mr. E. said he wondered whether all these feelings we were talking about were not due to the hurt inside the parents. The child, he thought, does not suffer so much as the parents. Mr. T. agreed, "It is because you feel there is something wrong with you that you should have a retarded child."

Mrs. F. spoke of knowing a 19-year-old retarded boy whose parents take him everywhere. "Maybe it is our fault when our child embar-rasses us. Maybe he picks up our feelings about him."

Eventually, the group enters a period of alternating grief and solace: themes of loss and death alternate with themes of how gentle and lovable retarded children are and the solace they offer the family. The parents' fears that the children might die are based on reality, for many retarded children have other con-genital defects that add to the difficulty of caring for them and fill their parents' days and nights with apprehension.

The parents praise each other's children, and during the ex-pression of such positive feelings they slowly venture to speak of their anger and fright at the persistent intrusion of intense death wishes. Many say in effect, "Having a retarded child is like having a death in the family, only worse; at least you can get over a death, but this is never behind you. You have to live with this—for the rest of your life."

When the group members become aware of the intense feel-ings this theme arouses, they move away from it. Many indicate they do not want to look ahead very far. Groups are often quite free from expecting false assurances and are quick to challenge platitudes. The retarded child is an inescapable reality. The fu-ture is feared because the child must surely present more difficul-ties as he grows; his faults and defects will be magnified. Some parents express the wish that the child will remain an infantile love object to be cuddled and pampered, of whom little need be demanded. Conversely, some parents note that in remaining like an infant the child will be an ever-increasing burden, tyrannical in his need for attention and care.

Each parent in a couple seems to fear that the other will be drawn to the retarded child so strongly that all others in the family will be neglected. This leads to anger and a sense of guilt in an alternating repetitive cycle.

Parents often screen their doubts and misgivings about the extent to which they might express their innermost thoughts in the group with expressions of concern about what to tell their other children, relatives, friends, and other persons in the community. However, parents frequently say they feel both relieved and surprised after they *have* expressed a strong negative feeling or fear. They wonder that they have been able to say things in a group that they had never been able to say to a husband or wife or a best friend. Their feeling of relief, however, is soon followed by further doubts and fears of revealing deeper feelings.

So great is the need among such parents to protect their self-esteem that a group sometimes subtly divides into sections: one, parents of children who are only mildly or moderately retarded and have only slight or no physical defects; the other, parents of children who are severely retarded or whose retardation is also apparent in their physical appearance, as with mongoloid children.

Signs of Strength

Each member of the group feels defeat, but many have also had experiences that have given them a sense of victory—moments of small triumph whose import they feel the "outside world" is not equipped to understand. For example, a parent may say, "Our retarded children are different; we can shed tears together. But we are alert to and take pride in every sign of small improvement in them. Every slight step forward, which would be unnoticed in our normal children, is a major triumph in the handicapped child."

The group members usually identify with one another in an intense and binding fashion. They seem to feel that since their children are unusual, they themselves are unusual also and belong together. Sometimes they are united against the "outside world"; sometimes against the leader of the group, a representative of that outside world.

Mrs. T. said that for 2 years she would not admit to herself that her child was retarded. She recalled the first doctor she had consulted about the child, and she said she hated him. Mrs. N. suggested that perhaps Mrs. T. hated the doctor because he was the first person to tell her about her child's retardation. Mrs. T. agreed. The discussion then became heated as the group members spoke of doctors, how they were told about their child's handicap, and their need for someone to talk with.

For the first time, two or three parents spoke at once. The worker, raising his voice slightly to be heard, pointed out that the parents were saying three important things: first, that the doctor, by giving them the diagnosis, had hurt them; second, that the doctor had failed to help them in the way they had wanted at the time of their first deep shock; third, that they had found consolation in talking with others with the same kind of problems through the parents' association and that outsiders did not understand and could not help very much.

The parents agreed to this. Then the worker pointed out that several times previously he had tried to get into the discussion but that they had been so intent on getting their points across that he had not been able to do so. He asked whether they were aware of this and, if so, whether they could understand why.

Mr. P. quickly said, "You are an outsider, too." The worker said he thought this was an important point. Mrs. T. pointed out that one of the "professionals" on the staff of the parents' association was supposed to attend a meeting of the school board but had been "too busy" to do so. If he were a parent of a retarded child, he would have been there, she added, but professionals did not have the same kind of concern as parents. Mrs. N. said that the man's absence probably had nothing to do with his being a professional person; even some parents had to be pushed to attend meetings.

When the group session ended, the parents remained standing outside the building as the worker drove away. Mrs. S. waved goodbye, saying, "You see, we are going to continue outside in the cold."

As the discussion explores the labyrinth of feelings, the parents grope toward mature ways of viewing behavior in an attempt to find a value system that is right for them, one that will sustain and nourish them. They support one another, bring out feelings for the scrutiny of the group, question irrational ideas, point up the inefficiency and dubious value of certain kinds of behavior, and gradually increase the ability of each person in the group to look realistically at the problems presented by his retarded child and ways of dealing with them. The worker must have faith in the inherent ability of the individual parent to release his capacity to do this—a capacity previously blocked by anger, conflict, and fantasies. If he does not have such faith, he will intervene hastily in the group's discussion and become authoritative and didactic, and in doing so dilute the emotional intensity of the experience for the parents.

The Leader's Role

Using the group process to help parents is an increasing clinical practice in service to the mentally retarded. The worker who attempts the process must be skilled in dealing with persons in one-to-one interviews, *preferably before* he attempts to deal with them in groups. If he chooses the group method because he is discontent with the one-to-one method, he should know that in trying to help individual parents through the group process he takes on a task of greater complexity, one requiring an understanding of the dynamics not only of individual behavior, both normal and abnormal, but also of the behavior of groups. If he is discontent with the slow, cautious movement in the one-to-one process and expects a more rapid progress in working with a group, he will be disillusioned. In either method the worker must be aware of the recurrent nature of grief in parents of retarded children and of the adhesive quality of their inner conflicts. He must know that he will win the group's confidence and trust only after repeated trial and error and that each member of the group grows at his own pace.

It is tempting to use the group meeting to teach parents facts about mental retardation, to answer their questions about their children, and to discuss at length the reasons for their children's slow development. Listening and observation, however, will quickly show the worker that many parents in the group are very well read on the subject of retardation and that some have become learned on specific aspects of the problem and are much closer to being masters of the subject than the worker. Instead of teaching, the worker helps the parents deal with their inner problems by using his knowledge that sorrows can be borne if they can be put into words or into a story; can be absorbed or dissolved if they can be expressed in words to those who face the same inescapable adversity and who wish to examine that adversity as it affects their inner selves. His task is to help the parents see the import of what they are saying and feeling as the discussion weaves back and forth between the way individual members feel about being parents of a mentally retarded child and how and what they understand about their world, themselves, and each other.

To the group the worker is an outsider. As the parents speak about professional people not understanding, about their treating parents abruptly and harshly and not helping in the way the parents want and expect, the worker must use the strictest self-discipline to control his anger, for it becomes clear that the parents also consider him an outsider incapable of helping them and unable to understand their feelings because he has not had the same shattering experience as they.

The worker is like a screen against which are projected the parents' feelings toward all outsiders as critical, uncaring, judgmental, and punitive. He represents all authoritative figures who have failed to protect the parents from an irrational and malignant fate, who will not give answers, and who force them to think for themselves.

"Will no one give us answers to our grief, will no one hear us?" The cry, at first silent, is soon voiced more and more. The language of the group is commonplace. It is concerned with the ordinary aspects of experience, but suddenly, and sometimes without warning, it slips into expressiveness or expressions that give the speakers themselves a shocking glimpse into their deeper feelings—

"Do you ever get over it, the depression, I mean?"

"I felt that being around friends who were pregnant was like some curse."

"What did I ever do to have had this happen to me?"

"Sometimes, I wish he had died at birth; the doctor should have killed him and not told me."

"When I did bring the baby into the store, the clerks all admired her and cooed. I wondered whether they knew she was retarded and they did that just to please me. Then, when I didn't bring the baby, they asked about her. I felt guilty and wondered whether I had left her home because I was angry. Maybe the fact is, I'm too sensitive."

The conversation is sometimes drab, superficial; the speakers grope to convey information, search restlessly for contact, for understanding, for an illuminating explanation of the myths, theories, and conflicting beliefs about retarded children. In this search they express fear that the worker will see them as damaged, inferior, and ill and will not see their strength. Then, of course, they hesitate as though wondering how much it is safe for them to see and understand.

They become angry and seem to feel that the group process means they are to devote their lives and their dreams exclusively to the retarded child, to the neglect of their other children and themselves.

They seem to wonder: Are they in bondage? Will the worker let them go? If they express the full measure of their thoughts, their anger, will they be able to control those feelings after they leave the group and do not have each other for support?

They seem to wonder, too, about the worker and his relationship to them: Will he, because of the intensity of their concern and anger, become overburdened and ill? Is he preoccupied with his work, too professional, insensitive, and unobservant to know how they really feel? When a meeting is canceled because he has to be away, where does he go and to whom does he give the words of wisdom that he is denying them? How can they make him do their bidding and gain mastery over him so that he can gratify them more?

These and other questions the parents sometimes ask directly, sometimes imply in their questions or statements about their retarded children, their families, and their lives outside the group.

But little by little they delve beneath the cliches and superficial questioning to deeper layers of meaning until they can see the hitherto undreamed of nature of their own true feelings.

Time and time again, parents express surprise about their former narrow views of their families, other people, and the institutions of society and what needs to be done about them. They also express hope about finding ways to handle the tasks ahead of them.

The end of these sessions is like the termination of a voyage. The passengers have come together; have talked, laughed, cried, struggled to share feelings and to achieve deeper, wider understanding of themselves and their children. They have formed close friendships. Now it is time to say goodbye.

The members of the group express regret that the group cannot continue in its present form. They express fear of letting go of something that has been helpful and of being alone again. Each member, however, as a member of the larger association of parents of retarded children has an opportunity to help formulate and work in behalf of retarded children. Having, through the group process, focused his attention on himself and on others in a series of interactions in which he both gained insight and lost some of his exclusive preoccupation and self-interest, he is the more ready for social action. For as Aldous Huxley has noted, "The more inward we are, the more we may undertake outward activities; the less inward, the more we should refrain from doing good."[3]

[3]Huxley, A.: The devils of Loudon. Harper & Bros., New York. 1953.

The Crisis Group: A New Application of Crisis Theory

Martin Strickler
Jean Allgeyer

Over the past few years social workers have become increasingly interested in crisis theory and intervention. Crisis-oriented clinics and services attached to social agencies are being established in mounting numbers in conjunction with the growing emphasis on prevention. Furthermore, the need has been created for additional information so that theory may be applied to definitive treatment.

Reprinted with permission of the authors and the National Association of Social Workers from *Social Work*, Vol. 12, No. 3 (July 1967), pp. 28–32.

The Benjamin Rush Center in Los Angeles, California—a multidisciplinary, community-based, walk-in crisis clinic—acknowledged this need and thereby sponsored a pilot study in 1965 to develop and test the feasibility of a new type of group instrument that would make use of modern crisis theory.

This study, using key concepts of crisis theory, was a collaborative effort by the authors who designed and implemented the operation of one short-term test group of people in crisis and evaluated its performance over a six-month period. The special function of this group required a radical departure from the usual group treatment model. Much consideration had to be given to the unique role of the group therapist and the dynamics of the group process in this new modality. Also, the group instrument had to be so structured that it would lend itself to the characteristic phases of crisis resolution and thereby facilitate working through of the crisis.

The results of this study were gratifying—the majority of patients made obvious and often dramatic progress. Moreover, the crisis group was accepted as the model for the group program now used by the center in its community-wide service as well as in its Venice branch, which serves primarily minority groups and the hardcore poor. By these means, more people now can be offered crisis help than was heretofore possible.[1]

Admissions Policy

The membership and structure of the pilot group reflected the admissions philosophy of an adult walk-in service—an inclusive intake approach as well as limited treatment period. The only criteria for denying application for treatment at the center are age (17½ and up) and whether a patient is in treatment elsewhere. Therefore, no person is excluded because of severe pathology or marginal treatability—crisis treatment is problem-solving not pathology-oriented. There is a maximum of six weekly interviews for individual and conjoint treatment and the pilot group was designed with the same time limits.[2] This particular time limit coincides with the findings of Caplan and others that a crisis is resolved for better or worse in four to six weeks.

In the pilot group, however, it was found necessary to exclude two other categories of people—those so seriously suicidal or

[1]Martin Strickler, Ellen B. Bassin, Virginia Malbin, and Gerald F. Jacobson, "The Community-Based Walk-In Center: A New Resource for Groups Underrepresented in Outpatient Treatment Facilities," *American Journal of Public Health and the Nation's Health*, Vol. 55, No. 3 (March 1965), pp. 377–384.
[2]Martin Strickler, "Applying Crisis Theory in a Community Clinic," *Social Casework*, Vol. 46, No. 3 (March 1965), pp. 150–154.

homicidal that they needed the high degree of therapeutic attention of individual crisis treatment and those displaying severely
impaired ability to communicate (i.e., psychotic individuals unable to relate or patients unable to communicate in English). The
presence of acute anxiety, depression, or psychosis was not in itself a reason for exclusion. The patient could choose individual
treatment over the crisis group treatment if he preferred, but this
occurred infrequently.

Therefore, the pilot group was a heterogeneous one in age,
ethnic, sociocultural, intellectual, and diagnostic characteristics.
Because patients resolve their crises at different speeds, an open-
ended group was necessary, which led to changing kinds of
patient interactions and group constellations.

The pilot group served thirty patients over the six-month test
period with an average weekly attendance of four to five. The
size of the crisis group in each session varied from four to eight
members with five to six considered the optimum number for
treatment purposes. The weekly attendance fluctuated, depending on the number of new walk-in patients requesting treatment
and ongoing patients actively involved in the process of crisis
resolution. The therapist regulated the maximum attendance by
the number of pregroup interviews scheduled per week.[3]

Theoretical Aspects of
Crisis Intervention

The therapeutic task is to treat individuals experiencing disturbances based on various crises. Research has found that the
particular type of disturbance associated with crisis is not, in itself,
an illness.[4] Rather, crisis is a condition that arises when an individual faces an obstacle to important life goals that his coping
mechanisms cannot deal with satisfactorily.[5] (Coping mechanisms are those aspects of ego functioning designed to sustain
psychic equilibrium by regulating and controlling the intensity of
anxiety-producing perceptions of real or fantasied external dangers that involve loss or threat of loss.)

When the homeostatic balance is upset, a high level of tension
is generated and the person is considered to be in crisis.[6] A crisis
occurs only if the individual senses that he does not possess

[3]Since the pilot study the clinic has increased the number of pregroup interviews per week
from one to two per group to enlarge the over-all group size. However, group attendance will
always vary with the number of walk-in patients requesting treatment at any given time.

[4]See, for example, Lydia Rapoport, "The State of Crisis: Some Theoretical Considerations,"
Social Service Review, Vol. 36, No. 2 (June 1962), pp. 211–217.

[5]Gerald Caplan, Principles of Preventive Psychiatry (New York: Basic Books, 1964).

[6]Howard J. Parad and Gerald Caplan, "A Framework for Studying Families in Crisis," Social
Work, Vol. 5, No. 3 (July 1960), pp. 3–15.

available means of coping with the hazard, which is seen consciously or unconsciously as a vital threat to his narcissistic, libidinal, or dependency needs and supplies.

The crisis state, although dangerous because usual ways of coping are ineffective and there is vulnerability to further ego disorganization, offers adaptive opportunity as well. A unique opportunity exists for the person to be challenged and motivated to attempt different solutions to his current problem.[7] Moreover, since the threat that triggered the crisis most likely occasioned previous stress reactions, he has another chance to learn to cope with this repeated threat.

An adaptively resolved crisis is one that will restore the individual to a new psychic equilibrium with an enlarged coping repertoire to deal adequately with the kind or degree of threat that precipitated the current crisis. Conversely, resolutions that are of a stopgap, unrealistic nature may soon lead to intrafamilial conflicts and to the development or intensification of neurotic or psychotic symptomatology.

The goal of crisis intervention is preventive, since the outcome can be affected significantly by the presence of timely help. As Caplan states: "A relatively minor force, acting for a relatively short time, can switch the balance to one side or another, to the side of mental health or the side of mental ill health."[8]

The treatment focuses necessarily on the immediate problem, not on long-standing pathology or well-established character patterns. General psychodynamic understanding of the person is as indispensable for effective treatment in crisis therapy as in ongoing treatment, but since the crisis situation is the main focus, what is communicated to the person relates essentially to clarification of the crisis impasse.

Crisis Group

The crisis group at the center is structured to correspond to three sequential phases of crisis resolution. The first phase involves the formulation of the crisis situation for the patient—a difficult and highly specific diagnosis that can best be accomplished in a pregroup individual interview. It entails the following: (1) Active exploration of the current situation to identify the precipitating stressful event. To arrive at this, the therapist pursues such significant clues as recent or anticipated losses of important "others," points of noticeable change in af-

---

[7]Gerald Caplan, *An Approach to Community Mental Health* (New York: Grune and Stratton, 1961).
[8]*Ibid.*, p. 293.

fect, memories of analogous stressful events stirred up by the current crisis, the approximate onset time of the acute upset, and so forth. (2) The therapist tries to discover why the patient cannot handle the present problem by using previous coping mechanisms. He needs to formulate the dynamics of the current situation against the background of genetic material offered by the patient. (3) The impasse brought about by the present insufficiency of habitual coping with a particular kind of emotional hazard must be explained clearly to the patient.[9]

When an impasse has been defined validly, there is a noticeable lowering of the tension level and a renewed sense of hope is fostered in the patient. The patient's ego will have regained its capacity for problem-solving and preparation for entering the group is the final step in the individual interview. The same therapist will continue when the patient enters the group.

In the second phase of crisis intervention the group is used to help the patient attempt to solve his problem. In the third phase the group reinforces and helps sustain the patient's confidence in his new way of coping. More specifically, the treatment activity begins with encouraging each patient to share the impasse he is facing with the group. This is vital if the group and the patient are to understand clearly what must be resolved. If the patient cannot formulate his crisis clearly, the therapist assists him, and it is important for the therapist to clarify for the patient and the group which coping device had been used to deal with the particular threat or loss and why this was not effective.

This search for a better means of coping is facilitated by the therapist who solicits group help and fosters a group atmosphere of empathy and support for change. Crisis has the effect of lowering, at least temporarily, psychological barriers between people of diverse social and cultural backgrounds and creates a feeling of unity ("we're all in danger") that tends to counterbalance differences in age, personality types, and other characteristics.[10]

Another feature of the crisis group process is that the individual's functioning in the group often reveals the type of faulty coping that has caused his current difficulty. The therapist can urge the group to comment on such behavior and discuss alternate ways the patient might use to handle his current situation.

[9]Gerald F. Jacobson, Daniel M. Wilner, Wilbur E. Morley, Stanley Schneider, Martin Strickler, and Geraldine J. Sommer, "The Scope and Practice of an Early-Access Brief Treatment Psychiatric Center," *American Journal of Psychiatry*, Vol. 121, No. 12 (June 1965), pp. 1176-1182.

[10]Gerald F. Jacobson, "Crisis Theory and Treatment Strategy: Some Sociocultural and Psychodynamic Considerations," *Journal of Nervous and Mental Disease*, Vol. 141, No. 2 (August 1965), pp. 209-218.

Then there is the need to maintain the group's support while the patient is "trying out" these new ways.

The therapist discourages the group from lapsing into a discussion of chronic character problems that can serve as a detour from the main focus of treatment. Also, such discussion risks promoting regression that can interfere with crisis resolution and termination.

When more adaptive behavior has been achieved, the therapist moves the patient toward terminating treatment. Throughout, the therapist's role is an active one in focusing and limiting discussion to problem-solving around the crisis situation. This active role can also serve as a model for the patient in his efforts to extricate himself from his dilemma.

Miss X

The following case summary will illustrate some of the processes described previously (e.g., identifying the precipitating event, the patient's typical coping devices, the failure of these devices, the search for a more adaptive way of coping, the group's pointing up of ineffective coping mechanisms, and its support of the patient's efforts):

Miss X, a 30-year-old unmarried schoolteacher, had insomnia, was depressed and unable to concentrate on studying for her master's degree. After intensive exploration, the precipitating event was found to be the recent discovery that her ex-boyfriend was engaged to another woman. She had dated this man for many months, had her first sexual affair with him, and expected him to marry her. When she broached the subject of marriage indirectly, his response was cold and evasive. She was unable to express her anger to him and broke off the relationship precipitously hoping he would pursue her. When he did not pursue her, she turned to her studies. However, her coping methods—denial and avoidance—broke down when she learned of his engagement. Her stereotyped way of coping with affectional deprivation was no longer capable of sustaining psychic equilibrium. When her problem was defined during the pre-group interview, her anxiety subsided appreciably.

In the crisis group she acted out her life role—that of a helping person. In her parental home she was so busy ministering to the verbal demands of her mother and sister that there was no time to express her own needs. Therefore, in affectional relationships she had never learned to ask that her needs be met and had carried this into adult relationships including the unsuccessful love affair. This was in contrast to her professional behavior as a teacher when she was able to assert herself verbally not for herself but when a student's welfare was involved. The group quickly perceived her denials of frustration and anger over losing her lover and continuously reminded her of them. It thereby afforded her a substitute family that would not allow her to function only as a helping person or ignore her affectional longings. With the group's support she began to recognize and express verbally the recent, intense frustration of these longings and to marvel that she could do so without the "earth swallowing me up." She realized that she never told her boyfriend that she wanted to marry him or to seek this goal actively. Thus, the group provided a corrective emotional experience in which she was put in touch again with her affectional longings and strongly encouraged to express and pursue them without finding the dreaded punishment. She summarized this new knowledge by saying, "All my life I have been swallowing my feelings and now I know I can't get what I want by swallowing; I must ask!" At termination of the treatment (in the sixth session) she was symptom-free.

Assessment of Outcome

Criteria for measuring improvement in the pilot group were geared to the authors' evaluation of outcome based on the following graded criteria.

Minimum improvement. When an individual achieves at least his precrisis level of functioning through the regaining of homeostatic equilibrium that restores his problem-solving capacity.

Moderate improvement. When a patient uses his regained problem-solving capacity in the course of treatment to find an adaptive way of coping with the hazard and demonstrates this in his current life situation.

Maximum improvement. When the patient displays a cognitive understanding of (1) what coping device he has used in the past to deal with the hazard, (2) why this method has not been effective in coping with the recent threat, and (3) why the coping means he now uses are more effective in handling this threat and, therefore, any similar threat that could arise in the future.

In the pilot study, twenty-five of the thirty patients evinced one of the three levels of improvement — of these twenty-five patients, two-thirds were in the maximum category, one-sixth in the moderate category, and one-sixth in the minimum category. In contrast to this rate of improvement in the crisis group, two-thirds of the patients receiving individual or conjoint treatment at the center were rated improved.[11] (However, those ratings were not differentiated into the three categories.) The average number of interviews per patient in the crisis group was similar to the other modalities—i.e., 4.0 as compared to 3.9 visits per patient. Therefore, in the pilot study the economies of group treatment were used and a similar number of treatment interviews achieved slightly higher rates of improvement.

Summary

Crisis group treatment is different from traditional forms of group treatment because of the special nature and process of

[11]Jacobson et al., op. cit.

crisis resolution. Crisis, with its time limitation and sense of urgency, is helped toward resolution by the limit of six weekly visits. The universal feeling of crisis quickly welds the group into a working unit. The focus on a high degree of cognitive as well as emotional recognition of the dilemma sets the stage for problem-solving. Specific clarification and awareness of the patient's coping device that is now failing him complete the cognitive picture. The group functions both by prodding and stimulating the patient into awareness that his way of coping must change and then by supporting his efforts to try out new ways. The therapist implements this by giving open and enthusiastic support to the patient's efforts. Together, group and therapist generate an atmosphere of hope and trust that growth can take place. Both work hard in a highly focused and intensive manner and experience considerable gratification from the ability of group members to grasp the opportunity for change.

Social Group Work in the
AFDC Program

Louise C. Youngman

A recent one page pamphlet from the U.S. Department of Health, Education, and Welfare describes the Aid to Families with Dependent Children program as "reflecting the belief that strong family life benefits every child. AFDC is the nation's largest child welfare program. Through AFDC all of us share in providing money and other welfare services for children who lack support because of a parent's prolonged absence, death, incapacity or unemployment. Thus we help needy children to develop normally in spite of conditions beyond their control." Why are other welfare services necessary? What social problems are created or are present where there is financial need? Do these families have within themselves the potential to use other welfare services to maintain or develop a *strong family life*?

My experience first as a caseworker in public assistance, and then as a supervisor of caseworkers in the ADC Special Unit of the Baltimore Department of Public Welfare, has given me the opportunity to become familiar with some of the social problems which are every day realities in the lives of both the parents and the children of needy families. It has also given me the opportunity to know through experience the strengths in these families.

Reprinted with permission of the American Public Welfare Association from *Public Welfare*, Vol. 23, No. 1 (January 1965), pp. 25–31, 59–61.

Sometimes these strengths are used constructively, sometimes destructively, sometimes they seem dormant and sometimes they are overshadowed by the weaknesses. But because of family strengths, there is the potential for these children to have a home life conducive to their healthy growth and development.

Services to Meet Needs

In most instances these AFDC families need, want, and use social work services to help them channel these strengths toward a fuller life. However, change from drifting and hopelessness to facing the reality of their future with hope toward independence, doesn't just happen. Change demands creativity of the social work profession and use of all its knowledge, skills, and methods.

The Baltimore Department of Public Welfare administration is sensitive to developing services to meet the social needs of the client within the intent of the program. The function of the caseworker has always been to help parents face responsibilities to themselves and to their children; help people use the resources available within the community; help them value themselves and their potential for change and growth as they moved towards independence. In 1958, social group work was introduced:

> In its concern with new and more comprehensive ways of helping mothers maintain satisfactory homes for their children (in 1958) five groups of ten one-hour meetings were held to supplement the regular casework service. A trained social group worker was in charge. About a dozen mothers enrolled in each group. Attendance was voluntary. In the brief three month experience with the program, the Department gained evidence of the success of this group work experiment. It will be continued and expanded in the future.[1]

As might be expected, there were questions and doubts in the minds of some caseworkers. How could this social work method, associated with recreation and play, have any place in the AFDC program? In the past six years as caseworkers have become more informed of the social group work method, they have begun to value the help offered the AFDC clients through a group experience in meeting social needs that could not be met in the caseworker's one-to-one relationship.

AFDC Mother Isolated

The social work staff has learned through experience that, "The use of the group meetings and the AFDC clients' reactions

[1] 1958, *Twenty-fourth Annual Report*, Department of Public Welfare, Baltimore, Maryland, p. 12.

point up the dearth of social contacts for most of them. Even in the public housing project the frequent isolation of the public assistance client is appalling. The experience in the agency-sponsored group often helps the client gain enough strength to step out into community, such as PTA and church on her own."[2] Can family life be strengthened through social contacts in a group experience? Can the intent of AFDC be implemented more effectively if these mothers share their social problems in a group?

My own convictions were so sincere that I sought professional education in social group work at the University of Pennsylvania School of Social Work in Advanced Curriculum, with a field work placement at this agency working with groups of AFDC clients. The purpose of this paper is to highlight some of the social problems involved in the life of the AFDC family that deter a child's normal development, and then to describe my own experience in using social group work services to supplement traditional social casework services in an attempt to meet some of these social problems.

A Family Needs More Than Dollars

In any family where a parent is absent, dead, incapacitated, or unemployed, relationships among its members are threatened. What is the answer for families that are faced with this abnormal situation? Can we expect normal development of the children under such adverse circumstances? Is the inadequate welfare grant which provides money for shelter, food and clothing the answer? We cannot underestimate the importance of money. Parents and children need to be protected by a shelter from the elements—cold and heat, rain and snow; and enough food to prevent starvation which in some cases is all the welfare check can offer. This money grant is essential to provide for basic needs, and since 1935 the Social Security Act has authorized financial assistance through the AFDC program. The term "needy families" so often is interpreted as meaning families needing only financial relief. The need for help with their social problems, which in some cases is a *result* of their financial problems and in other cases is the *cause* of their financial problems, is seldom recognized, understood, or adequately served.

[2]Shoemaker, Louise P., "Social Group Work in the AFDC Program," *Social Work*, National Association of Social Workers, 2 Park Avenue, New York, New York 10017, January 1963, Vol. 8, No. 1, p. 39.

Home Is School of Human Relations

Although AFDC is a child welfare program, the client is the parent. It is only through the parents that these children can be helped to develop normally, for the climate of the world in which children live is dependent on the standards and the attitudes of their parents. The home is the child's world in miniature; here he learns to trust or to distrust, to be confident or to fear, to be honest or deceitful. The parents are the teachers. Their values are his values.

In most AFDC families the client is the mother and the family is in need because the father is absent. This is a most serious break in relationships for a family. We know that a mother cannot be both mother and father to her child, but without the father her role as mother becomes more demanding. One AFDC mother expressed the fact that she was all her children had to cling to against the world. It frightened her to think that if she should let them down, they would have nothing.

This mother had been let down by *her* mother. Born out of wedlock, her childhood had been spent moving from one relative to another. In each home she felt like an added burden, rather than being wanted. She married at an early age seeking a home where she was wanted. Her husband deserted her and their four children, perhaps because he couldn't meet the financial burdens; perhaps because of interest in another woman; perhaps because they had little in common and quarrel followed quarrel. Because this mother's relationships had been shrouded in uncertainty and she had felt completely rejected, how could she, without the help of a caring person, begin to trust either herself or others and develop a home climate that would be conducive to normal healthy growth of her children?

The Guilt of Individual Unemployment

Although the greater number of AFDC recipients are mothers rearing their children alone, there are many families receiving assistance where both parents are in the home. The father is either incapacitated or unemployed and not eligible for either OASDI or UNEC. Both incapacitation and unemployment deprive a man of fulfilling his role as a breadwinner. He may feel defeated and worthless. As a recipient of AFDC he does not have the satisfaction of earning the welfare check, as he would if he received an OASDI or UNEC check. Unable to meet his financial responsibilities, a father's attitude can change from understanding and patience to apathy and bad temper toward his family. Friction and misunderstandings between husband and wife may result from this change and the relationships within the family circle might become tense and unpredictable thus damaging the children.

These social problems of weakened and broken relationships within the family circle are serious and deep seated. Without the help of a sustained relationship, these parents can drift aimlessly, unable to give their children a sense of ongoing security or family solidarity.

It is not only within the family circle that social problems of conflict and rejection are present. The public's attitude toward the members of the AFDC family is frequently critical and suspicious. Some members of the community set AFDC clients apart as "those people" suggesting they are all alike and all bad.

A Mirage of Nonchalance

It is not difficult to understand that in self-defense, some AFDC mothers build up a public image of indifference in an attempt to live within a community that labels them "free riders." Members of a group of AFDC mothers who had been discussing their lack of friends readily acknowledged that some of their neighbors called them "free riders" to their faces, while others made unkind remarks because these clients were being supported by taxpayers' money—the neighbors were taxpayers. One client explained that when she asked her sister if she could use her washer to wash the children's clothes, the sister told her that as long as she was getting everything else free, she had plenty of time to wash on a washboard and she could expect to do so as long as she was on welfare. The sister was doing her share by paying taxes. As she told of this experience she evidenced no resentment or indignation. It seemed as though she had grown accustomed to this kind of treatment. But does a human being ever become accustomed to insults, to being labeled a "free rider," to living in fear of neighbors' accusations? Although the bitterness and anger can be hidden by an attitude of indifference as the AFDC client faces the public, these frustrations encountered in the community may be taken back into the family circle, where the children learn through the criticism and hostility of their parents, to condemn and to hate.

Poverty Yesterday and
Today

Today AFDC families isolated through financial dependence have much in common with those for whom the first group-serving agencies were established.

In many respects, the agencies were protective associations against the problems created by city life in a rising industrial society. They ranged themselves against the mobility and rootlessness, the stultifying, noncreative work, the rising rates of delinquency and crimes, the patterns of neighborhood segregation, and pervading all, the inability of transient and disorganized populations to pool their interests and take action in their own behalf—people in groups were more teachable, more reachable, and more susceptible to change; small groups in particular were crucibles of attitude and value formation.[3]

Meeting Human Need for
Social Contact

In considering the social problems created for the AFDC family through threatened or broken relationships, both within the family circle as well as in the community, there is in social group work, "the possibility of meeting at least part of the human need to find a balance between the inner and outer forces—the individual and social—that make up the reality of life. It holds the potentiality for relating people in small encompassable parts, not only to each other, but to society, as opportunities develop through programming."[4]

Social group work services offered to AFDC clients at the Baltimore Department of Public Welfare are short-term discussion groups. During the past winter, I have served six groups of between six and ten members. These groups met for one hour per week for six weeks. Caseworkers selected and interviewed the clients whom they felt could use a group experience in accordance with the purpose of the specific group. Participation was voluntary. One group was formed for mothers who had made a satisfactory plan for their children, wanted to find a job, but had not been successful. Their common problem was employment. Another group were mothers who had children committed as delinquents to a Maryland training school. Their common problem

---

[3]Schwartz, William, "Group Work and the Social Scene," Kahn, Alfred J., ed.,*Issues in American Social Work*, Columbia University Press, 2960 Broadway, New York, New York 10027, 1959, pp. 114–115.

[4]Phillips, Helen U., *Essentials of Social Work Skill*, Association Press, 291 Broadway, New York, New York 10007, 1957, p. 27.

was to understand better the child's behavior and their own responsibilities in preparing for his return home. Another group were mothers who had severe difficulty in providing a satisfactory home for their children on the assistance grant. Their common problem was that the agency questioned their ability to give their children adequate care and to use the available help.

Another group was made up of parents who were both in the home. The husband was incapacitated, but physically able to attend agency group meetings with his wife. Their common problems were those that arise during whole family adjustment to the illness of the breadwinner, and those economic adjustments to the AFDC grant. Two groups of mothers were new recipients; they had been receiving AFDC for only a month. Their common problem was recent financial dependence, facing their present social situation, and planning their future.

Group relations, characteristically unique to social group work, have several specific qualities that enhance the social functioning of group members. There is an opportunity for professional relationship with the social group worker as well as the relationship with peers. An opportunity exists for members of the group to give help as well as to take help. Motivation for change is stimulated as the member tries to live up to the expectation of the group. Making social contact and universalizing the problem helps the member feel less alone, a part of a whole.

An Example of Group Work Discussions

The following example will demonstrate these aspects of group relations. It is case material from the sixth and last group meeting of six mothers who had recently become AFDC recipients.

When I asked them how they wanted to handle this review of the group meetings, they all said that I should start it off. We discussed the first meeting, when both Miss Elliott and Miss Watson had expressed their choice of coming to the agency and asking for assistance, rather than trying to live off relatives who seemed to resent it. Their feeling of independence now, even though they were receiving welfare, was better than being "beholden" to their families.

We discussed the second meeting, in which all but Mrs. Pierce had expressed how lonely they were, and the problems they had with relatives. During this discussion, Mrs. Thompson interrupted to say that somehow there has been a change in her relationship with her mother-in-law. In her motherly way, Mrs. Pierce commented that you had to do your part, and that was why she could always get along with her mother-in-law. She tried to understand her, rather than just criticize her. Mrs. Thompson said that you could always blame other people when you were unhappy, because you were so busy thinking about yourself.

Mrs. Pierce said sometimes you had to think about yourself and find out what you thought about different kinds of things. She said it was after the third group meeting, when we had been talking about what you tell your children about their father, and she didn't agree with everything that was said at that meeting. She said that she knew it was right to tell the children or anybody else the truth, but she didn't see any reason to make the children feel badly by telling them that their father and she didn't live together any more. She said as she thought about herself and why she felt this way, she began to wonder if it wasn't because it would be harder on her than it was on her children. She had decided that you don't take the easy way out for you, but tell your children the truth when they ask and let it go at that. Miss Watson said, "But nobody ever gave me an answer to my question, since my children's father and I weren't married!" Mrs. Pierce expressed agreement and said that was true, and Miss Elliott nodded and they all looked at me.

I said perhaps there wasn't a specific answer to Miss Watson's and Miss Elliott's problem, but is the truth any different for one than for the other? Can we make a mistake right by denying it? All nodded in agreement and we talked about the fact that one cannot make a wrong right, but we can move on from that mistake and be different, if we recognize and face the mistake.

Mrs. Thompson said, "You know what? I've told my kids that their father and I have had a disagreement and that is why we aren't living together." She explained that the children seemed to understand and accept this, and laughingly told the story of her little boy who asked her later, "when are you two going to get over your disagreement?" Everybody laughed and Mrs. Thompson giggled as she continued, "and you know what? My husband and I are talking things over like we have never done before." She went on to say how mad they used to get at each other whenever they differed or one criticized the other, but now, they seemed able to discuss and differ and explain to each other the things that used to make them angry. The group members were very much interested in this and Miss Watson said knowingly, "remember, I told you it wasn't all the man's fault—that we have a lot to do with it!" Mrs. Murphy said that she didn't know about that. She said, "All these nine years I have just stayed at home and been nice and taken care of my children and all my husband ever did was make another baby for me to take care of and then go off and leave." Again, there was laughter and knowing acceptance.

Mrs. Thompson said, rather hesitantly, "But maybe you have to do more than just take care of the home and the children." She said that she had been thinking about the times she used to find excuses when her husband would come from work and suggest that they go to a movie or to some friend's house; she would always make the excuse that she was too tired from taking care of the children. She said that it was a lot easier to just sit in front of the television set and she'd do this over and over again and then be mad when he went out alone. She turned to Mrs. Murphy as she said, "you just can't forget yourself and your husband and do nothing but stay at home." She turned to me and laughingly said, "You may not like this, but do you know why I come to these meetings?" She went on to say that they were very interesting and she liked talking things over with these people, but it also was to get away from the kids and be free for a while.

I said that this was very understandable and every mother needed some time free from the children and that was one of the reasons why I had suggested that they make a plan for their children so they would have this hour for themselves, "but sometimes this was impossible and several of you did bring your children. What a lot of effort to plan, get dressed and get here, particularly on a morning like this, with the heavy snow. Why did you all bother to do it?"

Miss Watson said that it was worth it; that she'd learned a lot in this group. She said that she was able to say things and ask questions that she would have been afraid to do if it was just one person. She said she remembered her caseworker had told her that it would be like this and that we'd learn from each other. She had never thought about a lot of things we had talked about here; having strength, and being weak, and it made her think about things like self-respect, and the excuses one makes and what you can do if you really want to, because some of them had done things better than she had. Miss Elliott said that it was the first chance she'd ever had to talk about deep things. I asked the group if they had found this to be true—that these group meetings had helped them think about things they had never thought about before and they found encouragement and understanding in each other, what are they going to do about it now that these group meetings are ending? Are they going to put forth this same effort to be part of other groups, like the schools, churches, and other organizations in their community? Miss Elliott said that was the strength part and if you wanted to, you would. Mrs. Murphy said that maybe, like Mrs. Thompson said, you have to do more than look at television for fun, and she shrugged her shoulders as she concluded, she didn't know why she bothered because she knew all the programs backward and forward. Mrs. Pierce agreed with this, saying she gets so tired of television, and coming here gave her a chance to meet these people and, like Mrs. Thompson, it had been very interesting. She said that she felt different about the agency, too. She smiled, as she said that she was really scared to death when she first came and hadn't said much because she didn't know what one would be allowed to say. She said that as the others asked questions and talked, it gave her courage and now, she felt she could ask her worker anything that she didn't understand. She said "Last week, we talked about responsibility to the agency and about standards, and now I understand them better."

Miss Elliott turned to Mrs. Pierce and said, "I wasn't there then, what are the standards?"

Mrs. Pierce explained that the standards of the agency seemed to be just like any other way of doing the right things. Because you're poor, doesn't mean you can't be clean and honest and be responsible to yourself and your kids. Welfare standards are raising your children right, so they have a chance when they grow up.

"We all know the right way," Miss Watson said. "It isn't right to just sit home and keep on taking Welfare if you could get off and work." Her face lit up as she said that she'd been thinking about the kind of work she would like to do and she would like to be a hairdresser. With pride, she pointed to her head and said, "I did all this straightening and fixing myself and my mother is letting me work on her hair too." The group admired her accomplishment. Miss Watson said that she was going to ask her worker about getting some training and see how she could become a hairdresser.

Mrs. Thompson turned to the members of the group and said, "But don't expect your workers to all be like her," pointing to me. I laughingly said that one could hardly expect that! We all at the agency are different, just as each one of you is different. But as we are one group here together, this is one agency. For instance, in this group we had one reason for being together, which was to discuss and, with each one helping the other, look at the problems that had brought them to this agency, thinking about themselves and their children and how they can best work on these problems. We had discussed how they could use the agency's help, having a better understanding of the rules and regulations and the expectations. Each one of them has a worker, who can continue with this help. "Naturally, it won't be the same, but as you begin with your worker, because of this group experience, it can be more useful—it's up to you all what you want to do with it." Perhaps because we had so much to cover in considering the past five meetings, there had been many things we had missed. Mrs. Pierce said that one thing we had missed talking about was the good and the bad things about these meetings and she wanted to say that she hadn't found any bad things. Miss Elliott said that she agreed with her and like she said before, she'd like to have it go on and on. She said that one doesn't get much of a chance to talk like this and things go round in your head and you don't know what to believe until you hear others talk and have a chance to say just how you feel. Mrs. Murphy said that sometimes she didn't talk too much, but she sure had learned a lot listening.

Hesitantly and with a few more comments the members left together.

From this material, one can gain some insight into the members' use of this short-term group experience for change and growth. The relationship between these mothers was enhanced as they became aware of the similarity of their problems. They were all alone, rearing their children alone, had broken relationships with husbands and relatives and were dependent on public assistance. For all of them these experiences had been very recent; they felt they had reached rock bottom, and were unique in their distress. But here in this group were women with similar problems, and each in her own way could offer help as well as take help. "As the member fulfills his part in the group, he helps the group move to a new or more qualitative place in its development; the member thus can see himself as a force affecting others. Seeing his force is seeing himself; recognizing the use of that force on behalf of purposes which seem valid to him helps place value on himself."[5] Thus Miss Watson, affirming her contribution in a previous meeting said, "remember I told you it wasn't all the man's fault." Mrs. Murphy feels free to disagree at this point. This is motivated by the other member's freedom of

[5]Lodge, Richard, "Individuality through Belonging," Unpublished doctoral dissertation, School of Social Work, University of Pennsylvania, 2410 Pine Street, Philadelphia, Pennsylvania, 1958, p. 80.

expression. As she later says that she hasn't said very much, but has learned by listening, it was from what she heard and a sense of trust and belonging through a relationship with her own "kind" that freed her to express her difference. Throughout this material, likenesses and differences are expressed and accepted. "To value the other members as they are, and to trust their unique natures need not be a threat to either himself or his group are no small gains in social maturity and self-realization for the individual group member."[6]

The Group Worker Adds
Focus and Control

Group relations do not develop just because six people with common problems are together in one room. The social group worker identifying with agency function carries the role of the professional helper. "For it is the worker whose presence and activity add focus and control to the process of group relationships. To carry the control of a process that allows and enables group members to have their full and appropriate part in the process, so that the outcome is their own, requires skill."[7]

The need for skill in social group work presents a serious problem in implementing this method in the AFDC program. Public welfare agencies have been traditionally casework agencies and between group work skill and casework skill, "too much that is different and distinctive remains to deny that difference."[8] Although the workers at the Baltimore Department of Public Welfare are not professionally trained, those responsible for their supervision have professional training in casework. Social group work methods were not used at this agency until a professionally trained social group worker became a member of this staff. Through in-service training and supervision by trained caseworkers, agency-trained workers do offer AFDC clients casework service. It is just as essential to recognize that a trained social group worker is necessary to supervise agency-trained group workers, if service to AFDC clients is to be offered through this social work method. We know this is a serious problem and needs to be faced realistically.

When Peers Are a Threat

In our enthusiasm to encourage social group work services in the AFDC program, let us not claim this method as *all things for*

[6]*Ibid.*, pp. 67, 68.
[7]Phillips, *op. cit.*, p. 144.
[8]Smalley, Ruth E., "Discussion of the Social Worker in the Group," *New Perspectives on Services to Groups,* National Association of Social Workers, 2 Park Avenue, New York, New York 10017, 1961, p. 33.

all clients. There are some situations where casework, the one-to-one relationship, can better meet the AFDC client's social problem. The problem may be one that the client can share only in a one-to-one relationship. Lack of confidentiality, although emphasized in the group, can be too much of a risk for some group members to share with other members.

There are also clients who are not emotionally ready to use group relations. Some clients who have experienced broken relationships, who have trusted others only to find their trust misplaced, can be so emotionally damaged that a group of peers may seem threatening rather than helpful. This was evident in the group of AFDC clients previously mentioned, where the agency had real question of their ability to constructively use their assistance grant to provide a healthy home for their children.

As evidenced by this excerpt from the case material—

I said that I knew today we were going to discuss health, but I had been wondering what it was that made it difficult for them to talk and say out loud what they were thinking? This was our fourth meeting; we had only two meetings left, and by this time, I felt we knew each other pretty well. They smiled and Mrs. Brown said, "The reason I don't say much is I'm afraid I won't say the right thing and maybe what I say will be stepping on somebody else's toes."

I asked how the rest of them felt about this? They smiled, but there were no answers. I said that at our first meeting several of them had said that they wanted to come to find out what these meetings were all about and now that they had been together for four meetings, did they know what the meetings were all about? Again, they looked disconcerted and Mrs. Acton shrugged. I asked them why they came? Mrs. White said that she wanted to come. Now that she had been here a couple of times, she liked it and she had learned things, and she liked to hear me talk.

This is hardly a good example of group relations! Although during the six group meetings, there was occasionally some interaction, some engagement with each other, these AFDC clients probably would have been better served by casework. Before they could effectively use a short-term group experience, they needed to experience through the help of a caring person some trust in one human being so that they could move out with trust in a group of people.

To Achieve a Sense of
Self-Worth

There are many ways, lay and professional, to enhance social functioning. Social group work is one of them. Its specific effectiveness lies in the psychological make-up of human beings: two basic needs—the need to belong and the need to have self-respect—are dependent on fulfillment of positive group experiences. A third need is located in the totality of human society, namely the need to cooperate with each other. For the

individual it means taking responsibility for one another, and this includes—and requires—group interaction.[9]

Social casework and social group work are both needed in the
AFDC program if we are to most effectively help these clients with
their social problems. A child's normal development is dependent on the normal development of his parents. The parent
needs to have self-respect and to have a sense of belonging before he can create a climate in the home that is conducive to
healthy development of the child. The social group work method
offers AFDC parents, through democratic and responsible participation in a group, an opportunity to achieve a sense of self-
worth and belonging.

[9]Konopka, Gisela, *Social Group Work—A Helping Process*, Prentice-Hall, Inc., Englewood
Cliffs, New Jersey, 1963, p. 163.

Selected Bibliography

Alissi, A. S., "Social Influences on Group Values," *Social Work*, 10
(1), 1965, pp. 14–22.

Barnwell, J. E., "Group Methods in Public Welfare," *International
Journal of Group Psychotherapy*, 15 (4), 1965, pp. 446–463.

Carter, W. W., "Group Counseling for Adolescent Foster Children,"
Children, 15 (1), 1968, pp. 22–27.

Churchill, S. R., "Social Group Work: A Diagnostic Tool in Child
Guidance," *American Journal of Orthopsychiatry*, 35 (3), 1965, pp.
581–588.

Cyrus, A. S., "Group Treatment of Ten Disadvantaged Mothers," *Social Casework*, 48 (2), 1966, pp. 6–8, 23.

Dall, A. G., "Group Learning for Foster Parents. II. In a Public Agency,"
Children, 14 (5), 1967, pp. 185–187.

Falck, H. S., "The Use of Groups in the Practice of Social Work," *Social
Casework*, 44 (2), 1963, pp. 63–67.

Finck, G. H., Reiner, B. S., and Smith, B. O., "Group Counseling with
Unmarried Mothers," *Journal of Marriage and the Family*, 27 (2), 1965,
pp. 224–229.

Frey, L. A., and Kolodny, R. L., "Illusions and Realities in Current Social
Work with Groups," *Social Work*, 9 (2), 1964, pp. 80–89.

Goldstein, H., "Group Learning for Foster Parents. I. In a Voluntary
Agency," *Children*, 14 (5), 1967, pp. 180–184.

Konopka, G., "The Generic and the Specific in Group Work Practice in
the Psychiatric Setting," *Social Work*, 1 (1), 1956, pp. 72–80.

McGee, T. F., and Larsen, V. B., "An Approach to Waiting List Therapy
Groups," *American Journal of Orthopsychiatry*, 37 (3), 1967, pp. 594–597.

Osman, M. P., and Hobbs, D. B., "Consideration of Group Therapy for

Recently Released Offenders," *Corrective Psychiatry and Journal of Social Therapy,* 12 (5), 1966, pp. 363–370.

Rowitch, J., "Group Consultation with School Personnel," *Hospital and Community Psychiatry,* 19 (8), 1968, pp. 261–266.

Scheidlinger, S., "Therapeutic Group Approaches in Community Mental Health," *Social Work,* 13 (2), 1968, pp. 87–95.

Schwartz, W., "Toward a Strategy of Group Work Practice," *Social Service Review,* 36 (3), 1962, pp. 268–279.

Shapiero, J., "Group Work with Urban Rejects in a Slum Hotel," *Social Work Practice,* New York, Columbia University Press, 1967, pp. 148–164.

Shoemaker, L. P., "Adaptation of Traditional Methods in Services to Individuals in Families and Groups," *Perspectives in Social Work, Mothers-at-Risk,* 1 (1), 1966, pp. 103–115.

Solomon, B. B., "Social Group Work in the Adult Outpatient Clinic," *Social Work,* 13 (4), 1968, pp. 56–61.

Vinter, R. D., and Sarri, R. C., "Malperformance in the Public School: A Group Work Approach," *Social Work,* 10 (1), 1965, pp. 3–13.

Weiner, H. J., "Social Change and Social Group Work Practice," *Social Work,* 9 (3), 1964, pp. 106–112.

Weiner, H. J., "A Group Approach to Link Community Mental Health with Labor," *Social Work Practice,* New York, Columbia University Press, 1967, pp. 178–188.

5

Community Organization

The organizational approach to social work focuses on the performance of institutions in meeting human needs. An aim of the social worker in this area is to improve that performance. Moore sees the organizational approach as "A method of effecting *social change* in all or any part of a community through the modification of the *behavior of its institutions* and its *ways of using resources* in social welfare matters."

One possible path for the practitioner is to work to change the institutions directly, that is, to concentrate on the "providers" of social welfare. Effecting change in institutional structure presents difficulties, of course, due to the tendency of past policies and procedures to preserve. Feldman and Jacobson discuss some approaches to this problem of limited flexibility.

An alternative means of working for improvements is to organize the people who require institutional services, that is, the "consumers." In her article, Piven discusses efforts to organize such consumers. Grosser describes the use of hometown clubs, civil rights groups, and storefronts to achieve such consumer organizations.

Of course, both community planning and social action are necessary concerns of the social worker. With an eye to the relationships among the components of the institutional system of services, the social work generalist attempts to involve both consumer and provider in the task of improving social services.

The Practice of Community Organization

Norman R. Moore

This paper is intended to introduce some of the content of community organization as a field of specialized learning and as a form of professional practice. A brief history of the nature of practice in community organization is presented in the first part as a means of providing some understanding of the status and character of contemporary community organization practice. The second part, then, attempts to provide a conceptual orientation to some of the major "elements" of practice (i.e., role process, techniques, etc.) and to some of the broader "contextual aspects" (i.e., social change, community patterns, etc.) in community organization. A number of the basic tenets of current community organization are identified, leading to an effort to unite conceptually the current diversity of community organization.

Some Historical Orientation

This paper shall attempt to present a brief account of the evolution of community organization as a field of practice in an effort to place its current form in the perspective of its history. Much of the history of community organization, of course, closely parallels that of all social work practice. Community organization naturally would claim allegiance to the great social reformers of the early 1900's and their crusades to improve social institutions and social conditions. Many of the events in our social history which influenced the development of community organization also influenced other aspects of social work practice.

A couple of broad points should be made as a way of beginning a discussion of the evolution of community organization practice. These are:

Reprinted with permission of the author and The University of Tennessee School of Social Work (mimeographed, 1967), pp. 6B–31B.

a. Over the past 90 years or so there have been a great many "social inventions" which have contributed to the development of modern community organization. Some of the more important of these social inventions have been identified by Heath and Dunham as follows: the Charity Organization movement; the social service exchange; the community welfare council; joint financing of social welfare agencies, and to a lesser extent, statewide agencies; surveys and studies—particularly broad community social welfare surveys; community development—an international and interdisciplinary movement.[1]

b. Community organization is not the sole product or prerogative of social welfare. In Schaller's view, community organization is like a thread woven from many different strands. Social work, in particular, is the oldest strand, and has produced the most systematic understanding of community organization. Other important contributors to the development of community organization are the institutions of organized labor, religion, political parties, government, and the social experiments in community development, civil rights, and urban renewal. Experience in each of these, Schaller maintains, has produced some lessons, good and bad, for the "art of community organization" as it might be used for a variety of purposes.[2]

In other words, that which has gone on around social welfare in the vein of community organization has had considerable influence on the nature of community organization in social work.

Community organization in social welfare emerged as a necessary extension of the whole pattern of social services, rather than as a distinctively separate movement toward a desired end in social work practice. It evolved from the growth of the whole charity movement, was stimulated by war-time and depression era social needs, was shaped and reshaped by social legislation, was "reformed" by ideological and pragmatic considerations, and, even now, appears headed for still further alteration.

Different students of community organization come up with different ways of classifying the eras of community organization, but most end up with three to five significant eras. We shall use four periods for examining the evolution of community organization.

1. Charity Organization Societies

The COS's, prominent in the country for about 40 years, are credited with providing the origins for modern social work, particularly with family welfare services, and community organization. The Societies were quite frequently dominated by the

[1]Heath, Monna and Arthur Dunham. *Trends in Community Organization* (Chicago: University of Chicago, School of Social Service Administration, 1963), p. 60.
[2]Schaller, Lyle H. *Community Organization: Conflict and Reconciliation* (Nashville: Abingdon Press, 1966), pp. 50-71.

wealthy leisure class who were intent upon reforming the "relief system" of their day—for the same reasons as reform is called for today. What concerned the COS's was that a great many agencies were operating with the same functional field, namely, family welfare. They were concerned that the autonomous operation of the relief agencies was leading to the evils of case duplication, client abuse and waste of funds, and of less than possible coverage of need and helpfulness to clients. Their first objective became one of *coordinating the work of private agencies*. To achieve this they developed ways to divide the work, integrate intake policies, exchange case information, and for the central clearance of cases. Out of such developed the practice of the case conference and the social service exchange. The societies also published local directories, and operated information bureaus about charities. These are still common activities of community organization agencies. The COS's were typically authoritarian in their approach, but did meet with some success.[3]

Soon COS's themselves became engrossed in trying to cope with social and economic problems: tenant reform, sanitation, child labor, vagrancy, health, and housing. Part of the effort of COS's was to close gaps through benevolence, legislation, and the extension or creation of organizations. They also began to organize and operate programs, as employment bureaus, day nurseries, wood yards. In these activities, the societies were competitive with existing agencies, if not contributory to the duplication they sought to avoid. More importantly, however, such direct services programming apparently lessened the effectiveness of their original coordinating role. It should be noted that today most community organization agencies try zealously to avoid operating direct services programs for anything more than demonstration. In sum, most students agree that the COS provided the foundations for community organization. In fact, two observe: "The emphasis on cooperation and coordination, on fact-finding and exchange of information and experience, on working on the underlying causes of social problems, have been retained in modern social welfare planning bodies."[4]

2. Federation of Social Agencies

Within a few years, the COS's began to foster councils of social agencies and gradually shifted the leadership for community welfare planning to them. Councils of social agencies began to de-

[3]Murphy, Campbell C. *Community Organization Practice* (Boston: Houghton-Mifflin, 1954).

[4]Johns, Ray and David DeMarche. *Community Organization and Agency Organization* (New York: Association Press, 1951), p. 85.

velop around 1910, the first in Pittsburgh. They were still primarily concerned with *the coordination of programs among the various voluntary agencies*. But councils were intended to have some advantages over a direct-service agency (i.e., the COS), such as objectivity and neutrality, in effecting such coordination.

The early councils themselves were limited in scope and effectiveness. While some attempted, and others showed desire to engage in community planning and social action, councils largely concentrated on the provision of central services and operated as clearinghouses for information, etc. There was *no clear focus on interagency planning*, which was a partial consequence of the councils lack of any authority over the standards of service.[5] Much of the reason for this lay in the fact that councils were organized on "delegate body" plans, whereby the council membership was made up of representatives of the agencies. Agencies dominated the councils leaving them without any effective sanctions against the agencies. The initial growth of councils was very slow; by 1917, they existed in only seven cities. The impetus of WWI had brought this number to 20 by 1923.

Another aspect in the federation movement was that of "federated fund-raising". Federated financing originated in England and was adopted in America in 1888, in Denver, and in 1913, in Cleveland, but did not really catch on until during WWI. As early as 1906, principles were being suggested for a "financial clearing house to assume responsibility for the support of local charities" which included *a central budget committee and a comprehensive annual campaign*, both mainstays in our contemporary model.[6] At that time, each agency conducted its separate fund-raising drive which it was reluctant to relinquish, and a period of controversy ensued until WWI. What is now the Cleveland Welfare Organization is considered the first modern community chest. Interestingly, it evolved from some charity policing activities of the local chamber of commerce. This was perhaps the origin for the support as well as control of the business sector so common in United Funds today.

Financial federations expanded tremendously at the stimulation of WWI. "War Chests" developed as if by tidal wave across the country, and were converted to community chests in postwar years. By 1925, such federations existed in some 250 cities. Chests of this era were typically weak: They had *little authority over the allocation of funds raised or the standards of agencies being supported*, and hence little control over the use of charity

[5]Murphy, *op. cit.*
[6]Heath and Dunham, *op. cit.*, p. 23.

funds.[7] Councils of social agencies continued to develop and most affiliated in some way with the chests, for the emergence of the *chest-council concept* in community organization. Some councils exercised some influence over agency allocations through the planning function. Many councils concerned themselves with only the member agencies of their local chest. The characteristic weaknesses of councils throughout the 1920's was that they (a) lacked "community representativeness", i.e., were still dominated by social agencies; and, (b) excluded largely the public services from their planning and coordinating efforts.

McMillen termed these developments as the emphasis in community organization on the *"cultivation of community support"*, as opposed to the earlier emphasis on the *"problems of coordination"*[8]. Social agencies consolidated such common activities as fund raising with the chests, and research and interpretation with the councils, in an effort to widen the rather narrow and esoteric bases of support which individual agencies normally had.

3. Advent of Public Social Services

The spread and development of councils were stimulated by social legislation of the depression era. Community chests had experienced another period of rapid growth during 1929–31, as local relief campaigns attempted to meet depression needs in a fashion similar to the war chests a decade earlier. This time, however, they were overwhelmed by the magnitude of the needs. The Social Security Act of 1935 created public services which supplanted the programs of the private agencies. This event ushered in an *era of reorientation and reprogramming* for the voluntary social services.

Councils were pressed into service to aid in planning for this transition within the community social welfare system. This task necessitated a *shift in focus by councils* to the tax-supported programs rather than voluntary ones. This was to become a lasting ingredient for council affairs in the future. Another change typically occurred: The participation of laymen in the work of the councils was greatly expanded. "Citizen participation" was to become a council motto within the next 15–20 years.

[7]Murphy, *op. cit.*
[8]McMillen, Wayne. *Community Organization for Social Welfare* (Chicago: University of Chicago Press, 1945), p. 33.

World War II produced additional beneficial effects on the development of chests and councils. It ushered in the greatest period of expansion for federated financing, as "war relief" chests became even more widespread than during World War I. Depression relief expenditures diminished drastically, and national revenues were absorbed by the war effort. The War Relief Board organized the National War Fund, modeled after the community chest, and raised large sums of monies for war-related programs. The war fund formation led to the merger of a large number of war-relief agencies which were later converted into community chests—which by 1950 numbered about 1300.

Council development was likewise stimulated through the creation of defense councils and war-service councils under the auspices of the Office of Civilian Defense. The federal government provided funds to create facilities and services to meet social needs in the "war impacted" areas as large influxes of military-related populations created hardships on local communities. Local planning was necessary to cope with these social welfare needs, and defense councils were established. In some cases, existing councils of social agencies were entrusted these responsibilities, in others they were designated for participating roles. Many of the newly created councils survived after the war as community planning councils. By 1950, about 500 councils existed, with nearly every city of 100,000 population having one.

4. The "Problem-Solving" Planning Approach

Community organization experience during the Depression and World War II largely fostered the notion of "planning for the solution of social problems in the community" as the desired direction for practice. Much experience in planning had been gained and community councils were set on a course of developing their modern role. McMillen reported that a shift in emphasis was occurring in the mid-1940's toward efforts by councils "to formulate programs to provide for unmet needs."[9] In this shift, the interrelations of agencies ceased to be of dominant interest. Rather, "problem-solving" became the dominant interest, for which it became more important to arouse citizen concern for community needs.

In recent years, this community organization role emphasis has been sustained by social legislation for the development of public

[9]Ibid.

services, by private philanthropy, and the success of fund-raising for health and welfare. For instance, the planning task of community organization has increased tremendously with the passage of federal acts dealing with mental health (1947), housing (1948), juvenile delinquency (1962), public welfare (1962), poverty (1964), and health care (1965), and the many federal grant programs. Since World War II, state and local governments have also expanded their activities in education, recreation, youth services, health, and welfare programs. These actions have made tremendous resources for social welfare available to communities. They have encouraged councils, particularly, to develop ways of directing these resources to social needs in their community—i.e., planning. In the 1960's, it has become rather popular for councils to describe their function as "comprehensive community-wide planning" and to pursue more ambitious social planning projects.

Councils have not, however, given up their earlier function of coordinating social agencies in favor of broad social planning. The nature of a considerable amount of planning is that of resolving problems which are created by the structure of community services itself, or which arise when that structure must make adjustments to stay abreast of changing social needs.

In post-war years, the fund raising task of community organization has also expanded tremendously. Private agencies have proliferated rapidly since World War II, reaching well over 100,000 by 1958. Most of these, particularly the myriad health agencies, have developed outside the structure of federated financing. Early in the 1950's, the "United Fund" movement started to spread to counteract the multiplying number of fund-raising campaigns. The concept of a United Fund was designed to improve the structure of the Community Chests, primarily by widening the scope for voluntarily combined fund drives and by creating community sanctions for controlling the spread of independent campaigns. United Funds have now superseded nearly all except the smaller Community Chests. The problem of multiple campaigns, however, continues to be a struggle. For even today with some 1500 Funds and Chests raising about $600 million, upwards of three-fourths of all voluntary agencies are not participating members. The United Funds have on the whole proven reasonably successful as community organization agencies for "cultivating public support" of community health, recreation, and welfare services. They have tended to develop into rather sophisticated business-like enterprises for financing social welfare.

Later on in the 1950's, the concept of the "United Community Services" agency became popular as a new structure for community organization. The UCS approach combines the United Fund and the Planning Council into a single organization. It represents an attempt to integrate more effectively the functions of financing and planning in community social welfare decision-making. In part, at least, the UCS plan was also conceived as a way to overcome the "friction" which had developed between Funds and Councils in many communities. The United Community Services approach has been adopted rather slowly, but such agencies now exist in a fair number of communities. Whether or not UCS offers superior merits for more effective community organization has not been investigated or generally reported.

Community organization, then, has passed through these stages of development in evolving its current primary functions of community planning and fund-raising for social welfare purposes. In recent years, the interest of most educators, writers, and researchers, as well as many practitioners in community organization has centered predominately on the social welfare planning approach for community problem-solving and program development. A great deal of interest has been generated in such aspects as the process, methods, and strategy in planning, the role of the planner, the non-technical aspects of planning, community influences on planning, etc. At the same time, more attention has been given to certain issues created by contemporary pressures on community planning councils. Planning for social needs has been expanding and proliferating fairly rapidly in recent years. Specialized problem-centered planning (e.g., aging, mental health, recreation, poverty) has been growing as a function of agencies and organizations within functional fields. New social planning structures have come into being and governmental agencies have ventured out further into social planning. The modern scene now contains what Warren calls a "plurality of planning centers" which raises issues and problems for centralized planning.[10]

The central question, then, concerns the probable future role of the community planning councils, and hence the role of organization practitioner. Will other forms of social planning supersede council-type planning, or what will be the new relationships? Some suggest that councils might become "super planning centers" for communities; while others envision councils as agents for coordinating pluralistic planning. Another

---

[10]Warren, Roland. "The Impact of New Designs of Community Organization," *Child Welfare*, 44(9): 494–500, 1965.

possible alternative would be for community organization practitioners to work within specialized planning agencies and attempt coordination through their relationships. At the moment, the movement in council practice tends to be toward community-wide planning.

But planning is not the whole of community organization, just as Funds and Councils were not the whole, although it became convenient to think in those terms. There has always been some community organization work directly with the people in their neighborhoods or in similar social problem situations for neighborhood development or social action purposes. The settlement house movement, beginning with the Neighborhood Guild in New York (1886), and the Hull-House in Chicago (1889), is probably the historical precedent for this aspect of community organization in social work. The settlement approach was a total identification with the disadvantaged neighborhood and its people, and an attempt to elevate socially whole groups of people (e.g., housing, sanitation, education, recreation, medical care). In recent years, there has been a renewed interest within the field in community organization practice at the neighborhood or client level. Much of this interest has been stimulated by the Civil Rights Movement and the War on Poverty of the 1960's. At least a part of community organization practice seems to be moving in the direction of direct organizational work with low-income populations who are not affiliated with the major institutional systems and are not using available services in the community. It would seem that community organization is approaching still another juncture in its evolution.

A Conceptual Orientation

It should be recognized, first off, that there is no "theory for community organization" as a social work method. The literature of community organization does contain a collection of theoretical concepts for guiding practice, but even these are not highly developed nor well-integrated. What are often regarded as "principles" for community organization are usually untested propositions, which might be better described as normative beliefs, traditional assumptions, or the like. In Ross' view, the principles and methods of community organization are "sensitizing concepts" (unvalidated clues) rather than "definitive concepts" which have been tested in practice.[11] Later students have been

---

[11]Ross, Murray G. *Community Organization: Theory and Principles* (New York: Harper and Brothers, 1955. Revised second edition, 1967).

more critical. Morris, for instance, believes that the "global nature" of concepts in community organization renders them of "limited assistance" in dealing with problems in the real world. To Morris, the intellectual task is one of developing practice theory to fill the gap between "philosophy and action" in community organization.[12]

During its history, community organization has been defined by several educators and practitioners, and, yet, has seemed to defy or elude definition at the same time. Currently there is not a universally held or used definition of the community organization method in social work. Nor has there been great continuity in conceiving the objectives of community organization, which, of course, is important to a definition. In the 1920's, Jesse Steiner searched for a technology to support a "specific method of social organization" in communities.[13] By 1940, the landmark "Lane Report" had declared the central aim of community organization as a "process" was to secure "a progressively more effective adjustment between social welfare resources and needs".[14] This implied that community organization should be concerned with the "discovery and definition of need," the "elimination and prevention of social needs and disabilities," the "articulation of resources and needs," and the "constant readjustment of resources" to meet changing needs. These functional obligations have continued to be cornerstones in the general conception of community organization.

The Lane Report recognized that "organizing a community" takes place outside as well as inside social work, and a thorough scrutiny was needed before "the field in which the community organization process operates" could be accurately circumscribed. But, it stated, what distinguished community organization in social work from all other was the social welfare nature of its objectives when "coupled with its general content and setting". Here the Report made a key statement, saying "the justification of the community organization process is improvement in the coverage and quality of service to clients which the community is enabled to provide". This kind of orientation has been particularly strong in the thought and practice of community organization. In later years, the emphasis was to stress that the *practitioner enables the community* to provide improvement in ser-

[12]Morris, Robert. "New Concepts in Community Organization," *Social Welfare Forum, 1961* (New York: Columbia University Press, 1962), pp. 128–145.

[13]Steiner, Jesse F. *Community Organization: A Study of Its Theory and Current Practice* (New York: Century Co., 1930), p. 323.

[14]Harper, Ernest and Arthur Dunham (eds.), *Community Organization in Action* (New York: Association Press, 1959).

vices as the concept of "the community as the client" began to emerge.[15]

By 1954, Murphy viewed community organization as "a set of processes and skills" and "a field of activity". For Murphy, the *field* was largely comprised of those agencies which specialized in community organization. These were the "coordinating agencies" (planning) and "promotional agencies" (fund-raising, educational) which had reached high peaks of development. It was these specialized agencies which constituted the primary *setting* for practice. The *skills* of community organization were those of the social work method (e.g., using self and relationships, diagnosis) and rested on the same body of values and principles (e.g., acceptance, self-determination). The practitioner was essentially in an "enabler" role, using what Murphy termed "professional discretion". The *processes* were those of social change through democratic procedures which seek to unite rather than divide groups, and to plan "with" rather than "for" people. Here Murphy upheld one of the basic tenets of community organization, saying it "is not the work of a directive few; it is a matter of representation and participation by all concerned". Murphy's orientation is well summarized in his own words, which underscore the "community as the client" concept, as follows: "Community organization practice attempts to meet the community where it is, to help it determine its own needs, to move at its own pace, and decide its own solutions". The similarity of this conception to that for other social work practice is apparent.[16]

In the most complete theoretical treatment of the community organization method, Ross in 1955 challenged much of the existing theory. For Ross, neither *setting* nor *content* determined the nature of the community organization *process*. Ross conceptualized almost entirely free from any agency referents, such as Murphy had done, so that the notion of a "field of activity" was unimportant. Community organization to Ross was a "distinctive pattern of work" which had "wide application" in community work, including the fields of community development and community relations as well. What was essential was the process itself, and its end product—which must always be to enhance "community integration". By "integration" was meant the community's "capacity to function as a unit in solving its own problems". Integration constituted the "process goal" of the community organization method, and always took precedence

[15]Murphy, *op. cit.*
[16]*Ibid.*

over the "content goals" of any specific project or endeavor. Community organization, then, as Ross defined it, was:

. . . to mean a process by which a community identifies its needs or objectives, orders (or ranks) these needs or objectives, develops the confidence and will to work at these needs or objectives, finds the resources (internal and/or external) to deal with these needs or objectives, takes action in respect to them, and in so doing extends and develops cooperative and collaborative attitudes and practices in the community.[17]

Ross differed little with Murphy with respect to role and method. Community organization has a "unique frame of reference" which was a composite of the "particular value orientation" of social work philosophy, a "particular conception of community problems," and "certain assumptions influencing methods". Ross was particularly emphatic about the latter, saying they constitute the "foundation of community organization", i.e., its nature, its methods, its principles. For instance, a couple of Ross' assumptions were that "communities of people can develop the capacity to deal with their problems", and that "people should participate in major changes in their communities". Communities of people, Ross held, will change their ways only if forced or highly motivated to change. Community organization must be committed to "indigenous plans" in preference to "externally imposed plans", since communities do not develop problem-solving capacity when there is imposition rather than desire.[18]

Ross, in 1955, apparently saw no need to restrict community organization to social work practice nor to narrowly construed social welfare concerns. His concern was "community integration" rather than the achievement of a preconceived social welfare program, and in this reflected the considerable influence from the field of international community development. In 1956, however, Ross attempted to "distinguish community organization in social welfare from all other approaches to community work". The concept of community organization lacked clarity with respect to the "essentials of a social work process" and the "discipline of method, including the relation of ends and means". Ross reasoned that the "reform" and "planning" orientations to community work were not *per se* social work processes, and therefore not the whole of community organization. The process orientation", however, did meet the criteria of social work, but was probably only appropriate for use within the social welfare community. In his words, "the planning council within the

[17]Ross, *op. cit.*
[18]*Ibid.*

welfare community should be committed to the use of the community organization process, to the end that there may be movement toward a strong, cohesive welfare community with increasing capacity to plan and act". The welfare community in seeking objectives in its geographic community, however, does not have to rely on the "slower and gentler methods" of community organization, but may use any approach appropriate to the endeavor.[19]

The foregoing, I believe, is the essence of the traditional conception of community organization in social work. Much of it seems to have been fairly well captured in the 1959 Curriculum Study: While community organization is "only beginning to be considered a 'basic' method of social work" it is increasingly "conceived to be a direct service method" whose aim is "to provide services to community agencies for the enhancement of community life and the functioning of community groups, and thereby indirectly contribute to the enhancement of the social functioning of individuals".[20] Social work literature contains several works directed at the twin questions of whether community organization is a "method" and whether it is "social work". All would require that it embody the "core" values, goals, knowledge, and methods common to casework, and group work to be part of the "social work practice family."[21] Newstetter, for instance, wrote that the "social process" of community organization becomes a social work process when "it has social work objectives" and it is "consciously effected" by a person whose professional role is primarily that of "bringing social work knowledge and methods to bear on the solution of a problem".[22] Beyond this basic qualification, Carter held that it was the use of the "core elements" of the social work method in a "problem-solving process" with phases which produced "a system of ordered activities" for the community organization method. The core elements were identified as "social study and diagnosis" which leads to shared goals; "a change process" directed toward social change for better functioning; and "evaluation of the changed situation" for accountability to the profession and the public. The phases of the problem-solving process, on the other hand, were the "reconnaissance phase" in which the problem's treatment feasibility is assessed; "the diagnostic phase" in which an ap-

[19]Ross, Murray G. "Conceptual Problems in a Community Organization," Social Service Review, 30(2): 174–181, 1956.

[20]Boehm, Werner W. Objectives of the Social Work Curriculum of the Future, Vol. 1, Curriculum Study (New York: Council on Social Work Education, 1959), p. 136.

[21]Carter, Genevieve. "Practice Theory in Community Organization," Social Work, 3(2): 49–57, 1958.

[22]Harper & Dunham, op. cit., pp. 179–191.

proach or strategy to the problem is formulated; the "planning phase" in which the change process is initiated, the problem analyzed, alternative solutions developed, and a group decision reached; and the "implementation phase" in which a plan of action is formulated, strategic and tactical factors considered, action is completed and social change is evaluated. Carter and others have maintained that the method of community organization is limited to "project-centered activities" where the problem-solving process has "a recognizable case beginning and termination".[23] Ross, as we have seen, does not share this view. Others, notably Newstetter and Pray, have maintained that the quality of social relationships between the people and groups engaged in the community organization endeavor is just as important as the goals pursued. Both agreed that the primary role of the practitioner was to enable people to find and use constructive and satisfying social relationships in the intergroup process, and this is the social work function. Both the "project-centered" and the "social relationships" positions have become strong tenets in practice. Practitioners have sought to create cooperative, integrative, harmonious, "consensus-type" relationships within a problem-solving process focused on a particular situation in the community.[24]

Another fundamental belief in community organization is that it is a *process of social change.* In its simplest definition, such as Schaller uses, it may be nothing more than "a method of effecting social change".[25] Even Boehm, in social work language, has said that community organization "attempts to help collective man change his common environment to permit better social functioning of individuals".[26] Enlarging on her 1958 article in Friedlander's book, Carter stated that the practice of community organization involves "(a) social work intervention in a given situation, which (b) initiates or guides (c) a movement or change process toward (d) a goal".[27] A number of key concepts guide and influence this practice, including those of goal movement, enabling community readiness, representativeness and need. In oversimplified form, these concepts may be interpreted as follows: a community, itself, (1) must recognize that a social need exists, for it to be a real need, and (2) it must focus on some specific attainable goal, (3) toward which the worker facilitates the

[23]Carter, *op. cit.*
[24]Harper & Dunham, *op. cit.*, pp. 179–191.
[25]Schaller, *op. cit.*
[26]Boehm, *op. cit.*
[27]Friedlander, Walter A. (ed.). *Concepts and Methods of Social Work* (Englewood Cliffs: Prentice-Hall, Inc., 1958), p. 240.

work of a group, (4) which is representative of the interests affected by the problem, (5) through activities geared to the readiness to move of the people involved and the community, (6) which must result in some progress toward the goal. These are not sequential steps in a change formula, however, but rather are factors which must be occurring or in evidence almost simultaneously. These are a few of the things which the literature tells us of social change with respect to the community organization method.

But the questions arise: Who shall change and who shall be changed?, and What shall be changed and how shall it be changed? Traditional community organization has, since World War II, premised that the "leadership" in the community shall decide, plan, and activate social change. In the last several years, there has been a particularly strong emphasis on "lay" or "citizen" leadership, as opposed to that of professionals or officials in social welfare. The attendant assumption has been that community social welfare policy should be under lay control. Citizen participation and decision-making should precede any change in the community's policy and provisions for social welfare. In this approach, community organization functions to organize people as "providers" of social welfare goods and services for the community.

With the momentum of the Civil Rights Movement and the War on Poverty in the 1960's, however, has come a rather spirited interest in community organization practice on the neighborhood or community sub-group level. The idea of neighborhood organization is by no means new, although its context and thrust seems to be changing. Previous neighborhood organization has had various orientations, such as "planning" (District Welfare Councils), "action" (The Woodlawn Organization), "common-interest" (tenant associations), "special problems" (juvenile delinquency, voter registration), "development", etc. Current neighborhood and sub-group organization seems to combine the action and common or special-interest orientations with a stronger commitment to action, a stronger ethic of participation and a bolder set of tactics (e.g., conflict, protest). It emphasizes the role of the indigenous people or sub-group members and the task of influencing the larger community to act in ways beneficial to the people represented by the organization. In this approach, community organization functions to organize people as "consumers" of social welfare goods and services in the community.

The "providers" and "consumers" approaches represent opposite bases for community organization practice. One could probably find other bases in between, such as "neighbors" for neighborhood development, which would have some characteristics of either pole base. But the basic question would seem to be: Can the pole bases be reconciled for community organization in social work? They can, if we take *social change for social welfare* as the primary objective and essential property of community organization practice. In the writer's view, social change through deliberate efforts using competent methods is the key to the refinement of community organization. In order to reconcile the pole bases, then, we would need a conceptual framework something like this:

Community Organization: A *Method* of Effecting *Social Change* in All or Any Part of a Community through the Modification of the *Behavior of Its Institutions* and Its *Ways of Using Resources* in Social Welfare Matters

People may be organized as:	Providers	Consumers
	Of social welfare foods & services Around some social value (s)	Of social welfare goods & services Around some material objective (s)
To work through:	Decision-makers, in:	Needs-makers, in:
	Service-systems (health, housing, welfare, recreation) Institutionalized systems (political, economic, religious) Socio-economic systems (status, role, power)	Recipient-groups (housing, welfare, education) Institutionalized systems (churches, settlements, schools) Neighborhood social systems (clubs, organizations, friendship & leadership)
On the institutional & resource problems of:	Scarcity	Scarcity
	Creating new resources Expanding present resources	Demanding new & expanded resources Creating & expanding own resources
	Allocation	Allocation
	Rational pattern of use Planning & organization of use	Equity in distribution Reorganization of use patterns
	Delivery	Delivery
	Agency coordination Policy integration Program operation standards	Rights of beneficiaries Participating in policy control Changes in policies & program

This framework obviously strives only to be conceptually complete, and not exhaustive of all concrete manifestations in community organization. An instructive word is perhaps needed here. The elements in the above chart may be read in several different combinations. For example: People may be (1) organized as (a) providers of social welfare goods and services around some social value to (2) work through (b) decision-makers in a particular service system (3) on an institutional and resource problem of (c) allocation to obtain a more rational pattern of resource use. Similarly, the elements identified in the "consumer" column may be linked in various combinations to describe the essence of a community organization effort. What the chart indicates is that while the elemental content of community organization with providers and consumers may obviously and necessarily vary, the essential characteristics of the process and objective need not vary.

An orientation such as this is useful in several ways. First, it calls attention to the fact that the problems in the community social welfare system are related to the supply and utilization of resources. One aspect is the scarcity of resources, and hence the problem of discovering, developing, expanding or creating resources. Another is the pattern of resource allocation to the community's various programs and services, and hence the problem of securing the most rational and equitable distribution for maximizing community social welfare. A third aspect is resource utilization, and hence the problems of delivering social welfare goods and services in accordance with social needs and community capabilities.

Second, it suggests that these problems of resources may be approached by community organization efforts on two levels in the social welfare system: Those with the "providers" of social welfare, and those with the "consumers". This is so because the general problem is one of effecting change in one or more of the aspects (scarcity, allocation, or delivery) of social welfare resources. Many resource problems may be, and some should be, approached on both levels, either in joint or separate efforts for change.

Third, it suggests that a community's resource problems are frequently related to the nature and behavior of its institutions, since they control the major social welfare resources in the community system. "Lag" occurs whenever institutional behavior is not in accord with the current social needs or conditions of the community. Community organization efforts must be oriented toward reducing "institutional lag" in social welfare, and this is a focus on social change.

What the foregoing suggests is not a radical departure in community organization. In important ways, community organization has long been concerned with the need for deliberate social change, and the problems of resource supply and utilization and of institutional lag and behavior. What is suggested as needed is a sharpening in its focus on the problems of social change in the community, and the development of concepts, methods and skills more adequate for dealing with those problems in a professional practice. This doubtless would be a difficult goal to realize. For one matter, it would imply that the practitioners role repertoire should be expanded (e.g., to include the roles of "advocate", "activist", etc.) as well as his ability to use a wider variety of social processes (e.g., competition, adversary, conflict). For another, it would imply that the practitioner should have a broader foundation for understanding, using, and dealing with community "dynamics" (i.e., social forces, elites, politics, economic dominance, etc.). In this respect, community organization would need to draw more heavily on the social sciences. It is somewhat difficult to tell exactly where community organization is in its thought and practice and the direction in which it is moving. In the writer's estimation, these few pages represent the status of its development and its efforts toward greater sophistication in its methodology.

A Modern Council Point of View

Frank W. Harris

This paper undertakes a discussion of two important controversies in the field of community planning.[1] The first has to do with the role and relationship of a health and welfare council to comprehensive community planning. What role should the council play? Where do the physical, economic, educational, political, and other planners fit in? What should be the relationship among these planning groups? The second controversy relates to the practice model of staff in the council. Is a staff person an enabler or a leader or both? Can he be only nondirective or is he both directive and nondirective?

Reprinted with permission of the author and the National Association of Social Workers from *Social Work*, Vol. 9, No. 4 (October 1964), pp. 34-41.

[1]For the purpose of this paper, the term "community planning" means educational, economic, physical, political, and social planning to meet the needs of people. In turn, "social planning" is another term for health, welfare, and recreation planning. Also, when a health and welfare council is referred to, let us visualize an urban area council with a minimum of two full-time workers dedicated to social planning with a community organization base.

The comments and point of view that follow are based on several years of life in a climate of change. The New Haven area has undergone both a physical and a social transformation. The Community Council of Greater New Haven, responding first to the need to relate social planning to the physical changes taking place through a comprehensive redevelopment program, developed new relationships. Building on these, the council underwent change in its own structure, followed by sharing in the creation and activation of a program aimed at attacking causes of poverty. This program is carried out through Community Progress, Inc., which was initiated through the joint action of the New Haven Board of Education, the New Haven Redevelopment Agency, and the community council.

The Issue of "Bypass"

Of late, councils frequently complain they are being "bypassed" by the newer and more comprehensive approaches to solving problems in urban communities. In turn, many people associated with government, foundations, and other groups take a dim view of the present effectiveness and strength and power of health and welfare councils. But are councils really being bypassed? Can they be if they do not want to be?

The complaint of being bypassed is like pouting in the corner. Community planning is complex and no council can know all that is going on. In such cases, the omission of the council from a planning effort is usually easy to correct by an assertion of interest. When a council is omitted intentionally, the council may have to be more forceful in stating its responsibilities. In any event, one assumes that the council should already have created an atmosphere in which public and voluntary agencies seek it out. If the council image is a positive one, then overtures from a council will command attention.

So, if an idea or a plan germinates without the council involved in the initial stages, an assertion of council interest and competence is all that should be needed to open the door. But— one's foot has to be there first! Relationships based upon confidence and respect with planners in other fields, as with the health and welfare field, do not happen overnight. For quite a while in New Haven, the community council had to run hard to catch up with the physical planners, who responded immediately to the mayor's leadership. Urban renewal, with all its benefits and problems, problems that cried for the thinking and the action of social planners, was off to a running start while the council was still debating whether it should support it.

Nevertheless, it was relatively simple to pick up the initiative, to demonstrate not only interest but willingness to work with the redevelopers in terms of the human needs they were attempting to meet, and to bring the council, the renewal planners, and the city government into a close working relationship. This relationship placed the council in a natural position to continue as the need to involve educators became apparent. Preliminary thinking on how to tackle the problem of hard-core families who carried blight to new neighborhoods through relocation quickly gave way to a more comprehensive planning effort that involved the New Haven Redevelopment Agency, the Department of Education, and the council.

In other cities, in one way or another the opportunity presents itself to councils to become part of the over-all planning structure. Even the advent of federal vertical planning need not do without the assistance that a council's comprehensive perspective can bring to planning if the council will but insert itself into the situation.

The idea inherent in "bypass" implies that the health and welfare council is *the* organization through which comprehensive community planning—embracing educational, political, physical, economic, and social (health, welfare, and recreation) planning—can take place. The New Haven group questions this assumption.

Planning and Action Tool

In such across-the-board planning the council should be prepared, through use of its staff, to utilize its community organization skills to help create an effective planning and action tool, designed to meet the peculiarities of the specific community. The tool may take the form of a voluntary association of planning groups as in Washington, D. C., a special agency as in New Haven, a governmental body as in Oakland, Calif., or an as yet untried form. But it is unlikely that this planning tool could or should operate under the aegis of a health and welfare council itself whether or not the council takes the initiative in its establishment. Several reasons can be advanced for this position:

1. To assume the over-all responsibility for such an agency weakens a council's ability to carry out its own primary charge—health, welfare, and recreation planning.

2. It is already difficult for a council to keep up with all the specialized planning within its own area of competence, e.g., hospital councils, mental health groups, and the like.

3. Another inhibiting factor is the difficulty of obtaining sufficient funds for a social planning agency. In New Haven the council already has a larger professional staff than similar councils in areas this size. The author questions the willingness of a community to support and maintain a substantially enlarged council. (Community Progress, Inc., had a professional staff of forty, a total staff of seventy-five, as of November 1963.)

4. Councils do lack the power, political and otherwise, to pull and hold together a planning mechanism including the diverse disciplines of educational, economic, political, and physical planning.

5. A council can be just as effective by influencing and guiding rather than by including the whole comprehensive program in its own operation.

This last point merits elaboration. The fact that the New Haven council played a major part, together with the redevelopment agency and the Department of Education, in the creation of an "opening opportunities" program immediately placed the council and its staff in a close working relationship with the new agency, Community Progress, Inc.

Council staff participated vigorously in recruiting for CPI. Council staff and lay leadership enjoyed the confidence of the key leadership of CPI. Council planning became part of CPI planning. Conversely, CPI planning begins to become part of council planning. Staff attend each other's staff meetings. It is agreed that in all areas directly affecting mutual interests there will be collaboration and joint planning. Council advice and suggestions are welcomed with respect to CPI programs in which the council's direct stake is not as great but its knowledge and ability to relate the various components and their effect upon people has great value.

Today, one year after CPI opened its doors, the council continues its close working relationship with it, the Department of Education, and the redevelopment agency in planning and carrying out programs in the inner city. The council staff are not educational or physical planners, but they are trained to recognize the relationship of other planning to health and welfare planning and vice versa. The council is essential to the team.

The Council as a Partner

For all these reasons councils should participate as partners in newly burgeoning community planning efforts. And if steps are under way for the creation of an over-all planning body, formal or informal, the council should become part of such steps, with or without an invitation.

Council people well know, in dealing with agencies that undertake unilateral planning, that it will not always happen by invitation. The council should assert the same interest and responsibility in the area of comprehensive community planning as it would on evidence of unilateral planning by an individual agency. It helps if the council has a past record of interest, performance, and directness, plus staff relationships founded on frankness and mutual trust.

Some members of The Ford Foundation and the President's Committee on Juvenile Delinquency and Youth Crime have said they believe community health and welfare councils have a place in the scheme of things. But they qualify this statement, publicly and privately, with the expression of an underlying concern about the effectiveness of councils, of councils' ability to move decisively, of councils' dedication to group decision and self-determination. They sometimes imply that they believe councils do not even qualify for partnership.

What are the prerequisites for a council to become a partner in comprehensive community planning? The ticket of admission includes:

1. A council ready and willing to be a member of the team, at the same time retaining the freedom to be critical.

2. A council interested in and involved in planning public programs with public agencies as much as in planning voluntary programs with voluntary agencies, if not more so.

3. A council with a positive image, based upon both sound planning and effective action.

4. A council ready and willing to be part of the power structure, the decision-making apparatus of the community. The council cannot flee this responsibility. It must play its role in carrying out broadly conceived plans.

5. A council with capable staff, prepared to shun jargon, state their opinions, stick their necks out, and respect confidences.

The council has an indispensable contribution to make to the team. Of what does this contribution consist?

The Overview

The ability to encompass the total community, within and outside the disciplines of health, welfare, and recreation, and to relate one planning function to another. The council is accustomed to taking a comprehensive view. It can assist other planners in understanding and using the interrelationships among physical, educational, and social planning and their effects upon people.

Community Organization Skill

The ability to use staff community organization training in the development of an effective interdisciplinary planning organization. Council staff should be leaders in helping to weld an effective partnership out of the team members.

Social Planning Competence

Just as the physical planner or the educational planner has his special area of competence, so the social planner has know-how in the areas of health, welfare, and recreational needs and services.

Continuity

The council has been on the scene for many years. It will continue. Many of the planning organizations are temporary in nature, affected by the withdrawal of grant funds, an adverse election, and so on. The council will be there to provide continuity for whatever groups are doing the broad comprehensive planning this year, next year, and a decade hence.

Thus far we have spoken about the council, but of what does a council consist? A council is its volunteers—both lay and professional—and its staff. In much of what has already been said mention has been made of the staff role. Let us examine it more closely, especially the second area of conflict—the ends versus the means.

Ends versus the Means

Is the community the client of the health and welfare council or are the citizen volunteers its clients? In New Haven the primary purpose of the council is the achievement of a better, healthier community, a community in which each citizen has maximum opportunity to realize his potential for self-development. The 300,000 individuals living in the area are the council's clients. Council leadership—volunteers, professionals, and council staff—are the tools for achieving action on previously accepted goals and must determine how the action is carried out.

Robert MacCrae concluded an address in 1962 by saying:

One thing is increasingly clear to me. We cannot aspire to this larger role [partnership] on a business as usual basis. We shall need to *adapt* some traditional approaches and methods of work. We shall need to build staffs of a higher degree of competence. We shall need to *revise* our scale of values in many instances.[2]

Robert Morris dealt with one of these values in speaking before the annual meeting of the Council on Social Work Education in 1963 when he said:

Although we recognize that much may have to be altered in the environment, we are deeply committed to citizen self-determination which has thus far concentrated our action efforts on freeing others to bring about change. By comparison with this primary commitment, our own efforts to bring about major social changes have been sharply limited.[3]

We cannot be blindly dedicated to consensus, to inclusion of all parties to an issue, to avoidance of imposing change—without often unnecessarily shackling ourselves to compromise solutions and inability to move on major problems. Our social work scale of values has been too long overly tilted in the direction of the volunteer and his development of self-determination.

David Hunter, after a series of observations in an address outlining what he sees as the weaknesses of councils to take on the whole community planning responsibility, concludes by challenging all the planners to look at the social, economic, and political structures and systems that produce human wreckage and noting the need "to look at them unsentimentally, with the facts and with theory; to analyze how they need to be changed; to assess realistically *how they can be changed and by whom.*"[4] (Author's italics.) He goes on to say:

The council itself may have the power. If it has only the vision but not the power, it must ascertain who has the power, who's got the action, and then exploit its own resources to activate that power toward raising the levels of community welfare.[5]

Here is stated the *action* role of the council. It is a role based on knowledge, understanding of how to work with individuals and groups, how to achieve action through the council's own effort and power or *through those who do have the power to effect change.* The New Haven staff has a saying: "We do not propose to lose friends unnecessarily but if everyone likes us, we are

[2]Robert H. MacRae, "The Challenge of Change to Community Welfare Councils." Unpublished paper presented at a meeting of the "Million and Over Club," September 1962.

[3]Robert Morris, "Social Work Preparation for Effectiveness in Planned Change." Paper delivered at the annual meeting of Council on Social Work Education, January 1963, Boston, Massachusetts.

[4]David R. Hunter, "Who's Got the Action?" Paper presented to the Midwest Regional Conference of United Community Funds and Councils of America, February 1963, Springfield, Illinois.

[5]*Ibid.*

probably not doing our job." This holds equally true for the council. A council cannot be action oriented, cannot be a decision-maker, cannot disturb the status quo, without ruffling some feathers.

Councils must flexibly utilize volunteer and staff talents and power and leadership to achieve the *ends* agreed upon. Decisions on how to attain the ends—the means—should be planned decisions. More and more in New Haven the council seeks to move in the direction of deliberate decision on how it will attain its goals, knowing full well that too often the action is determined by fortuitous circumstance. Even this, however, is preferable to a primary emphasis upon total involvement, the automatic invoking of committees, an emphasis on the advisory role of a council, requiring group decision for all minutiae.

Although the New Haven organization is far from perfect, each year the council's Board of Directors, upon recommendation from the Project Planning Committee, agrees upon the "workable program" in which is outlined the council's assignments and the specific recommendations upon which action is sought. This committee is the intake valve for the council. The program becomes the guideline within which there can be relative freedom of movement—especially in determining strategies of accomplishment. In carrying out the program council staff play a key role. How they play this role leads directly to the next question.

Staff Role: "Enabler" and Leader

Capable, informed, and effective council volunteer leadership is important to the program of a council. The adequacy of the staff ingredient is *vital*. The New Haven group believes, as MacRae and many other leaders in the field have stated, that a council must recruit highly competent staff. These must be staff capable of a flexible approach to the solution of problems, unafraid to use themselves in direct action, negotiation, and decision-making within the context of over-all goals and objectives. The staff has responsibility to lead as well as to enable. Robert Morris aptly stated it when he said that social workers should not be just engineers of consent but engineers of change.

It is singularly true that we cannot equivocate, evade, or defer as we participate in the broader circles of community planning. Here communication is most frequently between professionals. It is a council responsibility to provide the guidelines for staff action, but staff must be permitted the freedom to express opinions, to promote action.

Even within the circle of health, welfare, and recreation planning the same can be said when considering planning and action with respect to public agencies. More often than not direct staff relationships with key public department professionals and political leaders can achieve more toward reaching council goals than attempts to produce committees. Policy frameworks for public departments are broad and subject to interpretation. If the broad policy needs change, the entire weight of the council may have to be thrown into legislative action. If the interpretation needs to be changed, a council staff member, alone or with a few other professionals, may effect the desired change.

Much has been written and said on this question of the role of staff, especially in the past several years. Jack Rothman summarized the conflicting theoretical approaches and stated a point of view. He began by citing Kenneth L. Pray, whose view was that "the weight of professional intervention should be directed toward the *process* by which decisions are made, not toward the *decisions* themselves."[6] Here is clearly stated the position of focus on means, not the end.

In 1955, Murray Ross attempted to maintain a more flexible posture and yet swung toward a means-oriented judgment that said:

Increased practitioner activity in this sphere [intervention related to problem-solving] ipso facto means diminished freedom of movement and consequently *reduced educational payoff* [result of process] for the participants.[7]

Later he states:

His work [the professional's] is always being regulated by the awareness that at the point at which he takes responsibility away from the community, the possibility of learning and growth in the community is thereby reduced.[8]

Is not responsibility a question of degree? What is meant—ultimate responsibility or responsibility for each and every detail? Do we want involvement of citizens for the citizens' sake with a strong possibility of little or no accomplishment, resultant frustration, discouragement, and the creation of the present impression that councils are ineffective? Or do we want involvement, self-determination, direction, and leadership in appropriate helpings when needed?

[6]Jack Rothman, "An Analysis of Goals and Roles in Community Organization Practice," *Social Work*, Vol. 9, No. 2 (April 1964), p. 26.
[7]Murray G. Ross, *Community Organization—Theory and Principle* (New York: Harper & Brothers, 1955).
[8]*Ibid.*

What of the professional's knowledge, insights, and leadership abilities? Are these to be exercised only in helping others to develop their leadership abilities? Is the professional not to lead in his own right? Cannot the staff member in a council be a decision-maker, an implementer of agreed-upon action programs? He can and must be!

Rothman succinctly rejects an "all-purpose, invariant role for practice" and suggests "an array of intervention roles as part of the practitioner's intellectual equipment which can be drawn upon diagnostically as appropriate to a designated community problem and situation."[9] This suggests the model the New Haven group attempts to follow—the practitioner who consciously chooses the most appropriate means of reaching an agreed-upon goal. This approach is followed energetically. The council is problem-solving oriented. The community is seen as the client, not volunteers. Staff have freedom to lead as well as enable under the eyes of a knowledgeable and working board of directors, which periodically reviews staff and committee activity.

Weight of Staff Opinion

There is another assumption implied in the professional's supposed unwillingness to point the way, to advocate a course of action, in carrying out community planning. It assumes that the expression of his opinion amounts to imposing it upon members of the committee or other group in which the professional is functioning.

On the contrary, a council staff member has a responsibility to bring his own thinking to the table. He must permit others to view it squarely. They may accept or reject it, but if they accept it blindly there has been a poor choice in the members of the committee or poor timing in the expression of the opinion. It is obviously true that in specific situations, especially in the beginning stages of committee activity before the committee has achieved its own body of knowledge and exercised a decision-making role, the professional should be more nondirective, more enabling. Otherwise he may take advantage of an element of deference in which the layman sometimes holds him and lead without the right to do so. But in most situations he should not be hesitant to state his point of view as long as he is equally prepared to listen to others and to accept rejection.

[9]Jack Rothman, *op. cit.*

Rothman says that if lay people unswervingly accept the professional's direction, then the professional had better take stock. However, he states:

The practitioner himself may have considerable freedom of action in making decisions regarding the implementing of community policies. It may appropriately fall to him to make a wide array of professional, administrative and technical decisions within the context of a previously made broader policy decision.[10]

If council staff are to lead as well as to enable, where is their accountability? The public agency executive is accountable to a higher public official or board and is usually removable by same. The political leader in turn is accountable to the voters at each election. This provides the political leader willing to grasp it the freedom to lead, to act, to be a decision-maker, subject eventually to the will of the voters and public opinion.

Council staff also have accountability, namely to the board of directors that employs them and may just as easily fire them if staff actions are contrary to council policy, ahead of council leadership, too individualistic, and inappropriate to the working relationship between the council and all affiliated agencies and organizations.

Situation Determines Role

Have we, then, discarded the enabling role? Do we single-mindedly follow a problem-solving orientation? Hardly! The situation should determine the role. Different community problems require different approaches. In many instances, moving a situation toward resolution will call for a variety of approaches.

For example, the New Haven council has had to use several strategies in furthering the full development of the community school concept and a council policy suggesting that neighborhood group service agencies move away from building orientation and maintenance of expensive facilities and toward more flexible use of staff in providing services in public facilities, especially the community school. Since the planning with respect to three of the four neighborhood agencies involved relocation, the co-operation of the redevelopment agency was obtained in insuring that no site would be provided that was not mutually agreed upon among the council, the involved agencies, and the redevelopment agency. In other words, the redevelopment agency agreed to participate in joint planning.

[10]*Ibid.*

A special committee was created. Its chairman is the vice-president of a major utility. If there is an implication of power in its membership, there should be. The committee includes the president of the Board of Education, an official representative of the redevelopment agency, the chairman of the Youth Activities Section of the United Fund Budget Committee, a vice-president of the United Fund, a member of the city Board of Finance, and so on. With staff service—including staff willingness to express and help develop a point of view—the committee evolved the policy outlined above and began the task of implementing it. Its primary role is negotiation with the boards of the voluntary agencies. It also provides support to the Department of Education in moving the community school idea forward.

At the same time, in order to insure that schools will have facilities the agencies can use and without which the policy would not be worth anything, a council staff member suggested to the superintendent of schools that the Board of Education appoint an advisory committee on community school facilities. The city is currently engaged in a thirteen-million-dollar school-building program.

The committee was appointed and a council staff member works with it as a consultant. At the same time he works closely with the director of community schools and the school construction coordinator. The result is ability of the council to influence decisions on type, location, and number of facilities built for either dual school-community use or exclusively for community use.

Summing Up

The health and welfare council is just one of many groups competent in community planning. Its particular competence is comprehensive health and welfare planning.

The council should be a partner in joint planning with the economic, educational, physical, and political planners.

The council has an essential contribution to make but it is *not* the organization under whose banner all planning should or will take place.

The achievement of the goals and recommendations—the action—of a health and welfare council is of primary importance. The focus of the means, the determination of the tactics and the strategies, should be upon the accomplishment of the goal, not upon the value of the means.

The council staff member must be an enabler and a leader, a tactician and a decision-maker. He must be directive or nondirective as the situation dictates and as the program of the council requires.

Health and welfare councils are essential to sound social and community planning. They must be recognized as such and included in community planning ranks.

In New Haven, as elsewhere, community planning is the order of the day. Planning requires implementation. Implementation requires decisions. Decisions require community acceptance. The Community Council of Greater New Haven, through its lay, professional, and staff leadership, applies its special skills in the area of community organization and health, welfare, and recreation planning so that this broad planning may continue and achieve results. The New Haven council is a partner in the total effort. It would not have it otherwise.

Participation of Residents in Neighborhood Community Action Programs

Frances Piven

The widespread advocacy of participation by residents of local communities in public programs by no means reflects agreement regarding the goals of such participation, the forms it should take, or the means for its effectuation. Some of the different concepts comprehended by "resident participation" and the problems these entail are suggested by a review of recent experiences with urban renewal and the early community action projects, predecessors of the antipoverty program.[1]

Both urban renewal and the antipoverty program can be viewed as policies for underdeveloped areas. They represent a new move forward in the developmental functions of government, as distinguished from its more traditional regulatory functions. It follows from the tasks of these programs that they have extraordinary — and differential — impact on selected local communities.

An Issue in Urban Renewal

Resident participation became a major issue in local areas earmarked for rebuilding under urban renewal programs. The dilemmas regarding resident participation followed in part from the fact that although local areas were selected as targets for redevelopment they were to be redeveloped in terms of

Reprinted with permission of the author and the National Association of Social Workers, from *Social Work*, Vol. 11, No. 1 (January 1966), pp. 73–80.

[1]Community action projects were initiated by the Ford Foundation's "Grey Areas Program" and by the President's Committee on Juvenile Delinquency and Youth Crime several years before the current spate of projects funded under Title II of the antipoverty legislation, according to which a "community action program means a program which mobilizes and utilizes resources, public or private of any . . . 'community' . . . in an attack on poverty." Public Law 88 452, Title II, Part A, Section 202.

assumptions about the welfare of "the city as a whole." Whatever diffuse benefits such a program might indeed come to have for the larger community, an immediately disruptive impact was felt by groups residing in the target area.[2] It was these groups that were hit most sharply by the costs of renewal, but it was not necessarily these groups that were to benefit from the new development. Economic and cultural revitalization of inner city areas was spelled out for slum residents by clearance and dislocation. The new developments chiefly included high rental housing. Existing residents in areas scheduled for renewal were confronted with the distress of upheaval, the loss of neighborhood, and the prospect of greatly increased rentals.[3] In consequence, adamant local protests came to be an earmark of renewal programs, often spelling political turmoil for the projects.[4] These experiences resulted in a growing concern with resident participation in renewal and also influenced the kinds of participation that were advocated and solicited by those responsible for the programs. In order to avoid local protests, which often rocked the projects when they were already well under way, steps were taken to initiate resident groups at an early stage in order to educate and win them to the plans.

Efforts to bring about resident participation in urban renewal were thus marked by an irony reflecting the dilemmas of renewal policy. Programs for resident participation were developed to offset the spontaneous—but disruptive—participation of local protest groups. Critics came to describe such programs cynically as a mere "cooling-off" tactic. However, so long as renewal plans were oriented to the welfare of the city as a whole they would almost surely generate acute protest and conflict in local areas. Only the most blithe and happy faith in the democratic consensus could permit a program geared to the community as a whole to promote participation by *and influence of* local residents in renewal areas. It was virtually inevitable that educational forms of participation would be emphasized in renewal programs.

[2]Considerable outrage has been occasioned among the advocates of government action in housing and urban renewal by publication recently of an extremely critical study of urban renewal by a conservative economist. *See* Martin Anderson, *The Federal Bulldozer* (Cambridge, Mass.: MIT Press, 1964). For a general but more judicious review of urban renewal policies and problems, *see* Herbert J. Gans, "The Failure of Urban Renewal," *Commentary*, Vol. 39, No. 4 (April 1965), pp. 29–37.

[3]For a review of problems in relocation, *see* Chester Hartman, "The Housing of Relocated Families," *Journal of the American Institute of Planners*, Vol. 30, No. 4 (November 1964), pp. 266–286.

[4]For a discussion of the political dilemmas created by renewal programs, *see* James Q. Wilson, "Planning and Politics: Citizen Participation in Urban Renewal." *Journal of the American Institute of Planners*, Vol. 29, No. 4 (November 1963).

Difference in Poverty
Projects

The community-based poverty projects that are already under way also emphasize the place of resident participation. These projects have, however, been given a different public mandate than renewal programs in that they are oriented to the problems of the poor in the project community rather than to the larger urban community. Moreover, they have developed at a time when the civil rights movement has lent new force and meaning to political and organizational activity among the minority groups that form the bulk of the urban poor.

The new concern with resident participation reflects a characterization of the low-income urban community as disorganized and politically ineffective. Low-income people tend not to belong to organizations and do not participate in community affairs. They are relatively uninfluential in the formation of policies and practices of the major institutions that affect the course of their lives. This kind of social and political inactivity is viewed as an aspect of social disorganization and is closely linked, therefore, with many of the problems of the low-income community— having to do particularly with socialization of the young and also with the social preconditions for individual and family effectiveness generally.

Consistent with this characterization, new objectives and strategies are being associated with resident participation in the antipoverty projects. Three interrelated objectives can be identified:

1. Fostering the participation of low-income people in a variety of local associations.
2. Enhancing the effective influence of low-income people on the policies and practices of institutions that serve the low-income community.
3. Establishing the conditions for effective individual and family life by altering the social context of individual behavior.

These objectives for resident participation reflect the concern of the poverty programs with political problems pertaining to democratic participation and influence, as well as concern with the social welfare problems to which the programs are principally addressed. The conception attributed to urban renewal programs, in contrast, emphasizes another kind of political problem—that of integrating local groups to the support of a larger public policy. It should be noted, however, that the poverty programs are only less immediately charged with the problem of reconciling divergent group interests. To the extent that the programs do pursue objectives oriented specifically to the interests of the poor they will, as they develop, require changes and accommodations from larger institutions. Problems of political conflict and integration will inevitably arise and rebound on the objectives of local resident participation and influence.[5] Recent contests between city officials and neighborhood leaders for control of the local poverty program structures may be an anticipation of these developments.

Characteristics of the Urban
Poor

While the poor are obviously composed of diverse groups, certain attributes can be identified that are pertinent to any efforts to encourage resident participation among the poor, in terms of the objectives outlined above.[6] The discussion which follows is addressed specifically to the urban poor. The problems and potentialities in involving the rural poor would appear to be quite different and to require examination in their own right. Several aspects of low-income urban life contribute to disorganization and political ineffectiveness.[7] Low-income people are overwhelmed by concrete daily needs. Their lives are often crisis ridden, deflecting from any concern with community issues. They often have no belief in their ability to affect the world in which they live, and so they are not easily induced to try to affect it.[8] Frequently they lack the necessary resources of knowledge and information to enable them to scrutinize social policies. Leadership capabilities are also scarcer among the poor. Moreover, when leaders do emerge, the poor have few incentives to offer them and means of controlling them are scarce. Potential leaders therefore tend to take advantage of opportunities for their own advancement that move them quickly away from low-income concerns. Finally, the institutions whose ser-

[5]There is already evidence of such probems in the controversy over Mobilization For Youth, an action-research project on New York's Lower East Side. Recent testimony from local leaders before a Congressional committee suggests, moreover, that such problems may smolder without becoming so publicly evident.

[6]For a discussion of the different class and status factors used to identify the lower class see S. M. Miller, "The American Lower Classes: A Typological Approach," in Frank Riessman, Jerome Cohen, and Arthur Pearl, eds., *Mental Health of the Poor: New Treatment Approaches for Low Income People,* (New York: Free Press of Glencoe, 1964), pp. 139–154.

[7]For a review of the sociological literature on the lower class see Herbert Gans, "A Survey of Working Class and Lower Class Studies," in Riessman, Cohen, and Pearl, *ibid.,* pp. 119–127.

[8]*See* Walter B. Miller, "Lower Class Culture as a Generating Milieu of Gang Delinquency," *Journal of Social Issues,* Vol. 14, No. 3 (July 1958), pp. 5–19; and Albert Cohen and Harold Hodges, "Characteristics of the Lower Blue-Collar Class," *Social Problems,* Vol. 10, No. 4 (Spring 1963), pp. 303–334.

vices might offer incentives for low-income interest and activity are often effectively insulated from the low-income community by their structure, practices, and cultural style.[9]

These several aspects of low-income life are interrelated and cumulative in their effects. Thus, lower-class interpretations of the world stress the inability of most men to affect the conditions under which they live.[10] These beliefs take form in a sense of political inefficacy, which discourages political participation and thus further reinforces conditions of actual powerlessness. Low-income people have little to offer in the way of material resources as political inducements, and they are separated by their social location from the exercise of personal influence on decision-makers. Therefore they are not easily able to obtain the benefits of political influence that might serve as inducements for political participation and to overcome the disadvantages in education and skill that inhibit participation.

The organizational life of the low-income community both reflects these individual attributes and serves also to maintain the conditions that produce them. Participation and influence do not consist only of the relations between disparate individuals and official decision-makers. The influence of individuals is mediated by organizations. It is through organizations that diverse individual resources are co-ordinated into coherent patterns of effective influence. But lower-class people have few of the requirements out of which stable organizations are generated: they have less organizational skill, less professional expertise, less money, and fewer personal relations with officials.[11] In any case, they do not have the resources lent by a stable livelihood that are required merely for regular participation in

[9]This has been a major theme in recent criticism of social welfare services, and a problem that the employment of "indigenous" or "nonprofessional" workers in neighborhood service centers is designed to alleviate, by helping to bridge the cultural and bureaucratic gaps between client and agency. For a description of public welfare practices and how they are countered by such a service center, see Richard A. Cloward and Richard M. Elman, "The Storefront on Stanton Street," to be published in *Commentary*. For a critique of the service patterns of the private social welfare agency, see Richard A. Cloward and Irwin Epstein, "Private Social Welfare's Disengagement from the Poor: The Case of Family Adjustment Agencies" (New York: Columbia University School of Social Work, 1964). (Mimeographed.) See also Herbert J. Gans, "Redefining the Settlement's Function for the War on Poverty," *Social Work*, Vol. 9, No. 4 (October 1964), pp. 3–12.

[10]For a discussion of the interrelationships between real powerlessness and attitudes of powerlessness, see Warren C. Haggstrom, "The Power of the Poor," in Riessman, Cohen, and Pearl, *op. cit.*, pp. 205–223.

[11]For a political scientist's discussion of the requirements for organizational influence in city affairs, see Wallace L. Sayre and Herbert Kaufman, *Governing New York City* (New York: Russell Sage Foundation, 1960), pp. 481–515.

organizations. The instability of lower-class life and the character of lower-class beliefs further discourages the poor from organizational participation.[12] It is, in turn, partly because of the meagerness of organizational life that the poor community is so little able to retain or control its potential leaders.[13]

This characterization of low-income urban life may be modified or even overcome when, for example, a community is bound by a strong ethnic culture.[14] It is a characterization that tends to apply to vast numbers of the urban poor today, however, and one that marks those groups who share least in organizational and political life. The meager success of traditional approaches to involving the poor, which rely on exhorting them to participate or on civic education, can be understood in terms of the interlocking and reinforcing relationships between actual powerlessness, apathetic beliefs, and scarce skills and resources. These circumstances, in turn, both produce and are maintained by the paucity of organizational life in the low-income community.

Program Strategies

The antipoverty projects can address these problems in resident participation in two different contexts. They can attempt to facilitate resident participation in a variety of areas of community life and with regard to a variety of institutions. This is typically the approach of community organization efforts. The antipoverty project is, however, also itself a public policy arena. The focus may, therefore, be specifically on resident participation in the policy and program of the local project.

Various strategies for facilitating resident participation in community life generally are being used by projects already under way. These can be identified and reviewed in terms of early experiences.

[12]In fact, instability in occupational or family life has frequently been the criterion used to distinguish the lower class, or the poor, from the working class. See, for example, S. M. Miller, op. cit.; and S. M. Miller and Frank Riessman, "The Working-Class Subculture: A New View," Social Problems, Vol. 9, No. 1 (Summer 1961), pp. 86-97.

[13]The sparse social texture of the poor community is suggested by a survey conducted by Mobilization For Youth on the Lower East Side of New York City. Over half the residents reported no informal group participation and only 15 percent got together with a group more than once a week "just to talk, play cards, go bowling, or something else like that." "Codebook: Mobilization For Youth, Vol. I. Adult Survey" (New York: Research Center, Columbia University School of Social Work, 1962). (Mimeographed.)

[14]See, for example, Herbert J. Gans's study of an Italian community in Boston in The Urban Villagers: Group and Class in the Life of Italian-Americans (New York: Free Press of Glencoe, 1962). See also William F. Whyte, Jr., Street Corner Society (Chicago: University of Chicago Press, 1955).

1. Concrete services are provided, such as help in processing housing complaints or in consumer problems. These services are located in places easily accessible to local people and are expected to attract low-income people as recipients. The effort, however, is to induce recipients to take on more active roles through associations formed around the provision of service. Thus tenant associations may be organized in housing clinics, with the aim of interesting tenants in sponsoring and operating the clinic and the hope that eventually, as a group, they will become more articulate and aggressive concerning the issues in housing policy that their daily problems reflect. Mobilization For Youth, for example, opened storefronts where residents could get not only advice on housing problems, but the intervention of staff in dealings with landlords and housing agencies. The staff first gave individual help and then attempted to induce the tenants in a building to get together in order to register joint complaints and in some instances for joint withholding of rent. These different building organizations were, in turn, invited to join a neighborhood-wide tenants' council for further group action.

2. Existing low-income organizations in the project area are helped with staff and facilities. It is expected that adding to the resources of these groups will enable them to attract more participants and will also encourage them to take more alert and forceful positions on social issues of concern to the membership. The Haryou-Act project in New York's Harlem tries to do this by subcontracting many of its programs, with the idea that program resources can thus serve in building local organizations.

3. A short-term approach to the problem of scarce leadership resources in the community is the engagement of professional staff in community organization activity. This is, of course, not a new role for social workers. Whether the engagement of professionals in this role is indeed merely an interim solution depends on success in the development of local leadership.

Potential leadership is sought among local people. Efforts are made to interest persons who seem to show leadership qualities in organizing activity and to educate these persons about issues considered critical to low-income people. These individuals may be paid as a kind of "community worker," or they may be coached and encouraged to perform actively as volunteers. Some projects have actually developed "community action institutes" to train neighborhood people who will be employed as block workers or organizers.

4. The social contiguity provided by ethnic, religious, occupational, or residential groups is a natural basis for affiliation and therefore is a reference in organizing group activity. Residential groupings—the building or block association—and racial or ethnic groupings seem particularly important among the poor. Many projects are located in ghetto neighborhoods and therefore work only with a racially and ethnically homogeneous client population. In a mixed community such as the Lower East Side of New York, however, groups are often formed according to the racial and ethnic lines along which people divide themselves.

5. Participation in social protest action is sometimes encouraged by staff assigned to local organizations. Facilities required to pursue such actions may also be provided to these organizations or even to formally unaffiliated individuals who seem to play a leader role. These protest actions may range from participation in nationwide or city-wide events to demonstrations over specific grievances involving perhaps only a few residents.[15]

Barriers to Participation

Some early experience with these program strategies reveals persisting problems in overcoming barriers to low-income participation and influence in community affairs.

When concrete services are the incentive for initial participation they tend to remain the focus of activity. The extent of need for such service among the poor seems to overwhelm any less urgent activities and the provision of services consumes the energies of staff and recipients alike. Thus staff assigned to help with housing or welfare problems find that emergency housing violations or delayed welfare checks are so widespread and compelling as to require their direct and continuing efforts at obtaining service, deflecting them from organizational activities.

Existing low-income organizations are weak and seem often to be mere emblems of power for leaders whose personal ambition is tied, not to a low-income following that has little to offer them, but rather to the service organization. Thus these organizations may use facilities or funds they receive to acquire the furnishings of respectability: typewriters, furniture, and the like. And new resources can merely precipitate bickering among leaders, deflecting rather than impelling their attention to membership.

[15]It should be noted that while protest actions by the poor have received wide interest and attention, they have not generally been risked by the community action project. Mobilization For Youth in New York City and the Syracuse University training program for community organizers, inspired largely by Saul Alinsky, are two exceptions.

The role of professionals in community organization remains problematical. Local people tend to regard them with uneasiness, as strangers. The professionals themselves must accommodate a strain between the style and actions indicated by their role in low-income organizations, the dictates of their professional training, and the organizational requirements of the antipoverty project itself. Thus the professional worker is expected by the community group with whom he works to take clear and support- ive positions on issues that arise. If instead he defers to direc- tives from his supervisors or to the dictates of professional neutrality, he may lose the confidence of the community group.

Other problems seem to reside in the strategies for selecting and cultivating indigenous leadership. When these individuals are paid, in an effort to compensate for the absence of incentives for leadership in the low-income community, they tend to orient themselves predominantly to the organization that pays them. Volunteers, when they can be cultivated, come to expect similar compensation.

Social protest actions, because they offer simple and dramatic definitions of problems, may penetrate apathy and override the puzzled disengagement bred of lack of information. These actions also require less personal and economic stability than sustained organizational participation. It should be noted that urban re- newal programs elicited protest action from local groups in response to the threats posed by renewal. Social protest is likely, however, to incur hostile and repressive reactions from other groups in the community and from public authorities. Low- income groups may in consequence be even further cut off from channels to influence and also from the services that can serve as a basis for more stable organization. Experience with anti- poverty programs testifies dramatically to this risk.

Different Ways of Participating

The antipoverty project itself is a potential arena for resident participation. This has lately become something of a public issue and several different organizational forms of participation are being recommended:

1. Resident should participate on policy-making structures—ordinarily the board—either on the city-wide or local level. These residents are regarded as representatives of the resident population in the areas served. It is this kind of participation that has usually been associated

with the legislative mandate for "maximum feasible participation of residents." A certain proportion of the seats on these structures are allocated to residents, with different schemes—elections, appointments, or conventions—for selecting them. These arrangements have often been the occasion for tugging and hauling among various groups, local and city-wide, for controlling influence.

2. Residents should participate as staff. These programs, generally referred to as the employment of indigenous or nonprofessional workers, are among the most widely used of the poverty program strategies.[16]

3. Residents should be formed into active constituent groups. These groups are sometimes recommended as a program resource for professional staff, providing feedback for program evaluation, or they may be regarded as pressure groups that properly influence the project in its activities.

The "neighborhood boards" of Haryou-Act, planned also by the Youth-In-Action project in Brooklyn, are organizational devices intended to provide for all three of the foregoing forms of participation. These boards are supposed to be independent of the parent project—though funded by it—and governed by neighborhood people. The boards are supposed to develop service functions and will presumably make policy in that regard (at least within the limitations set by the terms of their contracts with the parent project and within the overall limitations set by the city's poverty structure). The boards will employ local people in service-giving functions. And, finally, since the boards are composed of independent groups of residents they are potentially active constituents for the parent project.

These proposals can be reviewed for problems and potentialities in the light of the foregoing characterization of low-income urban life:

1. Persons from the resident community who are selected to participate in policy-making structures will, if they are to be effective, ordinarily be distinguished by superior abilities or resources. To this extent their representative character is qualified. Moreover, what has been said about the scarce resources for control of leaders in the low-income community applies to the control of these representatives as well. The community has little in the way of an alert and able citizenry or organizational resources to review, control, and direct what its ostensible spokesmen do. The antipoverty program, on the other hand, and the organizations with which it is affiliated constitute an active source of pressure and inducement to the presumed representatives.

2. To some extent these problems also pertain when residents are employed as staff. Their sense of themselves as employees, however—

---

[16]They are often interpreted in terms of other goals than resident participation, however: they provide employment for local people, for example, or are intermediaries to bridge the cultural and organizational gap between clients and service bureaucracies.

facilitated by unionization—may create something of a bulwark enhancing resident identity. The tendency of supervising professionals to become overly protective and directing with resident staff, usually in the name of professional guidance and training, may also strain against the goals of participation and influence. This may be mitigated if the resident staff are organized in cadres enhancing their resident identity and providing group support.

3. When constituent groups are restricted to "feedback" participation there may be little incentive for their continuing viability. Feedback in the form of more active pressure and influence by these groups, in the course of which the project could deliver incentives for continued engagement, might be more successful. This requires organizational arrangements that try to insure the project's responsiveness to constituent groups. For example, local public hearings can be held on various program practices provided these practices are deemed appropriately reviewed and changed in response to constituent groups.

Conclusions

Whatever patterns are developed in the antipoverty projects for resident participation will reflect answers to two sets of questions:

1. Who should participate? In what actions should they participate? Where should this participation be located in the organizational structure? What conditions should govern this action?

2. How can participation by the specified groups, and in the prescribed forms, be elicited and maintained; i.e., what are the effectuating mechanisms for the forms of participation prescribed by the answers to the first set of questions above?

Decisions made in antipoverty programs will initiate patterns of participation and influence, and these questions should be confronted. Decisions pertaining to program activities designed to foster resident participation in community life generally will imply answers that properly vary with the kinds of participation considered and the institutional contexts of participation. The full scope of such decisions will reflect the political philosophy of the antipoverty program, as well as a range of assumptions regarding the conditions of social action. Insofar as these decisions pertain to participation in the project themselves, they will imply answers that describe the antipoverty program as a political subsystem and the place of residents of the local community in this political subsystem.

The answers to these questions must reflect some of the fundamental ambiguities of our political values and must take account of the fluidity of social and political arrangements. Moreover, they require knowledge of processes of social and political change that does not yet exist. For these reasons, the questions will not be answered entirely explicitly or comprehensively.

The essential dilemma in gaining participation, however, and the problem that underlies many of the difficulties detailed here, is that participation and influence depend on a range of social and economic capabilities. Strategies intended specifically to induce participation may set directions. Sustained and effective participation, however, will finally depend on the allocation to these communities of the social and economic benefits that are the resources for participation and influence in a complex society.

Community Development Programs Serving the Urban Poor

Charles F. Grosser

A discontinuity exists between the theory and the methodology of community organization. Recognition of this is evidenced in the recent literature. Kahn notes:

> One cannot plan for the education, job training, placement, or counseling of deprived inner-city youth without new concentration on the public sector generally. What was often tokenism in welfare council participation would not do for these endeavors. . . . One must learn to deal with, involve, plan with, bring pressure upon, or even to cause changes in, local and state governmental bodies. . . .
> . . . until recently, the community organization method was conceptualized entirely in relation to the enabling role. . . . The enabling took the form of facilitating leadership development of consensus about direction to be taken or winning local assent to leadership-sanctioned direction and plans—not of shaping planning out of true community-wide involvement in goal setting.[1]

Morris and Rein similarly indicate that "the requirements of the new community demand skill in invoking special points of view and in living with other professionals who advocate competing points of view."[2]

One major factor impelling new developments in community organization practice is the increased attention by the field to the client group with which it is engaged: specifically, beginning

Reprinted with permission of the author and the National Association of Social Workers from *Social Work*, Vol. 10, No. 3 (July 1965), pp. 15–21.

[1]Alfred J. Kahn, "Trends and Problems in Community Organization," *Social Work Practice, 1964* (New York: Columbia University Press, 1964), pp. 9–19.

[2]Robert Morris and Martin Rein, "Emerging Patterns in Community Planning," *Social Work Practice, 1963* (New York: Columbia University Press, 1963), pp. 174–175.

to work directly with the recipients—rather than exclusively with the providers—of social welfare service. As the term is used in this paper, *neighborhood community development* means community organization efforts being made with lower-class, minority group, urban slum residents. The goals of these efforts are to engage the poor in the decision-making process of the community, both to overcome apathy and estrangement and to realign the power resources of the community by creating channels through which the consumers of social welfare services can define their problems and goals and negotiate on their own behalf. Much of the experience gained from these efforts can be generalized for application to most groups of deprived persons.

The purpose of this paper is to explore some of the consequences emerging from community organization's growing engagement with the poor man. Briefly discussed are (1) the substantive areas and issues with which community organization practice will have to deal, (2) a consideration of the role of the community worker, and (3) a brief review of the issue of the organizational forms that practice will take.

Substantive Areas and Issues

Community organization in neighborhood development programs signifies direct engagement with the problems of the poor man. More than any other group in our society, the poor expend a major portion of their efforts to achieve the "good life" through interaction with agencies of city government. It is with the local branches of the department of welfare, the police, the housing authority, the board of education, and similar agencies that the poor man negotiates for his share of the community's resources. Striving toward the equitable distribution of these resources is the programmatic strategy that must accompany any bona fide effort to encourage the residents of the inner-city slum to help themselves. If neighborhood development denies or ignores this fact, in the eyes of the local residents it is at best sham and window-dressing, at worst, deceit. Lower-class, minority group individuals cannot be expected to feel that they have a part in the determination of their own destinies in the face of such grievances as denial of welfare to nonresidents, forcing parents to take legal action against their child under the relatives' responsibility laws, categorization as an "undesirable tenant" with no right to face one's accusers and no recourse to appeal, arrest and interrogation characterized by prejudice and brutality, and an inferior, segregated school system. To attempt to facilitate a client's adjustment to such a social system is to betray his interest. Therefore, if local community development programs are to be successful, it must be recognized that local efforts at self-expression will be directed at the agents of government in an attempt to bring about solutions to such injustices as these.

Further, in order to arouse people who have been systematically socialized into apathy and inaction—in some cases, over several generations—it may be necessary to teach them that the solutions to their problems lie in the hands of certain governmental agencies, and that these agencies are sensitive to well-publicized mass efforts, particularly in election years. Lower-class, alienated, nonparticipating people will not be induced to organize by appeals to their sense of civic duty, patriotism, or morality, or other exhortations to exercise their obligations of citizenship. Such individuals will organize only if they perceive organization as a means to an immediate end. It should be pointed out—without becoming involved in a means-ends, process-content discussion—that these programs require a great deal more attention to material objectives than has been true in the past. Community development in slum neighborhoods is, after all, essentially a process for the redress of grievances that are the cumulative result of the differential distribution of community resources. To avoid partisanship in the name of objectivity and service to the "total community" is, in effect, to take a position justifying the pittance that has been allotted from the health, educational, and social welfare coffers to the residents of the inner-city slum.

An applied example of the foregoing was a voter-registration campaign conducted in New York City by Mobilization For Youth last summer and fall.[3] Geared to the registration of eligible minority group nonvoters, the campaign was not run on the model of the League of Women Voters, which presses voters to fulfill their civic duty. Instead, it was focused on the ballot's Proposition I, which provided for additional low-income housing, and on the recently enacted "stop-and-frisk" and "no-knock" laws. Because these issues have great pertinence for the Lower East Side slum community, they were used to encourage voter registration. MFY was careful to avoid creating unrealistic expectations of immediate success regarding these issues; rather, it argued that Proposition 1 was sure to be defeated unless the people of New York City carried it by a large enough plurality to overcome the upstate oppositon, and that the "stop-and-frisk" and "no-knock" laws violate the rights and dignity of the suspect and are a reflection of

[3]Betty Jo Bailey and Sidney Pinsky, "1964 Voter Registration Drive." Unpublished report, Mobilization For Youth, New York, 1965.

Community Organization

a general lack of political accountability and of abstinence from voting by the poor man, who is more often arrested and interrogated than any other citizen.

The Enabler Role

The traditional stance of the community organizer as enabler is based on two assumptions, one valid, the other invalid. The valid assumption is that self-imposed actions growing out of a community's assessment of its own needs have a value and permanence that do not inhere in actions imposed from the outside. The invalid assumption is that the enabling role is the only one by which this desirable end may be brought about. In this section several alternatives are suggested that are believed to be viable.

It should be noted, first, that the role of enabler, geared to process, may itself be limited as a strategy for facilitating community self-help. For example, one text on community organization method draws on the experience of a special governor's committee set up in Colorado to deal with pervasive problems in the state's mental institutions as illustrative of proper work by a community organizer. Conditions within the institutions were unsatisfactory, and individuals were being improperly and illegally committed:

. . . the legislation [directed at the problems] recommended by the governor's committee did not get very far in the ensuing session of the state assembly, although a more substantial program might have resulted if the committee, or even a considerable bloc within the committee, had been willing to manipulate or use undemocratic methods. It was rightly felt, however, that this might jeopardize future working relationships—in short, that process or means was as important as the immediate goal.[4]

Although such judgments may be possible in statewide interdisciplinary committees, direct contact with those immediately affected by such decisions in a neighborhood community development program precludes any such cavalier determination of the client's fate.

The "Broker" Role

Familiar in such non-social work contexts as real estate and the stock market, the role of "broker" was instituted in the Mobilization For Youth program in 1962. It appears to have been first suggested for social work practice by Wilensky and Lebeaux

---

[4]Campbell Murphy, *Community Organization Practice* (Boston: Houghton-Mifflin Co., 1954), p. 22.

in 1958. These writers postulated a need for "guides, so to speak, through a new kind of civilized jungle," and spoke of social work as "an example par excellence of the liaison function, a large part of its total activity being devoted to putting people in touch with community resources they need but can hardly name, let alone locate."[5]

The community organization worker brings the component of collective action to the broker role, adding a potent factor to the process. Through collective "brokerage activity," the notion of collective solutions is introduced; that is, administrative and policy changes are undertaken to affect whole classes of persons rather than a single individual. The following comment, taken from a report of a Mobilization For Youth community organizer, illustrates the point:

Residents of the Lower East Side have brought their welfare problems . . . such as late checks, insufficient funds to pay large utility bills, no winter clothing, dispossess notices, and a host of others . . . to Casa de la Communidad, since it first opened in February 1963. These problems were handled by the caseworker . . . who shared the facilities with the C.O. worker. . . . All too often, no real change seemed to result either in the lives of the clients or in the procedures of welfare. The same clients tended to come over and over again from emergency to emergency.[6]

It was as a result of this experience that two community organization efforts in the welfare area were launched: a welfare information center and an organization of welfare clients holding court support orders. The latter group sought a collective resolution to the problems created by the determination of budgets on the basis of income ordered by a court but rarely received by the family.

The Advocate Role

It has been the experience of workers in neighborhood community development programs that the broker role is frequently insufficiently directive. Therefore the role of advocate has been co-opted from the field of law. Often the institutions with which local residents must deal are not even neutral, much less positively motivated, toward handling the issues brought to them by community groups. In fact, they are frequently overtly negative and hostile, often concealing or distorting information about rules, procedures, and office hours. By their own partisanship on behalf of instrumental organizational goals, they create an at-

[5]Harold L. Wilensky and Charles N. Lebeaux, *Industrial Society and Social Welfare* (New York: Russell Sage Foundation, 1958), p. 286.
[6]Daniel Kronenfeld, "Community Organization and Welfare." Unpublished report, Mobilization For Youth, New York, 1965.

mosphere that demands advocacy on behalf of the poor man. If the community worker is to facilitate productive interaction between residents and institutions, it is necessary for him to provide leadership and resources directed toward eliciting information, arguing the correctness of a position, and challenging the stance of the institution.

In short, the worker's posture, both to the community residents and to the institutional representatives with whom he is engaged, is that of advocate for the client group's point of view. While employing these techniques, the worker is not enabler, broker, expert, consultant, guide, or social therapist.[7] He is, in fact, a partisan in a social conflict, and his expertise is available exclusively to serve client interests. The impartiality of the enabler and the functionalism of the broker are absent here. Other actors in this social conflict may be using their expertise and resources against the client. Thus the community organizer may find himself arguing the appropriateness of issuing a permit while the police argue its inappropriateness, or the worker and tenant may take the position that building-code violations warrant the withholding of rent while the landlord argues their nonexistence. There may even be differences among social workers. For example, a community organization worker may claim certain welfare benefits for a group of clients over the opposition of a social investigator, or a community worker and a city housing authority worker may take opposite sides over the criteria the housing authority uses to evict tenants in city projects as undesirable.

In jurisdictional disputes or if organizational prerogatives are at issue, it is not uncommon to find social workers at odds with each other. When issues of professional ideology or politics are involved, vigorous advocacy is the rule rather than the exception, as a casual glance through the professional journals shows. Why is it not possible for such advocates to be recruited for the poor from the ranks of social workers? This is one of the orders of today's business.

Outside the courtroom, attorneys for defendants and plaintiffs often mingle in an atmosphere of congeniality and good fellowship. Social workers do not enjoy this kind of professional relationship. It is likely that the partisan advocacy postulated will evoke virulence from the public agency that is directed against the worker. The following charges were made by school principals of a local district as a result of the actions of a group of parents who were part of the MFY community organization program:

[7]Murray G. Ross, Community Organization (New York: Harper & Brothers, 1955), pp. 220-228.

We find that a group of its staff is fomenting suspicion and enmity toward the schools . . . this group is largely in the CO program. . . .

Mobilization workers have been engaged in a war on the schools. . . .

Parents and children are encouraged to make such complaints. This means that MFY is accumulating a secret dossier on the teachers in the area. . . .

The social worker from MFY began to assume the mantle of "guardian". . . .

It should be noted . . . how a controversy between MFY and the principals is transformed into a conflict between the community and the schools.[8]

Such a response is not surprising since advocacy, if effective, will cause public agencies to spend more money, create more work for their already harassed staff, and focus the community's attention on the agencies' shortcomings.

The Activist Role

Once the fact is recognized that community development efforts on behalf of the poor will produce partisan situations, it must be conceded further that the community organizer—or, for that matter, any other service worker in the urban slum—must choose which side he is on. The same logic that legitimates the roles of broker and advocate leads inevitably to another role, that of activist. Morris and Rein have pointed out:

Political knowledge and skill to achieve one's ends have often been considered by social workers to be unprofessional. We have somehow believed that strong advocacy of a particular point of view and the development of techniques to achieve those ends violate our professional commitment to the democratic process. The question for us is whether our commitment to professional neutrality and noninvolvement is to continue to sustain our professional practice.[9]

The traditional neutrality of the social work profession has much to recommend it, but it has been exercised to the detriment of certain client groups. Morris and Rein suggest that if this policy of noninvolvement persists, the function of community organization practice will be limited to coordination. If community organization is to find a role in community development, it cannot be exclusively neutral, hence the role of activist must also be embraced.

Except for the heroes of the American Revolution, this nation has had a culturally estranged view of the political and social ac-

[8]Report of twenty-six principals of Districts 1–4 (New York: City of New York, 1964). (Mimeographed.)

[9]Morris and Rein, op. cit., p. 174.

tivist. Despite their ultimate vindication, the abolitionist, suf-fragette, and labor organizer are still viewed as historical mutants by the community at large. Activists are characterized as "out-siders" and "agitators" to this very day, whether they play their roles in Selma, Alabama, or between Houston and Delancey Streets in New York City.

However, the activist role is and has been a legitimate stance for the social worker, especially the community organizer, and it must be available to be chosen from among other strategies when community needs require such activity. The passivity and objec-tivity of the service professions is after all something of a myth: people are urged to action of all sorts—to visit a dentist, sit up straight, curb their dogs, contribute to the Red Cross, and, in some communities, to register and vote and to support the PTA. In neighborhood community development, students are urged to stay in school, tenants to keep off project lawns, dropouts to join the Job Corps, and mothers to use well-baby clinics. Why should not tenants who are without heat also be urged to withhold rents, parents with grievances to boycott the schools, or citizens without franchise to take to the streets in legal public demonstration as a means to redress their grievances?

The answer to this point has been a matter of contingency, not reason. Some members of the profession have expressed concern that recourse to roles other than that of enabler—particularly that of activist—entails manipulation of the client group or commu-nity. The writer is convinced that the choice of role bears no rele-vance whatsoever to the issue of manipulation. As an attempt to achieve goals determined by the worker rather than the clients, manipulation can be accomplished by many techniques. Activists and advocates, no less than enablers and brokers, must make judgments on the basis of their professional appraisal of the cli-ent's needs, without regard to political expedience, personal ideology, or the vested interests of the agency.

Who is doing significant neighborhood community develop-ment with the impoverished today, and where? It is being done in the Negro ghettos of the North and South by nonprofessional ac-tivists in such organizations as the Congress of Racial Equality, Council of Federated Organizations, Student Nonviolent Co-ordinating Committee, and Southern Christian Leadership Con-ference. With few exceptions, neighborhood community devel-opment is taking place outside the field of social work, reflecting a narrowness of concept, not a paucity of resources in social work. Law students already have participated systematically in organizing drives for such organizations as SNCC and CORE. For a number of years, community organization practice and training of community organization students has taken place within such groups as the NAACP and the National Urban League. Therefore, it would seem appropriate for social work to place students in more activist areas within the civil rights movement.

Although techniques of activism are being sought, they are, in the main, unformulated. A body of literature is beginning to evolve, however, based on the philosophy and tactics of nonviolent direct action. For example, Oppenheimer and Lakey describe such techniques as haunting, renouncing honors, hartal,[10] boycott, demonstrations, leafleting, picketing, vigils, and role-playing.[11] They also suggest forms for record-keeping and typical budgets for voter-registration projects, provide notes on security in the Deep South, and offer advice on how to conduct oneself if arrested (including such specific suggestions as wearing two sets of underwear to absorb the shock of being dragged and using a bucket of water to remove traces of tear gas). Social workers should not be intimidated by the notion of incorporating some of these suggestions into their method: their strangeness stems largely from unfamiliarity. It might be noted that the many civil rights workers who have sought counsel and technique from social workers have frequently found social work methods somewhat strange also and have wondered how they might be incorporated into the methodology of nonviolence.

Organizational Forms of Neighborhood Development

Those in community organization practice who have wrestled with the problems of neighborhood development in urban slums have found the issue of the organizational forms that their efforts should take a troublesome one. In what form should slum residents organize to mount efforts toward self-help? When the forms that voluntary associations take in the middle-class community are examined, a proliferation of styles, purposes, and patterns of participation, as varied as the personalities and social circumstances of those who participate in them, is discovered. Social workers do not have the temerity to suggest that there is a single optimal form that middle-class voluntarism should take. The

[10]"Hartal" is defined by *Webster's Third New International Dictionary* (Springfield, Mass.: G. C. Merriam Co., 1961), p. 1036, as "concerted cessation of work and business esp. as a protest against a political situation. . . ."

[11]Martin Oppenheimer and George Lakey, *A Manual for Direct Action* (Chicago: Quadrangle Books, 1965).

assumption that such a form exists for collective action in the slum community is equally untenable.

Rather than debate on the relative merits of various alternatives, what is needed is to determine the strategies that will be most effective.

Forms of organization, their structure, and their affiliations if any will depend on the job decided on and the personnel available. The worker may want to join an existing group in order to influence it; he may want to set up an ad hoc or temporary group composed either of individuals or of representatives of other groups; or he may want to create a new group.[12]

Neighborhood work has been conducted with groups on the basis of common cultural patterns (hometown clubs), common social problems (welfare or housing organizations), physical proximity (building or block organizations), social movements (civil rights groups), specific task orientation (voter-registration campaigns), and the operation of a resource center (storefronts). If it has not yet created the technology or method of neighborhood community development work, social work efforts at community organization in urban slums have at least established the legitimacy of such efforts.

Commenting editorially on this issue as reflected in the MFY experience, the New York Times stated:

If Mobilization For Youth is to do more than merely ameliorate the lot of the poorest elements of the community, it must teach them to help themselves by concerted efforts. . . . Any form of social protest is bound to generate controversy, and some forms clearly raise serious questions of propriety for an agency that draws so much of its support from government funds. . . . But the poor must be encouraged to believe that there are ways to express their views on the need for social betterment. . . . The right to fight City Hall is as much a prerogative of the poor as of any other group of citizens; it is only when those who dwell in the slums and have too little to keep themselves and their families in dignity surrender to a supine sense of total futility and helplessness that the community has real cause to worry.[13]

[12]Ibid., p.43.
[13]Editorial, New York Times, November 11, 1964.

Intake Policy as a
Community Organization
Tool

Solomon E. Feldman
Marshall Jacobson

In many instances the policies regarding the flow of cases handled by an agency are unevaluated products of the Topsy-like growth and synthesis of professional zeal, the unique competencies and preferences of the staff, momentary expediencies, and tradition. Often it is assumed that intake policy procedures have only one purpose, the statement of who is eligible for service and the specification of the available services. There is minimal articulation of potential effects of the development, communication, and implementation of an agency's intake policy upon community organization (CO). By CO in this context we are referring to an interdependent involvement of local, lay, and professional persons in the planning, execution, and maintenance of comprehensive services providing continuity of care to those needing it. It is the major thesis of this paper that the pattern of CO will have both short- and long-term consequences upon the realization of an agency's goals and that the impact of intake policy upon CO must be weighed heavily if an agency hopes to maximize its potential ameliorative and preventive effectiveness.

Among the several ways in which a community and agency may relate, three models can be identified which reflect basic, but not mutually exclusive, goals that may be entertained with regard to community development. The models to be elaborated upon are the direct service, extended community management, and extensive community development models.

Direct Service Model

This model has a minimum of identifiable CO goals. Very simply, the basic consideration is that the agency has a mission to provide direct services. The agency's intake policy is not developed to initiate any change in the community's social structure as it bears upon mutual problems. Under this model, community participation is narrow and primarily limited to the members of the board of directors who may aid in developing general agency policy.

The agency's accountability to the public for financial support requires it to maintain professional standards congruent with an

Reprinted with permission of the authors and the publisher from the *Community Mental Health Journal*, Vol. 5, No. 1 (January 1969), pp. 76-81.

aura of efficient output of services to the entire community. Toward this end, the agency's program often is communicated to the community as being broad and extensive. Since the lay community may be led to believe that total programming is present and that most, if not all, needs are being met, a "comfortable community" is a natural consequence.

An "open door" intake policy is frequently belied by the fact that for many clients the door is a revolving one. Obviously there will be instances of individual cases which fall outside the province of the actual resources of the agency. The handling, or rather lack of handling, of these cases is a potential source of community discomfort. However, an agency will typically adopt coping mechanisms that stave off full feedback of its limitations to the community. As with many defensive strategies, they will be minimally articulated by their users. Among the various techniques employed are second-rate substitutes, going through the motions of remediation, selective use of the waiting-list, passive resistance via such ploys as impractical scheduling of working clients, and too rapid institutionalization. While direct refusal of service may be an infrequently used technique, it is more likely to be employed for those cases who, because of socioeconomic status, are least likely to be effective in fermenting community discomfort.

Thus the delusion of all-encompassing service may persist, and the anxiety required to initiate change in the community care apparatus is slow in developing. The agency, to protect its image, will be reluctant to initiate change in intake policy as a CO tool. The agency can fear that the community will not only become concerned with the situational deficiencies pinpointed by intake change, but will also become angry at the agency. This anger is justified in the sense that the agency was at least partly responsible for some of the inappropriate assumptions developed in the community.

The most likely and comfortable vehicle for change, under this model, is through the role of service giver. The agency may attempt to initiate and publicize new services which are typically closely related to the ones that are presently given. It is unlikely that this agency will assume the lead in such things as promoting treatment alternatives and supports within the community or in initiating major innovations. Any participation in CO will be an afterthought which is seen as adjunctive to "major goals," rather than as an integral part of the agency's operative plan. As such it is hardly likely that the agency will be effective in fostering the community mobilization necessary for the development of a truly encompassing community care apparatus.

Extended Community
Management Model

This model has developed from the recognition of the critical shortage of mental health professionals and the growing understanding that case management can be extended to other types of professionals within the community, e.g., family physicians, educators, and others. The intake policy is clearly structured to include the mandate that referring professionals in the community have a sustained involvement in the diagnostic and treatment processes.

The primary, albeit short-range, CO goal that evolves from this intake policy is a focus upon change within the professional group of the community. The implicit assumption of this model is that change within the professional group will filter through the entire community and thus, in the long run, will foster the development of an encompassing and viable community care apparatus.

With this model the agency and collaborating professionals more readily can see themselves in a joint undertaking. Consequently agencies, having been provided sympathetic spokesmen, are less likely to sweep agency role deficiencies under the rug of professional isolationism. Conversely, the cooperating professionals are more likely to recognize community care shortcomings, be disturbed by them, and engage in constructive and cooperative attempts to implement change.

It should be noted that preceding this Valhalla of cooperation between agency and professionals there is a strong tendency for discord to occur regarding the agency's demands for case specific involvement by the referring professionals. In this "finger pointing" stage, the professionals are defensive about their own role and responsibility and often accuse the agency of negating its responsibility. Not until this "finger pointing" is openly identified and dealt with can the agency and professional move toward truly cooperative efforts.

One of the major problems in this model, however, is the secondary involvement of the social and political leadership outside the professional group. This is particularly an issue since it is the lay community which must bear the financial responsibility for any change in the community's care apparatus. Depending upon the ability of the professional to communicate as an individual or through a professional organization, this model may be a wise expedient as a transitional method of CO. However, its efficiency depends heavily on the continued motivation, the range of entries to the community, and the communication skills of the professionals involved. Finally, it runs the danger of encountering resistance within the community to the extent that this mode of attempting to institute change runs counter to the normal channels of developing community sanctions.

Extensive Community
Development Model

The agency which utilizes the extensive community development model is found at the polar end of the spectrum when contrasted to the direct service agency. While the former model includes a direct service program, this program is conceived as being secondary to the efforts of the agency to foster an integration of multiple treatment alternatives within the community. The realization that any one agency cannot, need not, and should not provide every needed service is the motivating force that will gear the agency to the development, communication, and implementation of an intake policy that will catalyze the process of CO which, it is hoped, eventually will produce a comprehensive community care system.

In addition to the possibility of sampling the prevalence of untreated cases within the community, careful study of the flow rates within an established agency and from the community to other agencies, e.g. state hospitals, provides ample evidence that the agency cannot provide all the ameliorative, no less preventative, services to all the population groups within the community.

Even without consideration of such things as flow rates, there are other reasons that argue against a sole emphasis upon a direct service mission. There are many resources within the community, e.g. schools, general practitioners, courts, and even the home, which potentially can be used more efficiently and effectively in changing symptomatic behavior than can a doctor-patient model of treatment. Although the direct service and extended community management models do not demand a commitment to a "medical model of treatment," the extensive community management model would seem to foster more flexible treatment approaches. Similarly, the conception of disordered behavior as occurring within a social context would be brought into focus more clearly.

Concentrating on an established agency, the realization that the services offered fall short of fulfilling the directive given or assumed by the agency, that many community members are either going untreated or are being extruded from the community, should make competent professions feel uncomfortable in their role as service givers. This discomfort in turn can motivate the agency to refocus its strategy and begin thinking through the use of intake policies in the development of a program that approaches total community service.

Any new policy that is to be instrumental in effecting community change must clearly delineate and communicate to the client population that will be served by the agency the services that will be provided this population. This is contrasted to individual decision-making and communication within the context of the planning of services for a specific client. It is suggested that the most effective vehicle for CO is a clear restriction on intake, a restriction in keeping with the actual effective treatment alternatives available to the agency, rather than a blanket offer of help.

Following a decision by the agency's staff and its board of directors that there will be restrictions upon populations serviced and services offered, the specific limitations must be set. Study of the agency's current services, the services provided by other agencies in the community, community needs, and who would best profit from various services, provide the grist for these deliberations.

Except for consideration of other community agencies and total community needs, what has been said so far minimally differentiates the strategies of an agency committed to an extensive community development model from the strategies of a restrictive agency which has no CO goals. It is in the communication and implementation of intake policy that differences are most evident.

In the extensive community development model, the restrictive intake policy is explicitly and loudly communicated to other agencies, adjunctive professionals, and the lay public. If the service mandate prior to the change was conceived as very broad, the initial negative reactions will include the complaint that these restrictions will tend to *increase* the number of untreated cases and the number of exclusions from the community. Anger and hostility toward the agency will be a common bond between the general lay community and other agencies and professionals within the community who are no longer able to find easy access to referral within the community. Most typically, attempts at CO prior to actual implementation of policy, where the change is clearly set in motion but is programmed in steps, do little to mitigate this anger. These attempts may, in fact, increase hostility as pressures upon the agency to alter the proposed policy changes are rebuffed.

To proceed toward its goal of CO, agency personnel must develop thick but not insensitive hides. It must be borne in mind constantly that the anger and hostility directed at the agency stem from the frustration that can be welded into an agent of community change. As discomfort was important in changing the service perspective of the agency staff, so too the agency can use this discomfort in effecting change in the network of services within the community.

The staff of the agency must prepare themselves for frequent tests of commitment to follow through on its new intake policy. "Inappropriate" cases must be rejected with an empathetic understanding of the resultant frustration. Interagency collaboration to find temporizing strategies to cope with the consequent gaps in the community care apparatus have to be tempered by the necessity for continued community ferment until effective CO has evolved. By standing firm within the context of its new program, the agency will demonstrate the kind of services it is giving and will at the same time highlight the areas where services are not being offered and should be. Although many of these gaps were present before the change in intake policy, they are now brought into bold relief, e.g. unwed mothers, learning disabilities, family crisis. Essential to the success of this attempt at CO is that the direct service offered by the agency be of the highest quality and provide the promised services to the client groups specified by intake policy.

The agency should be prepared to meet with other professionals and various lay individuals in the community to explain the new program in detail. The "finger pointing" must be redirected to a problem-solving orientation. The service gaps within the community must be identified and alternative ways of filling these gaps, whether by the development of new agencies or the refocusing of the service of existing agencies in the community, must be listed. To effect lasting CO and because it still remains the "source" of frustration, the agency must adopt a consultive role. It cannot dictate goals or means; the community must have final say on the priority of needs and the ways in which these are to be met.

The accusation that this strategy is a manipulative attempt by one group of individuals within the community cannot be rejected. However, it must be assumed that the justification is a competent appraisal of community needs and resources to meet the needs, if appropriate community mobilization takes place. Additionally, while one group may provide the prod, the mobilized community will select from the alternatives available and create new alternatives. In keeping with the legitimate use of community ferment, one could even suggest the creation and withdrawal of new services or the treatment of new populations, with the hope that the community can find ways to make permanent the best of these new approaches. Before long the agency should find a legitimate place in the community "power" structure so that more direct approaches are possible.

While the community gains an extensive care system, the agency gains a realistic mandate, broad community sanctions for its operations, and more direct access to feedback about its effectiveness. Certainly these conditions are important not only for professional satisfaction but in implementing treatment strategies such as limited hospitalization, continued community linkage, extended aftercare, environmental manipulation, and the teaching of the techniques of modifying disturbed behavior to various agents and members of the community.

While much of what has been said has referred to an established agency, many of the points can be applied readily in the planning of an agency new to the community. Countering the seductive temptation of bold promises of unlimited service, intake policy can and should be clearly delineated and communicated in terms of the goal of mobilizing CO to maximize the range and effectiveness of treatment alternatives. It is also possible that with creative planning a new agency may forego the luxury of being the target of community hostility and find other methods to mobilize community action. With either an established or a new agency, proper consideration and implementation of intake policies can only lead to greater satisfaction in the agency and the community.

The Impact of New Designs of Community Organization

Roland L. Warren

In considering the impact of new designs of community organization, I shall first comment briefly on some of the changes at the community level that are associated with these new designs and then raise some basic questions regarding citizen involvement and planned change in the community.

Reprinted with permission of the author and the Child Welfare League of America, Inc. from Child Welfare, Vol. 44, No. 9 (November 1965), pp. 494–500.

Changes at the Community
Level

Let us begin with the change that perhaps seems most dramatic, most challenging, and, from certain standpoints, most threatening. This is the huge input of funds and program development from the Federal government. Why is it so important?

First, it offers help, both in funds and in stimulation, to communities that are engulfed by the multiplicity and complexity of problems, many of which stem from sources beyond their control, such as the sweep of automation, the gradual reconversion of defense activities, and the growth of population in areas surrounding the central cities.

Second, Federal inputs usually come tied to specific program areas, with consequent limitations on their use and the necessity of tailoring community programs to these specialized Federal requirements.

Third, the problem areas in most cases turn out to be extremely complex, even though topically confined. This sets up a dynamic impetus to expand out from the core problem to encompass other, closely related ones. And since broad community conditions affect them all, each program is like a stone thrown into a pool—setting up waves spreading toward the perimeter and encountering waves from other programs.

Fourth, though not new to this decade, the number and magnitude of Federal programs have increased to the extent that the change is almost qualitative in nature.

Fifth, increasingly these Federal programs call for a community plan, or for extensive citizen participation, or for some other community organization component.

Sixth, the range and volume of these programs is so great that few, if any, conventional community welfare councils are able to incorporate them into a centralized and coordinated kind of comprehensive planning.

Seventh, the promise of Federal funds constitutes a stimulus, not only for the development of a program, but also for a competitive scramble for agency position with respect to the new program. The existing balance of community organization forces is vigorously agitated while the kind of organization that is to receive the funds and carry out the program is being decided. At the same time, the ferment created by the new activities continues to have important side effects.

A number of other changes are occurring, in more or less close association with this huge input of Federal funds and stimulation. Thus, even before the delinquency and poverty programs—ever since World War II, in fact—there has been a growing organization of attention and effort around specific community problems, each of which has broad ramifications. What seems to be emerging is the realization that, under current urban conditions, the balanced, administered approach to problems like housing, juvenile delinquency, services for the aging, school dropouts, and mental health is something that cannot be attained by any one agency under any one roof. Rather, specific *ad hoc* attacks on these and other problems have come to dominate the health and welfare scene. As mentioned earlier, though, each of these problem areas has aspects that overlap with others, providing a constant need to look toward the collaboration for mutual goals and the avoidance of mutually incompatible programs.

Coalitions

A closely related characteristic of the present scene is the development of *ad hoc* coalitions of agencies and organizations in relation to some of these specific problem areas. Often, these are not in the form of committees or divisions within the community welfare council, but are coalitions formed outside it, in a variety of relationships to the council. Each is, in some ways, a little council of its own, circumscribed by its specific problem area; limited, presumably, in time; and performing some, but not all, of the usual council functions. Each constitutes a potential threat to the council's ability to achieve a modicum of coordination in the health and welfare field, and each develops a degree of autonomy that can become a block to joint efforts.

Plurality of Planning Centers

Thus, at the very time when the need for coordinated, comprehensive planning in such fields as housing, urban renewal, and social welfare is being widely voiced, the problem is compounding itself through the appearance of the newer planning coalitions mentioned above. It is increasingly apparent that unified, centralized planning, whether or not desirable, is becoming more and more irrelevant to the current urban scene. A plurality of planning centers, each constituting a powerful coalition, becomes a challenge to conventional concepts of planning.

Meanwhile, another fundamental change is occurring. We have reached the point where the overlap of interest and activities emanating from specific agencies or specific coalitions is creating an increasingly competitive situation, with one agency's activities being much more basically affected by another agency's decisions and activities than was previously the case.

To oversimplify, we can think of an earlier stage when the client need for various kinds of service was very great and the number of agencies offering services rather small and spotty. The possibility of saturation of the client population was relatively remote. Each agency did what it could, and there was need for all. This is an exaggeration, since councils of social agencies have for decades been trying to avoid duplication of agency services. Nevertheless, the current picture is drastically different. The earlier stage could perhaps be visualized as individual agencies fishing in a placid brook, with relatively little competition or interference with each other. Now the brook has become agitated, various agencies and coalitions are interested in the same fish, lines get tangled, some agencies get the hook, others find difficulty casting in their lines—in short, an exciting turmoil! The need for coordination grows, but, at the same time, the difficulties of coordination multiply.[1]

I have admittedly oversimplified the background to the current new designs of community organization, which can be broken down into five rough categories: Federal programs, the single-problem approach, coalitions, a plurality of planning centers, and a more crowded field of agency interaction. In the light of these developments, several basic questions occur regarding the relation of these new designs to citizen involvement.

Citizen Involvement

The first concerns the concept of citizen involvement. Like love, citizen involvement is a many-splendored thing. And like love, citizen involvement calls forth certain sweet, tender feelings as well as certain gnawing implications that the relationship "never runs smooth." One more parallel: love of the wrong kind with the wrong person can involve a host of circumstances for

---

[1]An excellent analysis of this progression of organizations toward a "turbulent environment" has been given by F. E. Emery and E. L. Trist in "The Causal Texture of Organizational Environments," *Human Relations*, XVIII (1965), 21–32.

which we reserve some of the culture's most negative terms—incest, prostitution, homosexuality, frigidity, adultery. The term citizen involvement may offer similar problems of clarity of definition and appropriateness of application.

How vastly different are the implications of citizen involvement if one is talking about citizens at the board-member or policymaking level; citizens volunteering their services through agencies either to help clients or to raise funds; participation in neighborhood organizations dealing with local neighborhood improvement; the organization of clients to feed back into the agency's policymaking procedures; or the organization of protest and conflict groups. One must, in order to speak meaningfully in this field, be clear regarding the segment of the population that is involved, the purposes that presumably are to be accomplished, and the relationship of the citizens to the agency or coalition.

Each of these would require more extensive comments than could be given here. But let me cite a most significant article by Wilson, in which he points out that it is difficult to obtain the support of indigenous lower-class residents of renewal areas.[2] Although he does not elaborate on this point, it is apparent that citizen involvement in such neighborhoods is not for the purpose of a bottom-upward kind of goal definition and planning for execution, but, on the contrary, an attempt to gain their acquiescence to the changes that are to take place. These changes may have important positive value for the community as a whole, but, for the residents themselves, they may simply imply forcible eviction from one's own dwelling and the destruction of one's own home neighborhood.[3]

According to Wilson:

. . . planning with people assumes on the part of the people involved a willingness and a capacity to engage in a collaborative search for the common good. The willingness is obviously almost never present when the persons involved will be severely penalized by having their homes and neighborhoods destroyed by wholesale clearance. . . . But what is less obvious is that it may not be present, even when such clearance is not envisaged, because of important class differences in the capacity to organize for community-wide goals.[4]

In an earlier passage, he is more explicit on these differences. Speaking of the low-income sections that are to be renewed, he writes:

[2]James Q. Wilson, "Planning and Politics: Citizen Participation in Urban Renewal," *Journal of the American Institute of Planners*, XXIX (1963), 242–249.

[3]See, for instance, Marc Fried, "Grieving for a Lost Home," in Leonard J. Duhl, ed., *The Urban Condition: People and Policy in the Metropolis* (New York: Basic Books, 1963), pp. 151–171.

[4]Wilson, *op. cit.*, p. 247.

Such people are more likely to have a limited time-perspective, a greater difficulty in abstracting from concrete experience, an unfamiliarity with and lack of confidence in city-wide institutions, a preoccupation with the personal and the immediate, and few (if any) attachments to organizations of any kind, with the possible exception of churches.[5]

He thus concludes that, although some degree of citizen participation and involvement on the citywide level is relatively easy to obtain, the problems of citizen involvement on the neighborhood level in renewal areas in a "planning-with" relationship are highly complex.

Professor Wilson is more realistic and perhaps more forthright than some of the rest of us in tackling this "hot potato," and it is unfortunate that space limits a more thorough depiction of his analysis. Suffice it to say that his article dramatizes the importance of being clear on whether "involvement" is to be in goal-setting or in goal-receiving; whether it is honestly to broaden the basis of decision making or merely to get people to jump through the proper hoops; and whether it is for the purpose of policymaking, program development, legitimation, general acceptance, client cooperation, or whatever.

Aside from the instrumental purposes of citizen involvement—to get support, cooperation, or money, and the like—there seem to be two important value considerations. The first is to make social organizations sensitive to broad constituencies—in a sense, the democratic concept of representation. The second is to afford opportunities for creative growth through participation in community activities, a matter of individual enrichment and the good life. We often confuse these two, and we often blandly assume that we are motivated by one or the other or both when it is apparent to a detached observer that our overriding purpose is that of securing acquiescence to a preconceived program.

Relation of Individual
Agencies to a Coalition

My second basic question has to do with the relation of the individual agency to a coalition of agencies. I need only remind you that when it comes to tackling some broad problem, agencies often show a tenacious unwillingness to adapt their own programs to the presumably needed modifications, apparently preferring to continue their own comfortable, tried-and-true kind of program that is admittedly fragmentary and that may be highly

[5]*Ibid.*, p. 245.

ineffective. In addition, competition that involves seeking to protect or expand the agency's domain often looms larger than what the community might expect.

Thus, when Miller studied a delinquency-prevention program in a northeastern metropolitan setting, he found the agency behavior so obviously conflicting and ineffective that it could be accounted for only by realizing that "for the great majority of organized institutions which maintain programs directed at juvenile delinquency, the adoption of operating procedures and philosophies which would be effective in reducing juvenile crime would, in fact, pose severe threats to the viability of the institution."[6]

The agency-coalition problem that I mention is one of understanding the relation of agency function to the functioning of the more inclusive unit, the coalition. The coalition's goals are more inclusive than the agencies', and they are different from them. The coalition's function may be a comprehensive approach to juvenile delinquency, although the individual agencies may be performing specific functions with various degrees of relevancy to preventing juvenile delinquency.

If these agency functions in aggregate had constituted an effective approach, the coalition would be unnecessary. But the individual approach is fragmented, ineffective, at times self-contradictory. This does not indicate that the agencies themselves are in difficulty. Indeed, the greater their ineffectiveness, the more persuasive may be their appeal for more funds to do the job, for expansion, and for other prerequisites to individual agency well-being. The coalition, however, may face a responsibility that individual agencies usually do not—for making an appreciable impact on juvenile delinquency. Once such a responsibility is assumed, with its accompanying mandate to work for a rational, intermeshing, effective approach, changes are usually called for that threaten the domain, and sometimes the existence, of individual agencies.

We need to know more about how to relate agency goals to coalition goals—how to promote goal-attainment on the more inclusive level of the coalition. Eventually, we must have the knowledge that will enable us to make the optimum rational "mix" between agency survival needs and goal attainment by the coalition. Etzioni has made an incisive analysis of the relation of

[6]Walter B. Miller, "Inter-Institutional Conflict as a Major Impediment to Delinquency Prevention," *Human Organization*, XVII, No. 3 (1958), p. 20.

organization requirements to the performance of announced goals.[7]

In a highly important but largely ignored book, Ramsoy has attempted a systematic investigation of the relation of groups to more inclusive groups through the simultaneous analysis of the functions of the subsystem and of the more inclusive system.[8]

We are only at the beginning of a systematic attempt to expand organizational theory to include these complex levels of interorganization function and exchange.[9] When we know more about these things and have a better conceptual framework within which to analyze them, we shall perhaps cease flailing away at individual agencies for "resisting" broad community actions and shall cease asking the agencies to risk their own existence, or the professional status of their executive staffs, or their body of donor supporters, or their necessary body of service recipients for an unknown payoff to the community that may spell disaster to themselves.

Local Responsibility for Change

My third basic question relates to the issue of local responsibility for change. Is it true that social welfare organizations generally are principally concerned with maintaining society's equilibrium rather than instituting change? Many social scientists have come to this conclusion. The principal emphasis is on giving services to those whom present conditions and circumstances put at a disadvantage rather than on making basic changes in those conditions and circumstances. Joint planning takes place characteristically in noncontroversial areas. Where the need is such as to challenge present institutional power arrangements, the concern tends to become extruded into largely single-purpose organizations that further a "cause" more or less militantly or are torn between doing so and remaining "respectable."[10]

Simons raised the question recently at the National Conference on Social Welfare:

[7]Amitai Etzioni, "Two Approaches to Organizational Analysis: A Critique and a Suggestion," *Administrative Science Quarterly*, V (1960), 257–278.

[8]Cf. Odd Ramsoy, *Social Groups as System and Subsystem* (New York: The Free Press of Glencoe, 1963).

[9]For a ground-breaking study, see Sol Levine and Paul E. White, "Exchange as a Conceptual Framework for the Study of Interorganizational Relationships," *Administrative Science Quarterly*, V (1961), 583–601.

[10]Cf. Martin Rein and Robert Morris, "Goals, Structures, and Strategies for Community Change," in *Social Work Practice, 1962* (New York: Columbia University Press, 1962), pp. 127–145.

Where have we social workers been that we have allowed inherited poverty to develop in the wealthiest nation of the world? How have we allowed a caste system to develop in this land of the free? . . .

. . . Except for the neighborhood agencies and some new pilot projects, we are alienated not only because our offices are not accessible to the most deprived, but also psychologically and culturally. . . . In an age of conformity we have been conformists.[11]

It is questionable whether the profession of social work has as much impact regarding major institutional change as it did in the old days of fighting for minimum wages, tenement house laws, child labor laws, and the rest. Perhaps a few random observations on this assertion are in order.

First, it is widely realized that many of the problems that arise at the community level come from forces that are not subject to community control and that require state, regional, and Federal action. But once having said this, there remains the problem of developing methods through which the wishes of communities may be defined and expressed as distinguished from those of the state, regional, or national bodies with their relatively rigid programs for grant-in-aid to which community programs must be tailored.

Second, if local influence is to be brought to bear in effective ways on state and national policies, it is difficult to see how this can be accomplished without deep involvement in the political process. If agencies cannot become directly involved because of their essential equilibrium-maintenance function and because of the threat to their tax-immunity privileges, then it seems obvious that they must develop a closer relation to local politicians who can become so involved. The role of citizens on agency boards is crucial in this regard.

Third, it is questionable whether changes of the kind required can be effected by community welfare councils, largely because of the essentially conservative nature of their function. Generally speaking, centralized planning can occur only under conditions of basic consensus on goals—or at least on objectives—or under conditions where such goals and objectives are considered comparatively unimportant by the powerful groups in the community.

What are the alternatives to conventional health and welfare planning where value consensus is not obtainable and where the issues are not innocuous but highly controversial? Two of the most important alternatives come to mind. The first is that of en-

[11]Savilla M. Simons, "Social Change Implications for Policy and Practice Re: Deterioration of the Inner City—A First Step Toward Defining a Small Area Approach," paper presented at National Conference on Social Welfare, Los Angeles, May 1964, p. 5.

gaging in the political process, a process of negotiation among contending forces, where comparative strength and adroitness of tactics yield the highest payoff. The second is that of engaging in conflict. There are a number of issues—for example, racial segregation, birth control, fluoridation, and Medicare—in which "planning" has been inadequate and in which the conflict aspects of the situation have left many agencies in a dilemma regarding whether to enter the conflict or whether to remain as bystanders. Merely to mention such a list—and it could be extended—is to indicate both the dilemma regarding change through conflict and also the fact that some agencies actually do engage in such activities.

Change

My fourth basic question has to do with change in relation to the structure and functions of existing health and welfare agencies. Many agencies will have to change drastically if they are to be able to continue to exist in the face of such changes as were listed earlier. Some will be unable to do so, quite aside from the question of initiating change on their own account.

How do organizations tool up for change? If change is not the unusual but the normal, how can agencies so structure themselves as to undergo change with the least waste motion, the greatest effectiveness, and the greatest survival value? New concepts of organizational structure—not as something to be modified only in periods of grave crisis, but as something pliable, constantly in flux, but maintaining continuity—will be appropriate for the decades ahead. From agency executives, leadership, in the sense of restructuring, will be called for in addition to the usual administrative skills.[12] Much will depend on the willingness of citizen board members to take a flexible approach to community needs—even on their insistence that the agency do so.

Perhaps most agencies will be unable to effect such continuous flexibility and change without aid from outside consultants who can help them through successive sequences of change episodes, as Lippitt, et al., have described.[13] Likewise, such works as The Planning of Change offer executives and policymakers an opportunity to benefit from what is known—from what little is known, one must admit—about planning for change.[14]

[12]Philip Selznick, Leadership in Administration: A Sociological Interpretation (Evanston, Ill.: Row, Peterson and Co., 1957).

[13]Ronald Lippitt, Jeanne Watson, and Bruce Westley, The Dynamics of Planned Change: A Comparative Study of Principles and Techniques (New York: Harcourt, Brace and Co., 1958).

[14]Warren G. Bennis, Kenneth D. Benne, and Robert Chin, eds., The Planning of Change: Readings in the Applied Behavioral Sciences (New York: Holt, Rinehart and Winston, 1961).

Nature of the Planning
Process

My fifth basic question relates to the nature of the planning process. We are entering a phase in which numerous planning centers will each be planning for change in certain parts of the community's structure. As indicated earlier, the planning function in the health and welfare field has spilled over the narrow confines of domain and competency of the conventional health and welfare council. As Schottland said at the National Conference on Social Welfare in 1963:

> In spite of the 500 or more welfare councils which have engaged millions of citizens in cooperative community efforts, any analysis of where we stand today in the changing life of the American city raises serious questions about the ability of our traditional vehicles for social planning to cope with the kinds of problems we face and the impact of dozens of Federal programs upon them.[15]

It is not only the powerful Federal impact, but the pluralism of planning centers on Federal, state, and local levels that makes it impossible for any one agency to plan as though it alone were intervening in otherwise purely crescive social processes. If there is to be any degree of coordination among these various planning centers, even on the local level, it will occur less through a rational process in line with conventional concepts of planning than as a process of negotiation and bargaining and exchange among planning bodies, with politics, writ large and small, playing an important part in the final determination. Under such circumstances, survival and success and, let us hope, community betterment will go to those who are flexible and creative, who have a close ear for important constituencies, and who are adroit in the rugged process of political interaction.

Unfortunately, we seem to have few models for this kind of pluralistic planning *cum* politics. On the one hand, we seem to have a planning model that involves the rational adaptation of means to ends, but unfortunately in a social vacuum, conjuring up visions of the dust-gathering report or the ivory-towered master planner. On the other, we have some important chunks of practice theory about planning as a social process, about motivation, participation, and the like, mixed with large chunks of value assumptions.

Neither of these models has been systematically tested, though both have been followed on numerous occasions. The latter,

[15]Charles I. Schottland, "Federal Planning for Health and Welfare," in *The Social Welfare Forum, 1963* (New York: Columbia University Press, 1963), pp. 116-117.

more akin to the humanistic predispositions of the American social worker than the former, unfortunately contains no method for injecting rationality into the decision-making process. Interestingly, it is almost purely a political model, leaving the decision about rationality to the process of negotiated assent—thus providing that if the final planning decisions are less than logically convincing, they may be at least psychologically acceptable. Our two most widely used models of planning, therefore, call up either the complaint "It may be rational, but you can have it" or the empty satisfaction "It may not be rational, but it's ours, all ours!"

Perhaps we should insist on something better. What that something is, I do not know. I do feel, though, that Braybrooke and Lindblom are on the right track. They have developed a method for calculation that, unfortunately, they hide under a bushel by giving it the odious name "disjointed incrementalism."[16] Nevertheless, the book represents a milestone in that it presents one of the best attempts to deal with the rational aspects of planning as a social process.

In this process, the planner can assume neither omniscience nor omnipotence, but has to be in there pitching, trying to be coolly calculating, but making an occasional mistake; trying to have his way, but occasionally having to compromise; trying to make tentative formulations of next steps in a situation that is changing drastically, in part at least as a result of the planning activities of other constellations in the community, but also as a result of the unanticipated side effects of one's own activities.

It may be an uncertain path, but it is the path we will all have to follow if citizen volunteers and professional staffs want to keep up with the new designs that are changing the face of American communities and of American community organization.

Selected Bibliography

Bernard, S. E., Durtagh, E., and Johnson, H. R., "The Neighborhood Service Organization: Specialist Social Welfare Innovation," *Social Work*, 13 (1), 1968, pp. 76–84.

Davitto, B., and Schulman, T., "An Experience in Community Treatment of Delinquents," *Social Casework*, 48 (1), 1967, pp. 10–16.

Eugster, C., "Field Education in West Heights: Equipping a Deprived Community to Help Itself," *Human Organization*, 23 (3), 1964, pp. 235–244.

---

[16]David Braybrooke and Charles E. Lindblom, *A Strategy of Decision: Policy Evaluation as a Social Process* (New York: The Free Press of Glencoe, 1963).

Grosser, C. F., "Community Organization and the Grass Roots," *Social Work*, 12 (4), 1967, pp. 61–67.

Grosser, C. F., "Local Residents as Mediators between Middle-Class Professional Workers and Lower-Class Clients," *Social Service Review*, 40 (1), 1966, pp. 56–63.

Herre, E. A., "A Community Mobilizes to Protect Its Children," *Public Welfare*, 23 (2), 1965, pp. 93–97.

Kramer, R. M., and Denton, C., "Organization of a Community Action Program: A Comparative Case Study," *Social Work*, 12 (4), 1967, pp. 68–80.

Lourie, N. V., "Community Public Welfare Services," *Public Welfare*, 24 (1), 1966, pp. 65–72, 90.

MacRae, R. H., "Over-All Community Planning: How and by Whom?," *Social Service Review*, 39 (3), 1965, pp. 255–260.

March, M. S., "The Neighborhood Center Concept," *Public Welfare*, 26 (2), 1968, pp. 97–111.

Marsh, C. P., "The Structure of Community Power and Community Decision Making," *Adult Leadership*, 13 (3), 1964, pp. 71–72, 84.

Mogulof, M. B., "A Developmental Approach to the Community Action Program Idea," *Social Work*, 12 (2), 1967, pp. 12–20.

Morris, D., and Rothwax, H., "Partnership between Social Work and Law: An Essential for Effective Community Organization," *Social Welfare Forum*. New York, Columbia University Press, 1968, pp. 94–104.

Morris, R., and Randall, O. A., "Planning and Organization of Community Services for the Elderly," *Social Work*, 10 (1), 1965, pp. 96–102.

Palley, H. A., "Community in Conflict: Family Planning in Metroville," *Social Service Review*, 41 (1), 1967, pp. 55–65.

Peck, H. B., Struening, E., and Smith, J. J., "A Strategy of Intervention in a Low-Income Community," *Perspectives in Social Work, Mothers-at-Risk*, 1 (1), 1966, pp. 93–102.

Rein, M., and Riessman, F., "A Strategy for Antipoverty Community Action Programs," *Social Work*, 11 (2), 1966, pp. 3–12.

Ross, M. G., "Conceptual Problems in Community Organization," *Social Service Review*, 30 (2), 1956, pp. 174–181.

Rothman, J., "An Analysis of Goals and Roles in Community Organization Practice," *Social Work*, 9 (2), 1964, pp. 24–31.

Sieder, V. M., "The Community Organization Responsibility of the Social Caseworker in a Health or Medical Care Setting," mimeograph, NASW, Newport, R.I., May 1964.

Wachtal, D. D., "Structures of Community and Strategies for Organization," *Social Work*, 13 (1), 1968, pp. 85–91.

Zweig, F. M., and Morris, R., "The Social Planning Design Guide: Process and Proposal," *Social Work*, 11 (2), 1966, pp. 13–21.

6

Future Trends

From the previous sections, it should be clear that—at least from the generalist perspective—social work practice seems to be evolving from focus on a particular method to what Spergel here calls "a multidimensional approach." Problems are being seen in greater complexity and their solution is therefore thought to require an expanded problem-solving orientation.

The emergence of such an ecological emphasis in the field perhaps coincides with a trend toward seeing environmental or institutional change as a way of alleviating social and individual problems. Purcell and Specht consider the social worker responsible for "seeking a solution to social problems through institutional change rather than by focusing on individual problems in social functioning."

Thus, as the interdependence among the components of society becomes better understood, the social worker may be able to effectively improve the whole system by seeking to change various parts of it. An emphasis on improving the whole system demands a clear conceptualization of objectives. Bisno and Teare present models that can be used for defining these objectives (see the Introduction for details). These models can also be used for relating defined objectives to social work roles. Within this context, some of the possible roles for the social work generalist are discussed in the articles in this section.

The Changing Concept of Individualized Services

Carol H. Meyer

The concept of individualized services has been accepted by the social work profession and by leaders in the field of social welfare for almost a century, but throughout this period the concept has undergone many radical changes. These changes must always be viewed against the backdrop of the prevailing social and economic conditions and the preoccupations of the particular era in which they occurred, for it is the broad societal influences in each era that have shaped social legislation, agency programs, and professional methods and techniques. In this article, I shall present an examination of the concept of individualized services as it has been altered and reshaped by four kinds of change that have continually had an impact on the social welfare field—specifically, on social work practice. It is my thesis that the concept of individualized services has been inflluenced by changes in social values, changes in the structure and functions of family life, change in the concept of the unit of social work attention, and new developments in knowledge. Moreover, additional changes will inevitably take place, and the result will be further transformations in the practice of social work.

A prediction about the nature and place of individualized services in the social welfare programs of the immediate future must rest on a concept of the ultimate purpose of these programs. It is my conviction that this purpose can be summed up by this phrase: service to human beings. All our knowledge, including the knowledge that is increasingly being validated by research, and all our agency programs and professional commitments must be directed toward the primary goal of giving service. The acquisition of knowledge should not be an end in itself, and there is no social justification for an administratively tidy, but self-protective and nonserving, agency program. The hallmark of the profession of social work must be its readiness to commit itself to meeting human need before expending its energies on intraprofessional strivings that might compete for attention with its fundamental service aims. Agreement on this essential value will enable us to consider more profitably the changing concept of individualized services in social welfare programs.

Reprinted with permission of the author and The Family Service Association of America from *Social Casework*, Vol. 47, No. 5 (May 1966), pp. 279–285.

Changing Social Values

How have changing social values affected the concept of individualized services? In the nineteenth century, in both England and the United States, individualized services were provided for the wanton, the helpless, and the poverty-stricken by the charitable and benevolent souls of the period. Even before the western nations experienced the full impact of the industrial revolution and the subsequent increase in urban development and social isolation, individualized services existed to help or uplift those "deserving" unfortunates who lacked the capacity to be self-supporting and who failed because they were not strong enough or wellborn enough to cope with the surrounding social and economic pressures. Perhaps the particular concern for the individual that characterized the nineteenth century was the result of a universal hopelessness that social reforms could be effected. Working in the shadow of the Poor Law, the social worker of that day—the minister, the public agent, or the volunteer—provided food, shelter, and comfort to the impoverished out of religious or humane motives.

A paper presented at the fifth annual meeting of the National Conference of Charities, held in Cincinnati, Ohio, in 1878, put forward the view that if pauperism was to be eliminated, "the history and character of paupers as individuals must be carefully studied; the precise causes and influences that made them such must be ascertained. . . ."[1] Indeed, individualized services were accepted in this country at that time, but the social workers of the day seemed unaware of their social significance. That was before the robber barons were recognized for what they were and when people denied the existence of a classridden society. That was when Negroes could still remember their recent bondage, and civil rights legislation was more than two generations away. That was before two world wars and a great depression; before the emergence of new nations and the demise of colonialism. Today, in this era of space flights, atomic energy, and automation, it can be fairly stated that 1878 was centuries, not merely eighty-eight years, ago.

In the latter part of the nineteenth century, the concept of individualized services had the conservative flavor of the times. Notwithstanding the social action programs of the community organization society and the settlement house movement, this was the prevailing dictum: Caring for the individual will improve

---

[1]Nathan Allen, "Prevention of Crime and Pauperism," in *Proceedings of the Fifth Annual Conference of Charities*, A. Williams & Co., Boston, 1878, p. 117.

society—society cannot be changed, and it is the individual who must learn to adjust to society. According to this point of view, impoverished families were an insult to society; it was they who were at fault, never society itself, which seemed to be impervious to change. Perhaps it is a derivative of this view of the relation between the individual and society that has given casework the reputation of being a reactionary, narrowly defined method of service. Even today it is not unusual to hear that social casework is an antiquated, albeit technically effective, method of service designed to keep the poor in their place, to represent the establishment, and to keep out the social reformer. It should give us pause that social casework is so often viewed as a nineteenth-century anachronism when, in fact, tides of change in the twentieth century have swept casework along quite as quickly as they have the scientific quest in medicine, the space probes, and atomic research.

The changing role, substance, and characteristics of individualized services in the modern world may be accounted for to a large extent by changes in social values. Despite the fact that our nation has not yet dealt adequately with the surging problems of the day—poverty, unemployment, inadequate housing, the deterioration of the inner city, family breakdown, and so forth—our social values have changed drastically, and the intent of individualized services is quite different from what it was a century ago. For example, we no longer hold the individual totally responsible for his condition. Services are now viewed as the individual's right, not only because he makes a contribution to society but also because—unless he bands together with others—he is practically helpless to affect the social, political, and economic forces that govern his life. Today individualized health and welfare services are viewed not as an aid to those persons who are inadequate, but as a requirement for survival in a complex industrial society.

Whereas family members and residents of close-knit communities once provided each other with the supports that were lacking in their lives, today public and voluntary social services have to be organized to meet a variety of human needs. We have moved even beyond the point of providing services to alleviate problems that already exist and have begun to pursue the idea of establishing services to prevent the emergence of problems. Alfred Kahn's concept, "social utilities," suggests that individualized social services should become as much a part of the fabric of life in our highly automated and bureaucratized civilization as are the services of the police department, the fire department, and the parks department.[2] Social services should be available to all persons because of the "normal" conditions of their lives, not merely for those who are failures. The social values that have changed from those represented by the Poor Law to those that underlie social insurance and now social planning have swept us along with them. Social workers face the necessity of providing more, not fewer, individualized services. The character and premises of these services are changing and will continue to do so.

Changes in the Structure and
Functions of Family Life

The structure of family life has undergone such drastic changes in recent years that it is becoming increasingly difficult to find agreement even on the definition of *family*. Our concepts of family life and the nature of institutional responses to the family's functions have been revolutionized by the increase in the number of fatherless families; of families in which the mother is employed; and of nuclear, rather than extended, family units. Since 1900 there has been a 50 per cent increase in the proportion of manless households.[3] In 1962, over 60 per cent of all working women were married and living with their husbands.[4] In 1964, there were about 9 million children less than twelve years of age whose mothers were employed outside the home.[5] Of all divorcing couples in 1960, 57 per cent had children under eighteen years of age.[6] The divorce rate was 2.2 per cent per thousand population in 1960.[7] Per 1,000 total live births in 1962, 58.8 were illegitimate.[8]

We are all familiar with the assumed causes of the disruption in family life reflected in these startling figures: movement from the farm to the city, movement from the comfortable familiarity of the small community to the social isolation of the urban complex, increase in the population, and automation. Whatever the view of causation, the *effect* of the present social chaos has been felt by families who have, in turn, made dysfunctional accommodations to the severe impact of these conditions on the structure and requirements of family life. On the one hand, urban mobility

[2]Alfred J. Kahn, "The Societal Context of Social Work Practice," *Social Work*, Vol. X, October 1965, pp. 145–55.

[3]*Converging Social Trends: Emerging Social Problems*, Division of Research, Welfare Administration, U.S. Department of Health, Education, and Welfare, Washington, D. C., 1964, p. 55.

[4]*Ibid.*

[5]*Ibid.*, p. 60.

[6]Hugh Carter and Alexander Plateris, "Trends in Divorce and Family Disruption," in *Health, Education, and Welfare Indicators*, September 1963, p. x.

[7]*Ibid.*

[8]*Ibid.*, p. xvii.

and convenience have lessened the reliance of family members on each other to have their needs met. On the other hand, the highly organized, bureaucratized way of life that exists in the modern megalopolis has placed special demands on the family unit as the last resort for its members.

What is the significance of these seemingly conflicting statements? Today it is less necessary for marital life to be dependent upon the traditional (or rural) division of labor between men and women, and the resultant confusion of roles has placed the burden of marital adjustment almost totally on the emotional tie between the partners rather than on their separate but complementary functions as wage earner and homemaker. None of the previously defined marital functions is now clearly the responsibility of the man as husband and father or of the woman as wife and mother. Not only have these roles and functions become interchangeable within families, but many of them have been usurped by social institutions other than the family.

Surely the vast increase in programs, such as day care of children and Operation Head Start, and the new roles assumed by schools, hospitals, courts, and social agencies in the daily lives of all individuals are social responses to the changes occurring in family life and in the functions of family members. Day care centers for children have proliferated because mothers have become breadwinners. Operation Head Start, a program of uncommon significance, has come into being because the very poor and the culturally deprived family cannot give its children adequate care and education. Reliance on job-training programs, on public welfare, or on unemployment insurance has become a way of life for increasing numbers of men who once were wage earners but cannot now find continuity or dignity in employment because they lack appropriate skills or have been displaced by automation.

The social service of fifty years ago has become the institutionalized necessity of today. The client-recipient of the welfare programs of the 1930s has now become the citizen-participant of the poverty program and the social insurance program. And, indeed, he will be the citizen-participant of the public welfare program. For every aspect of family life that becomes dysfunctional in our complex and demanding civilization, some public or voluntary social service program arises to ease the problem.

Vast shifts in family roles and functions have indeed occurred. Accompanying these shifts have been the social phenomena of increasing behavior problems in children, divorce, unmarried parenthood, delinquency, crime, narcotics addiction, and so on.

To compensate in a rehabilitative, if not preventive, fashion for the weakening of family ties that underlies these social maladies, the court and the social agency have had to assume additional roles and responsibilities.

What, then, is left for family members to do for themselves? It would appear that the singular purpose of the family today is to provide a last stronghold of intimacy, love, and companionship in an impersonalized, mechanized, and merchandized society. This is a great burden for many persons to bear, for it casts the individual into the arena of close human relationships without his being able to receive the gratification provided by the opportunity to rear his children successfully, to work at a job he likes and can do well, or to be depended upon to carry out the essential tasks of family life. The countless material conveniences of life today may be welcome, but they also have forced family members to make an attempt to relate to each other emotionally and to try to sustain a family structure that is fast becoming obsolete.

Change in the Unit of Social Work Attention

Few would disagree with the assertion that the primary concern of social welfare is the well-being of man. This is indeed a global concern, and one that the social work profession shares with the disciplines of health and education. In fact, health, education, and welfare are looked upon as three distinct expressions of the concern for man because the concern is expressed through the functioning of separate programs, not because there can be such a separation in man himself. In other words, if it were feasible to integrate health, education, and welfare programs into a unified whole, the result would more nearly approximate the way in which a person visualizes or experiences his needs. Each of these fields of endeavor, however, has its own history, personnel, professional requirements, and expertise. Therefore, the division of labor is likely to be perpetuated, despite the fact that the services provided by each field ultimately result in the same benefit to an individual: his increasing intellectual, physical, emotional, and social well-being.

What does the social welfare field mean when it speaks of individualized services? Does it mean service to man as an individual, or does it mean individualized concern for a unit of attention, the definition of which will vary according to the kind of knowledge available and the prevalent social philosophy? I believe that it *should* mean the latter. For example, under the Poor Law, concern for the individual was just that. In that era man was not perceived as a *social* animal. Had social interaction been the overriding concept then, as it is today, man and society would have been viewed as having a mutual responsibility for the condition of each, and the separation of efforts in pursuit of social reform and efforts in pursuit of the modification of individual behavior would not have occurred.

Moreover, the concept of individualized services has been modified by the changing conditions in society that have been characterized by a growing interdependence. Obviously, the more complex a society, the more an individual must rely on significant others in his social sphere, on his government, and on other organized programs that enable him to survive. Today, the unit of attention can no longer be an isolated man, woman, or child; such individuation is no longer a reality. Human beings cling to one another in family units and in formal and informal social organizations of all kinds, because relationships with others are essential to the physical and emotional health of everyone. Moreover, the clusters of relationships that find their expression in family life, in neighborhoods, and in various kinds of groups are not separable from the society that surrounds them, with which they must interact.

Today's concept of individualized services, then, must embrace the unit of attention that is currently valid. This unit is not the individual man—who will nevertheless be the ultimate beneficiary of such services—but man in his family, in his group, and in his neighborhood; each unit continually acts upon society at large and is, in turn, being acted upon by it. This is not a statement of values; it is a description of the urbanized, mechanized, bureaucratized world of today, in which individual man's only chance to find expression and fulfillment for himself is in the company of others.

New Developments in Knowledge

In the past fifty years, social work has moved from the social sciences to the psychological sciences and back again in its search for reliable knowledge that would explain the psychosocial phenomena that are the objects of its concern. A characteristic of the social work profession, and one I view with fondness, is that it continues to act in a pragmatic fashion while it is seeking knowledge and building theory. Thus, in the periods of its history when it was seeking knowledge from the disciplines of sociology and economics, it was also going about the business of helping individuals with whatever tools were at hand. Even while caseworkers were going through the psychoanalytic phase of refining those tools, the cry for social reform was raised. Somehow, as we sought the correct ingredients of knowledge, those of us concerned with social action and those concerned with clinical mastery continued to practice despite the rough edges in all areas of work.

Not much more time should have to pass before the issues concerning the clinical emphasis *versus* the social emphasis, pathology *versus* normality, or the residual view *versus* the institutional view of social work's place in society are relegated to the same niche in history that the heredity-*versus*-environment issue occupies. Surely we now acknowledge that social work is basing its performance on knowledge gleaned from a variety of sources. We do not yet have an integrated theoretical understanding of human behavior in a society, but we are on the brink of capturing the essence of that knowledge. At least we know that the-person-in-society is the concept that forms the framework within which knowledge must be sought.

In truth, social workers have accumulated a respectable amount of knowledge about human behavior. In the practice of social casework, especially, this knowledge was accumulated at the risk of our being drawn into a form of psychoanalytic practice. We managed to avoid that pitfall and finally achieved a balance between clinical knowledge and social work activity. Now, pure Freudian psychoanalytic theory has given way to a new ego psychology that may yet bridge the gap between theories of human behavior and theories of social functioning.

What about social science theories? They have not, as an integrated whole, served us so well as have the theories of individual growth and development. Each of us selects a particular concept or theory from the social sciences and applies it where it appears to be most useful or relevant. Some caseworkers prefer the concepts of social role; some, the theories of class structure; some, the theories of reference groups; and so on. There is not yet a unified theory that offers a cohesive explanation of society and its adaptations. Social workers use what they can of the knowledge available, but there is not yet as high a level of theoretical development in the societal sphere as there is in the arena of individual behavior.

Nevertheless, theoretical knowledge that can support practice is growing rapidly, and practice, in turn, is contributing to the development of theory. The most useful meeting place of practice and knowledge today is in the realm of social interaction. The processes of family life, of group interaction, and of community interaction are being studied at the same time that they are being acted upon. In fact, all social workers, in the course of their daily practice, must both call upon and contribute to the existing knowledge of social interaction in order to do their work. Social interaction, therefore, is the unit of attention of almost all social work practitioners; it is the concern of almost all social agencies.

At last, all of us—the theoretician, the caseworker, the group worker, the community organization worker, the agency administrator, the board member, the taxpayer, the student, and the teacher—have converged on the same focus of concern. We have but one question: How can we explain and do something about the circumstances that support or hinder the interaction of man with his fellow man and with the institutions and provisions of society at large?

What Does Individualized Service Mean?

As a result of all the changes that I have reviewed, new modes of social work practice must be devised. The traditional separation of casework, group work, and community organization is no longer tenable. Even now there is no clear answer to the question whether the caseworker who works with a family group is doing casework or group work, whether a community organization worker who talks with a neighborhood leader is assuming a casework role, or whether a group worker who makes a home visit is doing casework. We cannot much longer justify the separateness of methods in social work.

The concept of social interaction discussed previously encompasses concern with human personality and concern with social functioning. Neither of these concerns is the prerogative of any one method in social work practice; both are the concerns of all methods. To offer individualized services means that a community organization worker may direct his attention to a particular neighborhood composed of people with singular characteristics and problems. Similarly, the group worker and the caseworker both select the particular units to which they will give attention. In each instance, the individualizing process is identical; only the unit of attention varies from one worker to another. Assuming a measure of agreement that the three methods of social work practice use the same knowledge base (perhaps with different emphases) and the same concepts and principles, one can speculate that eventually they will fuse. Currently, the dividing lines seem to be contrived on the basis of professional commitments rather than the needs of people to be viewed separately as individuals, groups, or communities.

Earlier I touched upon the changing values and commitments that have transformed the older concept of the client-recipient into the modern concept of the citizen-participant. It is, therefore, no longer appropriate for us to view the caseworker as acting *upon* the client and the community organization worker as acting *with* the citizen. Nor is it valid to view the work of the caseworker as the handling of clinical pathology alone and the work of the community organization worker as the handling of social problems. In present-day terms, the client and the citizen are one and the same. Consequently, since the individual's well-being is dependent on the nature of his interaction with society, clinical pathology and social problems are also inextricably intertwined.

Before considering some of the implications of this concept for social agency functioning, I think it important to affirm that the suggestion that practice be broadened in scope does not imply a dilution in professional competence. I am not suggesting that the social worker of tomorrow become a Jack-of-all-trades. Far from it. Rather, I am saying that a social worker who has integrated within himself a piece of casework, a piece of group work, and a piece of community organization will view the people whom he serves through a transactional lens; he will use his special knowledge of a variety of human behaviors interacting with a variety of social forces. Moreover, the social worker who adheres to the true concept of individualization will treat each person-in-situation differentially, thus calling upon relevant theory and classification schemes. He will need to be equally skillful in determining the presence of individual pathology, in assessing the degree of family breakdown, and in comprehending the cultural conflicts in a neighborhood.

In the light of the inevitable fusion of social work methods, we may question whether there will be the same boundary lines between fields of practice. I think it is doubtful that they will remain if we are to be concerned with social interaction wherever it appears. One can cite as an example the field of psychiatric social work practice. Community psychiatry is here at last. The role of the social worker in a preventive mental health program based in a neighborhood unit is a far cry from the role of the psychiatric social worker in the state hospital of the past who took the anamnesis for the psychiatrist. Case finding, marital counseling, treatment of parent-child problems, group education, and group therapy, as well as the mobilization of resources in the community, will be the practice concerns of the future social worker in a community mental health center.

The person-in-situation or persons-in-situation should be the unit of attention in all social agencies, albeit each agency will have a distinct emphasis. The boundary lines now separating fields of practice and social work methods must inevitably disappear as the significant issues are joined. Our concerns are not different. The well-being of man in his interaction with society and the necessity of individualizing a case—whether it is a person, a patient, a family, a group, or a neighborhood—are the goals we have in common. Logic dictates that we use our knowledge and skills earlier in the process of social breakdown, that we turn our collective energies to prevention even as we treat people who have problems. Our communities require the most judicious and disciplined use of the many talents of social workers in all social agencies. Only to the extent that we are effective in increasing the well-being of man will we meet the standards to which we have committed ourselves.

In summary, the concept of individualized services in social work practice reflects changes in social values, changes in family life, change in the unit of attention, and developments in knowledge. A new use of this concept must be accompanied by modifications in methodology and the disappearance of practice boundaries. We have the tools available; all we now require is a readiness to set in operation dynamic and effective programs to be carried out by our community of social agencies. The profession, the schools of social work, and the agencies themselves must get on with the task.

A Multidimensional Model for Social Work Practice: The Youth Worker Example

Irving Spergel

There has been growing interest in the development of an underlying or general model for practice in the field of social work.[1] As social work draws closer to the social and behavioral sciences, it tends more firmly to subscribe to the values of conceptualization, scientific method, and theory construction. This is not to deny the fact that social work, since its inception, has utilized, explicitly or implicitly, various models for practice. For in-

Reprinted from *The Social Service Review*, Vol. 36, No. 1 (March 1962), pp. 62–71, by permission of the author and The University of Chicago Press.

[1]Werner W. Boehm, "The Nature of Social Work," *Social Work*, III (April, 1958), 10–18; Gordon Hearn, *Theory Building in Social Work* (Toronto: University of Toronto Press, 1958), pp. 1–5.

stance, social casework until recently has grounded its understanding of human behavior and its development of professional skills largely on a psychoanalytic model.[2] Social group work, with its conceptual and practice roots in a variety of academic disciplines (sociology and social psychology) and professional practice fields (social casework, recreation, progressive education, adult education, and industrial management),[3] has derived a less clear model for theory and practice. In the past decade, both casework and group work have attempted to incorporate concepts from ego psychology, role theory, organizational theory, subcultural theory, class or stratification theory, reference-group theory, and small-group theory.

However, despite the infusion of new concepts from common sources of knowledge, social casework and social group work tend to remain distinctive, specialized, and mutually exclusive methods. Schools of social work continue, generally, to educate students as either social caseworkers or social group workers. Social agencies do not employ social workers; they employ social caseworkers or social group workers. Competence in both methods is neither expected, required, nor perhaps desired. Yet, in actuality, it is the rare practitioner who does not function, whether he recognizes it or not, as caseworker, group worker, and even community organization worker in the performance of his complex job.

This state of social work affairs in part reflects the current development of scientific understanding of human behavior and social organization. The reality is that the sociocultural and medicopsychological sciences or disciplines from which social work mainly draws its knowledge tend to regard man from different vantage points. Psychiatry and psychology view human behavior largely in individual personality terms. Attention is centered on inner psychic phenomena, ego functioning, or interpersonal interactions. Sociology and anthropology view man as an actor in a larger social and cultural drama. It is the social or cultural stage or system which acquires the major focus. Social psychology, in its effort to combine the two perspectives, has succeeded primarily in the development of a third perspective. The focus tends to be on small-group structure and process, often without notice of individual personality variables or broad sociocultural influences.

[2]Marcel Heiman, M.D. (ed.), *Psychoanalysis and Social Work* (New York: International Universities Press, 1953); Helen Harris Perlman, *Social Casework: A Problem-solving Process* (Chicago: University of Chicago Press, 1957), especially pp. 164-82.
[3]Clara A. Kaiser, "The Social Group Work Process," *Social Work*, III (April, 1958), 67-75; William Schwartz, "Group Work and the Social Scene," in *Issues in American Social Work*, ed. Alfred J. Kahn (New York: Columbia University Press, 1959), pp. 110-37.

Without doubt, certain psychologists or psychiatrists and social scientists have developed theoretical systems incorporating concepts and points of view from other disciplines. Yet each theorist seems fundamentally committed to a particular and partial perspective about the behavior of man in society. Efforts to integrate diverse models of man are increasingly undertaken, but a unified and systematic theory of man in society is not yet at hand.[4]

Ideally, the social worker requires a model for practice which systematically incorporates and integrates knowledge and directions for action derived from the various relevant bodies of understanding about human behavior and sociocultural organization. Although such a unified model is not present, it is at least possible to make fuller use of the segmented knowledge available. A multidimensional approach to social work practice is required at this stage. However, this kind of approach requires a major shift in the way social work is practiced. It requires a change from specific method orientation to human-social problem orientation. Instead of being largely developed within the context of a specific method, practice should derive from a broad orientation to the factors of the human-social problem. In the first instance, the problem is defined and confronted in terms of the limited range of perspective and skill which the worker has taken from a particular method; in the second, the problem is viewed and met on the basis of a broad orientation and multiple social work skills. In the first instance, diagnosis and treatment tend to spring artificially from a limited technical base; in the second, diagnosis and treatment arise and develop from the fulness or totality of the problem itself. Appropriate methodologies are sought and used to attempt solution of the problem. The shift in social work theory and practice emphasis does not detract from the importance of highly developed skills and techniques in managing stressful situations.

It is the thesis of this paper that at the present time the social worker should develop his practice according to a multidimensional model in as integrative a fashion as current social-science and behavioral-science theory permits. The following is an exercise in human-social problem analysis and in the application of social work practice theory within a multidimensional frame of understanding and action. The example utilized is that of the youth worker with the delinquent group. It is hoped that the relevance of the problem analysis to other social problems, such as

[4]Roy R. Grinker, M.D. (ed.), *Toward a Unified Theory of Human Behavior* (New York: Basic Books, 1956); Alexander H. Leighton, *My Name Is Legion* (New York: Basic Books, 1959).

alcoholism, drug addiction, mental illness, criminality, family breakdown, and unemployment, and the practice model to other social work roles, such as those presently defined as probation or parole officer, school social worker, welfare worker, family caseworker, medical caseworker, psychiatric caseworker, settlement worker, and community organizer, will become apparent. The exercise, although not a systematic conceptual analysis, attempts to present relevant ideas from three general streams of knowledge, i.e., the sociological, the social psychological, and the psychoanalytic. It is an effort to focus on the youth worker's role as he endeavors to cope with the problems of delinquent adolescents in a particular social context. The three dimensions of problem analysis—sociocultural, group, and individual—serve also to locate the major emphases, respectively, of the three types of social work practice—community organization, group work, and casework.

The youth worker ordinarily is assigned by a social agency to serve a group of delinquent boys in a neighborhood. His avowed goal is the facilitation of socially approved behavior and orientation and the restraint of antisocial behavior and orientation on the part of youths. Usually the worker is employed as a group worker and is expected to center his service on a particular group or groups. However, from the outset he is forced to perceive and deal with a multitude of problems which are not strictly amenable to social group work methodology. The following discussion is limited to the youth worker's role with one type of delinquent group—the conflict or fighting group.

Sociocultural Dimension

One aspect of the problem confronting the worker is the sociocultural. How are the delinquent group's values and activities related to community social and cultural processes? What are the larger societal pressures that may account for delinquent orientations? Which social and cultural conditions may result in different types of delinquent adaptations? In what way can social and cultural forces or the institutional arrangements which mediate them be modified?

There is some evidence that delinquency phenomena are located largely in the lower-class segment of society.[5] Certain sociologists have speculated that delinquent orientations originate as a response to anomie or to the structural condition of acute

[5]Albert K. Cohen, *Delinquent Boys: The Culture of the Gang* (Glencoe, Ill.: Free Press, 1955); Robert K. Merton, *Social Theory and Social Structure* (rev. ed.; Glencoe, Ill.: Free Press, 1957) pp. 144–45.

disjunction between culturally induced success goals and limited means or opportunities available to lower-class youth.[6] Specific types of delinquent adaptations may be based on the availability of alternative means for the achievement of status. When access to both legitimate and illegitimate systems of opportunity is extremely limited, a conflict or gang-fighting orientation may evolve among lower-class youth. Gang-fighting develops as the means for attaining the success goal. Such personal characteristics as "heart," strength, "coolness," daring, foolhardiness, "smartness" come to qualify individuals for eligibility in the competition to achieve "rep," or reputation. In the highly deprived slum areas of the city, the gang-fighting system is sustained until late adolescence when conventional opportunities may be made partially available. Legitimate lower-class styles of life tend to develop at this time, although a small number of former gang members continue to pursue criminal careers.

If this analysis is correct and if gang-fighting is a response to the unavailability of social opportunities, then the social worker is accountable for the provision of some of these conventional opportunities. Delinquent youth must be enabled to achieve a larger measure of status through acceptable means. Two institutions fostering conventional norms and providing acceptable means to the success goal are the schools and business or industry. The worker should, in relation to the individuals, groups, or the neighborhood that he serves, seek to develop and maximize opportunities controlled by the representatives of these institutions. Specifically, the worker may encourage or stimulate school authorities and organizational groups to provide enriched educational programs, including remedial reading classes, apprenticeship training possibilities, vocational guidance, sheltered workshops, and vocational placement opportunities. The worker needs to stimulate the development of jobs for youth either through direct contact with business and industrial officials or through existing employment agencies. On behalf of delinquent youths whom he serves, the youth worker participates actively in the organization and expansion of the community's resources through community groups. More often than not, the worker and his agency must risk, provoke, and utilize crises in the development of more socially significant opportunities.[7] The worker

[6]Richard A. Cloward and Lloyd E. Ohlin, *Delinquency and Opportunity* (Glencoe, Ill.: Free Press, 1960); Merton, *op. cit.*, chaps. iv and v, pp. 131–94.
[7]Hyman J. Wiener, "Toward Techniques for Social Change," *Social Work*, VI (April, 1961), 26–35.

must possess the time, competence, and will to fulfil these requisite community organizational and developmental functions of his professional role.

Since adults generally tend both to control opportunities and to exhibit the relevant norms and values for utilization of these opportunities, young people must be helped to learn appropriate roles mainly through interaction with adults. The conflict subculture is fundamentally non-adult in orientation. The extreme orientation of gang-fighting youths to the peer culture is dysfunctional to the process of adult adaptation.[8] The gang-fighting system tends to be encapsulated, and few channels to adult-controlled opportunities are available or used. Such youths should be helped to broaden and intensify interactions with significant adults. On the other hand, adult systems both within and outside the neighborhood must be helped or stimulated by the worker to greater responsibility for fruitful contacts with delinquent youths.

The youth worker is required to understand the sociocultural forces and the nature of opportunities conducive to the conflict orientation. He must know directly how to modify institutional arrangements mediating these forces and how to facilitate the provision of opportunities by the official representatives of key institutional organizations so that disabling social conditions are ultimately modified. He should also be expected to mobilize the opportunities which potentially reside in the relationships of a variety of conventional adults with delinquent youth.

The Small-Group Dimension

By the nature of his social-agency assignment, the youth worker is enjoined to work with delinquents as members of groups. Although certain social conditions appear to give rise to the conflict subculture, it is the group itself which activates and further develops the organized set of norms, values, and beliefs conducive to gang-fighting. The presence of the delinquent members of the group is the real or tangible manifestation of destructive, hostile, and conflict orientations so disturbing to the community. It is the delinquent group which engages in serious conflict behavior; it is not the delinquent subculture or the antecedent social or cultural forces which directly commit delinquent acts.

Focus on the small-group dimension requires that the worker perceive the group as a whole or as a system of norms and values

[8]Irving Spergel, "An Exploratory Research in Delinquent Subcultures," *Social Service Review*, XXV (March, 1961), 41-42.

and interacting parts. The system of role relationships of group members, mainly to each other and to other peer groups, is the center of attention. The worker's focus is neither on general neighborhood or community processes nor on the individual personality as a unique human entity. He views the environment in terms of its impact on a specific group. He sees the individual mainly in his role as a group member.

The major function of the conflict group is to meet the collective needs of its members for status.[9] Friendship and sociability appear not to be the major bonds that draw and hold members of the fighting gang together. The social identity or position of the member in the group is established mainly on the basis of his gang-fighting prowess and attendant characteristics. It is not uncommon for group members to know very little about one another in their family, school, and employment roles. Close ties in social activities are as likely to be with non-members as with members of conflict-gang groups. The gang develops and coheres primarily for the purpose of gaining, maintaining, and defending status or "rep" through fighting. Except for a small leadership core, the gang is not a solidary and permanent organization. It serves frequently as a stopping place for the ambitious youngster in his upward climb for status in the neighborhood system of conflict groups. The youngster seems almost to be graduated from one status- or "rep"-giving group to another which gives higher status or "rep."

It is mainly in times of crisis that the conflict group is closely knit. Autocratic leadership and decision-making prevail. During periods of peace and tranquillity, group cohesion decreases; leadership tends to be diffused and laissez faire or democratic decision-making processes are more common. At such times, subgroups may engage in a variety of activities unrelated to gang-fighting. Interaction of gang members with non-gang members increases. There may be even an increase of friendly interaction with members of opposing gangs. However, at certain points group members sense that continued quiescence and the further development of friendly relationships with members of opposing gangs threaten the group's basis for existence. Conflict is precipitated. One or more of a multitude of reasons—most of them inconsequential—may be given as the basis for the outbreak of hostilities. Organized and unorganized battles, skirmishes, and raids are sporadically carried out. After a period of days, weeks, or

[9]Data used in the next three paragraphs are from Irving Spergel, "Types of Delinquent Groups" (doctoral dissertation, New York School of Social Work of Columbia University, June, 1960), pp. 135–65.

months, the fighting and tension may be terminated by the ritual peace meeting, arranged by the youth worker, policeman, racketeer, or neighborhood adult or by gang members themselves. However, time itself seems to bring the greatest pressure for the cessation of conflict and the demise of the group. Group members who have reached late adolescence are no longer denied complete access to social opportunities and conventional roles. They find jobs, establish semipermanent liaisons with girls, and tend to be identified or to identify themselves as men. Ties with conflict groups are weakened or broken completely as new young adult roles are consolidated.

The youth worker is cognizant of group phenomena. He focuses on the collectivity of individuals as a small social system. The worker is aware that a group has certain avowed or manifest goals. Group members verbalize the importance of their achieving fighting status or "rep," protecting turf or territory, or taking girls away from rival groups. The group may also have unavowed or latent goals. For instance, group members also indicate that they occasionally like to play ball, to go on trips, or even to develop a social club.

A group has structure. It has leaders and followers, members of high status and of low status. Various roles are defined formally and informally which serve the group in the achievement of its goals and the maintenance of its structure. The group may be organized in various patterns: vertically, on an age or experience basis into seniors and juniors; horizontally, in divisions or "brother clubs."[10] The group may be self-contained, with no formal ties to other groups. The group has its norm and value system, largely derived from the prevailing conflict subculture in the neighborhood. Codes of behavior in regard to peers, adults, and friendly and unfriendly groups during periods of peace and war are developed. All these group processes, and others, are in flux—constantly shifting, sometimes slowly, sometimes rapidly.

Small-group research[11] and social group work experience provide directions for modification of some of the group processes. The youth worker strives through group discussion to make certain unavowed or latent goals in the group manifest. He seeks to increase the attractiveness of social goals for the group.

[10]Lloyd T. Delaney, "Establishing Relationships with Antisocial Groups and Analysis of Their Structure," British Journal of Delinquency, V (July, 1954) 34-45.

[11]Dorwin Cartwright and Alvin Zander (eds.), Group Dynamics: Research and Theory (2d ed.; Evanston, Ill.: Row, Peterson & Co., 1960); Eleanor E. Maccoby, Theodore M. Newcomb, and Eugene L. Hartley (eds.), Reading in Social Psychology (New York: Henry Holt & Co., 1958); J. L. Moreno (ed.), The Sociometry Reader (Glencoe, Ill.: Free Press, 1960).

He assists the members to redefine criteria for success status more in line with conventional expectations. The pressure to obtain "rep" by gang-fighting may be replaced in part by pressure to obtain "rep" as a ball team or a social club.[12] The provision of resources such as uniforms, a club house, transportation for trips, and varied social activities may facilitate the shift from antisocial to social group goals and norms.

Permissive group discussion rather than moralistic lecture by group workers may more readily induce the internalization of new group goals and standards of behavior. The process of democratic decision-making rather than autocratically imposed decision-making increases intragroup satisfactions.

The increased interaction of members from opposition groups, particularly through participation in joint projects requiring a high level of co-operation, may improve intergroup relations.[13] Such efforts are fraught with many hazards, but the rewards in improved social functioning for the various group members may be worth the risks of the worker.

The youth worker, depending on his assessment of the cohesiveness of the group and what it signifies, may determine to modify group structure by pulling off social or antisocial subgroups. He may try to increase the cohesiveness of the group, if group norms—particularly those of leaders—are sufficiently socialized. The strongly cohesive group has greater power than the weakly cohesive group to influence the behavior of group members. The youth worker may assist the indigenous group leader to exercise greater control over deviant members, particularly if the behavior of the deviates counters the new socialized norms of the group. On the other hand, when group norms are highly deviant, he may attempt to establish himself as a counter-leader or leader of a subgroup which subscribes to conventional norms. He hopes that a realignment of the group structure may bring more group members to a clearer and fuller commitment to conventional standards of behavior.

There are countless devices—differential use of program,[14] situational manipulations,[15] intensive worker relationship—which the youth worker may employ to modify group process, member orientations, and behavior.

[12]David M. Austin, "Goals for Gang Workers," *Social Work, II* (October, 1957), 43–50.
[13]Muzafer Sherif, "Social Responsibility and the Group," in *Social Welfare Forum,* 1956, pp. 219–34.
[14]Fritz Redl and David Wineman, *Controls from Within* (Glencoe, Ill.: Free Press, 1952), pp. 76–152.
[15]Howard Jones, *Reluctant Rebels* (New York: Association Press, 1960), pp. 109–26.

The Individual Dimension

The youth worker establishes contact and relationship with the individual delinquent both inside and outside the group structure. The individual delinquent is more than a member of a juvenile gang. He is a member of other groups and fulfils other roles. The worker is aware that the youth is a unique personality, fashioned through the complex interaction of social, cultural, subcultural, situational, family, interpersonal, intrapersonal, and biological forces. The social worker is especially interested in the individual's self-concept and his relationship to significant others in the environment. He is concerned with the way the individual delinquent reacts to external situations and becomes the person he is. The worker focuses on how the delinquent reacts to acceptance or rejection, frustration or stress, and security or insecurity, and on what his seemingly enduring patterns of personality and relationship are.

Knowledge of the individual requires especially an understanding of his current and previous patterns of family relationship. Basic and not easily remedied personality patterns are fashioned in the early years of experience in the family situation. Extreme and sustained affectional deprivation, overindulgence, and lack of supervision or guidance by parents appear to be factors highly associated with the antisocial or delinquent adaption.[16] Family breakdown or serious conflict, overt or covert, between parents seems to affect the adjustment of the child. It is possible that the individual who has derived little affection, security, or support from an unstable family group may seek substitute satisfactions through membership in a delinquent group. The gang serves in psychological terms both as a source of acceptance, affection, and security and, at the same time, as a means to vent anger, resentment, and hostility.

The youth worker confronts the delinquent in his current living situation. He centers diagnostic skill on the individual's present reactions to and feelings about his daily living experience. He seeks to understand the delinquent's past history only as it is significant to his current functioning. The worker strives to understand and modify the delinquent's modes of relationship and feeling which, without help or guidance, seem destined to be perpetuated.

[16]Kate Friedlander, M.D., *The Psycho-analytical Approach to Juvenile Delinquency* (New York: International Universities Press, 1947); Sheldon Glueck (ed.), *The Problem of Delinquency* (Boston: Houghton Mifflin Co., 1959), pp. 1003–51.

The psychoanalytic model, modified by current casework emphasis on ego functioning and interpersonal relations, appears peculiarly well suited to the youth worker in his efforts to change the behavior and attitudes of individual delinquents. The worker accepts the crucial value of the worker-client or one-to-one relationship. The worker tries to develop a positive, understanding relationship with the delinquent. He provides attention, interest, and acceptance. A relationship dynamic is established in which the youngster begins to trust, confide in, and depend on the worker. The youngster may gain security and develop self-respect from the relationship. He may see other persons and himself in more positive and desirable terms. Identification with the worker's values and acceptance of his perceptions of reality may also occur. If the youngster is amenable and if the worker is sufficiently skilled, the youngster begins to examine his motivations and feelings and to obtain insights into the dynamics of his own maladaptive behavior. A firmer base for new, more socially defined behavior and personally satisfying relationships may be established. In any case, the delinquent comes to perceive more clearly the implication of his own attitudes, interpersonal relations, and behavior. Consequently, he should be able to assess his opportunities more realistically and within a conventional frame of reference more congruent with that of the worker. The delinquent is taught at some level of understanding by the worker how better to help himself to achieve personal and social fulfilment.

The youth worker is expected also to intervene directly in the network of significant interpersonal relationships that the delinquent has developed, not just in the peer group but in the family and the employment or school setting. With the permission of the youngster, the worker may intervene, for example, in the family system and serve as a corrector of badly distorted perceptions and interactions, as a mediator of conflicts, and generally as a support and resource to the family in solving problems which affect the social functioning of the youth.

The worker, utilizing a distinctively social work model, serves as a bridge to community services that may more intensively assist the particular youngster and his family with their personal problems. He draws upon community resources and opportunities with which the particular youngster and his parents may be unfamiliar or which they need and resist using effectively, e.g., employment agencies and vocational training and retraining, recreation, and medical and rehabilitative services.

The worker exercises an authoritative function. Society and the agency have rights, responsibilities, and powers for effecting change in the particular youth identified as deviant. Although seeking primarily to help the youngster develop inner controls, the worker may be compelled for the youngster's own welfare to impose or secure the imposition of controls from without. For example, the worker may alert the police to the possibility of criminal behavior planned by a youngster. The worker may facilitate processes of arrest and court referral to a child-guidance clinic or casework agency, or institutionalization in a training school, residential treatment center, or mental hospital. The ambivalence, resentment, and hostility stirred up in youngsters by this aspect of the worker's role may be resolved only as the youngster fully understands and accepts the deep concern of the worker for the youngster's personal and social welfare.

In essence, the youth worker is concerned with the individual delinquent in the broad range of his interactions within the gang, the family, and community institutions.

Summary

The youth worker attempts to understand the problem of delinquency along three dimensions of knowledge about human behavior, i.e., the sociocultural, the group, and the individual. The absence of a unified theory of behavior prevents him from systematically integrating the various levels of knowledge into a simple, neat scheme for analysis and understanding. However, each human-social problem seems to require diagnosis and treatment along the different dimensions in which the problem exists. To neglect understanding and treatment of the problem at either the sociocultural, the group, or the individual level is to deny the full and complex measure of reality with which the social worker deals.

The foregoing exercise could as easily have utilized the example of the social worker in the juvenile institution or the mental hospital, the child welfare or public assistance worker, or the community organizer in a rural or urban setting. In each case, a variety of orientations and methods must be employed to cope with the problem confronted. In sum, the complex role functioning of the social worker may not be realistically exercised through employment of the casework, group work, or community organization methods in isolation from each other.

Various levels of practice may be carried on nearly simultaneously or at least successively in a human-social problem situation. However, there is a need for the development of clear-cut systematic practice strategies. It may be important, depending on the particular problem, to center attention on the sociocultural or group or individual dimension. Determination of practice emphasis varies with the analysis of the basic components or causes of the problem. In relation to certain problems, particularly those of lower-class delinquency, major attention may need to be paid to the sociocultural or institutional dimension. In the specific agency, the board of directors, administrators, supervisors, and practitioners should have ongoing collective responsibility for analysis of types of human-social problems as they are confronted and for the general practice strategies to be employed.

A multidimensional approach to social work practice calls for a broad base of understanding and technology. It calls for a shift from single-method orientation to social problem analysis and the broad use of social work skills and techniques in solving human-social problems. It is time to regard our methods as instrumentalities that facilitate the solution of the social welfare problems of people and society, and not as precious ends in themselves.

Finally, a multidimensional approach has at least three major implications for social work practice. First, it requires the social worker to know and be competent in the practice of the three principal social work methods. Second, it calls for the development of the position of general practitioner as the basic social work status unit. The so-called specialist—social caseworker, social group worker, or community organizer—must continually relate his special knowledge and skill to an evolving common body of social work theory, knowledge, and practice.[17] Third, the social work practitioner should be held responsible for systematically contributing data and insights about the reality of the human-social problem and how he confronts it, so that a unified theory of social work practice ultimately will be developed and tested.

[17]For a preliminary work on the integration of principles and techniques of different types of professional help, see Ronald Lippitt, Jeanne Watson, and Bruce Westley, *The Dynamics of Planned Change* (New York: Harcourt, Brace & Co., 1958).

Organization of the Poor—
Threat or Opportunity?

Leon H. Ginsberg

At the center of many new anti-poverty programs is the organization of the poor to solve their own problems. Advocates of this approach to the elimination of poverty believe that only through organization can the real problems of the poor be identified. No man or group can correctly define another's problems, they say. And this is viewed as even more true when solutions are sought, because solutions to social problems are effective only when those facing the problems choose their own answers.

If the objective is an end to poverty, the means to that end must deal with root causes—not only with consequences. Indigenous organizations may be a means for dealing with causes and are therefore often described as more likely to eliminate poverty than traditional social welfare programs.

This discussion will deal with the implications of various means for organizing the poor along with some examples of how low income people have been or could be organized. The strengths and limitations of these approaches are examined.

Of central concern in this discussion are the beliefs that organization of the poor poses either a threat to the society or an opportunity to resolve the problems of poverty. There are advocates for each idea as the probable result of organizational efforts. This writer would suggest that both results are possible and need not be seen as mutually exclusive. That is, threats are often a form of opportunities and opportunities for some groups may result in threats to other groups.

Small Group or Community
Effort?

It is of some value to distinguish between organizational efforts that focus on small groups and those that attempt to organize and change communities. Both approaches are being used systematically in anti-poverty programs and both have their effects. However, each is distinct, and careful thought should be given to which one will be used in a given situation.

Reprinted with permission of the American Public Welfare Association from *Public Welfare*, Vol. 26, No. 1 (January 1968), pp. 60–66.

The Small Group

Numerous efforts for small group activities with low-income people have already been reported. Perhaps the classic example is the group program for mothers whose families are recipients of Aid to Families with Dependent Children. Generally, the small group effort is educational, recreational, or designed to help people work together on mutual personal problems. That is, small group services are usually individual-oriented. They help people to cope with their living situations, to develop relationships with others, and to learn about internal and external resources that will help them meet problems.

Other examples are small recreational groups for children, basic education classes for adults, and training programs for unemployed adults.

These efforts are usually not threatening to the social structure of the community because they are focused on the individual. The change effort centers on the person in the group, not the community which surrounds the group. Of course, such efforts may enable people to develop capacities that will increase their chances of participation in wider social change endeavors. As Joseph E. Paull has noted,[1] some of the efforts to use group services in public welfare have led to the development of conflict-negotiation oriented organizations.

Programs of communal change usually involve large groups such as a neighborhood whose members are of an ethnic minority in a community, or a combination of small groups.

Such efforts may be as traditional as a neighborhood clean-up campaign or as change-oriented as a rent strike. That is, communal efforts may or may not threaten the established ways of doing things in the community. A byproduct of such efforts is often created in helping the person in the community develop individual capacities for participation in change endeavors, whether or not the communal effort is change-oriented. That is, involvement in itself is a learning experience. There is, of course, a wide range of communal change endeavors. Some attempt to revise the relationships between people and groups in the community while some simply work to maximize the quality of services given by existing agencies. In other cases, short range social change efforts may be made—such as those creating new services or revising, in some minor way, the structure or procedures of an institution.

---

[1]Joseph E. Paull, "Recipients Aroused: The New Welfare Rights Movement," *Social Work*, Volume XII, Number 2 (April, 1967).

Communities Are Structured

To appreciate the significance of organization of the poor requires some understanding of the fact that communities are structured. That is, communities are organized around groups of people, all of whom play some role in the community even when their role may be nonparticipation. There is power exercised in the community to determine who will get what and how they will get it. There is a "socio-economic structure," too. This refers to the distribution of wealth and resources in the community. Typically, those with the best jobs and the most money are placed at the top of the social structure; everyone else fits at one level or another.

Social science theorists say that when one role changes, other roles must change. Therefore, if a minority group that has been oppressed ceases to be oppressed, everyone else—including the oppressors—must have a change in role, too. The existence of minorities presupposes the existence of majorities. So all groups and individuals have their places in the community, and any change in any group means that there will be some changes in other groups.

Conflict-Negotiation
Approaches

Perhaps the most striking example of efforts to organize the poor is the Mobilization for Youth program which is concentrated on the Lower East Side of New York City. Richard Cloward and Richard Elmann described one phase of the organization effort in an article entitled "Advocacy in the Ghetto"[2]—as an organization of public assistance clients who believed they were being served inadequately by the New York City Public Welfare Department. Through the development of an organization which issued requests to the Department of Public Welfare, the position of the client was changed. Specifically, adequate allowances for warm winter clothing were made available in time for the cold weather, rather than later in the year, as had been happening in the past.

Of course, this is only one example of welfare rights groups which are being established in the United States. Joseph E. Paull describes the total movement in his article, "Recipients Aroused: The New Welfare Rights Movement,"[3] and says there are 173 such groups in twenty-three states and the District of Columbia.

[2]Richard A. Cloward and Richard M. Elman, "Advocacy in the Ghetto," *Trans-action*, Volume IV, Number 2 (December, 1966).
[3]Joseph E. Paull, *op. cit.*

"Conflict" groups follow, in some ways, the model developed many years ago by Saul Alinsky and his Industrial Areas Foundation.[4] They take the approach that only through organization can the poor obtain power and win the battles for human dignity, for participation in the society, and for adequate economic treatment.

It is these kinds of organizations that generally come to mind when the subject of organization of the poor is discussed. However, many other kinds of examples exist and these are equally important. For example, seldom mentioned are such activities as the Head Start parent advisory groups. Such groups exist in thousands of small areas of rural and urban America. They involve parents in policy making for Head Start child development centers; they provide an opportunity for parents to be involved in the Head Start program; they provide educational opportunities for parents who want to help their children in Head Start and in school.

There are also countless small neighborhood councils that have been developed by the settlement houses and by the Economic Opportunity Act's Community Action Programs. These often engage in conflict and negotiation, along the lines prescribed by Alinsky. Just as often, however, they engage in programs of education, community improvement, creation of community resources, and other kinds of nonthreatening but helpful activities.

Some of the Myths of Power

Many organizers believe the poor must be organized to deal with the "power structure." Proponents of such a position generally follow the theories developed by sociologists such as Floyd Hunter[5] and C. Wright Mills.[6] Typically, such theories say that a small group of powerful people direct most aspects of the lives of American communities. The power elite, according to these theorists, decides what will and what will not happen in the community; people are poor, ill-housed and ill-educated, because the top power structure sets the wage scale as low as possible and opposes low cost public housing and adequate taxation for education. The power structure is generally seen as a group of very wealthy people who govern the community's economic life.

[4]Persons interested in examining Alinsky's theories may want to read "Interviews with Saul Alinsky," *Harper's*, Volume CCXXXI, Number 1381 and Number 1382 (June and July, 1965), and *Reveille for Radicals* (Chicago: University of Chicago Press, 1946).

[5]Floyd Hunter, *Community Power Structure* (Chapel Hill: University of North Carolina Press, 1953).

[6]C. Wright Mills, *The Power Elite* (New York: Oxford University Press, 1956).

Because they will do only what they are forced to do, the power elite is viewed as an enemy of the poor. After all, each dollar earned by a poor person is taken from the wealth of a power structure member.

When one conceives of a community in this way, dealing with poverty is a fairly simple but threatening matter. One must organize the large numbers of poor people to overcome the stranglehold of the economically powerful power elite. Thus one makes efforts to organize the poor so that they may do battle in ways that will cause the top power people to change. Boycotts may be used, in addition to pickets, strikes, and other conflictual tactics.

The major difficulty with this theory and the approaches arising from it is that it simply may not be true. Granted, there may be some communities—large or small—in which all things are controlled by a small power elite. It is just as likely, however, that no absolute power structures exist. Power may be diffused throughout the community in a number of small power cells and power groups dealing with specific areas and issues. Thus an organization of the poor which harasses or otherwise attempts to intimidate a group it considers to be the power structure may find that it is unsuccessful—not because the power structure refuses to give in, but because there is, in fact, no top power structure. When this occurs the poor may readily lose any enthusiasm for the organization and for the agency working with it. It will appear to be simply one more phony and perhaps self-serving approach to the problems of poverty.

More Realistic Tactics

Probably a more realistic way to deal with community change on behalf of the poor is to identify all of the specific groups that hold power over specific areas in the community. For example, the Mobilization for Youth project did not attempt to take on any abstract power structure. Rather, it attempted to change welfare policies by dealing with the welfare department. Thus if a poverty group wanted to change educational practices— perhaps discrimination against minority group students in schools—it might well deal with the school board, administration, or whatever agency that was directly responsible for the issue concerned.

These notions are based upon research and writing by other "power structure" theorists. They suggest that there is more inertia in United States communities than there is centralization of power. There is simply no one directly responsible for or immediately able to handle problem situations which perpetuate poverty. Writers such as Robert Dahl,[7] Robert Presthus,[8] and Nelson Polsby[9] have indicated with some clarity that in most American communities there are many power cells rather than an elite power structure. If they are correct, some of the talk and action about taking on the powerful people of the community will only lead to frustration and not to the results desired.

Thus, more realistic tactics would be those which help the people to identify the problems of greatest concern to their organization. It may be a lack of sanitation; it may be inadequate schools. Or, it may be a lack of recreational facilities in the neighborhood or mistreatment by public officials. Whatever the problem, it would be the agency's job and the organization's job to determine exactly who could make the changes. People would learn about those groups which affected their lives and they would work to effect the necessary changes. Rather than attack a nonexistent power structure or the total community, the groups would attack specific agencies and organizations which could do something about the concerns of the people.

All this suggests that the efforts of organizations of the poor ought to be specific, rather than general. They ought to identify the issue and the "enemy" quite carefully and develop the strategies and tactics most likely to change them.

For example, buyers' strikes against grocery chains which have overpriced goods in low income neighborhoods have been publicized and dramatized in newspapers and other media. This has often resulted in an equalization of prices. In fact, most of the successful efforts at community change through organization of the poor have been based upon specific issues rather than generalized expressions of dissatisfaction. Even the civil rights movement began with the highly specific issue of bus seating in Montgomery, Alabama. This, along with the other efforts to integrate various institutions in American society, probably led to more concrete results than some of the mass rallies and organized efforts which followed.

[7]Robert Dahl, Who Governs? (New Haven: Yale University Press, 1961).
[8]Robert V. Presthus, Men at the Top (New York: Oxford University Press, 1964).
[9]Nelson Polsby, Community Power and Political Theory (New Haven: Yale University Press, 1963).

So the impetus of the organizational effort should be toward specificity of objectives and clarity about what can help most to achieve those objectives.

Other Groups Which May Be Organized

One other difficulty in discussions of organization of the poor is that the general public may think of only the welfare client or the underpaid fulltime worker or such others in the community who are deprived of full usage of its goods and services. There are still other groups, also poor, which should be organized if they are to achieve some change in their position and some improvement in their own conditions. For example, this writer has been interested in the problems of involuntary commitment of the mentally ill. Mentally ill people are probably one of America's least adequately treated groups. They are deprived of their rights to an extent greater than any group other than convicted criminals. Although this sounds appropriate because the mentally ill are supposedly irresponsible and unable to make judgments for themselves, the facts seem to indicate that there is a higher correlation between mental illness and poverty than between mental illness and factors such as dangerousness or irresponsibility. It would seem then that organizational efforts within institutions for the mentally ill among those who care about mentally ill people would be effective in coping with this issue. This does not refer to the official mental health movements, which focus on raising funds for institutions and programs. This means that the mentally ill themselves might be assisted in resolving some of their own problems and protecting their own rights through organization.

One might also consider students. The student rights movement has been gaining increasing publicity and recognition. College students want to have a voice in the colleges and universities. The want to break the powerful hold that these institutions have on them both socially and educationally. A strong high school student council in an impoverished neighborhood could do a great deal to counter mistreatment of and discrimination against students if such an organization was assisted by people who cared. Too often school student councils deal instead with the frivolities of sports, socials, and other elements which may be important but which may not deal with the most important concerns of the students.

The suggestion is that organization of the poor could be far more pervasive than is often imagined and ought to include much more than the notion of a neighborhood council or of a poverty commission involving the poor themselves.

Organization for the Sake of Organization

Much of what is said about organization of the poor is future oriented. People are told that if they work together as an organization they will achieve certain benefits, such as an end to their own poverty, an improvement in their schools or a change in their position in the community. Often neglected is the concept that organization in itself is a healthy element in the lives of human beings. One way to help the poor avoid alienation is to encourage participation in organizations.

In organizations people learn skills that they do not learn otherwise. They learn to work with others as a team; they learn leadership behaviors; they are likely to make friends, and they are likely to occupy their time in stimulating ways.

Thus, simple organizational endeavors can often do more to aid the social and mental health of individuals in poverty areas than many kinds of directly therapeutic services. Mothers may organize babysitting pools and participate in social or educational programs through this new-found service. Families can organize social activities on a regular or occasional basis such as barbecues, ball games, and dances. These will tend to add to the pleasure in living and also to the capacity of the participants to function in other ways. If the country club set is powerful in determining what the city's tax rate will be, it is just as likely that a folk-dancing group in a low-income neighborhood will be more powerful than unorganized poor people in demanding adequate streets and sanitation for their neighborhood. Activities such as these fit very closely into the framework of neutral organizational activities which neither threaten the existing community structure nor deal directly with the problem of poverty. Organization, in this context, is a potentially significant factor in genuinely aiding the people of the community.

Threats and Opportunities

Having examined some of the issues and factors involved in the process of organizing the poor, we may now ask the core question of our discussion—is organization of the poor a threat or an opportunity?

Some students of social science say that there is no valid distinction between problems and opportunities. That is, a stumbling block requires a solution; the mere requirement of a solution leads people to work toward one. Thus, a problem provides an opportunity. Therefore, although organization of poor people poses some threats, those threats must be seen as opportunities, too.

Of course, one person's threat is another's opportunity. For example, an organization of low-income people may provide "opportunities" to its members and some "threats" to nonpoverty groups in the community. However, these threats may be seen as opportunities to help integrate such poverty groups into the mainstream of community life. Organization of the poor may reduce the threats that low-income groups can pose to other groups in the community.

One of the difficulties with examining organization of the poor in terms of threats and opportunities is that it neglects this third potential result. That is, many organizations of the poor do not threaten the balance of the community. Instead they neutralize threats by helping unassimilated groups play a role in the community. At other times groups of the poor may meet social and emotional needs for the members without doing anything to threaten the nonpoor or the community as it is. These efforts are neutral in terms of their effect on the larger community.

In other cases, organizations of the poor hamper efforts to deal with poverty. Organizations are not always—perhaps not even often—change-oriented, dynamic entities. More typically they become self-serving, institutionalized, and sterile. For example, the largest and most influential organizational influences among the poor probably are churches. The churches which often serve the lower levels of the socio-economic structure are often oriented toward the status quo and toward rewards in an afterlife. They encourage the expenditure of congregational energy on matters far removed from the causes and consequences of poverty. Martin Luther King remains something of an exception among the minority-group clergy. While religious institutions which serve middle and upper class congregations are becoming increasingly focused on social action, the churches of the poor tend to center on more ritualistic activity.

Thus it is important to recognize that organization of the poor, alone, will not yield any specific results. Some organizational endeavors will pose threats to the existing community structure, while others will not. In some cases, organizations of poor people may interfere with social change or hold back progress which could otherwise be made.

The crucial issues are the objectives, composition, and motivation of the organization. Whether it will present a threat, offer an opportunity, or neutralize change endeavors depends upon these elements. Organizations, alone, are neither threatening nor creative. Whether or not they will become so depends upon who joins them, what they choose to do, and how they choose to do it.

It is axiomatic to the political scientist that people, unorganized, are virtually powerless. It is only through organized groups that the individual may influence his community and his society.

Solutions to the problem of poverty, and solutions to most other social problems, must come through organized efforts. If those solutions are to deal with the problems as they exist and develop solutions which are most appropriate to the people, then they must involve organization of the people affected by them.

This discussion has examined some examples of organization of the poor. Organization of the poor is viewed as including overt conflictual efforts to change public policy; efforts to force institutions to modify their behavior; and small-scale social, educational, and recreational activity. All three classes of efforts are seen as significant although the last is not directly threatening to the community as it exists.

Some practices in organization of the poor are viewed as based upon mythical notions about top power structures. It is suggested that the most lasting and effective efforts must deal with specific institutions and organizations for specific goals.

Threats and opportunities are seen not as opposites but as a continuum, with some threats serving as opportunities for change. One cannot logically separate the two. It is frequently the threat to things as they are which offers the greatest opportunity for change.

A Social Action Model for the Social Work Practitioner

Leonard Schneiderman

The goal of social work practice is enhancement of the social functioning of individuals and groups. Social workers do not view social functioning as an expression of the intrinsic properties of an individual but rather as a function of an interaction or

Reprinted with permission of the author and The Family Service Association of America from *Social Casework*, Vol. 46, No. 8 (October 1965), pp. 490-493.

transaction between persons and situations. Social functioning and social dysfunctioning are understood as expressions of a dynamic relationship between individual needs and functional capacities, on one side, and situational expectations, opportunities, and resources, on the other. Social dysfunctioning implies an imbalance in this relationship. The enhancement of social functioning—that is, the establishment or re-establishment of a workable balance, may, therefore, be effected by using any of the following approaches: (1) modification of individual need or functional capacity or both of them to bring them within the range of situational expectations, opportunities, and resources; (2) modification of situational expectations, opportunities, and resources to bring them within the range of individual functional capacity and need; or (3) a combination of these two.

Achieving a balance in this relationship is not in itself the ultimate goal of the social work profession. A qualitative consideration, introduced by the value commitment of the profession, mediates this process and determines the goals of professional intervention. Social workers are not, for example, simply in the professional business of improving the adjustment of people to their reality situations. No one ought to be permanently well adjusted to such conditions as living in a slum; having inadequate supplies of food, clothing, shelter, or medical care; or being the victim of punitive and restrictive public policies. Such conditions are inherently dehumanizing and pathological, and, consequently, demand change.

A combination of specific knowledge and a value commitment operates to determine the targets of social work intervention in the person-situation transactional field called social functioning. Facts alone cannot determine the purposes and goals of intervention. Before such a determination can be made, the facts must be combined with a commitment to some concept of what is right and wrong, good and bad, desirable and undesirable. Nor can values alone determine the targets of professional intervention. Values require the mediation of knowledge to connect them to, and to amplify, the human situation that invokes their application and makes them relevant.

This article explores the central issue, How can social work practitioners, as practitioners, engage in social action that contributes to the enhancement of the social functioning of their clientele? How can social work practitioners contribute to modification of situational expectations, opportunities, and resources for their clientele taken as a group, in a direction dictated by the unmet needs of people and by the value commitment of the profession relative to such unmet needs? Professional practitioners recognize, for example, the inadequacy of confining the focus of their intervention to helping clients adjust to inadequate public welfare grants, to a neater budgeting of their poverty. Although such "adjustments" may be part of the "proximate" goals of the case, they are inadequate as the "ultimate" goal of professional intervention.

The reason for focusing the discussion on the social action role of the social caseworker, group worker, and community organizer is not to eliminate or to minimize the importance of the other significant social action roles of the social worker as citizen, as researcher, as administrator, and as member of a professional organization. Rather, this focus was selected in recognition of the fact that the vast majority of social workers are involved in providing direct services to people—that while social workers have insisted upon the involvement of practitioners in social action, they have not developed a suitable model that can be used effectively for this purpose. When social workers have defined a social action role, for example, the role of a member of a social action committee of the National Association of Social Workers, there has been a tendency to view it as something separate and apart from rather than as something incorporated within, the method the practitioner uses daily. The result has been a sterile output of social action by the profession and a sense of guilt and uncertainty on the part of the practitioner concerning the social action role, if any, that he can play effectively.

Social Action Model

The social action model proposed for the social work practitioner constitutes a basic and important, but minimal, level of participation. The model assumes that each client, no matter how distinctive or unique his problem, is also a member of a population group of persons who share many things in common. Every case unit provides the practitioner with an opportunity to study both the specific and unique, as well as the general, features of the client's problems in social functioning. Consequently, the practitioner has an opportunity to test the adequacy of existing social policies and programs for members of a specific population. Every unmarried mother, every delinquent, every welfare recipient, every mentally ill person, in addition to being a unique person in a unique situation, is also a member of a population group having many things in common. Every case unit provides the practitioner with an opportunity to test the adequacy of existing resources for specific populations. Every case provides him with an opportunity to document the need, if any, for revising policies and programs to enable such persons to achieve the ends toward which social work's value commitments are directed. Every case provides him with an opportunity to begin identifying common etiological factors, the elimination of which might prevent the occurrence of certain problems.

By drawing from the same knowledge base that is used to rationalize methods of intervention at the case level, what conclusions can be arrived at about the adverse effects of present policies and programs upon the population that the client represents? What are the social, psychological, cultural, and organic consequences of failing to meet the needs of this population? What resources and facilities would make it possible for it to achieve optimum goals?

Every unit of practitioner activity represents not only an opportunity to provide service but also an opportunity to document at the practice level the present adequacy of all community policies and programs in relation to the needs and aspirations of an entire population.

The annual reports of agencies might well include, in addition to the number of persons served, the number of cases in which the need for social change was documented and the number of times that agency staff members, administrators, and board members presented documentation to appropriate legislative bodies.

There has been an unfortunate inclination to perceive recipients of social work services as individual case units without recognition that these persons are representative of specific populations whose members share many common problems and face many common obstacles to effective problem-solving. Such case unit perception as opposed to a group or community perception has tended to emphasize the unique rather than the common features of each case situation. The inadequacy of resources and opportunities for many clients and specific populations constitutes a collective indictment of the community's present way of doing business.

The individual client may derive substantial therapeutic benefits from recognizing the universal as well as the unique features of his situation and from feeling part of a social action movement designed to modify that part of his situation that many persons, including his social worker, find offensive. This type of approach makes it possible for the client to see the significance of his problem-solving efforts for others, now and in the future.

If social workers are to be professionals and not merely employees, they must be committed to purposes broader than the administration of an agency program. A professional, as opposed to an employee, is more than a purveyor of community-financed services to his client. He is a spokesman to the general community of the client's unmet needs and aspirations.

If social workers are to be professionals and not merely employees, they must do more than simply translate agency policies into services to clients. They must, in addition, systematically study their practice experience, which they can then use as the basis for advocating changes in agency policy and program. In this way they will more fully achieve the purposes of the agency and of the profession.

If social workers are to be professionals and not merely employees, they must have a viable connection with their agency *and* their professional reference group. The professional reference group commits the professional to a value system and set of professional goals and purposes with which the goals and purposes of the agency must be compatible.

The supporting community has a right to know not only about the practitioner's services to clients but also about the results of his experience. This information should be presented clearly and should meet high standards of accuracy, completeness, and honesty in reporting. This right of the community, and this obligation of the profession, cannot be met if practitioners continue to store their experience away in endless, nonabstracted records. Such a practice is, in addition, a betrayal of our responsibility to our clientele. We fail, thus, to speak effectively in their behalf. Practitioners, who have had the privilege of learning at first hand about the personal lives and problems of their clientele, have the sacred professional obligation to channel their collective experience into the main stream of community life. In advocating programs of social change, practitioners can use their experience to aid their clients and others in like situations. No definition of specific agency function can free professionals who possess knowledge from the obligation to put it to use. All practitioners have known clients who could have been better served if the community's resources had been more adequate. Failure to document the need for improving community services by not making use of case material (appropriately disguised, of course) is a serious professional failure. It is a failure in discharging our obligation to a population group of persons to whom our commitment is as strong and specific as it is to the individual client sitting before us.

That the social action model being advocated is not entirely new is of little or no concern. What does concern me is that it be clear that such a social action model should be incorporated as a minimum level of participation of all social work practitioners in a social action process.

The Responsibility of the Agency and the Professional Organization

The social work practitioner on the firing line has a unique and exciting opportunity to view each unit of service through professional bifocals. The microscopic lens defines the proximate goals to be achieved in the case. The macroscopic lens directs the practitioner's sight beyond the specific case to the needs of a specific population, which must be documented.

Such documentation will, of course, be meaningless unless the data are gathered together, analyzed, and employed effectively to achieve specific, relevant ends. Certainly, a major responsibility here belongs to agency administration. Beyond the translation of social policies into social services, effective professional administration includes using practice experience effectively in influencing policy-makers to accept the need for revising service programs and policies.

Certainly, social agencies and their lay boards must be important instruments for social action and social change. The agencies are, however, the creations of the general community and are an insufficient vehicle through which the profession can express its social action commitment. It is here that we come to the nub of a major obstacle to effective social action by the social work profession.

It is well and good to talk of the importance of systematic learning from our practice experience, of using our experience to document the unmet or inadequately met needs of people and the adverse effects of such a situation upon them. It is well and good to write of the professional organization as the professional's vehicle for social action. Our problem is that of putting the two together.

The professional experience from which we are to learn and to document takes place in the agencies. The professional organization has no clear ongoing relationship to the social agencies. To whom, then, does the professional's agency experience belong? Does it belong to the agency? Does it belong to the practitioner? Can he bring it in any organized form to the professional organization for reporting and action? Is the professional limited in the organized use that can be made of his own experience to that which a lay governing body will approve?

This is, I believe, a crucial issue. The experience and the knowledge that constitute the documentation for the social action positions we, as a profession, advocate, reside in the agencies. The commitment to act, to do as a profession, rests in our professional organization. How can these be brought together effectively so that our experience in practice will not be lost to the community and so that the profession may have a clearly documented base for its action?

There is no clear or complete answer to this question. It should be discussed, and alternative approaches should be considered. It is important, however, that any discussion begin by redefining the practitioner's function to include the dual obligation of serving clients effectively and of using practice to document the need for social change. Beyond this, the answer must include an extension of practitioner concern about agency setting, about the learning opportunities the agency encourages, and about the level of clinical practice it supports to equal concern with the agency's responsible use of documented evidence for inducing social change. Does the agency encourage the gathering and analysis of such data? Does it continuously and effectively publish its findings? Does it forthrightly seek the changes that the findings support? These must be part of the professional's expectation of his agency.

The documenting model provides all social workers with a meaningful beginning opportunity for personal involvement in a social action process—a process that must combine both a clear value commitment and solid, relevant supporting information. The personal commitment, the demand for follow-through, and the action that could result from any large-scale implementation of this action model would, I believe, greatly increase the effectiveness of the profession in this important, but largely undeveloped, area of its responsibility.

What Every Social Worker Should Know about Political Action

Wilbur J. Cohen

The interest of the National Association of Social Workers and its membership in social action and in the political process is well justified by the happenings of the last two or three years.

Reprinted with permission of the author and the National Association of Social Workers from *Social Work*, Vol. 11, No. 3 (July 1966), pp. 3–11.

There could not be any better affirmation of the value, importance, and increased significance of social action than recent events in the field of national legislation.

After ninety-five years of having a bill in Congress on federal aid to education, one was finally enacted last year; after a great deal of interest in various aspects of poverty, a specific piece of legislation was enacted two years ago; after thirty years of debate and controversy over legislation, a national health insurance program was enacted. These are certainly strong indications of the importance of sustained social action. There is no question but that more intense, wider social action in the future can produce even more of the kind of social legislation in which NASW is interested.

Recently a bill was introduced into the Congress by Representative Wilbur D. Mills [D.—Ark.], the chairman of the Ways and Means Committee, and Senator Abraham Ribicoff [D.—Conn.], which provides for a two-year program of federal funds for faculty expansion in the field of social work education. Two or three pieces of such legislation have been enacted before, but none has ever been funded—which illustrates one of the first lessons in any kind of political development, namely, that legislation by itself is not the solution to any problem. Not only does the legislation have to get through, but the money has to be appropriated, and then the program has to be administered—the "trinity" behind any successful legislation.

This bill provides for $750,000 for the first year for faculty expansion grants and $1,250,000 in the second year for similar grants to schools of social work; it covers both undergraduate and graduate education. It is the hope on the basis of the discussion with NASW, with the schools of social work, and with public welfare administrations that this rather small bill contains the seeds of important policy that will help the social work field expand even more rapidly than it has done already. It is my own hope that a substantial proportion of the people who will be trained by the expansion of the faculty will be working in social action, and that this recognition by the key social work organizations will help to put people on the faculty who can develop curriculum and entice students and place them in positions where they can be effective in the whole process of community organization.

Initially, legislation arises out of an awareness of the need for some kind of action to mitigate a social problem. Economic and social changes or other factors may create this need. Wars, depressions, technological changes, and changing institutions set the backdrop for the development of public policies.

Out of this need for social action, ideas are developed through a variety of channels in which the theories become political currency that in turn can be transformed into legislative proposals.

However, when one works in the field of social and political action it is not always possible to see the great long-range economic forces at work, even though they may be there. One sees the interaction and the political process of individual in relation to individual, and groups in relation to individuals at any one moment in time. If one wants to produce social legislation or social reform in his own lifetime, he has to learn that a great deal depends on the individual and his organization.

Elements in the Political Process

First among the elements in the political process is the *idea*, the essence of a proposal in its broad general outline. Most of the time the idea is vague and controversial, with a good deal of discussion yet to take place, but the idea itself is still the irreplaceable, irreducible, first essential in the political process.

This discussion will deal with controversial ideas in social policy and social reform, although in actuality a noncontroversial program or idea often turns out to be more difficult to attain than a controversial one. The controversial idea generates emotional response in the body politic. It starts a large-scale public debate that escalates fast, or at least escalates to the point when it becomes a major controversy and political people have to take a position. Ultimately, although the idea itself does not succeed, some aspect of it may.

Along with the controversial idea comes the period of germination. In this respect, social workers in their professional association play an important role because they give a forum to the idea; they speak about it; they write about it; and by so doing they aid in its development, no matter how inchoate or vague or unpopular it may be.

Organizations play an important part in this process for they can rework the idea into a more widely accepted policy. The impact of the idea on organizations and persons within organizations is a significant factor in the development of public policy. The public may become aware of the need for social action, but it is up to the organizations and interested groups—"the Establishment"—to develop the idea into a specific proposal on which the public can express its approval or disapproval so that a consensus, so to speak, can be developed. At some point, somebody's spark of will must transform the idea into a specific, viable legislative proposal.

Future Trends

The Legislative Proposal

Second in the development of the political process is the *specific proposal*. Such a proposal is necessary on which the views of organizations and individuals can be obtained, a wide consensus of opinion can be developed, and the proposal debated in terms of specifics rather than generalities. A major factor in the development of legislation is the leadership provided by the Executive Branch. The President recommends new proposals to the Congress in the form of messages and it is at this point sometimes that the Congress begins to focus on the specific legislation.

Sometimes, bills have been introduced over a period of years. Many of you have seen various versions of different bills and how subsequent thinking is incorporated in redrafts that ultimately produce the final law. Congress may hold extensive hearings, make extensive policy and technical changes in proposals, and vigorously debate controversial issues.

Successful legislative accomplishment requires the formation of a consensus in favor of a proposal. Political action, to be successful, depends on the support of many diverse groups and individuals with conflicting views and the action must be acceptable to the majority of those who will be affected by it. Otherwise, the action will not accomplish the goal it intended.

Let me illustrate from the current scene. At the present time there is no legislative proposal for the guaranteed income or the negative income tax, two of the major ideas that have been discussed at the NASW Seminar on Social Action here in Chicago with respect to income maintenance. This is still in the "idea" stage and there is no knowing at this moment whether the transformation of the idea into a specific legislative proposal is a week away or ten years away. While it is interesting to be in on the debate during the idea stage, unless a proposal is put into legislative form and has a legislative leader, it is really not yet a political proposal that can be seriously considered to have a priority on legislative debate in the social reform field.

Unless two conditions are met, unless the generalized idea is converted into a specific proposal that can be debated in detail —that can be attacked and criticized and supported and analyzed—and until it has a legislative leader, the idea of the minimum guaranteed income or of the negative income tax will not be really a prime factor in the political process or become a completed piece of legislation. When I first started to work on social legislation, I remember that we worked with a number of legislative leaders who were willing to introduce a particular bill, and they did so, but nothing ever happened to it. But then came the day when Senator Robert Wagner introduced the same bill and it became a banner headline on the first page of the *New York Times*. What was the difference? Mainly that many people thought that when Senator Wagner introduced a piece of social legislation it was really going to go somewhere—it was going to be successful. This was the difference.

The political process works not only with an idea, and then with a proposal, but also with a legislative leader who can command the respect not only of other legislative leaders but also can attract public attention to the proposal. All this gives the matter significance, and makes it appear to be moving. A proposal that people think is not likely to succeed is *not* likely to succeed! The same proposal—even a less significant one from the standpoint of social policy—if it has a legislative leader, if other people think it is going to succeed—is going to succeed faster by that very fact. The question of who will be the legislative leader of a proposal is an important one. The fact that a bill has a high-ranking leader automatically escalates its importance as a piece of legislation.

Period of Conflict and Public Debate

The next aspect of the political process that I think is important is what I call the *period of conflict and public debate*. This is probably the most exhilarating, exciting, and distressing period in the whole process. It is the period during which people make ridiculous statements. It is the period in which those who are against the legislation unleash all the possible objections that they can think of, hoping that one will strike home. And one of them usually does! It becomes the central issue among the people who debate, although it may not be the most important issue, but it may be the one that catches on. Second, the proponents of the proposal, responding naturally to this emotional appeal, will often give arguments that are not very important, or they may act in a ridiculous way themselves. The one thing to realize is that once the proposal is out and the conflict gets going, it is impossible to control what is said about this "elephant" in the public eye.

This is a crucially important period also because the social reform or the piece of legislation jells, and this has serious consequences for the administration of the program once it materializes. This is the way an institution may become formed even before it is created.

An example comes to mind in connection with Medicare. We are having to spend a great deal of time correcting the views that physicians have of what Medicare really is. They actually believed their own propaganda during the period of the debate, when the program was characterized in most unreal and unrepresentative terms. Today they are having difficulty shaking off the image and the feeling and the reactions engendered by their own spokesmen, who told them at the time that the program was going to regiment them, that it was going to tell them how to practice medicine, that they would have to sign many detailed forms, and so on. Now it is hard for the doctors to accept the fact that this is not so and will not be so.

This period of conflict is distressing for people who think that man is rational; that a good argument, as opposed to a bad argument, is going to persuade people. This is not necessarily so. This is not to say that one does not use rational arguments. Reason does tend to win out, but it is very easy to become discouraged during this period and to feel that all is lost. It is easy to feel that the forces of the Establishment are against one.

And this may well be true at any particular time. But the point is that anyone who wants to engage in the political process must accept the notion of perseverance. Without perseverance in the political process all is lost, because the essence of this process—at least under the system of government in the United States as distinguished from the British parliamentary system—is that one has to overcome every possible obstacle that is presented by the political system itself—the lack of party regularity and support, the existence of a House of Representatives and a Senate both with equal authority in this field, the fact of two committees in two houses, and perhaps even the fact that the Congress and the President may not be speaking to each other. In addition, there are individual senators and individual congressmen who will support or attack the particular piece of legislation, plus, of course, the great power of American lobbies.

Do not underestimate the fact that the political process increasingly involves important, well-financed, well-organized lobbies, directed toward pursuing the objectives of the group they represent. On the American scene, these organizations are becoming more important and more effective than ever before and, as a consequence, social workers also have to move into the political arena and get organized. Social workers too are just responding to the inevitable situation in America in which every interested group attempts to organize and to bombard the Congress. When social workers are doing that, they must realize that others are doing it too and with more money, more members, and more political influence than they can develop at any given moment in time.

So if social workers want to achieve results, they must practice and demonstrate perseverance in order to achieve successful political action.

Alliances

The next element is the making of *alliances*, the most ungentlemanly (or unladylike) part of the whole process! Practically no piece of important legislation adopted by the United States Congress has been achieved because one single group, all by itself, unaided by anyone else, has been trying to get it passed through the Congress. This is no longer feasible. American society is now so complex, so diffuse, so decentralized, so pluralistic that it is no longer possible for an American Medical Association or the veterans' organizations or the building and loan associations or the housing people to get legislation through on their own.

On the other hand, they are able single-handedly to *block* a piece of legislation. One single organization can have a great negative influence in blocking a piece of legislation; but a single organization, or profession, or group of people cannot get the controversial piece of legislation through the Congress unless it makes an alliance with some other group. These alliances always have a price that has to be paid, whether one likes it or not. "Price" does not mean money as a bribe or a transfer of funds. What it means is the need to modify the essence of one's own social principles, to take into account those social principles or social philosophies or priorities or goals of the other organization, if the other group thinks they are important!

Social workers have often made alliances with the labor movement, for instance, and have been successful on a number of occasions, whether the legislation has dealt with immigration, housing, social security, Medicare, or public welfare. This does not mean that they form an alliance with labor on every issue. Some labor interests are not of highest priority to social workers and vice versa. But in order to achieve a successful alliance with other groups, it should be recognized that often the priority or emphasis of one group must be tempered with that of the other group. It is not unlike a marriage. Both partners in the marriage cannot say—all the time, anyway—that the considerations of one person shall be the dominant ones all the time.

These alliances are both organizational and individual. Organizational alliances cannot be based on a paper facade—they

Future Trends

have to be real, right down at the local level, individual to individual. In the illustration offered earlier, the people in social work and social welfare and the people in the labor movement really have to believe that they have something in common, that they share common goals important to both groups. At all levels, both organizational and individual—national, state, local—the alliance has to be nurtured.

Period of Legislative Debate

At this point in the process, what do we have? Conflict exists, there are alliances, and now the *period of legislative debate* begins.

First, as the idea is being debated, it often turns out that the objections offered are ones that the sponsors could not possibly have thought of themselves! The legislators and political parties who want to oppose a measure are absolutely ingenious in thinking up objections that do not ordinarily come out into the public arena. These are the points discussed, not in the smoke-filled rooms, but among the political people who want to know what is important. Let me illustrate from my own experience.

When I first returned to Washington in 1961, one of the programs I was most enthusiastic about was federal aid for scholarships to able, but needy, students. Ted Sorensen and I talked with President Kennedy about it; I had only been on the job a few weeks, and I was very optimistic. I said to the President: "Well, this is one I am certain we can get through. We'll have a tough time on Medicare; we'll have a tough time on federal aid to elementary education, but federal aid for scholarships, Mr. President, that will be easy. We'll get going on that real fast."

So, we managed to get the bill introduced; and the department had the support of a lot of educational associations as well as other groups. I was called to testify before one of the congressional committees and as was to be expected the Democrats gave me a great deal of support and then the Republicans turned to ask me some questions. The first one was: "Well, Mr. Cohen, why are you so interested in federal aid for scholarships?"

I waxed eloquent and said, "The national interest demands that we see to it that every single boy and girl of talent in our society has the opportunity to maximize his contribution to his family, to the economy, to the society as a whole. We just can't afford to let one single boy or girl in this nation, regardless of race, creed, or color, go without an education."

I kept on in this vein—which I thought was very persuasive— and nobody interrupted me. Finally, the Republican legislator said: "Give me an illustration of what you think is a great shortage occupation that is in the national interest into which we ought to put a lot more money in scholarships."

I replied: "One of them is physicians. There is a tremendous shortage of physicians in the United States, and we can't have a great medical system that will bring the miracles of medical science to the American people even with all the billions of dollars we are putting into research unless there are more doctors, dentists, and nurses." And he said: "By the way, Mr. Cohen, how much do physicians get a year? What is their income?"

I said: "Well, the average is about $20,000 a year net at the present time," and he said, "And you think we ought to start a new federal welfare program"—that's what he called it, "a new federal welfare program"—"to help physicians get educated in order that they can make $20,000 a year or more?" I said, "Yes, I think we should."

And he went on: "What is the relationship of the physician's income to the rest of the population?" I said: "Well, it is about four times what the average worker gets," and he said: "Do you think the American taxpayers ought to spend money to help people get four times as much income as the rest of the population?"

"Yes," I said, "I do. You can't look at it in such a materialistic way. You have to look at it in terms of the national interest. That national interest is that mothers and babies need physicians." I proceeded this way, thinking I was still in the running when he said to me—and this was the coup de grace—"Mr. Cohen, tell me what you are going to do for us 'C' students who really run the country?"

I knew then that we had lost. And I may add that it took four more years before that bill went through.

This amusing story has in it an important lesson, namely, that the average congressman does not approach his political responsibilities in the way that a national organization such as NASW looks at national problems. After all, he probably is a lawyer who came up the hard way, who worked hard, who went to law school at night, who fought furiously in some small town or some small area or in a teeming metropolitan area to get nominated. He may have lost a couple of times. He may have had a tough time getting re-elected. He does not always approach the problem from an intellectual point of view or from the standpoint of the national interest. This is not to imply that a congressman does not think of the national interest but his conception of the national interest is influenced and molded in terms of the interests of his own congressional district. This is part of the American political process.

The process assumes that if everyone—including the lobbying groups—pursues his own political objectives, and if the congressman pursues the objectives of his district and of his state—out of this conflict of interest will come the national interest.

Another personal experience illustrates the unpredictable character of the discussion in the legislative arena. It happened in 1950 when Congress came to the conclusion that physicians should not be covered under social security for the cash benefits. Physicians were saying that if they were covered under social security, it was the beginning of socialized medicine. And since the doctors did not want to be covered, the committee decided to exclude them.

But then the committee members said: "If we just exclude doctors by themselves it may look as though we were subjected to political pressure so let's exclude some other groups, too." Which they did. By this time, the bill had reached the Senate, and an interesting development occurred with this exclusion of "self-employed professionals." Following this a group of people known as the "funeral directors" came to the Senate committee and said: "We want to be under social security. We would rather you would drop the whole idea of excluding self-employed professionals. But if you intend to keep the professional exclusion, please include us out—along with the physicians."

Senator Robert Taft, who was in my opinion the embodiment of a man who tried to be rational as a senator, sat up there at the committee table shaking his head and saying: "This is preposterous. This is preposterous." But when a fellow senator asked: "What shall we do?" Senator Taft replied: "We have to do what they want. We will exclude the funeral directors from social security." So the funeral directors went away happy that now they were included as professionals. When the idea was discarded a few years later, they were happy about that, too, of course!

But the point is that one has to be prepared for (1) objections that cannot be anticipated beforehand and (2) the unexpected. There are many possible illustrations of this but I shall give you just a few.

It would not have been possible to get disability insurance in 1956 if Walter George, dean of the Senate, were not going to retire. As one of the last acts of his senatorial career, he wanted something in the nature of a great social reform. If Walter George had not sponsored disability insurance in 1956, which won by the slim vote of 47–45, it is probable that the whole development of Medicare would have been postponed by at least another five or ten years. This was because, in the sequence of events, the passage of disability insurance was the necessary precursor to the whole Medicare program. The Senate might have passed it later in 1958 or 1960—no one knows. But it was passed in 1956—even if by only one vote—and that would not have been possible if Walter George had not been willing at that moment in time to do something for social reform.

Another example of the unexpected was the way in which the American Medical Association helped to get Medicare through. This was unexpected from their standpoint too. As you know, they took the tack that the Forand bill and the King-Anderson bill for hospital insurance were inadequate. And they had a point, because the bills dealt only with a small part of the total costs. The AMA said: "Here is the way for us to argue for Elder-care by saying the King-Anderson bill is inadequate and we can make a major attack on it. Our bill is so much broader and better."

What happened was both unexpected—and inexplicable. Congress added physicians' services onto the hospital insurance program as Part B, and made it an insurance program rather than an assistance or Eldercare program as the AMA had intended. So their own argument—which was the very heart of their attack—backfired.

One more unexpected event followed that one. Congressman John W. Byrnes (Wisc.), the ranking Republican on the Ways and Means Committee, did not introduce the AMA proposal because he thought the drain on the general revenues would be unpredictable. He favored, instead, a specific set of benefits which he developed from the government employees' benefits system. He proposed that a large part of the costs be taken out of general revenues. Congress accepted this provision and thereby adopted what is probably the most important principle involved in the financing of the program. The question of financing part of it out of general funds had not been seriously debated for thirty years, and no one had even thought it was achievable. But here was the Congress financing half the cost of the physicians' services out of the nonpayroll taxes (general revenues) simply through a combination of events in which the AMA was fighting for a broader program and the Republicans were trying to avoid financing it out of payroll taxes because that was the object of the AMA attack.

As you can see, through the kind of argument advanced by the AMA, we now have a new principle developed in regard to government financing of the social security program through general revenues.

Administration of the Program

Another element in political action on the American scene is that, after the period of conflict and after the legislation is enacted, there is a need for intelligent *cooperation in the administration* of the resulting program. The Civil Rights Act and the Medicare Act are both good illustrations of this. Once a law comes into being, the ideological antagonisms that occurred during the legislative debate can be forgotten. The key to future social reform is the successful administration of those institutions that have just been created.

In America, nothing succeeds like success. If something works, people are willing to add to it, to build on it; even if the basic idea was faulty, they are willing to perfect it and expand it. But if the idea does not work out in practice, the political process will not tolerate future social reform that tries to build upon it. If Medicare does not work reasonably well under the limited but crucial legislation that has just been passed, that fact will not be an argument for improving it. It will be an argument for modifying it and restraining it.

If Medicare works well, if the physicians and the hospitals say it is workable and practical, that a few changes are needed here and there to make it work a little better—then the idea will be expanded and developed. Thus, cooperation in the administration of a program once it is launched is obviously an important final element in developing social legislation in this country.

In any case, there is a natural antipathy among the practical politicians to social reform and social welfare and to redistribution of income, and perhaps to all the ideas that social workers have firmly in their minds as good and sacred principles. But the same practical politicians will forego their opposition if the principles work out in practice and are administratively feasible. It is important to keep in mind *what is feasible*, what can be carried out, when social institutions are being molded, new legislation is proposed, new social welfare programs developed. It is disastrous for future social reform as well as the maintenance of social goals to find that a great idea has been developed into legislation, has been enacted into law, has overcome all these obstacles, and that it cannot be put into effect.

Need for Consolidation

There are more elements in the process that might be described, but more than space allows. Let me add one final consideration. We have all just gone through a period of great social action in the social welfare field. We probably cannot expect to have as large and as concentrated a period of social reform right away and again as much as in the period from 1963 to 1965. I am not even sure this would be desirable. Frankly, there is more to do than we may be able to deliver. Now it is important to develop priorities about further social goals because there are not yet the doctors, the dentists, the nurses, the social workers, the librarians, or the teachers in this country to deliver all the education, the health, and the social welfare legislation that social workers, and NASW, and the Department of Health, Education, and Welfare can think up or that our platform says we want. Now is the time to concentrate on developing the manpower and the resources for training that are necessary to make future social reform possible.

This is not meant to be pessimistic. It is just to say that great social reforms in the seventies will not be realizable unless those of us today build the social institutions with the people in the sixties. This, then, will make it possible for those who come after us to continue to do what social workers have been trying to do in the last twenty years.

The Social Worker as Advocate: Champion of Social Victims

The Ad Hoc Committee on Advocacy

The new interest in advocacy among social workers can be traced directly to the growing social and political ferment in our cities in the past decade. Social workers connected with Mobilization For Youth[1] (which took its form in the context of this ferment) first

Reprinted with permission of the National Association of Social Workers from *Social Work*, Vol. 14, No. 2 (April 1969), pp. 16–22.
[1]Mobilization For Youth, Inc., started as an action-research program in juvenile delinquency control on New York City's Lower East Side.

brought the advocacy role to the attention of the profession.[2] But the notion that the social worker needs to become the champion of social victims who cannot defend themselves was voiced long ago by others, and has recently been revived.[3]

Present events are forcing the issue with new urgency. Externally, the profession is re-examining itself with an intensity that has few precedents. The profession's faith in its own essential viability is being severely tested. It is especially timely that social work turn its attention to the role of advocate at this time, both because of its clear relevance to the urban crisis and because it has been an integral part of the philosophy and practice of the profession since its earliest days.

What Is Advocacy?

The dictionary defines advocate in two ways. On one hand, he is "one that pleads the cause of another."[4] This is the meaning given to the legal advocate—the lawyer—who zealously guards the interests of his client over all others. Another definition describes the advocate as "one who argues for, defends, maintains, or recommends a cause or a proposal."[5] This definition incorporates the political meaning ascribed to the word in which the interests of a class of people are represented; implicitly, the issues are universalistic rather than particularistic.

Both meanings of advocacy have been espoused in the social work literature. Briar describes the historical concept of the case-worker-advocate who is". . . his client's supporter, his adviser, his champion, and, if need be, his representative in his dealings with the court, the police, the social agency, and other organizations that [affect] his well-being."[6] For Briar, the social worker's commitment to the civil rights of his *own client* "takes precedence over all other commitments."[7] This is, in essence, the orientation of the lawyer-advocate.

Brager takes another view. He posits the "advocate-reformer" who ". . . identifies with the plight of the disadvantaged. He sees

---

[2]See George A. Brager, "Advocacy and Political Behavior," *Social Work*, Vol. 13, No. 2 (April 1968), pp. 5–15; and Charles F. Grosser, "Community Development Programs Serving the Urban Poor," *Social Work*, Vol. 10, No. 3 (July 1965), pp. 18–19.

[3]See, for example, Nathan E. Cohen, ed., *Social Work and Social Problems* (New York: National Association of Social Workers, 1964), p. 374.

[4]*Webster's Third New International Dictionary* (Springfield, Mass.: G. & C. Merriam Co., 1961), p. 32.

[5]*Ibid.*

[6]Scott Briar, "The Current Crisis in Social Casework," *Social Work Practice, 1967* (New York: Columbia University Press, 1967), p. 28. *See also* Briar, "The Casework Predicament", *Social Work*, Vol. 13, No. 1 (January 1968), pp. 5–11.

[7]Scott Briar, "The Social Worker's Responsibility for the Civil Rights of Clients," *New Perspectives*, Vol. 1, No. 1 (Spring 1967), p. 90.

as his primary responsibility the tough-minded and partisan representation of their interests, and this supersedes his fealty to others. This role inevitably requires that the practitioner function as a political tactician."[8] Brager does not rule out of his definition the direct-service practitioner who takes on the individual grievances of his client, but his emphasis is on the advocacy of the interests of an aggrieved *class* of people through policy change. The two conceptions do overlap at many points, as for instance when the worker must engage in action to change basic policies and institutions in order to deal effectively with his client's grievances.

Social Work's Commitment to Advocacy

Advocacy has been an important thread running throughout social work's history. Some individuals have been elevated to heroic status because they have fulfilled this role—Dorothea Dix and Jane Addams come most readily to mind. However, it would be safe to say that most social workers have honored advocacy more in rhetoric than in practice, and for this there are at least two reasons.

To begin with, professional education and practice have tended to legitimate a consensus orientation and oppose an adversary one, and this has been perpetuated in the literature. A combative stance, often an essential ingredient in the kind of partisan alignment implied by the concept of advocacy, is not a natural one for many social workers. As a result, most social workers lack both the orientation and the technical skills necessary to engage in effective advocacy. Finally, the employee status of social workers has often restricted their ability to act as advocates.[9]

At the same time that the current upheaval in society adds a note of urgency to the issue of social work's commitment to advocacy, it also adds complications to the task of fulfilling that commitment because of the emotion surrounding many of the issues. For example, some members of the profession feel strongly that fighting racism and deepening the social conscience are the only means to combat these social evils; others—equally adamant—feel that social workers are not equipped to solve these ills, which are a problem of the whole society. There is still another group of social workers who tend to avoid involvement with

---

[8]*Op. cit.,* p. 6.

[9]It is not the intent to blame the agencies entirely for lack of advocacy in the discharge of a worker's daily duties. It is recognized that progressive agencies have already inculcated advocacy in their workers, often in the face of adverse community reactions and resistance by staff.

controversial issues at any cost. What is needed is a consistent approach on the basis of which each social worker can feel confident in fulfilling his professional commitment, an approach that can be responsive to the current crisis but must also outlive it.

Obligations of the Individual Social Worker

The obligation of social workers to become advocates flows directly from the social worker's Code of Ethics.[10] Therefore, why should it be difficult for a profession that is "based on humanitarian, democratic ideals" and "dedicated to service for the welfare of mankind" to act on behalf of those whose human rights are in jeopardy? According to Wickenden: "In the relationship of individuals to the society in which they live, dignity, freedom and security rest upon a maximum range of objectively defined rights and entitlements."[11]

As a profession that "requires of its practitioners . . . belief in the dignity and worth of human beings"[12] social work must commit itself to defending the rights of those who are treated unjustly, for, as Briar asserts: "The sense of individual dignity and of capacity to be self-determining . . . can exist only if the person sees himself and is regarded as a rights bearing citizen with legitimate, enforceable claims on, as well as obligations to, society."[13]

Each member of the professional association, in subscribing to the Code of Ethics, declares, "I regard as my primary obligation the welfare of the individual or group served, which includes action to improve social conditions." It is implicit, but clear, in this prescript that the obligation to the client takes primacy over the obligation to the employer when the two interests compete with one another.

The code singles out for special attention the obligation to "the individual or group served." The meaning seems clearest with respect to the caseworker or group worker who is delivering services to identified individuals and groups. It would appear to be entirely consistent with this interpretation to extend the obligation to the line supervisor or the social agency administrator who then is bound to act as an advocate on behalf of

[10]This code was adopted by the Delegate Assembly of the National Association of Social Workers, October 13, 1960, and amended April 11, 1967.
[11]Elizabeth Wickenden, "The Indigent and Welfare Administration," in *The Extension of Legal Services to the Poor* (Washington, D.C.: U.S. Department of Health, Education, and Welfare, 1964).
[12]"Code of Ethics."
[13]Briar, "The Social Worker's Responsibility for the Civil Rights of Clients."

clients under his jurisdiction. A collateral obligation would be the responsibility of the supervisor or administrator to create the climate in which direct-service workers can discharge their advocacy obligations. As one moves to consider other social work roles, such as the consultant, the community planner, and the social work educator, the principle becomes more difficult to apply. But how can an obligation be imposed on one segment of the profession and not on another?

The inherent obligation is with respect to the work role and to those persons on whose lives the practitioner impinges by dint of his work role. It is in this role that the individual social worker is most clearly accountable for behaving in accordance with professional social work norms. Through this role he is implicated in the lives of certain groups of people; thus his actions affect their lives directly, for good or ill. Similarly, his work role gives him authority and influence over the lives of his clients; thus he has special ethical obligations regarding them. Finally, there are expected behaviors inherent in the work role on the basis of which it is possible to judge professional performance.

At this point it is important to remind ourselves of the distinction between the obligation of the social worker to be an advocate within and outside of his work role, both of which constitute an obligation of equal weight. However, the obligation to be an advocate outside the work role is general, not specific, and does not have the same force as the obligation to the client. In a sense, this obligation is gratuitous, or, as some might say, "above and beyond the call of duty." An additional problem is that there are no external criteria for judging whether a person is fulfilling this broad responsibility adequately. To use an extreme example: voting might be considered a way of carrying out the role of the advocate-reformer, yet would one say that failure to vote was failure to fulfill a professional obligation? To lump together the two obligations, i.e., to be an advocate in one's work role and outside of it, might appear to reinforce the latter. In reality, it only weakens the former.

Yet tne profession as a whole has consistently treated the broad social responsibilities of social workers as important to fulfillment of their responsibilities. Schools of social work make an effort to provide their students with both the orientation and skills to become involved in social issues well outside their future assigned responsibilities. The difference between the two obligations is a moral, not a formal, one. In other words, enforcement of the obligation to be an advocate outside the work role would have to be self-enforcement.

Competing Claims

Until now, most discussions of the advocacy role in social work have limited their consideration of competing claims to those of the employing agency[14] or society as a whole.[15] These have overlooked the possibility that in promoting his clients' interest the social worker may be injuring other aggrieved persons with an equally just claim. Suppose, for instance, that a child welfare worker has as a client a child who is in need of care that can only be provided by a treatment institution with limited intake. Does he then become a complete partisan in order to gain admission of his client at the expense of other children in need? What of the public assistance worker seeking emergency clothing allowances for his clients when the demand is greater than the supply? Quite clearly. in either case the worker should be seeking to increase the total availability of the scarce resource. But while working toward this end, he faces the dilemma of competing individual claims. In such a situation, professional norms would appear to dictate that the relative urgency of the respective claims be weighed.

A second dilemma involves conflict between the two types of advocacy—on behalf of client or class. Such conflicts are quite possible in an era of confrontation politics. To what extent does one risk injury to his client's interests in the short run on behalf of institutional changes in the long run? It seems clear that there can be no hard and fast rules governing such situations. One cannot arbitrarily write off any action that may temporarily cause his clients hardship if he believes the ultimate benefits of his action will outweigh any initial harm. Both ethical commitment and judgment appear to be involved here. (Is it, perhaps, unnecessary to add that institutional change does not always involve confrontation?)

A third dilemma is the choice between direct intercession by the worker and mobilization of clients in their own behalf. This is less an ethical than a technical matter. One can err in two directions: it is possible to emasculate clients by being overly protective or to abdicate one's responsibility and leave them to fend for themselves against powerful adversaries.

Technical Competence

Questions of competence can compound these dilemmas, for good intentions are not enough for the fulfillment of the advocacy role. Workers must not only be competent, they must also be

[14]See George A. Brager, *op. cit.*
[15]See Scott Briar, "The Current Crisis in Social Casework," p. 91.

sophisticated in understanding the appropriate machinery for redressing grievances and skilled in using it. If social workers are required by the profession to carry the obligation to be advocates, they must be equipped to fulfill the role.

While any responsible profession constantly strives to improve its technology, the dissatisfaction of social workers with their skills at advocacy seems to go beyond this. For a variety of reasons, most social workers seem wholly deficient in this area. On the direct practice level, the traditional techniques of environmental manipulation have tended to become peripheral to the practice of social workers, as they have become more sophisticated in the dynamics of inter- and intrapersonal functioning. Second, knowledge of the law, which is vitally tied up with client entitlements, has had less emphasis in the social work curriculum in recent years. Even though increased attention has been given to the client in deprived circumstances—the one who is most likely to need an advocate—this emphasis in the curriculum must be further strengthened.

Regardless of the type of advocacy in which the practitioner engages, knowledge of service delivery systems, institutional dynamics, and institutional change strategies are crucial. Although great advances in this technology have taken place in certain sectors of practice and education, they must be disseminated to the field.

Among the basic content areas that need development and expansion both in school curricula and in continuing education of social workers are the following:

1. Sensitization to the need for an appropriateness of advocacy.

2. Techniques of environmental manipulation and allied practice components.

3. Knowledge of the law, particularly as it bears on individual rights and entitlements.

4. Knowledge of service delivery systems and other institutions that impinge on people's lives and from which they must obtain resources.

5. Knowledge and skill in effecting institutional change.

6. Knowledge and skill in reaching and using the influence and power systems in a community.

The relative emphasis on these different components would vary, depending on the specific work role, although all are necessary in some degree for all social workers.

Professional Autonomy and
the Role of NASW

But lack of technical skills is not the greatest deterrent to advocacy by social workers; actually, it is their status as employees of organizations—organizations that are frequently the object of clients' grievances. Unless social workers can be protected against retaliation by their agencies or by other special interest groups in the community, few of them will venture into the advocacy role, ethical prescripts notwithstanding. It would seem to be a sine qua non of a profession that it must create the conditions in which its members can act professionally. For the profession to make demands on the individual and then not back them up with tangible support would betray a lack of serious intent.

This does not mean that all risks for the worker can or should be eliminated. A worker's job may be protected—but there is no insurance that he will advance within his organization as far or as fast as he would have if he had not been an advocate. Rather, the object is to increase the social worker's willingness to take risks to his self-interest in behalf of his professional commitment.

This brings us to the role and obligation of the professional association—NASW—and once again back to the context of social unrest, social change, and militancy in which this discussion is taking place. In view of the need for the profession to act quickly and decisively to focus on advocacy as being germane to the effective practice of social work, a program is needed—one that should be undertaken by NASW as soon as possible.[16] This program would do the following:

I. Urge social workers to exercise actively and diligently, in the conduct of their practice, their professional responsibility to give first priority to the rights and needs of their clients.

2. Assist social workers—by providing information and other resources—in their effort to exercise this responsibility.

3. Protect social workers against the reprisals, some of them inevitable, that they will incur in the course of acting as advocates for the rights of their clients.[17]

---

[16]As the first step in implementing the program, the Commission on Ethics reviewed these findings of the Ad Hoc Committee on Advocacy and recommended that they be widely disseminated. The commission interprets the Code of Ethics as giving full support to advocacy as a professional obligation.

[17]This is the wording of the charge given to the Ad Hoc Committee on Advocacy by the NASW urban crisis task force.

Certain assumptions are implicit in these three program objectives, namely:

That the social worker has an obligation under the Code of Ethics to be an advocate.

That this obligation requires more than mere "urging."

That under certain circumstances, as discussed later, the obligation is enforceable under the Code of Ethics.

That the *moral* obligation to be an advocate is not limited to one's own clients, although this cannot be enforced in the same way.

That encouragement of advocacy and provision of certain kinds of assistance to advocates need not be limited to members of the professional association.

To return to the relationship of NASW to the social work advocate who gets into trouble with his agency because of his attempts to fulfill a professional obligation: NASW *has an obligation to the worker that takes priority over its obligation to the agency.* In effect, the worker is acting in behalf of the professional community. While the conditions of such responsibility of NASW must be spelled out precisely (to avoid misleading members or jeopardizing the interests of the profession), there can be no question about the member's prior claim on NASW support. Without this principle, the association's claim on the member is meaningless.

The Committee on Advocacy considered two extensions of NASW's obligation. One was in relation to the social work employee who is not a member of NASW. Should the same aids and protections be offered to nonmembers of NASW as to members? It was recognized that a majority of social work positions are held by nonmembers and that they are concentrated particularly in public agencies, which are often the object of client grievances. Furthermore, many indigenous workers in poverty and other neighborhood programs are especially likely to be performing an advocacy function. Obviously, the profession cannot impose a professional obligation on such persons, yet it is consistent with professional concerns that such efforts be supported even when NASW members are not involved. As is spelled out later, the committee recommends that certain types of help be provided, but states that NASW is not in a position to offer the same range of support to nonmembers as to members.

The other extension of NASW's obligation is the possible assumption by NASW of the role of advocate when a client has no alternative channel for his grievances. The committee agreed that NASW could not become, in effect, a service agency, offering an advocacy service to all who request it, although it was felt that the association should work toward the development of such alternative channels. The association should be encouraged to engage in selected advocacy actions when the outcome has potential implications for policy formulation and implementation in general. An example of this would be participation in litigation against a state welfare agency for alleged violation of clients' constitutional rights; in this instance NASW would be using the courts to help bring about social policy change instead of interceding in behalf of the specific plaintiffs in the case.

Broadly stated, then, the proposed program for NASW calls for concentrated and aggressive activities co-ordinated at local, regional, and national levels, to achieve the needed involvement by individual social workers, backstopped by members in policy-making and administrative positions and community leaders, through education, demonstration, and consultation in program planning; adaptation of NASW complaint machinery to facilitate the adjudication of complaints against agencies with stringent sanctions when indicated; and assistance to individuals who may experience retaliatory action by agencies or communities, ranging from intervention with employers to aid in obtaining legal counsel or finding suitable new employment.

A (New) Social Work Model

Bertram M. Beck

I share the impression of the preceding speakers that professional roles become increasingly blurred as we address ourselves to particular social problems. This, to me, is a healthy thing. The most meaningful conversations we can have will come about, not through attempting to define relationships between professions or disciplines or fields, but through addressing ourselves to what over-all contributions may be made to the solution of some of the key social problems in our nation today.

Mobilization for Youth has a social-problem focus; i. e., it is a program that is established plainly and clearly to reduce juvenile delinquency. Mobilization for Youth has an articulated theory upon which it is based. It is the theory originally enunciated by a sociologist and a social worker, Lloyd Ohlin and Richard Cloward. Essentially it holds that, in a slum neighborhood, delinquency is caused among young people who do not

Reprinted from *The Social Service Review*, Vol. 40, No. 3 (September 1965), pp. 270-274, by permission of the author and The University of Chicago Press.

have ready access to the opportunities for upward social mobility. In other words, the theory is that, if these young people can gain the status and materialistic goods of society the way their peers can in more favored neighborhoods, they will get them through socially sanctioned means rather than by turning to deviant means.

This theory has two advantages. First, it sets for our program a conceptual framework. In other words, it sets our objectives. Whether the theory is right or wrong remains to be seen and will be seen within the next five or six years. Second, it allows us to originate a program that steers away from what might be an effort to induce conformity. Essentially, the theory says that, to produce desirable social changes so that these youngsters can get up and out of the ghetto, we must in fact make the American dream come true. We must find a way to make social institutions work so that these young people who are born and bred in these ghettos can find their way out through the educational system, through the job system, through the welfare system, and so on. The focus, therefore, in this social work endeavor is on "changing environment" rather than "changing individuals." This represents a common focus in current thinking about the problem of juvenile delinquency, and it is one that is easily defensible.

Mobilization for Youth was not born out of local community interests. In a sense, it was actually superimposed on the community by the welfare agencies operating within the area. After funds were granted for the project, there were interviews with a sample of the population to be served to find out the nature of their problems and what changes they would like to have made. These interviews had consequences to which I shall allude later.

The community in which MFY is working is the Lower East Side of New York City, the original port of entry for wave upon wave of immigrants. Although this area contains one hundred and fifty thousand people, MFY serves only about forty thousand or fifty thousand people who live within our sixty-seven-block area. Like the inner core of so many other cities, the Lower East Side has a group of in-migrants who cannot move out. They cannot move out because job opportunities are lacking and the color of their skin erects a barrier for them.

The population with whom we work is largely composed of Spanish-speaking Puerto Ricans. Our aim is to work with the most put-upon population, not with the population "most likely to succeed." In our early history, we were picketed by youngsters in the neighborhood who said they could not use the coffee houses that had been established because they were not gang members. While the story is a little more complex than that, these issues were properly put.

We stand firm on serving the particular segment of the population that I have defined, because of the nature of our theoretical concept. That is, we want to work with people who need help to get up and out, not with people who might make it by themselves. There is a temptation to use the public health model of prevention in social work. This model would allow us to work with those who are easiest to work with on the basis that by early intervention we are preventing deterioration. Above all, I think, in the antipoverty programs, one must be extremely careful to be sure that the preventive efforts do not lead us to abandon the responsibility of working with the people who are in sorest need. These are not the people who are the easiest to work with, and they are not the people who fall within the conventional public schemata of prevention. I do believe, however, that there is a way of viewing prevention so that they may be included.

MFY has encountered many problems in trying to operationalize its theory in this community. One of the early findings of the MFY is that the holy trinity of social work—casework, community organization, and group service—has no relevance when addressing a social problem with this population. One finds it impossible to departmentalize things this way. Nevertheless, I have attempted to organize my paper in that way to lead into discussion. What we usually call casework, I prefer to call work with individuals.

Locale is a key issue. Whenever studies are made of who uses what agency, we usually find that the customers come from around the immediate area where the service was offered. Hence, we have established throughout our area storefront helping stations where people can "drop in." In these store fronts we attempt to provide for the particular needs of those to be served. For example, in conjunction with each helping station we must have some baby-care facility, since the people we are serving have no place to leave babies and young children. We operate, for example, a drop-in day-care station— much to the horror of many of the authorities—where we take very young children for two or three hours while the mother goes to the clinic to get prenatal care for the next child. Without these facilities, we do not see how we can make the services work. The people who drop in do come at a point of crisis, and the crisis is usually a bread-and-butter one. They come with the eviction notice in their hands or because their son has been arrested; or a cop has beaten their son; or their welfare check has not come. We therefore attempt to make an immediate delivery of service.

In the helping stations, we have social workers, lawyers, vocational counselors, public health nurses, and psychiatric consultants. We find a blurring of lines between these various persons.

One of the barriers to the success of the helping station is the securing of adequate personnel. Because we give genuine help with real-life probems, in one of these store fronts there were four thousand interviews over the course of one month last summer, and there were only thirty persons on the staff handling that number of interviews, including the clerical, professional, and whatever other labels you have to give the staff.

A second problem has to do with crisis theory. Because of the bread-and-butter nature of the issues, it is likely that crises will be recurrent. In that case, I am not sure we are making a genuine contribution to people's ability to handle the next crisis.

We were based, and remain based, on the idea that we must produce institutional change. Instead of doing that through our helping stations, we first moved toward what was first called "social brokerage"—that is, standing between the client, or the customer, and the bureaucracy that is supposed to deliver the service. We moved from "social brokerage" to what is now called "the advocacy role," whereby the social worker or other helper stands next to the client and fights with him in partnership. Usually the battle is with the Police Department, the Welfare Department, or the Department of Housing and Buildings. While this service is extremely significant, it does not in itself necessarily contribute in a major way to institutional change. One of the things that we found we need is to develop a vision of social change. If the Welfare Department does not deliver services (or the Police Department, or the Board of Education, to take the toughest one), how would we envisage organizing these major services so that they would do a better job? Then the really tough question becomes: What are the strategies of intervening into these local community systems that would change them, other than the route we have taken in these helping stations, in which it seems—if you take it to its logical extension—that there is one social work type for every client type, fighting with the other social work types to get the services for the client?

I view the helping stations as platforms leading to ladders which are extended down into the ghetto. There are certain ladders that have been constructed by MFY. We have, for example, an expensive work-training program. We run a filling station; we also run a luncheonette, as well as a sewing factory and a woodworking shop. These are all job-training sites for young people, to whom we try to impart a job skill. Of course we run into the problem you would expect when you begin a larger problem of institutional change. That is, can you train the youngsters with whom we work for jobs other than "dead-end" jobs? We are beginning to move into a kind of work-study plan, equally emphasizing remedial education and work.

As we move forward, I hope that we can deploy the social worker at the opportunity ladder so that when a youngster fails in a job situation there is a social worker there, at that point, to help him.

Another dimension of our program, in addition to the individual services, concerns community development. I use this term advisedly, distinguishing it from community organization and meaning to represent the actual involvement of persons resident in this local neighborhood and the effort to help them come to grips with some of their own problems. Here we have shifted from what was at the beginning largely a social-protest notion to what is now a somewhat less dramatic form of involvement that we hope to sustain. During our early years, we found we could organize a picket line; we could get people to demonstrate. We also found that the skill required to organize the dramatic demonstration is not the same as the skill required to sustain the interest of local people after the picket line ends. Today, we are again operating out of store fronts in block organizations. A typical program (and these programs vary, depending on the interests of the residents) is a consumers' co-operative organized by public assistance recipients, one of whom gets up early in the morning and goes to market—for example—and buys eggs which are sold to the other public assistance recipients at markedly lower prices. Obviously this plan has benefits in terms of the self-concept of the people as well as practical benefits in terms of how to get along on a welfare budget.

Another typical program coming out of our numerous store fronts was our voter-registration program. In the course of trying to help the residents with whom we work (particularly the Puerto Ricans) to register, we encountered, of course, a markedly different situation from that in the more favored neighborhood. The registrars tend to push these people around; they are rude; they are unfeeling; they do not take account of the fact that people are engulfed with difficulties; and our workers get into fights with the registrars. As a consequence of their experience throughout the registration period, the neighbors held a demonstration at voter registration places, which encountered some press publicity. We then, however, set up a conference with the Commissioner of Elections, local residents, and members of the MFY board, who are not local residents.

There is a constant effort at institutional change that is to combine what I call the elite social-change process through negotiation with action by local people so that they begin to feel their own democratic privileges and their own potential. The relationship to the theory I have cited is fairly self-evident. We are not reaching people before they have problems; on the contrary, we are working with people with the most dire problems. But we are attempting, through them and with them, to change their society so that not only do they have opportunities for a richer life, but so do their children. Though I am not comfortable with the primary, secondary, tertiary kind of prevention schemata, I believe that this kind of problem orientation brings us to a genuine preventive emphasis.

In its beginning our program suffered from the fact that it was imported into this area from Columbia University, and it continues to suffer from the fact that it is not truly an instrument of the local community. In New York City, after a great fight over the slogan about involvement of the poor, it was agreed that in thirteen poverty areas there would be an election of a local committee that would have substantial control over the Community Action Program. In three areas (of which the Lower East Side is one), the authorities turned to an existing organization (MFY) and said that no election is needed here. But, in a rare social gesture, the MFY board of directors said to the authorities that they did not think we could do this; that we would instead develop a process—and I still do not know what that process is to be—whereby the residents in the Lower East Side will select their own committee, which would have a policy-making (not advisory) role in respect to the Community Action Program. This is rare because it is an instance in which a group that has power gives up power. It is practically unbelievable.

Having told the city fathers this, we had the problem of how to keep our promise. We decided to organize a series of meetings with a group that had already been formed. It was a beautiful day in New York that Sunday and yet, at two o'clock in a high school on the Lower East Side, one thousand people came out to elect, not the community committee, but a steering committee charged with the responsibility of suggesting, perhaps, different ways of selecting a community committee, that will then be voted on. At this meeting, one saw registering side by side (and this was actually recorded by photography for posterity) a man with an American Legion hat, an Orthodox Jewish rabbi with beard and beaver, a nun, and a local Progressive Labor party leader right in a row. This meeting, typical of the whole sequence we have had, was very lively and to some people very distressing; it depends on your tolerance for difference and heresy. For one thing, many of the people with whom MFY works do not have a tradition of Robert's Rules of Order, nor do they have a tradition of gracefully accepting a majority opinion. So, when a decision went against them toward the end of the day (and the meeting extended—as they all do—right into the night), violence was quick to erupt.

A great deal of bitterness is stirred up in this whole process, and MFY is criticized. We are asked why we are dividing the community, and the criticism comes from social workers. I believe that we are not dividing the community; we are only making manifest the divisions that have long been there. Various interests—including some that had never heretofore really been heard from—are now fighting for control. They include social welfare as a definite interest. They include different church groups, Puerto Ricans, and Negroes, as well as divisions within divisions. All of this poses for us a problem that I want to leave with you. It poses the problem of how we can combine community involvement with therapeutic services and new opportunity structures. There is today, because of this ferment in this country, a new hostility, a new fractionalization because new groups are coming up. This, then, poses the question of how to bring out of this a reintegration, a new sense of community. As a consequence of our experimentation with new social work models, with community psychiatry, and with social psychiatry, the long-term goal we all share is the evolution in local communities of a true sense of community, not based on the in-group suppressing the out-group, but based on a true participation in the economy and in the better things of society.

The House on Sixth Street

Francis P. Purcell
Harry Specht

The extent to which social work can affect the course of social problems has not received the full consideration it deserves.[1] For some time the social work profession has taken account of social problems only as they have become manifest in behavioral pathology. Yet it is becoming increasingly apparent that, even allowing for this limitation, it is often necessary for the same agency or worker to intervene by various methods at various points.

In this paper, the case history of a tenement house in New York City is used to illustrate some of the factors that should be considered in selecting intervention methods. Like all first attempts, the approach described can be found wanting in conceptual clarity and systematization. Yet the vital quality of the effort and its implications for social work practice seem clear.

The case of "The House on Sixth Street" is taken from the files of Mobilization For Youth (MFY), an action-research project that has been in operation since 1962 on New York's Lower East Side.[2] MFY's programs are financed by grants from several public and private sources. The central theoretical contention of MFY is that a major proportion of juvenile deliquency occurs when adolescents from low-income families do not have access to legitimate opportunities by which they can fulfill the aspirations for success they share with all American youth. The action programs of MFY are designed to offer these youths concrete opportunities to offset the debilitating effects of poverty. For example, the employment program helps youngsters obtain jobs; other programs attempt to increase opportunities in public schools. In addition, there are group work and recreation programs. A wide variety of services to individuals and families is offered through Neighborhood Service Centers: a homemaking program, a program for released offenders, and a narcotics information center. Legal ser-

Reprinted with permission of the authors and the National Association of Social Workers from *Social Work*, Vol. 10, No. 4 (October 1965), pp. 69–76.

[1] Social work practitioners sometimes use the term "social problem" to mean "environmental problem." The sense in which it is used here corresponds to the definition developed by the social sciences. That is, a social problem is a disturbance, deviation, or breakdown in social behavior that (1) involves a considerable number of people and (2) is of serious concern to many in the society. It is social in origin and effect, and is a social responsibility. It represents a discrepancy between social standards and social reality. Also, such socially perceived variations must be viewed as corrigible. See Robert K. Merton and Robert A. Nisbet, eds., *Contemporary Social Problems* (New York: Harcourt, Brace, and World, 1961), pp. 6, 701.

[2] A complete case record of the Sixth Street house will be included in a forthcoming publication of Mobilization For Youth.

vices, a housing services unit, a special referral unit, and a community development program are among other services that have been developed or made available. Thus, MFY has an unusually wide range of resources for dealing with social problems.

The Problem

"The House on Sixth Street" became a case when Mrs. Smith came to an MFY Neighborhood Service Center to complain that there had been no gas, electricity, heat, or hot water in her apartment house for more than four weeks. She asked the agency for help. Mrs. Smith was 23 years old, Negro, and the mother of four children, three of whom had been born out of wedlock. At the time she was unmarried and receiving Aid to Families with Dependent Children. She came to the center in desperation because she was unable to run her household without utilities. Her financial resources were exhausted—but not her courage. The Neighborhood Service Center worker decided that in this case the building—the tenants, the landlord, and circumstances affecting their relationships—was of central concern.

A social worker then visited the Sixth Street building with Mrs. Smith and a community worker. Community workers are members of the community organization staff in a program that attempts to encourage residents to take independent social action. Like many members in other MFY programs, community workers are residents of the particular neighborhood. Most of them have little formal education, their special contribution being their ability to relate to and communicate with other residents. Because some of the tenants were Puerto Rican, a Spanish-speaking community worker was chosen to accompany the social worker. His easy manner and knowledge of the neighborhood enabled him and the worker to become involved quickly with the tenants.

Their first visits confirmed Mrs. Smith's charge that the house had been without utilities for more than four weeks. Several months before, the city Rent and Rehabilitation Administration had reduced the rent for each apartment to one dollar a month because the landlord was not providing services. However, this agency was slow to take further action. Eleven families were still living in the building, which had twenty-eight apartments. The landlord owed the electric company several thousand dollars. Therefore, the meters had been removed from the house. Because most of the tenants were welfare clients, the Department of Welfare had "reimbursed" the landlord directly for much of the unpaid electric bill and refused to pay any more money to the electric company. The Department of Welfare was slow in meeting the emergency needs of the tenants. Most of the children (forty-eight from the eleven families in the building) had not been to school for a month because they were ill or lacked proper clothing.

The mothers were tired and demoralized. Dirt and disorganization were increasing daily. The tenants were afraid to sleep at night because the building was infested with rats. There was danger of fire because the tenants had to use candles for light. The seventeen abandoned apartments had been invaded by homeless men and drug addicts. Petty thievery is common in such situations. However, the mothers did not want to seek protection from the police for fear that they would chase away all men who were not part of the families in the building (some of the unmarried mothers had men living with them—one of the few means of protection from physical danger available to these women—even though mothers on public assistance are threatened with loss of income if they are not legally married). The anxiety created by these conditions was intense and disabling.

The workers noted that the mothers were not only anxious but "fighting mad"; not only did they seek immediate relief from their physical dangers and discomforts but they were eager to express their fury at the landlord and the public agencies, which they felt had let them down.

The circumstances described are by no means uncommon, at least not in New York City. Twenty percent of all housing in the city is still unfit, despite all the public and private residential building completed since World War II. At least 277,500 dwellings in New York City need major repairs if they are to become safe and adequate shelters. This means that approximately 500,000 people in the city live in inferior dwelling units and as many as 825,000 people in buildings that are considered unsafe.[3] In 1962 the New York City Bureau of Sanitary Inspections reported that 530 children were bitten by rats in their homes and 198 children were poisoned (nine of them fatally) by nibbling at peeling lead paint, even though the use of lead paint has been illegal in the city for more than ten years. Given the difficulties involved in lodging formal complaints with city agencies, it is safe to assume that unreported incidents of rat bites and lead poisoning far exceed these figures.

The effect of such hardships on children is obvious. Of even greater significance is the sense of powerlessness generated when families go into these struggles barehanded. It is this sense of helplessness in the face of adversity that induces pathological

[3]Facts About Low Income Housing (New York: Emergency Committee for More Low Income Housing, 1963).

Future Trends

anxiety, intergenerational alienation, and social retreatism. Actual physical impoverishment alone is not nearly so debilitating as poverty attended by a sense of unrelieved impotence that becomes generalized and internalized. The poor then regard much social learning as irrelevant, since they do not believe it can effect any environmental change.[4]

Intervention and the Social Systems

Selecting a point of intervention in dealing with this problem would have been simpler if the target of change were Mrs. Smith alone, or Mrs. Smith and her co-tenants, the clients in whose behalf intervention was planned. Too often, the client system presenting the problem becomes the major target for intervention, and the intervention method is limited to the one most suitable for that client system. However, Mrs. Smith and the other tenants had a multitude of problems emanating from many sources, any one of which would have warranted the attention of a social agency. The circumstantial fact is that in individual contacts an agency that offers services to individuals and families should not be a major factor in determining the method of intervention. Identification of the client merely helps the agency to define goals; other variables are involved in the selection of method. As Burns and Glasser have suggested: "It may be helpful to consider the primary target of change as distinct from the persons who may be the primary clients. . . . The primary target of change then becomes the human or physical environment toward which professional efforts via direct intervention are aimed in order to facilitate change."[5] The three major factors that determined MFY's approach to the problem were (1) knowledge of the various social systems within which the social problem was located (i.e., social systems assessment), (2) knowledge of the various methods (including non-social work methods) appropriate for intervention in these different social systems, and (3) the resources available to the agency.[6]

The difficulties of the families in the building were intricately connected with other elements of the social system related to the housing problem. For example, seven different public agencies were involved in maintenance of building services. Later other

[4]Francis P. Purcell, "The Helping Professions and Problems of the Brief Contact," in Frank Riessman, Jerome Cohen, and Arthur Pearl, eds., Mental Health of the Poor (New York: Free Press of Glencoe, 1964), p. 432.

[5]Mary E. Burns and Paul H. Glasser, "Similarities and Differences in Casework and Group Work Practice," Social Service Review, Vol. 37, No. 4 (December 1963), p. 423.

[6]Harry Specht and Frank Riessman, "Some Notes on a Model for an Integrated Social Work Approach to Social Problems" (New York: Mobilization For Youth, June 1963). (Mimeographed.)

agencies were involved in relocating the tenants. There is no one agency in New York City that handles all housing problems. Therefore, tenants have little hope of getting help on their own. In order to redress a grievance relating to water supply (which was only one of the building's many problems) it is necessary to know precisely which city department to contact. The following is only a partial listing:

No water—Health Department
Not enough water—Department of Water Supply
No hot water—Buildings Department
Water leaks—Buildings Department
Large water leaks—Department of Water Supply
Water overflowing from apartment above—Police Department
Water sewage in the cellar—Sanitation Department

The task of determining which agencies are responsible for code enforcement in various areas is not simple, and in addition one must know that the benefits and services available for tenants and for the community vary with the course of action chosen. For example, if the building were taken over by the Rent and Rehabilitation Administration under the receivership law, it would be several weeks before services would be re-established, and the tenants would have to remain in the building during its rehabilitation. There would be, however, some compensations: tenants could remain in the neighborhood—indeed, in the same building—and their children would not have to change schools. If, on the other hand, the house were condemned by the Buildings Department, the tenants would have to move, but they would be moved quickly and would receive top relocation priorities and maximum relocation benefits. But once the tenants had been relocated—at city expense—the building could be renovated by the landlord as middle-income housing. In the Sixth Street house, it was suspected that this was the motivation behind the landlord's actions. If the building were condemned and renovated, there would be twenty-eight fewer low-income housing units in the neighborhood.

This is the fate of scores of tenements on the Lower East Side because much new middle-income housing is being built there. Basic services are withheld and tenants are forced to move so that buildings may be renovated for middle-income tenants. Still other buildings are allowed to deteriorate with the expectation that they will be bought by urban renewal agencies.

It is obvious, even limiting analysis to the social systems of one tenement, that the problem is enormous. Although the tenants were the clients in this case, Mrs. Smith, the tenant group, and other community groups were all served at one point or another. It is even conceivable that the landlord might have been selected as the most appropriate recipient of service. Rehabilitation of many slum tenements is at present nearly impossible. Many landlords regard such property purely as an investment. With profit the prime motive, needs of low-income tenants are often overlooked. Under present conditions it is financially impossible for many landlords to correct all the violations in their buildings even if they wanted to. If the social worker chose to intervene at this level of the problem, he might apply to the Municipal Loan Fund, make arrangements with unions for the use of non-union labor in limited rehabilitation projects, or provide expert consultants on reconstruction. These tasks would require social workers to have knowledge similar to that of city planners. If the problems of landlords were not selected as a major point of intervention, they would still have to be considered at some time since they are an integral part of the social context within which this problem exists.

A correct definition of interacting social systems or of the social worker's choice of methods and points of intervention is not the prime concern here. What is to be emphasized is what this case so clearly demonstrates: that although the needs of the client system enable the agency to define its goals, the points and methods of intervention cannot be selected properly without an awareness and substantial knowledge of the social systems within which the problem is rooted.

Dealing with the Problem

The social worker remained with the building throughout a four-month period. In order to deal effectively with the problem, he had to make use of all the social work methods as well as the special talents of a community worker, lawyer, city planner, and various civil rights organizations. The social worker and the community worker functioned as generalists with both individuals and families calling on caseworkers as needed for specialized services or at especially trying times, such as during the first week and when the families were relocated. Because of the division of labor in the agency, much of the social work with individuals was done with the help of a caseworker. Group work, administration, and community organization were handled by the social worker, who had been trained in community organization. In many instances he also dealt with the mothers as individuals, as they encountered one stressful situation after another. Agency caseworkers also provided immediate and concrete assistance to individual families, such as small financial grants, medical care, homemaking services, baby-sitting services, and transportation. This reduced the intensity of pressures on these families. Caseworkers were especially helpful in dealing with some of the knotty and highly technical problems connected with public agencies.

With a caseworker and a lawyer experienced in handling tenement cases, the social worker began to help the families organize their demands for the services and utilities to which they were legally entitled but which the public agencies had consistently failed to provide for them.

The ability of the mothers to take concerted group action was evident from the beginning, and Mrs. Smith proved to be a natural and competent leader. With support, encouragement, and assistance from the staff, the mothers became articulate and effective in negotiating with the various agencies involved. In turn, the interest and concern of the agencies increased markedly when the mothers began to visit them, make frequent telephone calls, and send letters and telegrams to them and to politicians demanding action.

With the lawyer and a city planner (an agency consultant), the mothers and staff members explored various possible solutions to the housing problem. For example, the Department of Welfare had offered to move the families to shelters or hotels. Neither alternative was acceptable to the mothers. Shelters were ruled out because they would not consider splitting up their families, and they rejected hotels because they had discovered from previous experience that many of the "hotels" selected were flop-houses or were inhabited by prostitutes.

The following is taken from the social worker's record during the first week:

Met with the remaining tenants, several Negro men from the block, and [the city planner]. . . . Three of the mothers said that they would sooner sleep out on the street than go to the Welfare shelter. If nothing else, they felt that this would be a way of protesting their plight. . . . One of the mothers said that they couldn't very well do this with most of the children having colds. Mrs. Brown thought that they might do better to ask Reverend Jones if they could move into the cellar of his church temporarily. . . . The other mothers got quite excited about this idea because they thought that the church basement would make excellent living quarters.

After a discussion as to whether the mothers would benefit from embarrassing the public agencies by dramatically exposing their inadequacies, the mothers decided to move into the nearby church. They asked the worker to attempt to have their building condemned. At another meeting, attended by tenants from neighboring buildings and representatives of other local groups, it was concluded that what had happened to the Sixth Street building was a result of discrimination against the tenants as Puerto Ricans and Negroes. The group—which had now become an organization—sent the following telegram to city, state, and federal officials:

We are voters and Puerto Rican and Negro mothers asking for equal rights, for decent housing and enough room. Building has broken windows, no gas or electricity for four weeks, no heat or hot water, holes in floors, loose wiring. Twelve of forty-eight children in building sick. Welfare doctors refuse to walk up dark stairs. Are we human or what? Should innocent children suffer for landlords' brutality and city and state neglect? We are tired of being told to wait with children ill and unable to attend school. Negro and Puerto Rican tenants are forced out while buildings next door are renovated at high rents. We are not being treated as human beings.

For the most part, the lawyer and city planner stayed in the background, acting only as consultants. But as the tenants and worker became more involved with the courts and as other organizations entered the fight, the lawyer and city planner played a more active and direct role.

Resultant Side-Effects

During this process, tenants in other buildings on the block became more alert to similar problems in their buildings. With the help of the community development staff and the housing consultant, local groups and organizations such as tenants' councils and the local chapter of the Congress of Racial Equality were enlisted to support and work with the mothers.

Some of the city agencies behaved as though MFY had engineered the entire scheme to embarrass them—steadfastly disregarding the fact that the building had been unlivable for many months. Needless to say, the public agencies are overloaded and have inadequate resources. As has been documented, many such bureaucracies develop an amazing insensitivity to the needs of their clients.[7] In this case, the MFY social worker believed that the tenants—and other people in their plight—should make their needs known to the agencies and to the public at large. He knew that when these expressions of need are backed by power—either in numbers or in political knowledge—they are far more likely to have some effect.

---

[7]See, for example, Reinhard Bendix, "Bureaucracy and the Problem of Power," in Robert K. Merton, Alisa Gray, Barbara Hockey, and Horan C. Sebrin, eds., *Reader in Bureaucracy* (Glencoe, Ill.: Free Press, 1952), pp. 114–134.

Other movements in the city at this time gave encouragement and direction to the people in the community. The March on Washington and the Harlem rent strike are two such actions.

By the time the families had been relocated, several things had been accomplished. Some of the public agencies had been sufficiently moved by the actions of the families and the local organizations to provide better services for them. When the families refused to relocate in a shelter and moved into a neighborhood church instead, one of the television networks picked up their story. Officials in the housing agencies came to investigate and several local politicians lent the tenants their support. Most important, several weeks after the tenants moved into the church, a bill was passed by the city council designed to prevent some of the abuses that the landlord had practiced with impunity. The councilman who sponsored the new law referred to the house on Sixth Street to support his argument.

Nevertheless, the problems that remain far outweigh the accomplishments. A disappointing epilogue to the story is that in court, two months later, the tenants' case against the landlord was dismissed by the judge on a legal technicality. The judge ruled that because the electric company had removed the meters from the building it was impossible for the landlord to provide services.

Some of the tenants were relocated out of the neighborhood and some in housing almost as poor as that they had left. The organization that began to develop in the neighborhood has continued to grow, but it is a painstaking job. The fact that the poor have the strength to continue to struggle for better living conditions is something to wonder at and admire.

Implications for Practice

Social work helping methods as currently classified are so inextricably interwoven in practice that it no longer seems valid to think of a generic practice as consisting of the application of casework, group work, or community organization skills as the nature of the problem demands. Nor does it seem feasible to adapt group methods for traditional casework problems or to use group work skills in community organization or community organization method in casework. Such suggestions—when they appear in the literature—either reflect confusion or, what is worse, suggest that no clearcut method exists apart from the auspices that support it.

In this case it is a manifestation of a social problem—housing—that was the major point around which social services were organized. The social worker's major intellectual task was to select the points at which the agency could intervene in the problem and the appropriate methods to use. It seems abundantly clear that in order to select appropriate points of intervention the social worker need not only understand individual patterns of response, but the nature of the social conditions that are the context in which behavior occurs. As this case makes evident, the social system that might be called the "poverty system" is enduring and persistent. Its parts intermesh with precision and disturbing complementarity. Intentionally or not, a function is thereby maintained that produces severe social and economic deprivation. Certain groups profit enormously from the maintenance of this sytem, but larger groups suffer. Social welfare—and, in particular, its central profession, social work—must examine the part it plays in either maintaining or undermining this socially pernicious poverty system. It is important that the social work profession no longer regard social conditions as immutable and a social reality to be accommodated as service is provided to deprived persons with an ever increasing refinement of technique. Means should be developed whereby agencies can affect social problems more directly, especially through institutional (organizational) change.

The idea advanced by MFY is that the social worker should fulfill his professional function and agency responsibility by seeking a solution to social problems through institutional change rather than by focusing on individual problems in social functioning. This is not to say that individual expressions of a given social problem should be left unattended. On the contrary, this approach is predicated on the belief that individual problems in social functioning are to varying degrees both cause and effect. It rejects the notion that individuals are afflicted with social pathologies, holding, rather, that the same social environment that generates conformity makes payment by the deviance that emerges. As Nisbet points out " . . . socially prized arrangements and values in society can produce socially condemned results."[8] This should direct social work's attention to institutional arrangements and their consequences. This approach does not lose sight of the individual or group, since the social system is composed of various statuses, roles, and classes. It takes cognizance of the systemic relationship of the various parts of the social system, including the client. It recognizes that efforts to deal with one social problem frequently generate others with debilitating results.

Thus it is that such institutional arrangements as public assistance, state prisons, and state mental hospitals, or slum schools

[8]Merton and Nisbet, op. cit., p. 7.

are regarded by many as social problems in their own right. The social problems of poverty, criminality, mental illness, and failure to learn that were to be solved or relieved remain, and the proposed solutions pose almost equally egregious problems.

This paper has presented a new approach to social work practice. The knowledge, values, attitudes, and skills were derived from a generalist approach to social work. Agencies that direct their energies to social problems by effecting institutional change will need professional workers whose skills cut across the broad spectrum of social work knowledge.

Selected Bibliography

Brager, G. A., "Advocacy and Political Behavior," *Social Work*, 13 (2), 1968, pp. 5–15.

Crow, M. S., "Preventive Intervention through Parent Group Education," *Social Casework*, 48 (3), 1967, pp. 161–165.

Deschin, C. S., "The Future Direction of Social Work. 1. From Concern with Problems to Emphasis on Prevention," *American Journal of Orthopsychiatry*, 38 (1), 1968, pp. 9–17.

Epstein, I., "Social Workers and Social Action: Attitudes toward Social Action Strategies," *Social Work*, 13 (2), 1968, pp. 101–108.

Gordon, William E., "Toward a Social Work Frame of Reference," *Journal of Education for Social Work*, 1 (2), 1965, pp. 19–26.

Gray, N. T., "Family Planning and Social Welfare's Responsibility," *Social Casework*, 47 (8), 1966, pp. 487–493.

Grosser, C. F., "Changing Theory and Changing Practice," *Social Casework*, 50 (1), 1969, pp. 16–21.

Kaufman, H., "Organization Theory and Political Theory," *American Political Science Review*, 58 (1), 1964, pp. 5–14.

Kidneigh, J. C., "Restructuring Practice for Better Manpower Use," *Social Work*, 13 (2), 1968, pp. 109–114.

Klein, M. W., "Juvenile Gangs, Police, and Detached Workers: Controversies about Intervention," *Social Service Review*, 39 (2), 1965, pp. 183–190.

MacRae, R. H., "Social Work and Social Action," *Social Service Review*, 40 (1), 1966, pp. 1–7.

Reid, W., "Interagency Co-ordination in Delinquency Prevention and Control," *Social Service Review*, 38 (4), 1964, pp. 418–428.

Roberts, R. W., "Social Work: Methods and/or Goals?" *Social Service Review*, 42 (3), 1968, pp. 355–361.

Salvatore, A., "A Family Agency Reaches Out to a Slum Ghetto," *Social Work*, 11 (4), 1966, pp. 17–23.

Specht, H., "Disruptive Tactics," *Social Work*, 14 (2), 1969, pp. 5–15.

Spitzer, K., and Welsh, B., "A Problem Focused Model of Practice," *Social Casework*, 50 (6), 1969, pp. 323–329.

Thurz, D., "Social Action as a Professional Responsibility," *Social Work*, 11 (3), 1966, pp. 12–21.

Wade, A. D., "The Social Worker in the Political Process," *Social Welfare Forum*, New York, Columbia University Press, 1966, pp. 52–67.

Willie, C. V., Wagenfeld, M. O., and Cary, L. J., "Patterns of Rent Payment among Problem Families," *Social Casework*, 45 (8), 1964, pp. 465–470.

Wright, M. K., "Comprehensive Services for Adolescent Unwed Mothers," *Children*, 13 (5), 1966, pp. 171–176.

Zweig, F. M., "The Social Worker as Legislative Ombudsman," *Social Work*, 14 (1), 1969, pp. 25–33.

Directions: Circle the number which seems appropriate

1. Understanding of the writing and utilization of behavioral objectives.

1	2	3	4	5
poor	fair	good	very good	excellent

2. Interest in the selected topic at the beginning of the semester.

1	2	3	4	5
none	some	moderate	especially	exceptional

3. The amount of satisfaction I found in pursuing my topic.

1	2	3	4	5
none	some	moderate	very good	exceptional

4. Intellectual and personal growth which occurred as a result of pursuing my objective.

1	2	3	4	5
none	some	moderate	very much	exceptional

5. The degree to which I am inspired to pursue some subjects or ideas which came from my learning in this course.

1	2	3	4	5
none	some	moderate	very much	exceptional

6. Utilization of opportunities for learning.

1	2	3	4	5
poor	fair	good	very good	exceptional

7. The degree to which your activities helped you in attaining your objectives.

1	2	3	4	5
poor	fair	good	very helpful	excellent

8. Active participation in sharing of learning experiences.

1	2	3	4	5
poor	fair	good	very good	exceptional

9. Utilization of faculty guidance when needed.

1	2	3	4	5
never	seldom	occasionally	usually	always

10. Degree to which you feel you assumed responsibility for your own learning in this course.

1	2	3	4	5
poor	fair	good	very good	excellent